Jazz, Rock, and Rebels

STUDIES ON THE HISTORY OF SOCIETY AND CULTURE

Victoria E. Bonnell and Lynn Hunt, Editors

Jazz, Rock, and Rebels

Cold War Politics and
American Culture
in a Divided Germany

UTA G. POIGER

University of California Press

BERKELEY   LOS ANGELES   LONDON

University of California Press
Berkeley and Los Angeles, California

University of California Press, Ltd.
London, England

Portions of chapters 2 and 5 have appeared previously in somewhat different form as "Rebels With a Cause? American Popular Culture, the 1956 Youth Riots, and New Conceptions of Masculinity in East and West Germany," in *The American Impact on Postwar Germany,* ed. Reiner Pommerin, 93–124 (Providence, R. I.: Berghahn Books, 1995) and "Rock 'n' Roll, Female Sexuality, and the Cold War Battle over German Identities," *Journal of Modern History* 68 (September 1996): 577–616.

Not in all cases was it possible to locate the holders of copyrights for illustrations.

Library of Congress Cataloging-in-Publication Data

Poiger, Uta G., 1965–
    Jazz, rock, and rebels : cold war politics and American culture in a divided Germany
       p.   cm. — (Studies on the history of society and culture ; 35)
    Includes bibliographical references and index.
    ISBN 0-520-21138-3 (alk. paper).—ISBN 0-520-21139-1 (alk. paper)
    1. Germany—Civilization—American influence. 2. Popular culture—Germany. 3. Popular culture—Germany (East) 4. Subculture—Germany. 5. Subculture—Germany (East) 6. Race relations—Germany—History. 7. Art and state—Germany. 8. Art and state—Germany (East) 9. Youth—Germany—Social conditions—20th century. I. Title. II. Series.
DD258.6.P65 2000
943—dc21   99-34558
                                                   CIP

Manufactured in the United States of America

08 07 06 05 04 03
10 9 8 7 6 5 4 3

Contents

Figures

Acknowledgments

It is a great pleasure to thank the individuals and institutions who helped me in the process of writing this book. Grants from Brown University, the Christian-Albrechts-Universität Kiel, and the German Historical Institute provided crucial research support in the initial stages, and a Charlotte W. Newcombe Dissertation Fellowship allowed me a year of writing. The completion of the manuscript was made possible by research support from the University of Washington, including a Junior Faculty Development Award, the Keller Fund of the University of Washington History Department, and a German Marshall Fund of the United States Research Fellowship. The staffs of numerous archives and libraries in Germany and the United States greatly assisted my research and filled extensive requests for copies. In Berlin, Leigh Love, Helfried Quint, Traute Schlabach, Matthias Kusche, Heike Stein, and Jan Kock offered me their hospitality. At various stages, Christopher Kemple, Colleen McClurg, Tuska Benes, and Vera Sokolova provided valuable research assistance.

Several teachers have shaped my intellectual path, and I am deeply grateful to them. Sara Lennox first showed me that the study of gender and history was an important intellectual and political project. She and Paula Baker were instrumental in my decision to continue graduate studies. At Brown University, Volker Berghahn and Mari Jo Buhle encouraged and guided my work on various aspects of American culture abroad. Their thought-provoking criticisms and unfailing support continue to be a source of inspiration. Mary Gluck urged me to think carefully about the relationship of culture and politics, while Carolyn Dean identified missing links in my arguments and helped sharpen my thinking as a result.

I am also grateful to my colleagues and students in the History Department at the University of Washington for creating a hospitable environment. In particular, I thank Teri Balkenende, Stephanie Camp, Madeleine Dong, John Findlay, Susan Glenn, Jim Gregory, Suzanne Lebsock, Laurie Sears, Vera Sokolova, John Toews, Lynn Thomas, and the members of the History Research Group and "Daughter of HRG" for comments and suggestions. The past and current department chairs, Richard Johnson and Robert Stacey, greatly helped in seeing this project through to completion.

Seventeen East and West Berliners generously shared with me their experiences of growing up and living in the divided city from the 1940s to the 1960s. Their memories led my research in important directions, more so than may be visible in the text of the book.

In the earlier stages of this project, I received expert guidance from "The Group," including Lucy Barber, Ruth Feldstein, Jane Gerhard, Melani McAlister, Donna Penn, and Jessica Shubow. On different occasions, Omer Bartov, Michael Ermarth, Michael Geyer, Edward Gray, Elaine Tyler May, and Alf Lüdtke provided useful criticisms. At the University of California Press, I thank Sheila Levine for her enthusiasm, advice, and patience. Jan Spauschus Johnson shepherded the manuscript through production, and Ellen Browning cleaned up my prose.

Several colleagues and friends commented on the entire manuscript. Molly Nolan's careful reading raised important questions. I am particularly indebted to Heide Fehrenbach, Melani McAlister, Bob Moeller, and Dorothee Wierling. Each of them gave invaluable criticisms on various drafts, and they, along with Ruth Feldstein and Lynn Thomas, also provided much appreciated encouragement in regular conversations and e-mail missives.

Special thanks go to my parents, Brigitte and Werner Poiger, for their unwavering support. Finally, I thank Kyriacos Markianos for (re)reading every page of the manuscript and for his companionship through all stages of this project. Its failings, of course, are entirely my own.

List of Abbreviations

AFN	American Forces Network
BBC	British Broadcasting Corporation
BFN	British Forces Network
CDU	Christlich Demokratische Union
CSU	Christlich Soziale Union
DEFA	Deutsche Film-Aktiengesellschaft
FDJ	Freie Deutsche Jugend
FDP	Freie Demokratische Partei Deutschlands
FRG	Federal Republic of Germany
FSK	Freiwillige Selbstkontrolle der Filmwirtschaft
GDR	German Democratic Republic
HICOG	Office of the U.S. High Commissioner for Germany
KPD	Kommunistische Partei Deutschlands
KVP	Kasernierte Volkspolizei
MPEA	Motion Picture Export Association
NATO	North Atlantic Treaty Organization
NSDAP	Nationalsozialistische Deutsche Arbeiterpartei
NVA	Nationale Volksarmee
OMGUS	Office of the Military Government for Germany, United States
RMK	Reichsmusikkammer
SED	Sozialistische Einheitspartei Deutschlands
SPD	Sozialdemokratische Partei Deutschlands
UNESCO	United Nations Educational, Scientific, and Cultural Organization
USIA	United States Information Agency
VdK	Verband Deutscher Komponisten und Musikwissenschaftler

Introduction

From the late 1940s until well into the 1960s, East German officials and the East German press attacked the influence of American popular culture on East and West German youth. First targeting westerns, gangster movies, and jazz, then rock 'n' roll, East German authorities claimed that American imports destroyed the German cultural heritage, that they "barbarized" both East and West German adolescents, and made them prone to fascist seduction. Particularly in the first half of the 1950s, many West Germans reacted defensively to these suggestions and sometimes wondered whether East Germans better protected their youth. West Germans, too, worried that the "hot rhythms" of American music or the "sex appeal" of movie stars like Marlon Brando posed threats—either to West German adolescents or to the broader project of West German reconstruction, or both. By the late 1950s, however, city officials were opening jazz clubs for adolescents all over West Germany, and Defense Minister Franz-Josef Strauß announced that jazz was a proper music for the West German army. West Germans now flaunted their own openness, criticized East Germany's continued repression of American influences, and ridiculed East German assertions that, for example, rock 'n' roll posed a political threat. Within ten years, the German Cold War had undergone a significant transformation, one in which cultural consumption played a central role.

This study investigates how and why, in the postwar period, East and West German encounters with American popular culture were crucial to (re)constructions of German identities in the two states. The project places the conflicts between adolescents and authorities over American cultural influences in the context of the legacy of National Socialism and the emerging Cold War. The Nazis had banned much of American popular culture, and after 1945, American movies, jazz, rock 'n' roll, dances, and fash-

1

ions remained hotly contested in East and West Germany. The study focuses on the most controversial U.S. imports, which constituted, at the same time, the most debated aspects of consumer culture for both East and West Germans.

Two interconnected concerns shaped battles within and between the two German states over American influences. First, East and West German authorities perceived American cultural imports as a threat to established gender norms. Second, in responding to American popular culture, which often had roots in African American culture, Germans confronted their own notions of racial hierarchies. Arguments between adolescents and authorities over American influences were contests over moral, cultural, and political authority; they illuminate the complicated ways in which East and West German authorities used conceptions of racial and gender difference both to contain Americanized youth cultures in their own territories and to fight the Cold War battle. In spite of many ideological differences, authorities in both German states made their citizens' *cultural* consumption central to their *political* reconstruction efforts.[1]

After 1945, with the Allied occupation and the opening of its market, West Germany experienced an unprecedented influx of American goods, from nylon stockings to popular music. The impact of these imports was by no means restricted to West Germany; especially via Berlin, it reached both sides of the Iron Curtain. Until the construction of the Wall in August 1961, a constant stream of people flowed back and forth between East and West Berlin. Large numbers of East Berliners and East Germans shopped and enjoyed themselves in West Berlin. Sometimes whole East Berlin school classes would cross into the Western sectors to watch movies. Many East Berlin boys and girls frequented West Berlin music halls, and young people from all over the GDR (the German Democratic Republic, or East Germany) would go to West Berlin to buy "boogie-woogie shoes" with thick soles, jeans, leather jackets, or records (in spite of prohibitive exchange rates). At home some of them would tune into Western radio stations, especially AFN (American Forces Network) and Radio Luxemburg, to listen to the latest American hits. And even after the building of the Wall, radio broadcasts and visitors continued to transport American popular culture into East Germany. Thus, America's impact was felt in both Germanies.

Given its increasing pervasiveness in daily life, American popular culture held an important place in East and West German attempts to regulate the cultural consumption of their citizens. While the two German sides of the Cold War developed their political and cultural visions in constant reference to each other, both German states also had a common focal point with America. Both Germanies were facing the difficult task of constructing national identities out of the rubble left by National Socialism and World War II, and under the conditions of the emerging Cold War separation. It was frequently in relation to the United States—long recognized as the most developed consumer culture—that each Germany laid claim to a German heritage and tried to define what it meant to be German.[2]

The divided city of Berlin was at the front lines of these battles. For each side, Berlin provided a showcase of its respective political, economic, and cultural systems. Because the two Germanies and their respective allies competed visibly for the allegiance of Germans in this city, Berlin is a major focal point of this study. Neither West nor East Berlin was strictly representative of all of West or East Germany, but what happened there reverberated throughout the two states.

Ever more visibly, American music and movies provided models of dress and behavior for young East and West Germans in the 1950s. In the first half of the decade, East and West German authorities were mainly concerned about American westerns, jazz, and dances like the boogie. After 1955 the arrival of American "young rebel" movies like *The Wild One* with Marlon Brando and *Blackboard Jungle* with Sidney Poitier, along with rock 'n' roll, exacerbated the worries of parents and officials about American influences. Especially unsettling were youth riots that shook East and West Germany in the years from 1955 to 1959. Although young men constituted the majority of rioters, the public visibility of many young women as fans of American film and rock 'n' roll stars further heightened anxieties.

In East and West Germany, adolescents' embrace of American popular culture caused anxiety because commentators linked consumption, sexuality, and femininity. These links have characterized discourses on consumer culture since the nineteenth century, when observers all across Europe began to comment on the voracious female shoppers in the new department stores who appeared to gain sexual pleasure from their activities. The links drawn were often rhetorical and did not mean that men did not venture into department stores, or for that matter, did not go to the movies. Nonetheless commentators have responded to almost every phenomenon of mass consumption, whether movies or dance fads, by reaffirming the usually negative connections with femininity. During the early days of cinema before World War I, bourgeois male German observers, for example, expressed worries about and fascination with what occurred on and off the screen. Alleging that prostitutes dominated movie audiences, these commentators also reported that they themselves felt sexually stimulated;

need to redefine "Germanness"
↳ gender roles = part of this
project

4 / Introduction

movies thus threatened, as Heide Fehrenbach has put it, their "masculine powers of discrimination."[3] Men like the Dandies of the nineteenth century, who showed too much interest in fashion, were quickly criticized as unmanly. At the same time particular "male" forms of consumption developed in the bourgeoisie. Since the nineteenth century, collecting in particular has been an acceptable leisure pursuit for men, and indeed has usually not even been labeled "consumption." And also since the nineteenth century, the negative connotations of consumption have been at opposition with its important "positive" function—that of representing, through the display of goods, one's family, one's class, and, increasingly, also one's nation and one's self.[4] This tension certainly persisted in Cold War Germany.

In fact, the alleged connections between the consumption of mass culture, the oversexualization of women, and the feminization of men were particularly worrisome to East and West Germans in the 1950s. After the defeat of National Socialism and in the face of the Cold War, authorities in both states saw the success of reconstruction as dependent on reconfiguring and revalidating Germanness. Defining normative gender roles was important to these reconstruction projects.

Many Germans understood the war and postwar years as a period of gender upheaval and even crisis. Women clearly outnumbered men in the population. During the war, women entered the workforce in unprecedented numbers, and once fighting had ended they were largely responsible for maintaining their families. Many German men did not come back from the war, many others returned with physical or psychological wounds, and some simply hid. While Germans did not discuss the atrocities that German men had committed as soldiers in the *Wehrmacht*, particularly on the Eastern front and in parts of Europe occupied by the Nazis, there was a widespread sense that men had failed as the defenders of and providers for German women and children. Commentators in East and West began to worry about overly powerful women and weak men. In all zones, climbing divorce rates and liaisons between German women and occupation soldiers exacerbated such worries.[5] These visions of overly sexual or overly strong women and weakened men coexisted with the specter of young men—whether postwar black marketeers, juvenile delinquents, or underground members of the Hitler Youth (so-called werewolves)—whose aggressive potential had not been tamed in the name of the state.[6] Such aggressive young men appeared as another threat to the renewal of social stability.

Attempts to resolve the gender crisis of war and occupation are indicative of differences and similarities between the two new Germanies.[7] The constitutions of both German states guaranteed the legal equality of men ① and women, but each state fulfilled this mandate differently. Whereas in *marriage* West Germany, women did not achieve legal equality within marriage until the late 1950s, and illegitimate children did not gain full legal recognition until 1969, East German laws had instituted these rights by 1950. In West Germany, legal equality for women and men proved compatible with the promotion of the so-called housewife marriage, in which wives stayed at home, preferably with children, while their husbands earned the family income. Politicians and social scientists, across party lines, hailed this ideal nuclear family as the one institution that had not been tainted by National Socialism and as the best guarantee for postwar social and political stability. Indeed these families, which were far from the reality for a great number of West Germans, would serve as a contrast to and line of defense against the encroachments of both Communism and American-style consumer culture.[8]

The East German government, under Soviet pressure, actively encouraged ② women to enter the workforce and also guaranteed "equal pay for *work* equal work." Like West German politicians, GDR leaders located their vision in the context of the Cold War. Already in the 1950s, they had announced that "equal standing" for women was an important achievement that proved the superiority of socialism over the capitalist system. But even though East German married women and mothers entered the workforce in significantly higher numbers than West German women, a gender division of labor persisted. Women were more likely to be employed in "maternal" occupations, including education, welfare, and health care. Even when more women entered technical education programs and jobs in the 1960s, they continued to shoulder the main burdens of homemaking.[9] And in the aftermath of National Socialism and war, in East Germany too the family appeared as a haven of stability. As in West Germany images of women constructing a homey place were a staple in the illustrated press.[10] The position of the family as an apolitical refuge, however, was never unproblematic for a regime that sought to undertake a fundamental transformation of German society in the name of socialism. Whereas "reprivatizing" the family in West Germany meant strengthening the role of the father both in legal terms and in public imagery, this did not happen to the same degree in East Germany.[11]

Nevertheless, similarities in gender norms and sexual mores in the two *single* Germanies did not simply disappear with the Cold War. The fact that ille- *moms* gitimate children enjoyed equal rights and that single mothers received *illegit.* preferential treatment in procuring daycare in the GDR shows that pre- *kids* marital sex and single motherhood were somewhat more acceptable there. At the same time, women's rights were clearly limited. As in West Germany, access to abortions was very restrictive after 1950.[12] Authorities in both states established heterosexuality within marriage and in the service of reproduction as the explicit norm for men and women.[13] And most East and West German women, like German women after World War I, considered their dominant role as providers for their families during the disruptions of the war and immediate postwar years to be temporary.[14] Although East German officials urged women to engage in wage labor, leaders in both states constructed ideals of male protectors and asexual female caretakers.

Young men and women with a strong taste for American music and fashions challenged these norms and exacerbated East and West German concerns about the consumption of American popular culture. Although young men were frequently the focus of debates about young rebels, authorities in East and West Germany invoked American and German women as instigators of the youth rebellion and also made them key to containing the problems they associated with consumer culture. And yet, in spite of all these worries, the 1950s were also the years of the "economic miracle" in West Germany, and the years when competition over which state could better provide its citizens with consumer goods became a central feature of the Cold War. Perhaps as never before, the negative connotations of consumption coexisted in uneasy tension with its ever more important social, national, and indeed international function. This led to many attempts to rechannel and redefine the consumer habits of adolescents.

In the first half of the 1950s, many similarities existed between the cultural visions of the two Germanies. In often vehement rejections of American culture, both sides conflated uncontrolled sexuality, African American culture, and German lower-class culture, and linked all three to fascism.[15] West Germans, in spite of their military and political alliance with the United States, were trying to separate themselves from Bolshevism in the East and from the allegedly emasculating powers of American-style consumer culture in the West. East Germans, who did not have to negotiate between their hostility toward consumer culture and westward political integration, even more explicitly directed their cultural policies against the "American way of life."

In the second half of the 1950s, West German strategies for containing Americanized youth cultures changed, and in turn transformed, the Cold War battle between the two Germanies. Facing young rioters with a penchant for American fashions, West German social scientists and politicians, influenced by American thinkers like David Riesman, increasingly accommodated the consumption of American popular culture. While East German authorities continued to attack and repress American influences, U.S. and West German policies toward East Germany now employed some forms of American popular culture as a Cold War weapon—to integrate their own adolescents and to delineate the communist "other." The cultural consumption of American jazz, for example, became part of the vision of liberalism and pluralism that West German authorities sought to transmit to both their own citizens and their Cold War enemies to the East.

These transformations in the reception and mobilization of American popular culture were accompanied by changing visions of racial differences, in particular between Germans and African Americans. Although many post–World War II attacks against Americanized youth cultures employed racial slurs and stereotypes, "race" has hardly been a category of analysis in histories of the German post-Nazi period.[16] Indeed, scholars are only beginning to explore the significance of race in Germany's encounter with the United States. Conflicts over American popular culture make it possible to examine how East and West Germans transformed their history of constructing racial hierarchies when the defeat of National Socialism had discredited a German national identity based on biological racial superiority. The issues of race and ethnicity deserve particular attention in the study of two societies grappling with the legacy of the Third Reich.

Since the nineteenth century, Germans had made race central to German national identity. German visions of racial hierarchies had manifested themselves most forcefully in anti-Semitism, but many Germans also saw blacks (along with other groups like Gypsies) as racially inferior.[17] While racism fueled all nineteenth-century European imperialism, German colonial rule in Africa was notoriously harsh, provoking such revolts as the Herero and Maji-Maji uprisings between 1904 and 1907, which were brutally crushed by German troops.[18] In the 1920s, Germans were unified in their antagonism toward blacks when the French occupation army in the Rhineland included many Senegalese. The Nazis forced children of unions between these soldiers and German women to undergo compulsory sterilization.[19] Anxieties surfaced again, when African American soldiers came to Germany as part of the American occupying forces after World War II.[20] Debates over American popular culture, and in particular its African American influences, also reveal that after 1945 many Germans continued to define Germanness in racial terms. East and West German authorities rejected many American movie and music stars and their German fans as transgressors of racial and gender boundaries.

Yet the terms in which Germans interpreted "cultural difference"—between Germany and the United States, as well as among different groups within Germany—changed. This study traces the shift from a biologically based understanding of human differences, with links to eugenics, to one that believed differences to be rooted in psychology. Eugenics as a "scientific" way of managing the reproduction of a "healthy" nation had permeated German debates on social policy as well as on culture since the turn of the century. Some of the terms linked to eugenics persisted in the years after 1945. For example, a West German youth expert described rock 'n' roll dancers as "wild barbarians in ecstasy," while East German authorities criticized the East and West German adolescents who adopted "decadent" and "degenerate" American styles of dancing allegedly rooted in brothels and gangster hangouts.[21] The use of terms like "degenerate" marked adolescents' deviations from norms of male and female respectability as unacceptable by invoking, often implicitly, a racial logic that believed Germans to be superior to Jews, blacks, and other groups like Gypsies.

However, National Socialism and its racist population policies that culminated in the Holocaust discredited eugenics. The horrors of National Socialism also coincided with and fostered the rise of a new antiracist social science discourse in the United States and Great Britain, often with participation of German émigrés. By the 1950s, West German social scientists, many of them drawing on American models, analyzed differences between groups of people in psychological terms. Although communists looked on the social sciences with much suspicion, these developments also had an impact east of the Iron Curtain. By the 1960s, expressions associated with eugenics had largely disappeared from East and West German discussions of social or cultural phenomena, such as juvenile delinquency or adolescents' fascination with American imports. Along with the acceptability of ideas about racial hierarchies based on biological differences, the idea that "race" mattered at all in Germany also vanished.[22]

Talking about race is not easy in the context of postwar Germany where people do not perceive themselves as "raced": Most East and West Germans reject the notion that German identities after 1945 were in any way racial. Indeed in both Germanies the term "race" became taboo. Yet, even this denial shows how potent the issue of race and racial hierarchies remained in the postwar period. This study not only traces how a terminology based on biological hierarchies disappeared, it also suggests how a psychologically based discourse could reaffirm and even reassert racial hierarchies.

In investigating the visions of German civilization that made young male and female rebels appear to be extraordinary threats in both Germanies, this study explores how gender norms were intertwined with concepts of racial and class difference. Jazz and rock 'n' roll were controversial because East and West Germans saw them as African American or African American–influenced music that undermined the respectability of German men and women. Conversely, asserting gender norms frequently served to distinguish civilized Germanness from the alleged threats of African American culture.[23] Moreover, commentators in both Germanies frequently associated adolescents' adoption of American styles with working-class culture. In response, West German elites sought to assert bourgeois respectability and bourgeois culture as an antidote to adolescent rebelliousness. For East German socialists the links between American influences and working-class culture posed special difficulties, since they saw peasants and workers, led by the party, as the main agents in the desired social and political transformations. Taken together, the discussions of American influence on German youth show the complicated intersections of gender, sexuality, class, and race in East and West German constructions of national identities.[24] Conflicts over Americanized youth cultures in the 1950s were part of a long trajectory of naming, containing, and rejecting "difference" in order to bolster domestic and international dominance.[25]

The end of the Cold War has fully opened the post-1945 period for comparative historical inquiry. This study uses newly available sources in East Germany and is one of few to look at East and West Germany *together*: it traces the flow of cultural styles from West to East, compares reactions on both sides, and explores struggles between them. While it draws on frameworks developed in gender and (sub)cultural studies, it also investigates the significance of state intervention, showing how opposing political systems contained youth rebellions. This approach is especially promising, since cultural studies have left East Germany largely unexplored.[26] Further, when examining differences between the two systems and their institutional frameworks, it is also important to show continuities between the two, which have been largely ignored in both political discourse and scholarship. The totalitarianism paradigm in the West, which posits a close analogy between socialism and fascism, and the fascism paradigm in the East, which declares fascist regimes and capitalist liberal democracies equivalent and which dominated in the Communist Bloc, have often rendered any similarities between state socialism and liberal democracies invisible. Careful attention to the constant interaction between East and West makes it possible to analyze the dynamics of socialist oppression *and* to investigate the fissures that the economic miracle and a liberal political culture obscured in the West.

Comparisons with the United States inform this project on several levels. For one, Germans reacted strongly to American influences because of
their respective assumptions about right and wrong in U.S. culture and society. American popular culture did not have a uniform or unifying effect,
but since it was commercial and mass-mediated it made America into an
ever more important reference point for both Germanies. Second, the study
details the impact of U.S. social-science research and U.S. government policies. It examines their impact on West German attitudes toward East and
West German youth cultures and on West German Cold War policy. Third,
comparisons of reactions to youth cultures between the two Germanies on
the one hand and the United States on the other make it possible to tease
out the specific visions of culture and politics that all three developed.

In spite of the significance of the 1950s youth rebellion, many scholars
of postwar East and West Germany have completely ignored youth cultures and have seen intellectuals as the only ones who resisted Babittry or
conformity in the 1950s. The existing accounts of 1950s youth cultures
have also underestimated their significance. Jost Hermand, for example,
has claimed that in West Germany, rock 'n' roll for the younger generation
was considered rebellious; however, he has used the Marxist idea of negative cooptation to conclude that this image of rebellion channeled the dissatisfaction of the lower classes, and their potential political resistance, into
the arena of compensatory entertainment.[27] Most Western analysts of East
or West Germany, both politicians at the time or scholars since, have failed
to look at 1950s youth cultures as a source of resistance, although adolescents rebelled in public and private and sometimes experienced severe persecution. Timothy Ryback has rejected the notion that rock 'n' roll could
have assumed any political significance for East Germany, other than highlighting the repressive stance of East Bloc authorities.[28] His interpretation
echoes liberal assessments that have evaluated 1950s West German youth
cultures not as misguided resistance but as apolitical from the outset.[29]
Kaspar Maase has recently tried to reclaim the significance of West German youth cultures in the 1950s and has shown how important American
cultural influences were in changing conservative value systems in West
Germany: young working-class men, he argues, used American popular
culture to develop a "civil" identity. Yet Maase, too, has explicitly located
the actions of male adolescents in the "semiotic wars of everyday life" and
"not on the political stage."[30] Western Marxists and liberals alike have
missed significant aspects of 1950s youth cultures.

As this study suggests, current assessments of the 1950s rebellion as
nonpolitical are the result of a Cold War liberal understanding of culture in

West Germany.[31] In the late 1950s, many West Germans ceased to see American influences as a danger, while East German authorities continued to fight them. The West German view that culture was not a central site of political struggle emerged in the years after 1957 when scholars and politicians like Helmut Schelsky and Ludwig Erhard employed psychological theories to explain rebellious adolescent behavior and to define it as nonpolitical. While recent scholarship has shown the interpenetration of culture and politics, this project considers the historical and political significance of efforts to define culture as nonpolitical—and thereby to affirm a division between culture and politics that liberalism assumes. The move on the part of West German Cold War liberals to define culture as nonpolitical did not simply amount to a "depoliticization" of culture, but rather was a renewed politicization of culture on different terrain.

The book investigates how this reframing of the consumption of popular culture as nonpolitical was related to efforts to accommodate and alter adolescent behavior. Scholars have usually left girls out of the histories of the 1950s.[32] Making gender and race central categories of analysis, and including young women, changes our understanding of politics and culture in the 1950s. The consumption of American popular culture and German reactions to it were important forces in changing gender mores in the two Germanies as well as in transforming the Cold War battle between East and West.

Americanization has in recent years become a contested framework for the study of West European and specifically West German postwar history. Some scholars view Americanization as a process of modernization by which the United States, through its political, economic, and cultural presence, manages the successful development of liberal democracies, market economies, and consumer cultures abroad.[33] Other studies of Americanization have analyzed American cultural influences abroad as a form of cultural imperialism. American culture in this view is a manipulative tool that bolsters American economic and political hegemony and that eliminates diversity.[34] This book pays attention to the baggage Germans brought to their encounters with the United States; it shows that the meanings of American culture abroad are often multivalent.[35]

With its focus on Americanized youth cultures in both East and West Germany, this study moves beyond the tropes of liberation, negative cooptation, colonization, or fascistization that have characterized many debates among cultural critics, social theorists, and politicians in the past and that many scholars have reaffirmed since. Conflicts over American cultural influences were an arena of contest and negotiation within changing relations of power: between the sexes, between adolescents and parents, between adolescents and the state, and between different social groups within the two German states, as well as between the two Germanies and their allied superpowers. This study only begins to untangle this complicated web. It focuses on how the politicization of culture in both states was interlinked with the reconstitution of gender and racial norms that were central to (re)constructions of Germanness on either side of the Iron Curtain. Battles over the meaning of American popular culture in the 1950s were sites for the reconfigurations of culture and politics in the two Germanies, even though the two states conceived these relationships very differently.

Such an approach requires taking into account a broad array of sources ranging from foreign-policy documents to oral histories. In analyzing the various responses to American popular culture, the study relies heavily on published materials including movie and music reviews, newspaper and magazine reports about concerts or youth riots, and sociological studies. Tracing the constant interactions between the two Germanies and the impact of American popular culture within East Germany would have been impossible without the materials now available in the East German archives. These collections contain statements on cultural policies and their enforcement as well as on the reception of American popular culture by adolescents east of the Iron Curtain. For West Germany, reports by local social workers, sociological studies, and parliamentary debates yield useful insights, not only into youth policies, but also into changes in West Germans' self-understanding in relation to both their Cold War enemy and the United States. Finally, records of the U.S. occupation of Germany, the U.S. State Department, and the U.S. Information Agency (USIA) include many reports about politics and cultural life in both East and West Germany; they also show the often contradictory means by which the U.S. government tried to influence policies and social change in postwar Germany.

The way the sources are weighted for each Germany says much about the different character of the two states. In East Germany, government and party reports from the local to the state-wide level contain a wealth of material on adolescents' consumption of American culture and on the reactions of state and party authorities to this perceived threat. The reporting in the East German press usually conformed with these reports. In West Germany, by contrast, the most important source of information is social-science scholarship. The words of social scientists reverberated throughout the press and government statements and policies. Thus the public spheres in the two states were quite different. In East Germany the party largely controlled the press, while there was more room for public conflict in West Germany. The same words uttered in East or in West Germany thus did not necessarily mean the same thing, and it is important to locate the speakers and actors in their political and institutional settings.

Two overarching questions tie the chapters of this book together: How was normality defined in the two German states? And how were visions of normality enforced? The first question allows for an analysis of continuities and ruptures between different systems, in this case between the two postwar Germanies. When supplemented with the second question, this approach can also take into account the different institutional frameworks. These questions, then, will allow us to relate the construction of identities to the construction of institutions in the two Cold War German states. In short, they will help identify similarities and differences between opposing systems.

AMERICAN CULTURE IN WEIMAR GERMANY

The 1950s were hardly the first period that American popular culture seemed subversive to Germans. A rather extensive look back at the pre–World War II discourses on American culture is necessary in order to fully appreciate the postwar battles. In both East and West Germany, commentators drew on terms and images that had been central to discussions of American influences in the Weimar and Nazi years. The themes of youth, gender, race, decadence, and degeneracy that were important in the 1950s resonated with earlier attacks on and valorizations of the United States.

During the Weimar Republic, many Germans equated America with modernity—an association that raised both hopes and fears. Germans were not just fascinated with American management methods and automation; in big cities like Berlin, American popular culture, especially music and movies, made a splash. After World War I, American servicemen and Hollywood movies introduced Germans to American products and mannerisms, and American-influenced fads such as the Charleston spread among some adolescents. By the mid-1920s, in the wake of the Dawes Plan and other American loan programs, "Americanization" and "Americanism" became buzzwords: Germans debated and adapted Taylorism and Fordism, consumed and discussed Hollywood movies or jazz music, and constructed and attacked American "types," such as the American "girl." Educated Germans tended to associate the United States with materialist *Unkultur* ("nonculture") and found it lacking a long tradition or a spiritual life.

criticism
race gender
class
(triad)

While American production methods were admired by various political camps, consumption proved much more divisive, raising anxieties about lower-class tastes, the feminization of culture, and the racial decline of Germany. Criticisms of American culture found adherents among all political groups, although nationalist conservatives and fascists were most vocal.[36]

Because of World War I, the German market was closed to American movies imports between 1916 and 1921, but only three years later, Hollywood gained dominance in the number of releases, although not in the number of viewers, in Germany. Not surprisingly, Germans quickly recognized it as the major transmitter of American products and an "American way of life." While many critics treated Hollywood films as "primitive" and "uncultured," and contrasted Hollywood sensationalism, sentimentality, and superficiality with German seriousness, others began to admire American society dramas and slapstick for their excellent acting, technical accomplishment, and dramatic impact and viewed them as serious competition for German movie production. In response, German movie producers engaged in a constant dialogue with Hollywood, some by attempting to maintain a distinct German national style, others by imitating the American star system or performance and production methods.[37]

Weimar critics and censors vacillated between seeing the "sensationalism" of American westerns and thrillers as harmless or as dangerous, because such movies encouraged lower-class men to crime and violence.[38] The National Motion Picture Law was enacted in 1920 with the support of all major political parties. The law prohibited censorship for political or philosophical reasons, but stipulated that movies that might "endanger the public order, injure religious sensibility, function in a brutal or demoralizing manner, endanger Germany's reputation or relations with foreign countries" could be censored.[39] Film censorship reflected intense anxieties about lower-class tastes and about the effect movies had on youth. In the 1920s the two censorship boards, which comprised representatives from education, the arts, the movie industry, and the state, declared a full third of movies off limits for adolescents under eighteen.[40] For example, censors banned one U.S. movie, *King of the Circus*, as "a serious social menace among the lower part of the populace."[41] Such criticisms were part of a tradition of associating American movies, lower-class culture, and overaggression among men—a tradition that would continue well into the post-1945 years.

German critics also faulted American movies for transmitting images of the American *girl*. Germans saw the American *girl* (they used this English word) not merely as a cinematic construction, but as an American reality. She was strong, fashionable, flirtatious, and often frigid. Movie images and travel reports reinforced one another in disseminating this view: American women failed as housewives, but were "goddesses" in their homes; they had a disproportionate influence on culture and consumption; they fell for every fad and were involved in a disturbing body culture, cutting their hair into short bobs and hiding their curves in short, loose dresses. To many German commentators, they seemed not so much masculine as gender neutral, but a threat all the same.[42] Conservative Adolf Halfeld, who published one of the most successful Weimar books on America in 1927 and who would join the NSDAP in May 1933, criticized American marriages as an "Amazon state in miniature." Nazi ideologue Alfred Rosenberg concluded that the "apparent low cultural level of the United States" was a result of its domineering women.[43]

"Girls" were of much interest to commentators, because they were discerning the presence of similar creatures, so-called "new women," in advertisements, department stores, and even some offices or factories of Weimar Germany.[44] Worries about female sexuality were central to German images of both "girls" and "new women." Social commentaries and movies (for example the 1928 German production *Pandora's Box* with American Louise Brooks in the main role) associated "new women" and "girls" with oversexualization, lesbianism, and sometimes also Jewishness.[45] Germans were fascinated with all-women dance troupes, such as the Tiller Girls (who were actually British). These dance troupes made their moves in synchronized unison, thus appearing as cultural manifestations of rationalization and the machine age, in short as a symbol of modernity. To many German observers they seemed, although scantily clad, curiously asexual, a manifestation of sexual dysfunction among American women who tried to attract men, but were unable to feel heterosexual pleasure.[46] These "new women" and "girls" disturbed different groups for varying reasons. Conservatives affiliated with the churches were concerned that women had become sexually expressive at all, whereas leftist reformers worried that these women did not develop a healthy heterosexual life that would lead to stable companionate marriages. No matter whether Americanized new women really proliferated to the degree that some contemporaries thought, these images had lasting power: the German view of American women as egoistic, manipulative, overly sexual, and ultimately unerotic, like the connection between American culture and male aggression, would be central in German assessments of America and of modernity more generally well into the 1950s.

While Weimar Germans felt captivated by American modernity, they were also fascinated with the American "Wild West," which had been a topic of interest in Germany since the nineteenth century. By the 1920s, many adolescents avidly consumed western movies and novels, particularly since bourgeois parents and educators looked down on them as low culture. Some groups of young male, often unemployed workers, the so-called "wild cliques" gave themselves "western" names such as "Trapper's Blood."[47] The disdain for westerns made Wild West imagery also attractive to artists, including George Grosz, Carl Zuckmeyer, and Bertholt Brecht. They played at being American Indians or outlaw heroes and integrated such images into their pictures and plays, always aware that this western world existed only in novels or movies. As Beeke Sell Tower has put it, "They protested against German high culture as much as against the rarefied 'primitivist' visions and posturing of many expressionist artists."[48]

 Under the influence of American production techniques and of Hollywood movies, images of an industrialized and modern America became more prominent than images of the Wild West in the 1920s, but these two poles—America as the incarnation of modernity and America as the land of the wild frontier—coexisted and even informed one another. Fritz Giese, in his widely read book *Girlkultur*, for example, interpreted the alleged dominance of women in modern urban and industrialized America as a result of the frontier experience where women had been scarce and therefore grew in power until a *Frauenstaat* (women's state) evolved.[49]

Jazz quickly became another symbol of modernity for Weimar Germans, and black jazz performers confirmed German visions of America as at once "ultra-modern and ultra-primitive."[50] The music made it to Germany at the end of World War I as the Allied occupying forces brought records and sheet music into the country. Postwar German cities were gripped by a series of dance crazes, beginning with the fox-trot and tango in 1918, continuing with the shimmy in 1921, and culminating with the Charleston in 1925. Few American bands came to Europe, but German jazz fans could listen to German bands, some of which, such as the Weintraub Syncopators (who appeared in *The Blue Angel*), became quite accomplished jazz groups. Fans could also find the music in the revues in the big cities or on some late-night broadcasts by German radio stations, the BBC, and, after 1930, Radio Luxemburg. Nevertheless in the 1920s and 1930s, jazz was not the taste of the German (or American) mainstream.[51]

Exoticizing America was a major thrust in German reactions to jazz. For many Germans, the few African American musicians who made it to Germany, such as Sam Wooding and dancer Josephine Baker (who, like Wooding, first arrived with the "Chocolate Kiddies" troupe) were attractive exactly because they were exotic; they were seen as improvisational, spontaneous, and wild. Their shows certainly reinforced such images and Germans had trouble picking up any possible irony on the part of the performers that was designed to subvert stereotypes. (African Americans or Africans, for example, were hardly sporting the banana skirt that made Baker famous.) Critics charged that black performers represented the primitivism of African Americans more generally and for some of them this held a promise of rejuvenation and renewal for German audiences. Fritz Giese applauded jazz music and dancing as an invention of African Americans, who had come to urban centers and there, with their naiveté and natural power to move, had given expression to the rhythms of the big cities.[52] One reviewer saw the music of the Chocolate Kiddies as "barbarically beautiful, full of primitive improvisations." Completely insensitive to the racism of the word "nigger," he gushed, "Humanity has returned to its origins in nigger steps, in the shaking and loosening of bodies. Only that can help us, we who have become too erratic."[53] Many reviewers imputed to the black performers a power that they saw missing among "decadent" or war-weary Europeans.[54] As Jost Hermand has explained, the "primitive," which certainly included Africans and African Americans, appeared "to embody authenticity in its purest form."[55]

Exoticization was in many ways a form of racial prejudice that created or reinforced racial stereotypes. Many Germans failed to see that associating African Americans with the jungle or even seeing them as authentic representations of Africa was problematic. Charges of blacks' alleged primitivism reaffirmed racial hierarchies, both in the avant garde, especially among the expressionists who viewed primitivism as liberating, and in the right wing, where celebrations of primitivism fueled a much more pernicious racism that saw primitivism as a cause of racial decline.

Open racism against blacks thus persisted in Weimar Germany. Black Germans from former African colonies found it difficult to get employment as anything but servants, waiters, or entertainers. And most Germans were outraged when the French sent Senegalese troops as part of their occupation into the Rhineland in 1919 and 1920; many Germans perceived being occupied by the formerly colonized as the ultimate defeat and spoke of the "black shame on the Rhine." An admiration for jazz was indeed compatible with racist attacks on the black French occupiers. Giese admired jazz and at the same time condemned these black troops as an attack on Germans' "natural, human racial sentiment."[56]

Commentators on different ends of the political spectrum employed a common language of degeneracy, decadence, and primitivism to respond to American influences. This cultural commentary, manifest in scholarly works as well as more popular articles, was shaped by a eugenics-based discourse on human civilization. Eugenics posited the need for social or racial hygiene and worried about "degeneration," that is, biological and cultural decline. It also claimed a close relationship between the degeneration of the individual and that of the nation. In the early decades of the twentieth century, the "science" of eugenics offered a language for analyzing and justifying social and cultural hierarchies in biological terms. Moreover, it promised to improve the population through scientific means. Relying on Darwinist, or pseudo-Darwinist concepts, elites all across Europe and the United States began to worry about the "health" of the "body" of "advanced" nations by the early decades of the twentieth century.[57] Measures promoted in the name of eugenics ranged from birth control and sterilization, to welfare, to the regulation of culture. In short, eugenics promised a scientific way for shaping nations and, as Frank Dikötter has put it, eugenics "gave scientific authority to social fears and moral panics."[58] In Germany, the racist variations of eugenics became ever more acceptable with the economic downturn and social unrest caused by the Great Depression after 1929.[59]

However, eugenics and degeneration were compatible with a wide range of ideologies. Max Nordau, a Jew and nineteenth-century liberal, first applied "degeneration" in cultural terms in the 1890s, in order to criticize modernist art and literature as unhealthy. Nordau, who became the major popularizer of the concept, believed in progress on a path to rationality through "natural" human evolution and discipline. Degenerate art and degenerate artists (who according to Nordau could be recognized by their physical abnormalities, including stuttering or a foaming mouth) endangered this process.[60] Unlike racists, most of them from the right, Nordau did not associate these characteristics with one particular ethnic group, such as Jews or African Americans, but rather saw them as a result of industrialization and urbanization.

Ideas about degeneracy and eugenics continued to be part of different political ideologies in the 1920s.[61] Fritz Giese, who tended toward the political middle in the 1920s but would serve the Nazis after 1933 until his death in 1935, admired America as the "land of well-built people, the nation with the best biological conditions." Americans had a "self-confident race sensibility" and "one of their most laudable achievements" was "constructive eugenics": rather than focus on biological origins, Americans worked on the conscious improvement of the "national race values" through education and body culture. According to Giese, the careful styling of the "girl" was part of this movement, but he also worried that

American women were overly powerful and American culture shallow. Giese, it seems, advocated social hygiene, that is, biological improvement through cultural change, and gave consumer culture a potentially positive role in this process. But he also did not question segregation, considered only whites to be Americans, and implied that whites were superior.[62]

Other commentators were more worried about the impact of American culture on German national health. German attacks on jazz, for example, used a language that numerous white Americans, from scientists to Protestant clergymen to educators and critics, also directed at the music.[63] Attackers across the political spectrum connected jazz to female and male weakness. Sexuality had a central place in this nexus, as in all discussions of degeneration. German eugenicist and anthropologist Fritz Lenz followed the findings of U.S. colleagues, when he described blacks' "infamous lack of sexual control" and linked it to their talent for jazz music.[64] A Social Democratic paper spoke of the "shamelessness" of the new "degenerate" dances.[65] "Nigger music," said one conservative critic, was designed to introduce obscenities into society. Another warned against the "idiotic decadence of Western dance rhythms," and a third spoke of "orgies of Negro jazz." Adolf Halfeld saw jazz as "socially acceptable barbarism and stimulated propaganda, displaying only inner emptiness and abandonment."[66] Conservative Protestant cleric and educator Günter Dehn criticized the predilections of proletarian youth for "primitive sexuality and jazz"—and for the bobbed haircut. National Socialists complained that jazz was sexually endangering Nordic German womanhood.[67]

Commentators made the connection between biology and mass culture in several ways. Continuities across the political spectrum should not blind us to important differences among those who used eugenics-based terms. "Degenerate" or "decadent" mass culture, such as jazz could be the cultural expression of people who were allegedly biologically "inferior." Also, mass culture could reinforce negative tendencies in people who were biologically "inferior" or at least "vulnerable." The "inferior" could include whole groups, such as the lower classes, adolescents, women, and/or ethnic minorities, for example, Jews or African Americans. And finally, mass culture could lead otherwise healthy people to degeneration, endangering sexual discipline, marriage, procreation, and the racial hygiene of the nation. Modern mass culture and modern women, and the forms of sexual deviance associated with both—including masturbation, homosexuality, promiscuity, and prostitution—thus could be both the causes and the symptoms of biological and cultural degeneration. And as most critics agreed, adolescents were the most vulnerable victims.[68]

Reactionary and fascist German critics of American influences saw degenerate culture, both "high" and "mass," as the cultural expression of biologically inferior people, which in their mind included whole ethnic groups as well as the "unfit" among allegedly superior races. Since the 1920s, reactionary Germans described jazz as created by "Negroes" and marketed by Jews. These attacks, which echoed similar statements made by such people as Henry Ford in the United States, viewed jazz as an expression of the biological makeup of its creators and promoters: the attackers saw blacks as playful, naive, and exuberant performers and Jews as cunning and manipulative businessmen. Many of the best Weimar musicians and composers were Jewish and this undoubtedly spurred the anti-Semitic sentiments against jazz in Germany.[69] The school teacher and SS Deputy Commander Richard Eichenbauer claimed in 1932 that with degenerate modern music Jews were following "the law of their race."[70] The Nazi Combat League for German Culture railed against jazz as the music of "intellectual subhumans" and "bordello singers."[71]

Catholic and other Christian commentators were likewise gripped by this moral panic. They were less influenced by eugenic ideas and in fact opposed birth control or sterilization. Instead they reiterated worries that had shaped Catholic social theory since the nineteenth century. The "materialism" that came with the industrial revolution threatened to destroy Christian values and the Christian family. In the 1920s, dance crazes and the more temporary heterosexual relationships between young people that increasingly replaced prostitution were all part of what one Catholic observer called the "extensive sexualization of public life." With the increasing significance of the United States after World War I and in the aftermath of the Russian Revolution, this corrupt materialism was now emanating from what many conservative Germans viewed as the two evil centers of modernity, U.S. capitalism to the West and Soviet Bolshevism to the East—or as one Catholic journal put it, the "two moral low-pressure zones: the United States and Russia."[72] Many German conservatives associated these dangers with Weimar democracy and the left, even though the SPD itself railed against "trivial" popular forms. After 1945 such attacks on materialism would be a central feature of conservative reactions to an emerging American-style consumer culture in West Germany.

Leftists, including both communists and Social Democrats, were perhaps most ambivalent about American cultural imports. Some of them, fearing that American consumer culture would dissipate the rebellious potential of the working classes, used a vocabulary similar to that of conservatives, in which "decadence" figured prominently. However, in contrast to critics who associated mass culture with lower-class culture, they saw it as a bourgeois product designed to manipulate the proletariat and to dissipate its revolutionary potential. Some communists dismissed the bourgeois American "new women" as one more perversion of capitalist culture, even as the communist press printed images of proletarian women who clearly looked like "new women."[73] One Communist agitprop group featured a "Niggersong" that criticized the performance of a black dancer in front of a bourgeois audience and suggested colonial exploitation and consequent rebellion as a more appropriate context for depicting blacks.[74] In 1932, leftist music critic and Frankfurt School member Theodor Adorno launched one of his attacks on jazz, announcing that "its rhythmic emancipation" had been deceptive and that its innovations, including improvisation and syncopation, were attached to "vulgar music."[75] And an SPD functionary complained about working-class tastes: "They are proud of the fact that they can imitate everything bourgeois, for the most part they have petit bourgeois ideals: drinking, trashy literature, jazz, boxing and so forth." As during the Wilhelmine era, SPD leaders continued to urge the working class to shed "improper" proletarian styles, including their adherence to "low" mass culture.[76]

Alternative left voices existed in Weimar. Left-leaning educators began to integrate jazz into the curriculum of primary schools and conservatories. Some left-leaning critics and artists, including Bertholt Brecht and Kurt Weill in their 1928 *Three Penny Opera*, came to admire jazz, as well as American westerns and comedies, as part of their rebellion against bourgeois cultural norms.[77] One commentator, Hans Siemsen, applauded jazz, for it "knocks down every hint of dignity, correct posture, and starched collars." Figures of bourgeois authority, such as the "German high-school teacher" or the "Prussian reserve" clearly were incapable of dancing it. To Siemsen jazz was a remedy against authoritarianism and even militarism: "If only the Kaiser had danced jazz—than all of that never would have come to pass!"[78] The Bauhaus in Dessau supported its own student jazz band, while jazz dances became wildly popular in the Soviet Union. The Soviet "Blue Blouses," whose variety shows included a jazz band, toured Germany with great success in 1927. Soon German agitprop troupes patterned their performance styles after this model, combining them in some cases with anti-Semitic lyrics.[79]

In the Soviet Union, tolerance toward the vibrant jazz music and dancing soon evaporated with the First Five-Year Plan in late 1928 and the ensuing Stalinist terror. In the 1930s and 1940s, when many of the future communist leaders of East Germany were in exile in the Soviet Union, periods of greater leniency were followed by vicious xenophobic persecution of jazz fans and musicians. Attackers associated the music with unbridled sexuality, homosexuality, degeneracy, and bourgeois decadence. Even so, American cultural influences did not disappear altogether from the Stalinist Soviet Union. And during the wartime alliance with the United States after 1941, Soviet leaders actively fostered American imports.[80] But ambivalence and outright hostility toward American culture would also characterize many leftist reactions after World War II.

Attention to the "health" of the nation and a biological language permeated the cultural criticism of various political camps during the Weimar years, but the most vicious attacks on American imports based on a biological racism came from the right. Many of these attacks continued into the Third Reich, even though American culture had already lost some of its power before 1933. With the arrival of sound, indigenous film productions regained a strong edge in the German movie market by 1930. Jazz too declined in significance. Under the impact of the Great Depression many jazz musicians were out of work, since Germans found going out too expensive. At the same time, opponents of jazz became ever more powerful. In 1930 the Minister of the Interior for Thuringia, the first Nazi appointed to a state cabinet, promulgated an ordinance titled "Against Negro Culture, for German Folkdom" that was directed against all forms of avant-garde art and prohibited all jazz performances in the state. And in 1932 the autocratic central government headed by Chancellor Franz von Papen, responded to racist critics of jazz by prohibiting the hiring of musicians of color. In the last years of the Weimar Republic, with the demise of governments that supported a liberal democracy, jazz thus came under government attack, a practice that would continue in the Third Reich.[81]

NAZI AMBIVALENCE AND PERSECUTION

The Nazis' relationship to America in general and to American popular culture in particular was complicated. While "Americanism" became an exclusively negative term, Hitler himself was fascinated with American production methods and with Mickey Mouse. Hollywood movies (although in reduced numbers and preferably only if they had no Jewish stars or producers) were shown in German theaters until at least 1941 and German papers regularly reported on American film divas such as Joan Crawford or Greta Garbo. Advertisements for that quintessentially American product, Coke, urged visitors to the Sportpalast, where Propaganda Minister Josef Goebbels gave many of his racist speeches, to drink "Coca-Cola ice-cold."

This was not necessarily a contradiction: the Nazis after all sought to gain a broad following or at least acquiescence among the population by providing consumer goods and entertainment. By giving Germans the feeling that they continued to be part of international entertainment circuits, they likely managed to produce a cross-class appeal among German audiences.[82]

Nazi propagandists continued to build the German entertainment machinery in conscious competition with and even imitation of the American model. This became clear both in movies and music. Classical Hollywood and Nazi cinema shared important features, especially in form and structure. Also many Nazi films did not carry a simple ideological message. Rather German filmmakers of the Third Reich produced diverse films that featured stars and upbeat scores popular with audiences in Germany and later in German-occupied Europe.[83]

In spite of much hostility toward jazz, bands continued to play some of the music in revue shows and dance halls, at least until Goebbels declared total war in 1943. The Propaganda Ministry prohibited jazz in broadcasting in 1935 at the time of the Nuremberg Laws that organized German society according to racial criteria. While Nazi officials made great efforts to keep "hot jazz" and the new American "swing" out of radio broadcasts, much confusion persisted. The Nazis continued to produce swing rhythms, often replacing brass sections in American originals with violins, thus "softening" and "Germanizing" the music. Such tunes might well have suited the tastes of the majority of Germans who likely never cared for jazz in its "hot" and improvisational modes. In some provinces, local officials prohibited jazz performances and dances, but no national policy emerged. The music of Jewish and black artists, such as Benny Goodman, Duke Ellington, or Benny Carter remained available on imported records until 1938. Moreover, prior to the war, white foreign bands would regularly visit German cities, keeping German audiences in touch with international tastes. Even in the 1940s, the National Socialists, caught between their racial utopia and the need to accommodate a population under the conditions of war, never banned jazz completely from the air waves. They formed new bands for troop entertainment, used the music to introduce anti-Allied messages in radio broadcasts, and even allowed American originals on the airwaves to boost morale and to prevent troops from tuning in to the BBC. The term jazz, however, carried exclusively negative connotations.[84]

Like jazz or Hollywood-style cinema, the "girl" or "new woman" also did not simply disappear under National Socialism. "Girls" continued to be featured in the kicklines of revue theaters, in movies, and in advertisements. The Nazis did promote the cult of the asexual Aryan mother, but they also fostered sports and a cult of the body for boys and girls. Undoubtedly such contradictions helped the Nazis maintain acquiescence among the German population.[85]

Some Nazi followers were disturbed by the continued presence of cultural forms that they perceived as a throwback to the Weimar era. In 1935 a Nazi women's journal protested the persistence of "Girlkultur." And in 1939 one party member wrote to the Propaganda Ministry, "Is it not disgraceful for us Aryans, when we allow the appearance of dancers whose 'costumes' lay bare with every movement the charms of woman—a woman who as a German mother should be holy to us, as we have intoned again and again?"[86] That same year another letter to the Ministry complained about the persistence of "stupid and Niggerish fox-trots."[87] The Propaganda Ministry was the correct address for such complaints. In this ministry, which wielded overwhelming influence over cultural production in the Third Reich, "pragmatists" around Propaganda Minister Goebbels had won out over comparatively more "radical," that is ideologically consistent, Nazis around the head of the Combat League for German Culture, Alfred Rosenberg.[88]

In spite of many continuities in language and some continuities in consumption patterns, National Socialism did represent a break in how American culture was treated. Continued evidence of Americanization under National Socialism—and continuities between Weimar and the Third Reich or between the United States and the Third Reich—should not distract us from the ruptures and violence that National Socialism brought about. Most Nazi films urged viewers, likely women as well as men, to identify with serious male heroes, who achieved their status through sacrifice and the subjugation of women. More frequently than Hollywood, Nazi cinema projected images of weak women. Eric Rentschler has shown that such movies replaced heterosexual relationships with more intense male bonds whose erotic character was not perceived as threatening, because these male connections served the cause of the German nation. The masculine German community was to be achieved through overcoming women as well as racial and political enemies, such as Jews, Gypsies, blacks, or communists, who were portrayed as culturally and biologically inferior.[89]

The Nazi racial state was geared toward eliminating the perceived "ills" of society, and cultural policies and production were clearly part of this vision. Various professional elites participated in this "scientific" project that drew increasingly strict lines between those deemed "desirable" and those deemed "undesirable."[90] While the language of degeneracy had been leveled against American imports well before the rise of National Socialism, a

Fig. 1. The threat of jazz. Cover of a Nazi brochure accompanying the 1938 Nazi exhibit "Degenerate Music." Reprinted from Barron, *"Degenerate Art,"* 1992.

state-sponsored exhibit such as the one on "Degenerate Music," which opened in Düsseldorf in 1938, would have been difficult to imagine during the Weimar years, at least until the authoritarian governments of the early 1930s. In this exhibit, as in attacks on "degenerate" cultural forms more generally, Nazi officials employed a logic that fascists and reactionaries had developed before 1933. They relied on a vision of biologically based racial hierarchies that linked American popular culture to alleged racial degeneration and to "racially inferior" groups, including blacks and Jews. This vision was exemplified on the cover of a booklet accompanying the exhibit. It depicted a saxophone player with stereotypically black features, including dark skin, a wide nose, and thick lips, who was bending his upper body and staring slyly at the viewer. Not only did the picture portray the saxophonist as unmanly and evil; a Star of David on his lapel also linked him, and by extension all blacks and jazz music, to Jews.[91] With this combination of antiblack and anti-Semitic sentiments, the Nazis attacked musicians and fans of what Nazis called "Nigger-Jew jazz."[92]

As Germans continued to drink Coca-Cola and to watch carefully selected Hollywood movies in the Third Reich, some musicians and fans of jazz music were persecuted in ways not imaginable in Weimar. The Reichs Music Chamber (RMK) played a significant role in this. The RMK was the Nazi professional organization of musicians; it was institutionally subordinate to the Propaganda Ministry and easily coopted as an instrument in the cultural coordination of the regime. After 1935 the chamber severely curtailed Jewish musicians' employment. Moreover, special agents of the RMK would make the rounds of bars at night searching for "distorted," "dissonant," or overly "hot" sounds. They could rescind musicians' work permits or alert the Gestapo. Such local officials did not always act on direct orders from above but rather exerted what amounted to censorship "from below."[93] Because the Nazis themselves were so confused about what swing was, clients in one Hamburg cafe danced to the music right under a RMK sign that proclaimed "Dancing Swing Prohibited." The Nazis attempted to develop new "Germanic" dance forms, and while these efforts remained mostly at the level of rhetoric, they were accompanied by verbal assaults on the part of Hitler Youth and culture officials who described jazz as "alien to the German taste."[94]

In the 1930s mostly upper-class jazz fans formed clubs in several cities, some of them with Jewish members. Most of these jazz fans were apolitical, but often even non-Jewish members refused to join Nazi organizations. By the late 1930s jazz and swing dancing became a way to express one's rejection of the uniforms and drills that the Nazi regime promoted. In the 1940s Hitler Youth patrols, school officials, and the Gestapo harassed, surveilled, and arrested "swing youths," groups of young women and men mostly from the middle and upper classes who listened and danced to jazz together and wore distinctive, "English" clothes in large German cities such as Hamburg and in German-occupied Paris.

Nazi officials were outraged by the dance styles and fashions of the swings. A report composed by the leadership of the Hitler Youth in 1942 described young men in unmanly fashions of long hair, "long, often checked English sports jackets, shoes with thick light crepe soles, showy scarves, homborg hats." Young women too, were criticized for "a long, overflowing hairstyle. Their eyebrows were penciled, they wore lipsticks and their nails were lacquered." To make things worse, they danced swing "linking arms and jumping, slapping hands, even rubbing the backs of their heads together." The dancers were dancing apart and not following social dancing conventions. Indeed, they "went into wild ecstasy." Many of these swings refused to become members of the Hitler Youth or to submit to the compulsory work service *(Arbeitsdienst)* and therefore had to be seen as political enemies, the report explained.[95]

Press reports in Hamburg criticized the hunched posture of the youths as an infectious "Anglo-Jewish plague" and an assault on the "healthy sensibility of the *Volk*," and urged citizens to denounce these adolescents to authorities, so that streets and establishments could be kept "clean." A cartoon featured a female swing who wore men's pants.[96] The leader of the SS and head of the police, Heinrich Himmler, complained in 1944 that swings "merely want to pursue their own pleasure and sexual and other types of excess through which they rapidly come into sharp conflict with the National Socialist worldview."[97] A number of the "swings" engaged in anti-Nazi activities and distributed leaflets or intoned songs directed against the regime, while others did not level such direct attacks. However, even the swings' fashions and dancing became political in the eyes of Nazi authorities. In March 1940, hundreds of them were arrested in Hamburg, if only for a short period. The Gestapo charged some of these youths with engaging in obscenities. After October of that year, several swings, men and women, Jews and non-Jews, were sent to prisons or concentration camps, where some of them were tortured. Jazz fans with Jewish parents died in the camps because of their ethnic background, as did numerous Jewish jazz musicians.[98]

Working-class youth, too, formed informal, spontaneous groups and drew on some American symbols to express their dissatisfaction with the drills of the strictly sex-segregated Hitler Youth. Adolescent blue- and white-collar workers, perhaps imitating bourgeois swing-youths, became known as "Swing-Heinis" or "Hotters."[99] Others, young men and women, used symbols of the "Wild West": in the Rhineland, for example, members of the Edelweiß opposition groups referred to themselves as "Navajos," thus identifying with American Indians. Under different labels—*Meuten,* "packs," in Leipzig; *Blasen,* "crowds," in Munich; Death Head's or Skull and Crossbones gangs in Hamburg—such groups sprang up in industrial centers all over Germany. Members held informal meetings, traveled, sang songs mocking the Nazi regime, and at times beat up Hitler Youth patrols.

As they had done with the swings, the Nazis accused such groups of uninhibited sexual activity. The behavior of group members was more than an expression of generational tension; rather, it brought them in direct conflict with the Nazi regime, whose authorities cracked down severely on these adolescents.[100]

A police ordinance for the "protection of youth" issued by Himmler in the fall of 1940 was part of the efforts by officials to destroy autonomous youth groups and more generally to discipline German youth. The ordinance sought to prevent adolescents from attending dances and cabarets after 9 P.M. It prohibited "loitering" after dark, smoking, and drinking. That same year, Nazi authorities introduced youth arrest as an "educational" measure. Himmler issued an even more restrictive ordinance for the "protection of youth" in June 1943. The focus of these measures was on punishment of adolescents rather than prevention. Clearly, Nazi authorities were worried about German male and female adolescents whose moves and bodies had not been successfully synchronized in the service of the nation. Like some swings, members of the informal youth groups fell victim to Nazi persecution, as several of them were sent to prisons and youth or adult concentration camps.[101]

After Germany declared war on the United States in December 1941, the Nazi propaganda machine stepped up its efforts to convince the population that American culture was inferior.[102] Goebbels ordered materials that would address "the broad masses in Germany" and "in particular the youth," in order to convince them "that the uncritical adoption of certain American measures, for example of jazz music and so on revealed a lack of culture."[103] Hundreds of newspaper and magazine articles, along with propaganda films, appeared after 1941 declaring that America had no culture. Likely many in the German audiences agreed. American president Franklin Roosevelt was depicted as an agent of Jewry, who had made an alliance with "Jewish Bolshevism." Germany, by contrast was fighting against "liberalist *(sic)* thought," including both Americanism and Bolshevism, against "cosmopolitanism" (*"Weltbürgertum"*) and "world Jewry" to preserve the "life right of Europe" and "a culture corresponding to the racial characteristics of each people," *"eine den Völkern arteigene Kultur."*[104] When German troops were retreating and German cities were being destroyed by Allied bombing in 1944, the propaganda machinery tried to foster fear of the "Anglo-American soldateska" and their alleged intentions of raping German women and putting them into army bordellos. This propaganda effort made some use of hostilities against African Americans among the German population, and rumors about German children lured with chocolate and then killed by African American soldiers were systematically spread. Overall, however, anti-American propaganda stressed that the Germans' main enemies were the Jews. In contrast to the anti-American propaganda, propagandistic efforts that talked about rape and brutality by the Soviets (so-called subhumans) were much more successful in the last year of the war, in no small part because Germans knew about the atrocities German soldiers and the SS committed on the Eastern front and in the occupied territories. As a result, many German soldiers and civilians preferred and even hoped to be captured or occupied by American troops.[105]

The different forms of negotiating American influences in the two postwar Germanies built on and revised a set of categories inherited from the discussions and battles of the 1920s, 1930s, and early 1940s. The following chapters explore how East and West Germans dealt with these legacies after 1945. They ask whether and how Americanized youth cultures destabilized the dominant political systems in postwar Germany; and they also examine how that potential for instability was contained.

Chapter 1 considers the visions of civilization and nation that shaped the regulation of popular culture consumption in both Germanies in the early 1950s. Both sides invoked antiblack, anti-Semitic, and misogynist sentiments to reject American influences ranging from jazz to movies to fashion. Chapter 2 demonstrates how East and West German authorities, responding to youth riots in the mid-1950s, linked American popular culture to the threat of fascism. They criticized young rebels' penchant for American fashions and their unruly behavior as dangerous to proper Germanness. Chapter 3 traces how West German social scientists, influenced by American thinkers, redefined adolescent rebelliousness as a psychological and nonpolitical problem in the second half of the 1950s. While East Germans continued to repress American influences, West German and American policies toward East Germany now employed cultural consumption as a Cold War weapon. Chapter 4 explores the gradual validation of certain forms of jazz in both Germanies. As jazz promoters worked to divorce jazz from associations with unbridled sexuality and lower-class culture, many West Germans, from youth officials to the defense minister, came to see jazz as an appropriate cultural expression for a democratic society. East German authorities, despite some vacillations in the party line, continued to reject most forms of jazz as "decadent." As chapter 5 shows, both East and West German authorities felt intensely threatened by the racial and gender transgressions that rock 'n' roll represented. The depoliticization of Americanized youth cultures, which was fostered by the West German entertainment industry, allowed for the increasing acceptance of rock 'n' roll in West Germany, but required containing aggressive young male rebels and the highly visible, sexualized female fans of rock 'n' roll in private "safe" heterosexual relationships. It also entailed a "whitening" of the products these adolescents consumed. The epilogue explores the implications of these shifts in Cold War conflicts and looks ahead to the roots of yet another youth rebellion in the 1960s. It also asks once again what concepts might help us in developing the comparative history of the two Cold War Germanies.

The significance of East and West German contests over American popular culture goes beyond changes in adolescent dress and behavior. Debates about American popular culture in the 1950s were not simply about Germany becoming more American, rather they played an important role in the complicated processes of reconstructing Germanness in the aftermath of National Socialism and in the face of the Cold War.

1 American Culture in East and West German Reconstruction

In 1953 Karl Bednarik published a book, which was widely read and reviewed in West Germany, on what he called a "new type" of young male workers. According to Bednarik these young men were characterized by two things above all: their love for westerns and other sensationalist films and their enthusiasm for jazz.[1] That same year East German officials and newspapers drew a similar image of male adolescents. In the aftermath of the June 1953, uprising in East Germany, they accused *"Tangojünglinge"* (Tango-boys) and other young males in "Texas shirts" and cowboy pants of having caused "provocations."[2]

In the decade following World War II, many East and West Germans came once again to believe, and fear, that American popular culture was shaping young Germans and especially young German men. From the late 1940s through the first half of the 1950s, debates over westerns, gangster stories, and jazz became vehicles through which Germans on both sides of the descending Iron Curtain discussed American influences and changing German identities. How to make German boys into men who were neither too weak nor too aggressive and how to make German girls into respectable women became one of the major challenges for East and West German authorities, as they were seeking to separate themselves from National Socialism and to rebuild their societies—and soon also their armies—in the face of the Cold War. The conflicts over American popular culture between East and West German authorities and adolescents became a central component in the cultural and political dynamics that shaped the growing division between the two Germanies.

Along with the ideas about America that Germans had developed during the Weimar and Nazi years, the experiences of U.S. and Soviet occupation, including fraternization, rape, denazification, and economic policies, were important in shaping ambivalent and often hostile East and West German attitudes toward American influences. In the midst of poverty and ruins, the Allies, and the newly appointed German authorities, began to ask how Germans should educate and entertain themselves. Because of censorship and economic constraints, Germans had relatively little access to American westerns and gangster movies in the immediate postwar years and adolescents instead avidly consumed dime novels. By the early 1950s, however, the U.S. film industry was delivering plenty of movies, including westerns and gangster films, to West Germany. Throughout the 1950s American films made up the majority of movies released in West Germany, and Germans flooded to see them.[3]

Even with the division of Germany, American influences could still be felt in the Soviet Zone and later in the GDR. Authorities there increasingly tried to prevent their population's exposure to American culture, but they could not control access. In East Germany, no American movies were released in the 1940s and only six American films were shown in the course of the 1950s, but East German authorities were well aware that every day

 thousands of East Germans, especially young people, crossed the borders to the Western sectors of Berlin where they watched West European and American movies.[4] East German papers even reviewed many American films as soon as they opened in West Berlin. By contrast, Soviet productions, which made up at least 50 percent of the movies released in the Soviet Zone, were "too heavy," too serious, or too militaristic for German audiences who complained that such movies provided little enjoyment. As one Soviet cultural officer concluded, Germans were interested only in films about adventure and romance.[5] American movies thus quickly proved more popular than Soviet productions. Also, Germans in all zones could listen to jazz on the radio and in clubs in the late 1940s, and many of them adopted American dance styles such as the boogie.

While many U.S. government programs in the 1940s and 1950s sought to prove to Germans that the United States was a land of high culture, East and West German officials, like authorities in the Weimar Republic and the Third Reich, grew increasingly worried about the impact that American movies, jazz, and boogie-woogie had on German youth. In the new German states, youth protection efforts varied, but both sides often drew on prewar discourses in their efforts to contain the impact of American-style consumer culture. At the same time, East German authorities made highly publicized efforts to exploit hostilities toward American culture that existed in East and West Germany. During the 1950 trial of Werner Gladow, whose gang had engaged in a crime spree across East and West Berlin, and the 1953 East German uprising, East German officials and the press linked American culture directly to juvenile delinquency and political deviance. This put West Germans, who were forging an alliance with the United States and who had plenty of Americans in their territory, into an awkward position. However, in both Germanies some officials also tried to use American or American-influenced cultural products, such as movies or jazz, to attract adolescents to their respective political causes. Under the conditions of the Cold War and in the context of diverging political and economic systems, such voices gained some, if always embattled, force in West Germany.

OCCUPATION AND FRATERNIZATION

In 1945, neither Germans nor the Allies who had defeated Germany had a clear vision of what the future would hold for the country. Most German cities lay in ruins, many people lived in cellars and destroyed buildings, often separated from their families. Millions of Displaced Persons (former concentration camp inmates and forced laborers) were awaiting repatriation or immigration visas. Moreover, millions of "ethnic Germans" who had fled or were expelled from the Eastern parts of the former Reich and the German-occupied territories were searching for new homes. Geographically and politically, Germany was divided into four occupation zones: American, British, French, and Russian, each with its military government. The Allies also divided Berlin into four sectors, although the city had a common administration.

During the following years, the four Allies shaped the political and economic reconstruction within their zones, even as they increasingly transferred control to German authorities. With the intensification of the Cold War, the Western Allies—the United States, Britain, and France—agreed to cooperate as they built a democratic state with a market economy in their three zones, which covered the Western two thirds of Germany and held over 70 percent of its population. In 1947 the United States and Britain formed "Bizonia." A year later "Trizonia," which also included the French zone of occupation, followed. In the Eastern zone, the Soviets, together with German communists, pursued the nationalization of industries, introduced land reform, and insured that the SED, the Socialist Unity Party, became the ruling party.

Even as the Allies repeatedly exchanged notes and held conferences about building a united Germany, the Cold War division of the country took shape. In 1947, the Soviets rejected the economic aid offered by the

United States through the Marshall Plan. The following year, in June 1948, the Western Allies reformed the currency in the Western zones, thus stabilizing economic activity there and also affirming the division of Germany. In response, the Soviet Union imposed a blockade on West Berlin, which lasted until May 1949.

Berlin would not remain unified in this climate. In November 1948, Soviet and East German authorities put an end to the united German local administration for all of Berlin and formed a separate Berlin government in their sector. Germans (and the world) came to think of the Soviet sector as East Berlin and of the three Western sectors as West Berlin.

The Allies continued to formalize the division of Germany over the next year. In May 1949, the Federal Republic was founded on the territory of the three Western zones, and in October the founding of the German Democratic Republic on the territory of the Soviet Zone followed. By 1955, both German states became formally sovereign while firmly tied to the two emerging political and military blocs: NATO in the West and the Warsaw Pact in the East.[6]

In the second half of the 1940s, Allies and Germans were very concerned with the provision of food and housing, but they were also trying to figure out how to reconstruct and reeducate a nation that had waged a terrible war and committed horrific crimes in an effort to forge a racial utopia. Many Germans were anxious and feared retribution; others hoped for radical change.

The experiences of occupation shaped German reactions to American culture in important ways. The American military presence in Germany changed with the developments of the Cold War. When Germany signed the declaration of unconditional surrender in May 1945, 2.6 million U.S. troops were deployed in Europe. The vast majority of them was quickly deactivated and replaced with a much smaller force necessary for the occupation of the American zones in Austria and in Germany (including Bavaria, Hesse, northern sections of Baden and Württemberg, and the city of Bremen). In 1950 American troop strength in Europe dropped to a mere eighty thousand. With the outbreak of the Korean War that same year, however, the U.S. government reversed this trend and by 1951 a quarter million American soldiers were again stationed in Germany, most of them in the West German state of Rhineland-Palatinate, which had originally been part of the French zone of occupation. Until the end of the Cold War in the early 1990s, the United States would retain similar or higher troop strength in West Germany as its central contribution to the NATO forces in western Europe.[7]

Fraternization of German women and American soldiers accompanied the American military presence and worried many Germans. In the West German press of the late 1940s, stories critical of female divorcees and "fraternizers" replaced laudatory reports about the brave *Trümmerfrauen* (women who were clearing the rubble of destroyed cities). Fraternizers were depicted as selfish and seemed to further weaken German male authority. In the West perhaps more so than in the East, the disruption and guilt of these years were thus frequently displaced onto women.[8]

West German commentators focused especially on those women who had relations with American soldiers. In spite of an initial U.S. ban on fraternization, aimed at reinforcing the notion of collective German guilt for war atrocities, many GIs struck up relationships with German women almost as soon as they entered German territory. American posters and literature gave dire warnings to U.S. troops about contracting venereal diseases from German women. Billboards showed a woman in a trench coat with "VD" stamped across her chest, and this acronym was further popularized with the song "Veronika, Danke Schön."

Nevertheless, more positive American views of German women soon prevailed, and in the minds of U.S. soldiers and politicians, the "rubble woman" replaced the male Nazi storm trooper as the dominant German image. Americans, like postwar Germans, did not view women as ardent followers of National Socialism and thus ignored women's contributions to the Nazi regime and the war effort. The apparently rapid rise of this view may have been aided by the fact that by December 1945, most U.S. troops who had seen combat were replaced by young men who had not fought the war in Europe. Official U.S. representations at home increasingly sought to desexualize relations between American GIs and German women in order to make German women and American behavior abroad appear respectable to domestic audiences. Popular German representations, in turn, did just the opposite. Germans used "Veronika" to label all women who entered relationships with GIs as prostitutes. Other derogatory expressions included *"Amiliebchen"* (Ami-lover) and "soldiers' brides." Drawing on the German stereotypes of powerful American women, called Amazons by some Weimar commentators, and playing with the term American zone, critics also referred to the German female fraternizers as *"Amizonen."* Particularly disturbing to these critics were no doubt the relationships between African American soldiers and white German women, who were often called *"Negerliebchen"* (Negro lovers). In the minds of Germans and of U.S. military authorities alike, such relationships once again raised fears about miscegenation, and after the fraternization ban was lifted, mixed-race couples found it much harder to receive marriage licenses from U.S. military commanders than their all-white counterparts.[9]

During the 1940s, many of the relationships between German women and U.S. soldiers were based on a need for food, consumer goods, and protection. That is not to say that mutual affection could not play a role; certainly numerous relationships ended in marriage. But in the minds of many Germans, the food or nylon stockings that German women received from their American lovers, or the dances they danced with them, confirmed a link that had a long history in German anti-Americanism: the link between consumption and the oversexualization of women. And even more so than in the interwar years, Germans now related these phenomena to the weakness of German men. Such concerns and the derogatory labels for German women who entered relationships with U.S. soldiers would continue well beyond the period of occupation. Over the next decades, reporting about American soldiers and their predilections for drinking, dancing, and/or German women would cement the link that most Germans made between America, consumption, and materialism.[10]

Overall, West German views of the United States continued to be deeply ambivalent. For many Germans, female "fraternizers" came to stand in for what they experienced as an emasculation and victimization first at the hands of the U.S. occupation force and then at the hands of the American military superpower. But alongside the criticisms of fraternizers and materialism existed a strong admiration for U.S. efforts to alleviate German deprivation, especially through the Berlin Airlift, the Marshall Plan, and CARE (Cooperative for American Relief to Everywhere) packages.

The images of fraternizers, wealth, and materialism, associated with one superpower, the United States, contrasted sharply with the images of the other superpower, the Soviet Union. Although hard to quantify, responses first to Soviet occupation and then to continuing Soviet influence in East Germany were more negative. Nazi propaganda that had portrayed Soviet soldiers as brutal subhumans appeared to be confirmed in the minds of many Germans when soldiers of the Red Army pillaged German towns and engaged in a campaign of mass rapes in 1945. In the Eastern Zone, the threat of rape continued for women until Soviet troops were confined to their barracks in the winter of 1947–48. To be sure, rapes also occurred in the West in 1945, but to a much lesser degree.[11] As with fraternization in West Germany, mass rapes in East Germany were part of the gender crisis caused by war and occupation. But ironically, mass rapes also facilitated a resolution of this crisis in East Germany. In 1945 many German men failed to come to the aid of women, but over the following years, their role as protectors against a (diminishing) threat of rape became part of a "remasculinization" that happened perhaps more speedily in East than in West Germany.[12] While Soviet authorities and the leadership of the SED successfully suppressed public discussions of looting and rape, these events undoubtedly contributed to hostility toward the Soviet Union. Likely they also led to lower rates of fraternization, although the Soviets initially did not impose a fraternization ban, and fraternization between German women and Soviet soldiers happened for much the same reasons as in the West. Reparations set by the Soviets, which sharply reduced industrial capacity in the Eastern Zone, and the Marshall Plan, which soon spurred economic development in the Western zones, exacerbated this contrast between a Soviet Union associated with deprivation and a United States associated with prosperity—a contrast that Western propaganda would certainly exploit as the Cold War picked up.[13]

The seeds of this contrast were already planted during the early occupation when Allied cultural visions still shared many similarities. In occupied Germany the four Allies determined cultural policies, although they began to return control to the Germans in 1946. Each in their own zone, the Allies seized and denazified the mass media; they licensed newspapers and radio stations and controlled movie programs. In the Eastern zone, Soviet and German communists tried to foster a classical German tradition (for example, the works of Goethe, Schiller, and Beethoven) and opted for some variety in cultural life, in order to effect an "antifascist democratic" transformation of Germany. Their programs featured folk dances, films, and public ceremonies, and included Soviet music and film, but in 1945 and 1946, they agreed that it was not yet time to adopt a Soviet model in Germany.[14] The Western Allies also hoped to counter Nazi ideas, which they believed were deeply ingrained in German society, through reeducation programs. As part of these efforts to turn Germans into democrats, they, too, sought to foster a classical German tradition, supplemented with modernist art.[15]

A major goal of the Office of Military Government of the United States (OMGUS) in occupied Germany, led by General Lucius Clay, was to prevent the renewed rise of German fascism through the establishment of democratic institutions and the "moral and cultural reeducation" of the German population. Although the U.S. government soon realized that full implementation of the "four D's"—denazification, demilitarization, decartelization, and democratization—was impractical, reeducation remained important. Reeducation measures concentrated in particular on educational policies, the media, and cultural policies; they included the reform of schools and universities (which quickly failed due to German opposition) and translations of American scholarship and literature as well as the establishment of American cultural centers. From 1946 to 1954, an ambitious exchange program brought about eleven thousand German politicians, bureaucrats, journalists, judges, clergy, trade union members, and functionaries of youth associations to the United States. Initially OMGUS officials watched carefully that they appointed no former Nazis to positions in the new bureaucracies. With the worsening of the Cold War, however, and with increasing efforts to integrate West Germany into a Western alliance, it soon became expedient to employ former Nazis. This contributed to the cynicism many Germans felt toward reeducation.

With the founding of the Federal Republic of Germany (FRG) in 1949, OMGUS was transformed into its civilian successor, the Office of the High Commissioner for Germany (HICOG), comprising representatives from the three Western Allies and led until 1952 by American John McCloy. West Germany remained under the Occupation Statute that made the new state into a self-governing dominion under Allied supervision. HICOG could theoretically intervene in any political issue in the new FRG, but McCloy pursued a cautious policy designed to bolster the authority of the newly elected government under Christian Democrat Konrad Adenauer. Under HICOG, some American educational and cultural programs, now geared toward "positive reorientation" were stepped up and extended to all of Germany. These efforts, including the exchange program and the American cultural centers, clearly focused on educating a new, democracy-minded West German elite. Almost half of the exchanges under HICOG involved elite groups of young people, including university and high school students, and youth leaders, among them numerous future West German leaders of the 1960s and 1970s. HICOG scaled back its activities in 1952 and was disbanded completely in May 1955 when the Occupation Statute formally ended and West Germany received full sovereignty.[16]

As they were seeking to liberate Germans into a Western-style capitalist democracy in the postwar years, American leaders themselves were ambivalent about the use of American popular culture in Germany. Hostilities toward American popular culture persisted in both Germany and the United States after World War II. In this context, the U.S. government did not include American popular culture in the reeducation programs for German prisoners of war and tried to control what cultural products entered postwar Germany. Often government officials found themselves at odds with the American entertainment industry. In the decade from 1946 to 1955, the American cultural centers, so-called *Amerikahäuser,* which opened in major West German cities with support from the American government, did little to spread American popular culture—be it popular movies or jazz—in Germany. The first of the "America Houses" grew out of a U.S. information center in Frankfurt in 1946; by 1950 their numbers had grown to twenty in the U.S. occupation zone including West Berlin, and by 1951 to twenty-seven in all of West Germany. Officials in the cultural centers established libraries with open stacks, organized lectures, offered concerts of "serious" music, and showed educational movies. Until the mid-1950s, they rarely sponsored jazz events, because most American elites themselves considered jazz low culture.[17] U.S. officials were busy convincing the German public that democracy and "culture" were not contradictions and that the democratic United States was indeed a haven of high culture. With their programs, they consciously catered to an audience they considered influential in German politics and society. In several reports, American officials expressed their satisfaction that those who visited American cultural centers were predominantly male and from the middle and upper socioeconomic strata.[18]

But American popular culture found its way into East and West Germany through other channels: American soldiers; Allied radio stations, especially the American and British Forces Networks; the increasing efforts of the American movie industry to gain access to the West German market; and German musicians and music fans who now shared their enthusiasm for American music publicly. At the same time German-produced visions of America circulated, especially in dime novels. All of these sources contributed to shaping German images of America.

Initially, the direct interactions between West Germans and American GIs were the primary source of cultural contact. In the American Zone, members of the American military began to provide adolescents with opportunities for sports and entertainment at the end of 1945. Formalized in 1946, the offerings of the army-sponsored German Youth Activities (GYA) ranged from baseball to lessons on how to behave as a democratic citizen. The activities differed depending on local conditions, but in many cases they exposed German adolescents to American music and movies—and consequently met with the resistance of local church officials who feared an "Americanization" of youth through these coeducational and cross-denominational activities.[19]

By the 1950s the channels of the American and West German entertainment industries became more important than direct contact with American troops in transmitting American popular culture to West Germany. In the 1940s, the influence of the U.S. film industry, and along with it the selection of American movies, was still quite limited. When, at the end of July 1945, U.S. military authorities allowed movie theaters to re-open in the American Zone, they showed American movies that were licensed to the Psychological Warfare Division and the Office of War Information. But since these movies could not meet the high demand for films, U.S. officials soon permitted theaters to show German features that American authorities deemed harmless. Film policy was originally organized on a zonal basis. By 1948, however, British and French authorities were following American policies.

In February 1948, the American Military Government authorized the Motion Picture Export Association (MPEA)—founded by major producers and distributors in the United States—to distribute movies commercially in the U.S. Zone. Until mid-1948, only eighty-three U.S. feature films were released in the three Western zones, and authorities and distributors could not meet the demand for copies. The MPEA delivered U.S. movies to Germany, but since most of the MPEA's German earnings remained frozen, it mostly distributed copies of old releases. Such movies included few westerns or other thrillers.[20]

While Germans still found it somewhat difficult to see American movies in the second half of the 1940s, a market for dime novels blossomed. Most of these were produced in the Western zones, but were also available in the Soviet Zone. In fact, along the border of the Western sectors in Berlin, "exchange" shops catered specifically to an East German pulp-fiction audience. Many of the most popular and most discussed dime novels were gangster or western stories set in the United States. Printed westerns actually ranged from the novels that the German author Karl May had written in the early part of the century to more recently produced dime novels. Adolescents, especially boys from the middle classes, avidly consumed May's novels, which were widely available in West Germany. Perhaps because these were book length, perhaps because they featured lengthy nature descriptions, or perhaps because they championed manly fictional heroes like the white man of the American West, Old Shatterhand and the chief of the Apaches, Winnetou (who both embodied the Christian maxim of love thy neighbor and fought bad American Indians and money-hungry whites alike), the May novels were absent from public discussions of westerns in the 1940s and 1950s.[21] Instead commentators—sociologists, church film leagues, policymakers, and the press in the West, and party and state officials and the press in the East—focused on dime novel and movies. The fact that most of the dime novels were German produced did not prevent Germans from debating and

Fig. 2.   Reading pulp fiction in postwar Germany, 1950. Photo: Gerd Mingram, courtesy Bildarchiv Preußischer Kulturbesitz.

rejecting them as American. In the late 1940s and early 1950s, these booklets worried East and West German authorities at least as much as the movies.[22]

Like dime novels, jazz, too, was widely available in all four zones. After years of facing possible persecution by the Nazis, German jazz fans brought out their jazz records, and German jazz musicians played in the midst of ruins. In 1945 and 1946 fans who had not given up their enthusiasm for the music during the Nazi years founded so-called "Hot Clubs" in several East and West German cities, including Leipzig, Berlin, and Frankfurt. They took their name from similar clubs that had existed in the United States since the 1930s. The American and British occupying forces also brought American popular music with them. Given the attacks on jazz music and jazz fans during the Third Reich, many Germans found it exhilarating after May 1945 to listen to jazz music on AFN or BFN. They saw the American tunes that could be heard in all occupation zones as a symbol of a more general liberation from Nazi oppression.[23]

In these years of flux, jazz music and fans crossed easily back and forth between the Western and the Soviet occupation zones. In July 1948, during the Berlin Blockade, Rex Stewart became the first American jazz musician to play in front of German audiences after the war. East and West German jazz fans welcomed him enthusiastically during his concerts in West Berlin. That same year, the East German state-owned label Amiga issued a recording of one of his performances with German musicians. Indeed, between 1946 and 1948, Amiga made more jazz recordings than all West German companies combined. And the activities of the East German state youth organization Free German Youth (FDJ), founded under communist leadership and with participation of confessional and bourgeois groups in 1946, included dancing to the music of Glenn Miller and Benny Goodman as well as to American boogie-woogie.[24]

The relative isolation of the war and postwar years meant that German musicians and fans had missed the latest musical developments in the United States. Picking up where they left off, they listened mostly to music inspired by the swing bands of the 1930s. In the postwar years, German fans defined jazz very broadly and many considered everything AFN broadcast—from bebop to country music—to be jazz. The same was true for most German bands: they also did not distinguish between jazz and other hits and played both. As one jazz aficionado remembered, these bands frequently encountered very noisy audiences, mostly of young people, who used the concerts to romp around.[25]

Not surprisingly, given the German history of attacks on jazz dating back to the Weimar years, German hostilities toward jazz music and its fans did not disappear with the defeat of National Socialism. In the cultural monthly *Aufbau*, published in the Soviet Zone, music critic Paul Höfer defended jazz against its critics: "Even today, in 1946," criticized Höfer, "there still exist in our society those who, still believing firmly in German superiority, dismiss jazz as *'Negermusik.'* "[26] When German musician Kurt Wege and his big band played jazz rhythms in 1947, the popular West German magazine *Hörzu* received petitions that contained hundreds of signatures complaining about the band's performances. In response, jazz fans collected even more signatures in favor of Wege.

In order to answer the question whether jazz was a "disgrace to civilization" *(Kulturschande)*, *Hörzu* published an article by the culture editor of the respected West German weekly *Die Zeit*. The author briefly criticized the prohibition of jazz during the Third Reich, and then responded explicitly to some of the accusations leveled against jazz before and after 1945. The objection that jazz was Negro music was both true and false, he explained. While its existence depended on the Negro bands of New Orleans, these "black-skinned musicians" had in fact reworked the European chorales that Christian missionaries had taught them. Negroes, "unmusical, as they are, and at the same time deeply naive," intended their music to be pious. The author claimed that Negroes had added improvisation to European-based music. Whether jazz was a disgrace to civilization, the author concluded, depended on how it was played: He criticized musicians who overused syncopation and thus achieved a "disturbing overheating" that was "often correctly reproved as 'squeaking, tearing, grunting, howling.' " But played in a somewhat calmer style, with much individual freedom, while stressing commonality, jazz "was almost a theme song for democracy." This defense of jazz thus depended on stressing the European roots of the music, while making clear that classical European music was superior. At the same time the author affirmed long-standing stereotypes of blacks as naive and as unmusical.[27] Other promoters of jazz, who were responding to continuing hostilities against the music, would often use similar, problematic arguments in the course of the 1950s.

ESCALATING COLD WAR TENSIONS

In 1947 and 1948, when the West reformed the currency and the Soviets imposed the blockade of West Berlin (which both represented and intensified the increasingly deep lines in the Cold War), political and cultural relations between the Soviet and the Western zones soured. East and West Germans defined Germanness more and more not just in relation to the

Weimar and Nazi past, but also in relation to one another. In this context uneasiness about the impact of (American) popular culture in postwar Germany took on new meaning. Concerns over jazz music and the effect of gangster and western stories told in movies and pulp fiction quickly became an important part of the Cold War battle.

After 1947 the Soviet military authorities and East German communists made concerted efforts to convince the Germans of the superiority of Soviet culture. While Soviet opera, ballet, and poster art were certainly successful—more so than Soviet films—the promotion of Soviet culture ran up against obstacles. For one, in spite of official pronouncements, German anti-Bolshevism and hostilities toward Soviet culture persisted, and second, the bureaucracy of the Soviet Union proved consistently too inefficient to even fill the requests for Soviet materials that officials from the military government or East German functionaries made.[28]

As the Cold War heated up, the press of the Soviet Zone began a campaign against the United States and the U.S. presence in Germany. In 1947 and 1948, for example, the Soviet occupation newspaper for Germans, *Tägliche Rundschau,* repeatedly reported alleged rape and pillage committed by U.S. occupiers and contrasted it with the cultured and generous Russians.[29] By 1950 posters produced for the East German government declared: "American High Commissioner McCloy on 4 July 1950: 'I feel at home in Germany!' Germany replies: 'Yankee, go home!'" That same year other propaganda claimed that "Yankee Beetles [a potato pest allegedly planted by U.S. planes] Are Set to Destroy Our Livelihood."[30]

As the communists strengthened their hold on power, they lashed out against American influences both in East and West Germany. The official newspaper of the East German SED, *Neues Deutschland,* asserted in 1948 that the cultural level of the West was sinking rapidly.[31] Also in 1948, the SED declared itself to be a "Party of the New Type," thus affirming its commitment to Moscow and to socialism. The way the SED defined its relationship to the Soviet Union appeared somewhat contradictory. On the one hand the SED gave out the slogan "To Learn from the Soviet Union Is to Learn to Be Victorious," but on the other hand the Soviet military administration encouraged the SED to pursue a "German road to socialism."[32]

Both impulses coexisted in the SED and in East German cultural policies. One East German official, Anton Ackermann, claimed in May 1948 that socialism did not mean a liquidation of national cultural forms. Drawing on Stalin, he further explained that the cultural forms of one country should and could not be exported into another.[33] Thus he stressed the necessity of a German national culture, and he implicitly criticized American influences increasingly visible in West Germany and West Berlin. At the same time, the "East German road to socialism" did not entail questioning Soviet policies or culture. Rather, East German officials reformulated their earlier policies and attacked American popular culture both inside and outside their borders as part of a campaign that was modeled on Andrei Zhdanov's efforts in the Soviet Union. Zhdanov had launched his attacks against American and other foreign influences and the forces of "decadence" and "cosmopolitanism" in 1946, and two years later East German officials adopted his arguments. This cultural campaign directed against both modernism and mass culture was part of accelerated Stalinization throughout the Communist Bloc. Neither East German officials nor their Soviet supervisors any longer supported the notion of cultural diversity.[34]

The vocabulary of "decadence" and "degeneration" was not the invention of Soviet or East German authorities. Rather, as we have seen, European and American writers and thinkers across the political spectrum had leveled such attacks against various forms of art as well as mass culture since the nineteenth century. "Decadence" had connoted deviations from civilization, from respectable manhood and womanhood, and critics had often used it along with "degeneration" to fight products or behavior they perceived as racial transgressions. This language had gained special significance in the 1930s and 1940s when National Socialists strove to exclude and extinguish what they perceived as different from a Germanic ideal by invoking "decadence" and "degeneration" as signifiers for gender disarray and racial decline. Both German and Soviet Communists had likewise used "decadence" and "degeneration" in order to attack American culture, especially most forms of jazz, as expressions of bourgeois decline. The term "cosmopolitanism" had a similarly problematic history; in both Nazi Germany and Stalin's Soviet Union it had clear anti-Semitic and xenophobic undertones.[35]

In postwar Soviet and East German attacks on mass culture and modernism, this vocabulary resurfaced. East German officials now used it to repudiate the National Socialist past and to attack their Cold War enemies. One of their intentions was to win East Germans over to their cause by appealing to what one might ironically call "bourgeois sensibilities." The attacks on mass culture and modernism once again established links to eugenics at a time when eugenic thinking was still prevalent, for example among members of the medical profession in East Germany. This language likely allowed East German officials to attract some conservative and bourgeois elements in society, especially among the intelligentsia, which had for the most part remained at a distance from the regime.[36]

On the other side of the Iron Curtain, West German authorities, in spite of their commitment to a Western military and political alliance, were trying to find a fourth "German" way, between the threat of Bolshevism, the self-destructive, sexualizing, and emasculating powers emanating from American-style consumer culture, and finally the dangerous secularism and materialism that according to many contemporary commentators had led to National Socialism. To separate themselves from all three, conservatives from the governing Christian Democrats (CDU/CSU) were promoting the notion of a "Christian Occident" *(Christliches Abendland)* in the late 1940s and early 1950s. Both the Protestant and Catholic churches seized the moral vacuum left by National Socialism and were able to influence public discourse as well as social and cultural policies of the national and local governments with their conservative visions. The churches founded film leagues and publicized their views of specific films. Representatives of church charities shaped the work of the influential Federal Working Group on Youth Protection *(Bundesarbeitsgemeinschaft Aktion Jugendschutz),* which also included representatives from government and nonconfessional charities. It operated as a pressure group and organizer of events at both the federal and the state level. The opposition Social Democrats (SPD) remained mostly outside the churches' realm of influence, but they, too, largely supported the national government's cultural conservatism. Concerns about respectability were apparently shared by large sections of the West German population, who bought a great number of manuals on "proper behavior."[37]

With mounting fears about consumption and American popular culture, West German cultural conservatives tried to fight, as one of them, Robert Brüntrop, put it in a welfare journal, "two epidemics that were mutually dependent and drove each other" and that were characteristic of all Western cultures: "the growing sexualization of our cultural life" and "the addictive love of pleasure."[38] Consumption and entertainment were once again associated with dangerous sexuality. Such postwar commentary used the language that Weimar conservatives, especially those influenced by Catholic social theory, had leveled against "materialism" in both its Bolshevist and American manifestations. Now such accusations were also directed against the Third Reich, which conservatives interpreted as an expression of the excess of the "mass age."[39] Brüntrop and others also worried about the present biological state of the nation. In the midst of continuing hunger and hardship, they urged a state policy of youth protection to mobilize against the alleged "self-destruction of the German people" through consumer culture.[40] Placing such a vision firmly in the Cold War context, officials from the West German Ministry of the Interior linked the need for youth protection, and the dangers of materialism, to the threats of socialism and National Socialism. "To protect the young person from drowning in a collective being is the purpose of youth protection," they announced.[41] Yet, another statement made by the chief administrator of *Aktion Jugendschutz* and released by the West German government made it clear that Western-style capitalism was just as dangerous, since it exposed adolescents to the "unrestrained drive for profit on the part of an entertainment industry that is extremely rich in capital."[42]

In 1951 and 1953, the West German parliament passed two youth protection laws. Unlike the Nazi laws of the 1940s, these did not threaten adolescents, but rather adults, and especially the entertainment industry, with punishment, although the police could pick up adolescents from "improper places" and take them back to their parents. All major West German parties supported the first law, which primarily regulated adolescents' access to dances, movies, and alcohol. The Social Democrats did not vote for the second, which provided for restrictions on printed matter, including pornography and pulp fiction, because they feared that the law could be used as a tool of political censorship. Nonetheless, the SPD, too, agreed that pulp fiction was dangerous. Officials in all West German states, including those governed by the SPD, sponsored events against pulp fiction throughout the 1950s, where children and adolescents literally buried their dime novels in a *Schmökergrab* (a pulp-fiction grave) or exchanged them for "better" literature.[43]

In these West German youth protection efforts, cultural conservatism was interlinked with gender conservatism. The 1951 law, for example, made the protection of marriage and family its explicit purpose. Believing that the West German family had survived National Socialism unscathed, the mainstream parties agreed that families of male breadwinners/protectors and female caretakers were central to postwar West German stability. Healthy families with traditional gender roles distinguished West Germany from its Cold War enemies to the East and from the dangers of American-style consumer culture arriving from the West. While the wording of the youth protection laws was gender neutral, the intentions and enforcement of the laws were in fact gender specific. Measures against violent gangster and western stories, in films or fiction, were geared toward curtailing male overaggression, and the restrictions on dancing were supposed to prevent the oversexualization of women.[44] As local officials made clear when promoting the law, dance events led girls into sexual delinquency and the dance provisions provided especially for the "protection" of girls.[45]

West German politicians thus constructed and asserted their views of proper femininity and masculinity not only in social policies, but also in their efforts to regulate cultural consumption. In fact, given their own misgivings about mass culture, West German authorities proved sensitive to East German charges that West Germany was being overrun by American popular culture.

"BERLIN IS NOT CHICAGO": THE GLADOW TRIAL

In 1950, increasing East German hostilities toward American influences found a focal point in the trial of Werner Gladow. In the late 1940s, Gladow's gang, made up of adolescent and adult men, had committed armed robberies in stores and private homes all across East and West Berlin; in the course of their crime spree, they had even killed some of their victims. The East Berlin police finally arrested the so-called "Gladow-gang." Gladow and nine of the gang members were put on trial in East Berlin in March and April of 1950. Although Gladow had not yet been eighteen when he committed most of his crimes, the court sentenced him to death and he was executed in December 1950.[46] Papers in East and West Berlin closely followed the proceedings of the trial, and East German officials and the East German press used the publicity for an all-out attack on American popular culture, especially on westerns and gangster movies and pulp fiction.

The East German press and some West Berlin papers put images of the Wild West and of American gangsters at the center of Gladow's story. As witnesses offered testimony, papers treated Gladow as a ruthless western hero and/or American style-gangster. One East Berlin article referred to Gladow's crimes as "Wild West adventures."[47] Other East German authors stressed that Gladow had modeled his crimes on stories about America told in dime novels. Gladow indeed seemed to be the perfect proof of East German accusations against the American "cultural barbarism" that allegedly led to overly aggressive German men. The East German press used images of an "uncivilized" America for a more general indictment of American culture and policies in postwar Germany.

The Gladow trial was marked by the oddities, and permeability, of the early Cold War division. Although it took place in East Germany, the court called a West Berlin psychiatrist to assess Gladow's behavior. Perhaps East German officials hoped to highlight that Germans on both sides of the Iron Curtain had misgivings about American popular culture.

The West Berlin psychiatrist testified that the legendary American gangster Al Capone had been Gladow's ideal. Gladow, who had consumed adventure dime novels from an early age, supposedly identified with the Al Capone presented in this literature: "a go-getter, despiser of mankind, and chivalrous adventurer in one person." According to the psychiatrist, a biography of Al Capone that had been published recently had strongly influenced Gladow. The accused himself confirmed this notion and declared that dime novels and movies had had a deep impact on him. He had modeled his crimes after them, while avoiding his heroes' mistakes.[48]

Showing Gladow's deviance involved associating him with "bad" women as well as with ruthless and untamed aggression. Papers focused on Gladow's "inadequate" mother with whom he had lived on the East side of the city and who was put on trial for misleading authorities about her son's whereabouts. Throughout the trial, East and West German papers portrayed her as hysteric and held her, rather than his father, who had been absent from the family for extended periods, responsible for Gladow's crimes.[49] Moreover, by focusing on what Gladow read (besides stories about Al Capone), East German papers linked him to pornography and women who lacked respectability, especially prostitutes. The East Berlin *Tägliche Rundschau* gave a sample of his readings, which ranged from "The Erotic Question Mark," to "Adventure of a Whore" to "Robbery in Chicago" and "A Colt in Each Hand." West German papers, on the other hand, rarely reported about such readings.[50]

East German papers linked the detrimental impact of American cultural influences to fascism. According to the West Berlin psychiatrist, whose testimony East German papers recounted, the combined impact of fascism and American popular culture had led Gladow to his crimes. The *Tägliche Rundschau* quoted the psychiatrist: "His fascist education, the deep impressions that the war left washed him down into the sluttish kitchen of American gangster movies, of crime stories, of murder and [other] sensational trials, to whose influence he succumbed."[51] A headline in the same paper went further: "Gladow's ideals: Wild West and Gestapo." Gladow supposedly had learned how to rob from gangster movies, how to gag his victim from American westerns, and how to torture them from the Gestapo.[52] This alleged connection between fascism and American popular culture defined a central position in both East and West German discourses on American influences.

However, stressing the manipulative influence of American popular culture put East German papers in a difficult position as they evaluated Gladow's guilt: the West Berlin psychiatrist proved how easily Gladow could be influenced, and consequently demanded that he be treated as a juvenile offender, rather than as an adult criminal. In that case Gladow could not have been sentenced to death according to GDR law.[53]

In spite of their hostility to American westerns and mysteries, East German papers resolved this problem by casting Gladow's story itself as a combination of western and crime narrative—one in which, however, the good guys won. Commentators imagined Gladow as a combination of the urban criminal Al Capone and western hero. One article described how "he races the asphalt of Chicago, as he leads his devoted gang with cowboy hat and revolver to one crime after the other."[54] However this western, unlike many of the dime novels and adventure movies, had what East German authorities regarded as a proper ending: in Gladow's case the authority of the state had prevailed. Papers stressed the testimony of high ranking police officer Schlädicke, who described Gladow as "society's deadly enemy."[55] Schlädicke claimed that he had put his own life on the line during Gladow's arrest, discounted the testimony of the psychiatrist, and demanded that Gladow be treated as an adult. While one West Berlin paper maintained that Schlädicke had not even been at the forefront of Gladow's arrest, East German reports stressed that he was "a man of action."[56]

The mixing of images drawn from two genres, the western and the gangster narrative, may seem surprising at first. The two genres represented two poles of negative images of America, the modern urban setting in the gangster film and the rural wilderness in the western. But often the audiences for both types of stories were young men, and East German commentators read them as promoting lawlessness and violence. A subgenre of American westerns of the late 1930s and 1940s, which celebrated the careers of famous outlaws such as *Jesse James* (1939) (and which Richard Slotkin has called the "outlaw" western), probably reinforced such associations. These westerns were just being released in West Germany around 1950. In their intense anti-Americanism, East German commentators failed to recognize that these outlaw westerns often located the source of social injustice in powerful capitalist institutions, such as railroads and banks.[57]

In his final statement, the East German prosecutor concurred with Schlädicke and demanded the death sentence for Gladow. He announced that "Berlin is not Chicago," a statement echoed in many papers.[58] Gladow had to die to set the GDR apart from the anarchism associated with capitalist urbanization. As the prosecutor explained, in the United States the "gangster king" Al Capone had been allowed to die of natural causes in bed. Although the psychiatrist recommended that Gladow not be tried as an adult, the court ruled in favor of capital punishment, and a few months later, Gladow was executed.

In summarizing the trial, East German papers leveled ever stronger attacks on American popular culture and American politics. As one East German paper put it, the sentencing of Gladow merely tackled the symptoms of the dangerous American way of life, but judicial measures alone would not suffice in rooting out this evil. The American imports and the American way of life posed a danger not just to German youth but to all German people. The paper demanded a unified democratic cultural policy for all of Berlin and asserted that the fight for the unity of Berlin and for Germany's unity was also the most effective fight against the "murderous economic, social and 'cultural' influences of the American imperialists."[59]

The East German press drew alleged parallels between German fascism and U.S. imperialism and made both responsible for past and present crime. "Dr. Goebbel's total war and Dean Acheson's total diplomacy are complemented by the total crimes of Al Capone and Werner Gladow."[60] Another paper suspected a conspiracy between Wall Street and Hollywood designed to educate millions of West German and West Berlin youths to brutality and killing. Preparation for war was the real objective of this American manipulation of youth.[61] Fighting the United States thus became a way for East German authorities to distance East Germany from the National Socialist past as well as from the West German state.

East German officials and the East German press tried to mobilize their vision of a unified German culture against American influences. As one commentator urged, a German *Volkskultur* (people's culture) needed to be pitted against the barbarizing influences of American mass culture.[62] In the context of a divided Germany, their focus on American cultural influences allowed East German authorities to stress what was evil about capitalism and Western imperialism, while leaving the door open for German rapprochement. This attitude was in tune with the official East German ideology that called for German unification. East German officials portrayed American politicians as manipulators and driving forces behind American popular culture. They probably appealed to anti-Semites by claiming that Washington officials promoted Wall Street and "Hollywood politics." Given these accusations, the West German government appeared as a mere puppet of the United States. In exposing American popular culture as an ideological tool of the U.S. and West German governments, East German authorities tried to alert Germans to the existence of a "true" popular German identity that could breach the Iron Curtain and connect people in East and West Germany.

WEST GERMANS AND WESTERNS

Such East German pronouncements were fueled by the increasing availability and impact of American popular culture in West Germany. With the Currency Reform in 1948 and the strengthening of West Germany's economy, U.S. motion picture distributors developed a greater interest in full access to the German market. The numbers of American films exported to

West Germany jumped up dramatically, from 64 in the twelve months from mid-1948 to mid-1949 to 226 in 1951–52, where they remained throughout the 1950s. Despite some disputes between U.S. distributors and West German authorities who wanted to reduce that number, an average of 225 U.S. films per year were released until 1959. In these same years, the number of German releases rose from sixty-five to over a hundred per year, but remained consistently well below American imports.[63]

With the growth of imports, the types of American movies released in West Germany also changed. Much to the concern of many Germans, westerns became particularly popular and appeared in great numbers in West German movie theaters. According to a report by the Catholic Film Commission for Germany, the number of westerns released in West Germany rose from two at the beginning of 1948 to one hundred by November 1951. Eighteen months later the Commission reported with some concern that this number had doubled.[64]

West German papers in 1950 had treated Gladow's actions mostly as the result of growing up in the poverty and disorientation of the postwar years. Yet in West Germany, too, strong voices existed that saw westerns as a cause of male juvenile misbehavior and juvenile delinquency. West Germans were increasingly convinced that westerns played an important role in forming male adolescent identities. One sociological study found in 1952, that 33 percent of twelve- to fourteen-year-olds had the western hero as their ideal.[65] The West German press occasionally reported on crimes that boys had allegedly modeled on western or gangster narratives. In 1951, a survey asked juvenile court judges about the effects of movies. Numerous judges gave examples of delinquents who had frequented "cowboy" and "gangster" films, but most judges felt that it was unclear whether the movies had led adolescents into delinquency. When they published these findings in 1954, the authors of the survey warned that adolescents themselves made this connection to excuse their crimes.[66] Nonetheless many articles in the West German press and numerous film reception experts and educators claimed that westerns and gangster films were a direct cause of juvenile delinquency.

West German attacks on westerns were often more insidious than East German indictments, because they identified Native American Indians directly with the evil effects of westerns. In East and West German newspaper reports, Gladow was usually cast in the role of a white bandit, but in at least one instance a West Berlin paper identified him directly with the faceless Indians besieging whites who were so common to westerns in this period. To describe Gladow's way of torturing his victims, the paper em-

Fig. 3. West German boys in front of a movie theater, 1948. Photo: Gerd Mingram, courtesy Bildarchiv Preußischer Kulturbesitz.

ployed the word *"martern,"* which Germans used mostly when they described American Indian behavior. Thus, readers could actually place Gladow in the role of the savage Indian. Similarly, Fritz Stückrath, one of West Germany's foremost film reception experts, published his critique of westerns under a headline that suggested that Indians were dangerous: "The Attack of the Ogallala on the Youth." With these images, these West Germans in fact racialized the alleged dangers of westerns.[67]

Stückrath reiterated criticisms of westerns that the East German press had highlighted during the Gladow trial. Westerns convinced children that the adult world was a mix of "deceit, maliciousness, fights, racketeering, and shallow eroticism." Moreover they made children think that the roughest behavior was also the "manliest and most appropriate." Stückrath stressed that these adverse effects were by no means offset by the fact that in most of these films the good hero won out over the bad. Linking westerns directly to male criminal behavior, Stückrath told the story of a young man who had shot his friend during a game of cards. Like the East German press and authorities, he complained that, by glorifying violence and mixing it with eroticism, westerns prepared humanity for war.[68]

Stückrath placed his critique of westerns in the context of the recent German past. He disagreed with those critics who had made German fairy tales responsible for the brutalization of the German people. Rather, he argued, these fairy tales paled in comparison to the "uninterrupted attacks of the Ogallala from the Wild West." In this outrageous move, Stückrath thus implied that American westerns, rather than indigenous German culture, could be responsible for Nazi crimes.[69]

In 1952 a West German Cold War propaganda pamphlet on movies in the GDR clearly revealed West German hostilities against both Stalinism in the East and consumer culture in the West. The pamphlet explained that "the exaggerated wealth of Hollywood stars and producers—for decades symbolic of an overheated and overpaid cult of banality—had its equally monstrous counterpart in the Stalinist *Filmkultura*." Even as the author indicted both Hollywood and Stalinist cinema, he implied that Hollywood's influence was even more dangerous. For, refugees from the Soviet Union, the satellite states, and the "Soviet Zone" were still able "to distinguish between *Filmkitsch* and film art." Like "every person of taste" they rejected "gangster, sex, revue, and mawkish *Heimatfilme*."[70] In the face of the onslaught of American-style consumer culture, it appeared in the first half of the 1950s that West German authorities felt politically even more vulnerable than their East German counterparts.

The American movie imports became a contentious issue between East and West German authorities, especially so in Berlin. Westerns, along with gangster films, increasingly constituted the main offerings of the so-called border theaters in West Berlin, which catered specifically to East German visitors. An American official urged in 1950 that theaters along the border with East Berlin should get special tax breaks to offer low-priced movies for East Germans. Following this suggestion, West Berlin officials supported ten theaters by February 1951 and twenty-three by 1954. In 1951, West Berlin and HICOG officials inaugurated the Berlin Film Festival that brought international movies and stars to Berlin and was designed to be a "Western cultural showcase." As one American cultural officer explained to West Berlin officials, it was scheduled to be "the necessary counterweight" to the "International Youth Festival" that the official East German youth organization FDJ, under firm leadership of the SED, was sponsoring for the same summer in East Berlin.[71] In fact American and West German officials hoped to draw youth from the Eastern people's democracies to West Berlin and HICOG even sponsored outdoor border screenings at the Potsdamer Platz. To downplay U.S. government involvement and to demonstrate West German independence, the West Berlin city government was listed as the sole sponsor for the festival, even though HICOG officials participated in the planning and made financial contributions. The presence of American movie stars during the festival, by contrast, was publicly celebrated by the press and by the German organizers. They could be used to demonstrate the greater openness of West German democracy.[72]

Nonetheless many West German government officials and cultural leaders remained hostile or at least ambivalent about the power of American movies. Beginning in the fall of 1952, East German citizens complained to West Berlin authorities in a letter-writing campaign about the low quality of the movies shown there. West Berlin authorities took these complaints to be the genuine opinion of the East German population and not just of East German authorities. Consequently they were concerned enough to try and persuade theater owners to improve the programs. In 1952, for example, they put together a list of "desirable" movies; however, these efforts were largely unsuccessful.[73]

Worrying that West German state authorities might restrict the import of American films, U.S. movie distributors saw such hostility as a threat to their profits. In 1951, they were so concerned about the anti-American bias of "religious and educational bodies" in West Germany that they sent a special emissary "to clear away presently existing misunderstandings regarding American pictures." West Germans never brought any economic sanctions against American movies, but the hostilities continued.[74]

East German officials tried to play on West German fears of cultural Americanization. When the two hundredth western opened in West Germany in May 1953, the West German Catholic Film Commission, which had its own ranking system, found that of the 200, 153 were unsuitable for adolescents. On this occasion, one East German paper stressed that in the previous year more than 50 percent of all movies shown, in Hamburg for example, had been American productions. A full quarter of the four hundred American movies the West German market "had to swallow" were westerns. In East Germany, the first American western would not be shown until 1963, and throughout the 1950s, East German authorities continued to attack West German and American authorities for exposing East and West German youth to westerns and gangster stories.[75]

JAZZ, BOOGIE-WOOGIE, AND GERMAN WEAKNESS

American movies were not the only object of concern for East and West German authorities. American music was likewise a contested issue. In the late 1940s, East and West German Hot-Clubs, founded in big cities, became notorious for jam sessions where musicians improvised and played long solos, while the audience danced and clapped. Although only a minority of Germans went to the Hot-Clubs, many people looked with suspicion at the jam sessions, where according to jazz expert Horst Lange, adolescents showed their enthusiasm for jazz without understanding that the music they listened to was often inferior.[76] While East and West German discourses on westerns centered on fears of male overaggression, debates around jazz and American dances evolved around worries about weak men and overly sexual women. Westerns, gangster movies, and jazz were the crucial parts in a cluster of cultural images that East and West Germans associated with the dangers of Americanization.

In 1949 one West Berlin commentator reported about a jazz event in the West Berlin club Badewanne, which featured a jam session every Monday. German musicians and American guests from the army broadcasting network AFN played mostly "hot American numbers, whose melody was overshadowed by exaggerated rhythms." The reporter complained, "only brass could be heard and none of the soft strings, which please the hearts of the friends of German dance music." He thus adopted the logic of the Nazis who had replaced brass sections with strings, when they adapted American swing for German audiences.

Even more than the musicians, jazz fans raised fears among cultural conservatives about a lack of respectability in postwar Germany. Critics of jazz employed vocabulary drawn directly from the Weimar and Nazi years. According to the West Berlin commentary on the Badewanne, the jam session led by German jazz musician Fredy Brocksieper satisfied the "jungle instincts" (*Urwaldinstinkte*) of the audience. The author thus reiterated the link between jazz and the African jungle that dated from the 1920s. Using language that the Nazis had employed to attack swing youths of the first half of the 1940s, he also derided the listeners as *"Swing-Heinis."* They jumped onto tables and chairs and let fly colorful balloons. The author marked the males in the audience as lacking in respectability not just in their behavior but also in their fashions: they were allegedly a mixture of members of the intelligentsia and blackmarketeers wearing rollneck sweaters and striped socks.[77] Along with short "brushhead" (bouffant) haircuts, and ankle-length pants, striped socks became the distinguishing signs of many jazz fans in East and West.[78] The dancing of some jazz fans also came under attack from many West German commentators. In the Hot-Clubs and other bars many of them danced boogie and jitterbug, which worried commentators because the dancers seemed to "dislocate their limbs," as they were moving their bodies and throwing each other through the air.[79] Some West

Germans clearly hoped that youth protection laws would curtail adolescent dancing of the boogie. *Die Zeit* recommended in 1952 that the owner of the Badewanne be prosecuted for organizing dance contests "among fourteen-to sixteen-year-olds." According to the article, the dances "drove the adolescent couples near physical breakdown, made the 'bourgeois' audience shudder, and brought the club excellent business."[80] While postwar attacks thus connected jazz to lower-class culture, they did not claim that the jazz fans themselves were primarily from the working class. Some reports about jam sessions, in fact, referred to jazz fans as "bohemians," thus indicating that they perhaps were bourgeois nonconformists.[81]

The jazz fans' fashions and dances ran counter to West German visions of male and female respectability. With their focus on fashions and expressive dancing, the young men appeared feminine. Along these lines, a West German education manual pointed to the emasculating and feminizing effect of "sultry Negro songs" for boys; it warned that boys had to restrain themselves, sexually and otherwise, in order to reach full manhood.[82] Such concerns were further exacerbated by commentators who worried about an addiction to jazz among fans.[83] Using expressions like "jungle instincts" and "sultry Negro songs," West German critics, like earlier critics of mass culture, associated male jazz fans with racial as well as with gender transgressions.

To some West German commentators, the respectability of female jazz fans was even more questionable than that of males. One West German official described the new dances as "intoxicating" and therefore as especially detrimental to young women.[84] Contemporaries criticized girls who hung out on streets and who danced boogie as potential sexual delinquents. The article on the jam session in the Badewanne described female jazz fans merely as "live dolls."[85] While male jazz fans were portrayed as rambunctious, female jazz fans appeared in this assessment as highly manipulated, passive beings.

Those who wanted to make jazz acceptable in the West German context tried to divorce it from an unmanly focus on fashions and from female sexual expressiveness. When one journalist reported about the opening of a Hamburg jazz club, he maintained that the male participants were all "obedient boys," whereas one could not be so sure about the girls who made up one third of the membership. In the end, however, he stressed that while some girls ended up on the laps of their *Dixiegalans,* everything was honorable, for "German jazz did not know eroticism." He went on to claim that the "ecstasy that German jazz caused has something abstract about it."[86] Ideally, jazz was to be an intellectual rather than a sensual experience.

Fig. 4.　Dancing in the West Berlin club Badewanne in 1952. The dancing couple may have been African Americans. Some of the men wore "striped" socks. Courtesy Ullstein Bilderdienst.

East German indictments of jazz and American dances used images very similar to those employed by West German critics. In September 1949 the East German daily *Neues Deutschland* criticized the club Badewanne as an expression of dire living conditions in West Berlin: those who frequented the club were artists without money, rich businessmen, crooks, "boogie-woogie-boys, who were wearing their shirts over their pants," and grinning Americans.[87] The United States had allegedly dumped "a mudslide of

E/W images of Jazz/swing similar

boogie-woogie" on Germans.[88] The American music industry, East German authorities claimed, produced swing and bebop as part of an imperialist strategy. The same was apparently true for bouffant (brushhead) hairstyles. As one East German culture official, Kurt Hager, explained in 1950, "The hair is styled in such a manner that it rises from the base of the neck like the mushroom cloud of an atomic bomb."[89] With such music and fashions, as with westerns, Americans were preparing people for war.[90]

Within East German borders, authorities began to repress jazz and American dances, following the Soviet example where authorities even prohibited the word *dzhaz*. By the early 1950s, East Germans were describing imports, like boogie-woogie, jazz, and samba as "decadent" or "degenerate" parts of "American cultural barbarism," which they saw at the root of American and West German imperialism.[91] One official declared in 1950 that East Germans were defending their "national cultural tradition" against "American imperialist ideologies" and against "barbarization by the boogie-woogie 'culture.'"[92] In March 1951 the SED's Central Committee announced a fight against formalism and called for a search for an authentic German national culture. East German officials defined as formalist all cultural expressions that put more stress on form than content; such art allegedly lost its humanist and democratic character and was characteristic of the imperialism of late capitalist systems, particularly the United States. Officials leveled accusations of "decadence," "cosmopolitanism," "naturalism," "modernism," and "formalism" against, for example, the literature of Kafka, abstract painting, and also undesirable music, like jazz.[93]

Hostile words were accompanied by administrative action. By 1950 the Radio Berlin Dance Orchestra was disbanded, along with other bands and informal groups that some avid jazz fans had founded. Authorities banned jazz from the East German radio waves, stopped jazz recordings, and even destroyed the Amiga originals of the Rex Stewart releases. The border police confiscated jazz records that fans tried to bring into East Germany. In 1952 authorities prohibited American names for bands. As a result of such repression many East German jazz musicians left for West Germany.[94]

Nonetheless jazz and boogie fans continued to ask for their favorite music at public events, and many bands continued to play it. Also East German jazz fans listened to the music on AFN, which they could receive particularly well in East Germany, and they even formed some illegal circles to discuss the music. These circles would play an important role when fans tried to promote jazz in times of greater leniency during the following years.[95]

Because of the anxieties about the allegedly negative impact of jam sessions and boogie dancing, authorities in both states used ballroom dancing in their efforts to transform adolescents into respectable heterosexual adults, who would be strong enough to forego premarital and extramarital sex.[96] In the 1950s, East and West Berlin youth agencies went out of their way to make dance lessons available to girls and boys from low-income families. The agencies sponsored folk dance groups and dance events where young people were to move "in a civilized fashion,"[97] and where education in social dancing was combined with instruction on how to behave toward the opposite sex.[98] Moving in a civilized fashion meant of course that the man was to lead the woman and that excessive movements of hips, arms, and legs—with possible sexual connotations—were avoided. Social dances were a means of "positive" youth protection designed to civilize asocial sexual drives that seemed to emasculate men while making women loose. As one West German social worker put it, delinquent youths would find life partners, "if they did not enter the 'neutral' dance floor, where they would disappear anonymously into the masses, but could choose good establishments, good company, and nice families."[99] One West Berlin social worker stated with some satisfaction in 1954, that not all adolescents were interested in boogie-woogie or jitterbug.[100] In West Berlin some commercial dance halls also furthered the establishing of a carefully monitored heterosocial world. In the club Resi young men and women invited each other for a dance via table telephones, as operators made sure that "nothing indecent" entered the lines.[101]

The similarities between East and West German assumptions about what constituted a viable civilization, and what role it should play in the construction of East and West German identities, led to a curious constellation. East German criticisms put West Germans on the defensive; even as the West German government was trying to forge a political and military alliance with the United States, many West Germans continued to be hostile toward American cultural influences and the transformation of West Germany into a consumer society. Neither the alliance with the United States nor American cultural influences were uncontested. The connections with the United States were indeed under attack from several directions. The leader of the SPD called Adenauer "the chancellor of the Allies." And on several occasions, West German church authorities, especially Catholics, pointed to the East, where, they claimed, adolescents were better protected from the dangers of consumer culture and from American imports. The authors of a West German Catholic church message worried in 1951 that the "unbroken youths of the Soviet Union" would "someday become the masters of the lustful boys in the West."[102] Perhaps even more dramatic was the remark of a politician who said: "The East wants to conquer the world, the West just wants to enjoy it."[103] Conservative West

German politicians echoed such charges to fight the supposedly damaging effects of consumer culture within West Germany. Family Minister Franz-Josef Wuermeling announced in 1953: "Millions of spiritually healthy families with well-trained children are at least as important for security against the peoples of the East with their numerous children as are all military installations."[104] The right sort of culture was crucial for preparing children to defend the "Christian West."

American government officials were likewise ambivalent about the development of a consumer culture and the impact of American popular culture in postwar Germany. In 1951 U.S. High Commissioner of Germany McCloy asked for an evaluation of existing American-sponsored youth programs. One official recommended that all programs focusing purely on entertainment should be discontinued. The efforts of the East German youth organization FDJ, who had staged mass rallies in East Berlin, needed to be countered with fewer "entertainment programs and less Americanization." This official suggested instead events highly compatible with the conservative vision of German government officials, such as "demonstrations for the mental and spiritual defense of the Christian West."[105]

"TEXAS SHIRTS" AND THE 1953 UPRISING IN EAST GERMANY

It was in the context of these shared hostilities toward American popular culture that East German authorities tried to use images of Americanization in their propaganda after the June 1953 uprising in East Germany. On June 16 and 17, thousands of people demonstrated across the GDR. The roots of these events were manifold, but demonstrators were clearly spurred on by the strikes of East Berlin workers who were protesting higher work quotas. The demonstrations were spontaneous and demands ranged from lowering quotas, to free elections, and even removal of the government. In Berlin demonstrators removed the red Soviet flag from the Brandenburg Gate and in many cities people tore down the party slogans plastered on walls and billboards. In some cases demonstrators freed prison inmates, in others they beat up members of the notorious secret service, the *Stasi*.[106] On the morning of June 17, Soviet tanks rolled into the center of East Berlin and by the afternoon troops opened fire, while demonstrators threw stones. At the same time the Soviet Military commander declared martial law over the radio waves, prohibited further demonstrations, and instituted a curfew. By 9 P.M. the Soviet army and East German paramilitary troops had gained control of East Berlin. Similar scenes repeated themselves in other East German cities.[107]

In the days (and years) after the uprising, East and West German officials were busy remaking its meaning for their own political purposes. Whereas East German officials were trying to redirect attention from the workers' demands for lower work quotas, a better standard of living, and democratic reform, most West German politicians were interpreting the uprising as a demonstration for national unity.[108]

Just two days after the Soviet army had brought the uprising to an end, the newspaper of the East German FDJ, *Junge Welt*, reported about adolescent "saviors of the culture of the Christian West," who, dressed in striped socks and half-long pants, had roamed through East Berlin streets. On June 21, 1953, the major SED daily *Neues Deutschland* published the picture of a "member of a group of West Berlin provocateurs" charged with disturbing the public order in Erfurt. Under the headline "This Is How the Fascist Spawn of [the West German politicians] Adenauer, Ollenhauer, Kaiser, and Reuter Looks," the paper described his attributes: "Texas shirt with cowboy [a T-shirt with a cowboy printed on it], Texas tie with a picture of nude women, Texas haircut, a criminal's face—these are the knights of the 'Christian West,' the typical representatives of the American way of life."[109]

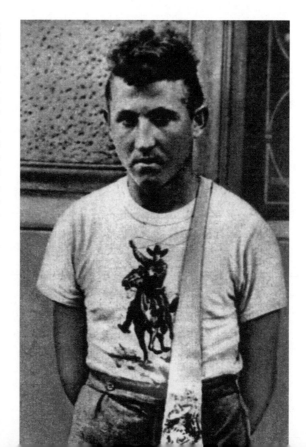

Fig. 5. "Fascist spawn, knight of the 'Christian West,' typical representative of the American way of life." Photo of an alleged provocateur of the East German uprising in June 1953. The picture was reprinted in East German newspapers and brochures. Reprinted from *Wer zog die Drähte?*, Berlin, 1954. Courtesy Bundesarchiv Berlin.

On June 26, 1953, the East German prime minister, Otto Grotewohl, echoed these statements when he assessed the uprising. As he put it, "The Western provocateurs with the colorful plaid striped socks [!], with cowboy pants and Texas shirts wanted to cause a large-scale political provocation" and thus attempted to prevent negotiations between the four big powers for a German peace treaty. Grotewohl's speech was part of an outright campaign in the East German press that put West German or West German–influenced youths who sported Americanized fashions at the center of the June events.[110]

The picture and the texts marked these alleged provocateurs as effeminate by stressing their interest in (unmanly) fashions. East German authorities drew on the discourses concerning westerns and jazz that had emerged in East and West Germany by the early 1950s: they associated the "provocateurs" with cowboys and with the striped socks that jazz fans wore. American culture had led Gladow to commit crimes against individuals. These rebels were even worse, committing crimes against the state.

The picture that showed the Western provocateur was reprinted on numerous occasions.[111] It is disturbingly similar to Nazi depictions of "inferior humans": the young man stood slumped over with an unfriendly expression on his face. Ironically, even as this East German propaganda in its aesthetic choices seemed to appeal to values of the Nazi period, East German officials were establishing a close connection between allegedly "Americanized" demonstrators and fascism and were in fact labeling the whole uprising an attempted fascist coup d'état.

In their propaganda campaign, East German authorities linked American popular culture, deviations from gender mores, and fascism. The list of alleged provocateurs was augmented in the following days. The "American imperialists" had recruited "*SS-Kommandeusen*" (female SS commanders), *Tangojünglinge,* and prostitutes.[112] Officials also alleged that the adolescent provocateurs had sung the Nazi Horst Wessel song.[113]

East German propaganda connected the "fascist provocateurs" to sexual deviance. For one, it portrayed female prostitutes as instigators of rebellion. Second, the expression *Tangojünglinge* was very similar to the "lustful boys" about whom West Germans worried. Both terms carried homosexual connotations. Thus East German officials, in their efforts to discredit the workers' rebellion, clearly hoped to place the rebellion within parameters of the discourses around juvenile delinquency that had developed in the two German states. With their allegations, they played on bourgeois fears of male delinquency and female prostitution associated with the streets and thus they catered to gender mores that East and West German officials shared. East German propagandists also hearkened back to a connection between homosexuality and fascism, that the SPD and KPD had employed during the Weimar years in its attacks on Nazis.[114]

The East German propaganda effort was in clear contradiction to the police reports about the roots and the events of the uprising. East Berlin police reports, for example, did not refer to adolescents as major participants in the uprising, but rather focused on the workers' mood. In fact there is no evidence that adolescents or West Berliners participated in the demonstrations in large numbers.[115]

While East German papers and police reports initially saw strikes by East German workers as one, if not the major, facet of the events around June 17, this view increasingly disappeared from public statements. The propaganda had some effect in rewriting the history of the uprising in East Germany. When policemen wounded on June 17 wrote home from their hospital beds around June 20, some of them boasted about the male youths in "half-long pants, striped socks, and Texas shirts" whom they had cornered.[116] Police reports in July likewise stressed that "fascist rowdies," many of them in "Texas clothes" had shaped the uprising.[117] At mass meetings held in all major East German cities at the end of June, officials emphasized that the "Day X" had been exclusively the work of Western provocateurs. Those party leaders who showed sympathy for the workers' demands were subsequently removed from their posts. And although thousands of GDR citizens were arrested in the aftermath of June 17, the press referred only vaguely to the work of fascist gangs, and with few exceptions did not report about trials or sentences.[118]

While East Germans put male youths in cowboy pants, that is jeans, at the center of the uprising, West German officials largely chose to ignore these allegations. A 1953 report published shortly after the uprising in the American-financed West German monthly *Der Monat* suggested a reason for this silence; "West Germans, too, would have been disturbed by the looks of the youth depicted in the picture [of the alleged provocateurs]."[119] West German politicians also mostly ignored the worker base of the uprising and instead remade it into a demonstration for German unity. Nonetheless, one picture reprinted over the following decades in the West showed two young men throwing stones at Soviet tanks. Since these young men were actively defying Soviet oppression, allegedly in the name of German unity, nobody in the West commented on their clothes which included shorter pants (possibly jeans) and short jackets—fashions that East and West Germans had identified as symbols of improper masculinity.[120]

Fig. 6.   Youths throwing stones at Soviet tanks during the East German uprising on June 17, 1953. This photo was frequently reprinted in West Germany. Courtesy Bildarchiv Preußischer Kulturbesitz.

A "NEW LINE" IN EAST GERMANY?

While East German authorities made an indictment of American cultural and political influences part of their efforts to contain the 1953 uprising, they changed their economic and cultural policies as part of the "new line" that they promoted beginning in 1953. Officials saw to it that more money was invested in the provision of consumer goods; they also allowed more space to maneuver in the cultural sphere and put a greater emphasis on entertaining their population.[121]

Nonetheless, hostilities toward American popular culture continued. In November 1953, for example, one East Berlin official sought to take measures to fight the American driven *Entartung* (degeneration) of social dancing and even wanted to purge the radio archives of Western "Hott-Music."[122] The FDJ tried to use "modern" entertainment to fight such American influences. Its magazine *Junge Generation,* for example, explained in the aftermath of the uprising that the FDJ had failed to provide sufficient opportunities for entertainment and relaxation and especially for dancing. Instead, criticized the magazine, young people resorted to hanging out on park benches and to reproducing the imported "Ami-Kultur" with their guitars. As an alternative, *Junge Generation* proposed dance events where adolescents would dance the waltz, the fox-trot, and folk dances of the Soviet Union and the other people's republics. Given such offerings, nobody would even want to dance the boogie, a dance that was proof of the evils of "the culture of the Christian West."[123]

Junge Generation soon celebrated the alleged success of such measures and printed a report from one local FDJ unit that, beginning in July 1953, offered dances three times per week. Apparently some young East German males showed up who, as the magazine put it, resembled the "exotic birds from West Berlin" in their fashionable "brushhead" haircuts and "Texas shirts." When reliable FDJ members saw them dancing boogie ("as if they had tooth pain"), they told the band to play a flourish and then asked the dancers to show that they were just as good at dancing the fox-trot. In other cases, FDJ "commandos" were emptying dance halls of *Texashemdenträger* (those wearing "Texas" shirts).[124]

Apparently such public ridicule and retrenchment led to a steep decline in FDJ popularity and membership, and the organization, under the leadership of Erich Honecker, came under attack from leading SED functionaries and government officials who saw the FDJ as a crucial tool to foster loyalty among youth to the new socialist state. An internal memo emphasized in late 1953 that by no means were the majority of adolescents "enthusiastic *Ami-Jünglinge*." The author asserted that "the adoration of the *Ami-Kultur*" resulted often from "a lack of other opportunities." He also concluded, probably incorrectly, that Western influences were strongest among the bourgeois youth. Ironically, the memo announced that "the Western influence in its ugly deviation" could be contained not just by offering dances, but also hikes such as those organized by confessional youth groups. The Protestant youth groups were according to this memo successfully warning adolescents "against all kinds of excesses."[125] In the year or so after the June uprising, the SED tended to leave the confessional groups alone, and indeed tried to learn from them but failed to attract a larger following.

While some East German officials tried to use entertainment to fight American influences, others found that some American imports could be part of East German entertainment. By 1954 the FDJ clearly tried once again to attract a broader membership by including American culture in its offerings. The youth magazine *Neues Leben*, for example, featured pictures of jazz bands. One photograph showed a percussionist surrounded by blurbs including exclamations like "boogie!", "rhythm!", "syncopations!", and "temperament!". They culminated in the pronouncement that one could recognize good, cool music in the percussion section: *"Dufte Musik man am Schlagzeug erkennt!"*.[126] Moreover, in 1954 and 1955, some jazz fans were able to promote the music all over the GDR.[127]

The flip-flopping continued. In 1955 East German authorities geared their youth protection efforts explicitly against the American *Unkultur*, resurrecting a German expression that altogether denied American imports the status of "culture." The East German youth protection law of that year made the containment of American influences its explicit purpose. The preamble of the law announced that East Germans were protecting their youth against the "American way of life" propagated in the "Adenauer-state," that is, in West Germany.[128]

While East German functionaries, at least in internal memos, saw the bourgeoisie as particularly susceptible to U.S. influences, West German social scientists and commentators viewed adolescent consumption of American popular culture increasingly as a working-class phenomenon. In 1953 the sociologist Bednarik linked the identity of the young male worker—"a new type"—closely to consumption and specifically to the consumption of American imports. Bednarik argued that nothing was more indicative of this generation than its relationship to film and jazz. Likely underestimating the attraction for middle- and upper-class adolescents, other researchers confirmed that westerns and gangster films were particularly popular among male working-class youth.[129]

Bednarik clearly had the outlaw westerns in mind when he claimed that after consuming westerns and gangster films, young male workers tried to relive "Wild West," "gangster," and "desperado" feelings for such an extended time and so intensely that they became their "basic outlook on life." Also, according to Bednarik, most young male workers liked jazz better than all other music. Bednarik saw jazz as the proper cultural expression of an industrial society and maintained it was not by chance that jazz came from highly industrialized America. Dancing to jazz music, including swing, and enjoying jam sessions, the young worker was able to overcome the functionalism of modern technology. In an attempt to experience adventures that would counter the atmosphere of boredom in the workplace, the "new type" was likely to engage in criminal activities. However, according to Bednarik, these young male workers were not trying to understand or even change their work conditions and, unlike earlier youth movements, they did not engage in political activities nor did they have revolutionary zeal.

Bednarik's evaluations of these young workers were somewhat contradictory. He recounted that fascism "and the successor powers" had fought such young men and the jazz music they preferred, and thus he was one of very few commentators who acknowledged that the Nazis had persecuted such adolescents. He acknowledged an antitotalitarian and antimilitarist impulse in these young men, but he also concluded that, "socially, the new type had to be seen rather negatively." In the end, Bednarik powerfully confirmed West German worries about male working-class youths made overly aggressive and manipulated by American popular culture.

At the same time, Bednarik was one of the first to suggest that this youth did not really pose a political threat. It would, however, take several years until this second part of his argument would be widely accepted in West Germany. When the West German weekly *Der Spiegel* reviewed Bednarik's book, it concluded the lack of a *Weltbild*, that is, a unified ideology, among these workers was dangerous; as before 1933, a state that offered them something they enjoyed, like motorbikes or shooting, could all too easily seduce them. In such judgments, adolescent male consumers of American popular culture posed totalitarian threats.[130]

West German authorities, like their East German counterparts, certainly attempted to contain American influences in the first half of the 1950s. In reaction to heavy East German complaints about the western, gangster, and pornographic movies shown there, one West Berlin official visited border theaters in October 1954 and found that East German allegations were correct. The programs of the specially priced screenings for East German visitors attracted an audience, complained the official, that was undesirable for West Berlin "for political and moral reasons." Eighty percent were allegedly adolescents who avoided work and "other donothings," while the "working population and the broad middle strata" of East Germany were appalled by their bad behavior and, in any case, did not want to see westerns or gangster movies. Improving the programs in the border theaters was especially important, urged the West Berlin official, since East German authorities had imported more West European movies in the aftermath of the June 1953 uprising.[131] The number of French and West German movies released in the GDR had indeed gone up in 1953 and 1954.[132]

In March 1955, West Berlin city officials tried again to pressure the owners of border theaters to improve their programs. One official drafted a letter explaining the political significance of the theaters: the border theaters were "responsible for providing the people behind the 'Iron Curtain' with cultural goods of the Christian West." According to the official this goal could hardly be reached with gangster movies and westerns. As he emphasized, "Screenings of such inferior-quality films had made the intended cultural policy into a boomerang against our interests and thus into a serious political issue."[133] Even though West Berlin officials threatened to withdraw the tax exemptions for the special screenings for East Germans, theater owners simply ignored official pressure. By the end of 1955, however, one West Berlin official report found that things had improved somewhat, if only for material reasons: since American distributors had increased their rental fees, theaters were screening fewer "American shooting and gangster movies" and had to offer more German films. Nonetheless, West Berlin officials remained dissatisfied with the situation.[134]

In first half of the 1950s, an alliance of local government officials, church groups, educators, and associations with links to the federal government and the churches (such as the *Aktion Jugendschutz*) discouraged and sometimes even prevented adolescents from reading pulp fiction, seeing certain movies, or dancing certain dances. Measures included government-sponsored dance lessons or letters to movie theater owners written by government officials. Not infrequently, the German entertainment industry and radio stations bowed to such pressures.[135] But unlike in the GDR, outright prohibition of American imports was rarely an option in the emerging West German capitalist democracy. Moreover, West Germans, sometimes under pressure from American government officials, also began to make popular culture, including American imports into a weapon against the Cold War enemy.

Already in 1949, one West German film company offered a movie that tried to come to terms with American influences in postwar Germany. *Hallo Fräulein* featured singer and actress Margot Hielscher, who had begun her career with some obstacles under the Nazis. After she had rejected the sexual advances of Propaganda Minister Goebbels, he had told her that her mouth was "too American" and her performances had been blacklisted as "too hot."[136] In *Hallo Fräulein,* which had the American occupation as its theme, Hielscher was a singer who gave concerts with a jazz band conducted by a white U.S. officer and made up of Displaced Persons, that is, of former concentration camp inmates and forced laborers. West German reviewers applauded the band as a symbol of speedy reconciliation between former enemies, ignoring the question of who had been the aggressors. The movie helped make jazz music, though as one reviewer complained only in its more tame version,[137] into a symbol of a new West German beginning, in which Germans, DPs, and Americans alike had been victims of National Socialism.[138] At the same time the movie resolved the challenges to gender mores that West Germans experienced in the postwar years, and that both fraternizers and jazz symbolized for many. For some West German reviewers, the film found its appropriate ending when Hielscher preferred the stiff German architect/mayor/former POW who called jazz "rhythmic epilepsy" over the nice American conductor with casual manners who put his feet on the table. As one West Berlin paper explained, perhaps not without irony, the successful German suitor was "pleasantly masculine," "*erfreulich männlich.*"[139] Jazz might be a good means of reconciliation in extraordinary times, but in the end it was incompatible with German masculinity.

Several East and West German papers found the ending and the self-confident resurgence of German masculinity over American men and music unrealistic. The East German *National-Zeitung* saw it as a worthy project to remind German women not to throw themselves at American soldiers, but did not believe in the happy end. And *Neues Deutschland* was even more critical: the movie "degenerated with jazz music, hits, and much love into banality." Not surprisingly this West German attempt both to validate and contain American influences was not entirely convincing, either for West or for East German commentators.[140]

In the decade after 1945, American culture once again had a powerful grip on East and West German imaginations. Cultural relations between the two states and their superpowers were hardly symmetrical. To be sure, Soviet military officials, the SED leadership and cultural functionaries in East Germany frequently praised Soviet culture, but it lacked the pervasiveness of American imports and their power to excite and repel—in short to raise controversy. Critics in East and West Germany feared that American popular culture contributed to the overaggression of men and the oversexualization of women, and thus ran counter to the values at the heart of both East and West German reconstruction. At the same time, East and West German debates over American popular culture in the postwar years foreshadowed how racial and class politics continued to be troublesome in these two opposing states, which, each in its own way, tried to define itself as classless and raceless in the aftermath of the Third Reich and in the midst of the Cold War.

2   The Wild Ones

*The 1956 Youth Riots
and German Masculinity*

An apparently new, disturbing social phenomenon preoccupied Germans in the mid-1950s: just ten years after the end of World War II, youth riots took place in East and West Germany, and the consumption of American popular culture appeared to be at their center. In September 1956 the West Berlin parliament discussed the riots that had erupted in various West German cities since 1955. One speaker asserted that the instigators of riots in a West Berlin working-class neighborhood had modeled their behavior "word for word, picture for picture" after the American movie *The Wild One*, starring Marlon Brando.[1] A few weeks later, West German education expert Hans Muchow warned against "nihilists," whom he compared to the white gang leader in the American movie *Blackboard Jungle*. These nihilists, he explained, consciously regressed into a "wild state" that evoked memories of the National Socialist rise to power. It was easier, he added, for East Germany to combat these dangers.[2]

When youth riots occurred with ever greater frequency in both West and East German cities after 1955, commentators in East and West quickly came to agree that the American "young rebel" movies served as models for German juvenile fashions, dances, and mannerisms, and even for the riots themselves. The arrival of movies such as *The Wild One* with Marlon Brando, *Rebel Without a Cause* with James Dean, and *Blackboard Jungle* with Sidney Poitier, along with the rock 'n' roll flick *Rock Around the Clock*, exacerbated parents' and officials' worries about American cultural influences.[3] Indeed, these "young rebel" movies quickly replaced westerns as the most controversial imports. German commentators discussed extensively the explanations for juvenile misbehavior suggested in American young rebel movies, which were themselves in a constant dialogue with the broader U.S. debates about American juvenile delinquency.[4] Strongly believing in the direct effects of films on audience behavior, most German authorities did not want adolescents to see these allegedly realistic depictions of worrisome American conditions. West German officials and educators did, however, sometimes recommend them as warning examples to parents. In both Germanies, these American films became new stepping-stones for the evolving debates on young German rebels.

East and West German observers and authorities focused their attention on young men, who made up the majority of rioters. The adolescents they worried about now were no longer the generation who had been teenagers in the mid-1940s (the so-called *Flakhelfergeneration*) or those just a couple of years younger who had still been subject to Nazi education. Rather these were youths who had at most begun elementary school in 1945 and whose formative years fell into the period of postwar reconstruction.[5]

The fact that riots occurred and American mannerisms spread just as German authorities were busy convincing their citizens of the necessity of rearmament and military service added to the anxiety of many East and West German observers. In the mid-1950s both East and West German officials tried to shape soldiers who were strong, appropriately aggressive, and loyal to their respective political system, yet not overly militaristic.[6] Young males, with their American-influenced fashions and their rioting, raised fears about both unmanliness and male aggression and thus challenged the fine line that authorities were walking.[7]

In response to these young German men who imitated dress and behavior from American movies, commentators in postwar East and West Germany once again linked consumption, femininity, lower-class behavior, and African American culture. Often they expressed these fears drawing on concepts borrowed from eugenics. Many East and West Germans also worried that young male rebels were challenging state authority and struggled to ascertain what political motivations, if any, were at the root of unruly behavior. While young men were the main focus of these discussions, American and German women were frequently invoked—as instigators of, victims of, and finally, solutions to the youth rebellion. The reactions to the young rebels, most of whom came from the working class, reveal persisting fears about working-class cultures both in West Germany, where the influential sociologist Helmut Schelsky had proclaimed the existence of "the leveled middle-class society" in 1952, and in East Germany, where socialists were striving to eliminate class hierarchies.[8]

REARMAMENT AND IDEAL CITIZENS

The two Germanies had embarked on the road to rearmament in the first half of the 1950s. With the beginning of the Korean War in 1950, the Western Allies were increasingly interested in West Germany as a partner in their defense system, rather than as an occupied country. In 1950, the Adenauer government had already appointed a commissioner for security matters and begun to lay the groundwork for rearmament. Against the opposition of the Social Democrats, the West German parliament voted formally in 1952 to join a European Defense Community. Rearmament became legally possible after a constitutional amendment passed in 1954. When France did not ratify the treaty on the formation of the European Defense Community, the Nine Power Conference signed the so-called Paris Treaties in October 1954, which specified that West Germany would become a sovereign state and a member of NATO. Five days after the Federal Republic joined NATO in May 1955, the Soviet Union set up its own military alliance, the Warsaw Pact, which included the GDR. The first West German soldiers joined the newly founded *Bundeswehr* in November 1955. In January 1956, GDR police units, which had been housed and trained in barracks since July 1948, were transformed into the National People's Army (NVA). Whereas West Germany introduced conscription with the right to conscientious objection in July 1956, East Germany did not take this step until 1962. Even as East German authorities put considerable pressure on young men to join the army, especially if they wanted to be assured of a higher education, the authorities claimed time and again that conscription proved West Germany to be the more militaristic and oppressive state.

Facing strong popular sentiment against rearmament and conscription, all West German mainstream political parties, including the governing Christian Democrats (CDU/CSU) and the opposition Social Democrats (SPD) had agreed since the early 1950s that the new democracy required a new male citizen and soldier who would undertake the military tasks with "sobriety" and "reliability."[9] With this new masculinity, West German politicians sought to resurrect a positive German tradition of brave and obedient soldiers. On the one hand, West German politicians tried to reject a militarist German history in which, as they put it, the military had escaped civilian control. On the other, they tried to overcome the immediate postwar period when the soldier allegedly had been "undervalued"; some even worried about an army that was "too democratic."[10]

One advertisement for the West German army suggested in 1956 that this new soldier could assert his manly individuality in the process of defending "his people": "He who wants to remain master of his decisions and his time joins voluntarily." West German officials defined this new German man in part by contrasting him with women's militarization under National Socialism. As the CSU politician Richard Jaeger put it in the West

German parliament in 1955: "The BDM [the Nazi association of girls] marching in cadence, that was the triumph of militarism and the perversion of true soldiery." The new West German citizen/soldier was to protect German families and homes, especially women and children. Officials thus were reasserting the role of the male protector and provider that women's labor in and out of the home during war and postwar emergencies had shattered.[11]

West German authorities resurrected old hostilities against mass behavior and mass culture in order to fight the danger of militarism, on the one hand, and to construct a restrained male "citizen in uniform" on the other. As Jaeger announced: "Against the mass technology and the mass army of the East, only the spiritually and intellectually educated individual fighter of the West can withstand and be superior."[12] This logic linked "mass," femininity, and overaggression with both fascist militarism and the Cold War enemy. To counter these dangers, the moral education of the new citizen/soldier required the rejection of styles associated with the working class and with American mass culture that simultaneously feminized men and made them overly aggressive.

This new West German soldier was not a resurrected soldier of the Third Reich. The very label "citizen in uniform" connoted that this soldier was to relate to his state in a different way. The discourse of the Weimar and Nazi years had shaped a militarized image of German men whose public identity was founded on their role as soldiers. By contrast, the primary public identity for postwar West German men was to be based on their role as civilian husbands and fathers. It was as protectors of German families, not as promoters of a nation organized according to racial categories, that postwar men were to join the *Bundeswehr*. Just as the first West German soldiers moved into their barracks, this new ideal of West German male citizenship also became visible in the treatment of the last POWs returning from the Soviet Union in the fall of 1955. West German politicians and the press depicted them as men whose allegiance to their present or future families at home had allegedly helped them survive largely unscathed through years of totalitarianism, first under National Socialism and then under communism. Indeed, the aging Adenauer himself, a widower with numerous children, successfully embodied this new ideal of a West German "patriarch."[13]

"Remasculinization" in East Germany took somewhat different forms. Giving younger men positions in the new administration, in political organizations and in the police and the army, the East Germans created what Dorothee Wierling has called a "state father," whose authority was based not on his role in the family, but on his loyalty to the socialist cause.[14] Depictions of returning POWs did not focus on their fatherhood or their integration into families, but on their role as workers or as members of the police force (which many of these men entered under coercion). Even though denazification was initially more thorough in the Soviet Zone, public allegiance to the socialist system could soon make up for any past involvement in National Socialism. The version of German history that East German socialists told claimed a complete disjuncture between National Socialism and the antifascist GDR. Loyalty to one party and military values of obedience appeared less problematic to East German leaders than it did to their West German counterparts. And unlike West German leaders, East German authorities did not see the family as a guarantor of German continuity that had survived National Socialism unscathed. Rather, the family could be a potential threat to complete socialist control; it was a building block of socialism only if its members showed their public commitment to this system. This made fatherhood less important for the public identities of East German men.[15]

MAKING WESTERNS RESPECTABLE

In West, but not in East Germany, certain types of American westerns proved compatible with the processes of "remasculinization" in the first half of the 1950s. In contrast to the westerns that made outlaws into heroes, westerns that could be interpreted as asserting the power of brave men and of the state became respectable in West Germany. The figure of the sheriff, in particular, personified this vision of manly courage and obedience to the state. In 1949, for example, the 1946 John Ford movie *My Darling Clementine* (*Faustrecht der Prärie*) was released in West Berlin theaters. Although the sheriff participated in a shoot-out, the West Berlin paper *Welt am Sonntag* summarized the plot this way: "The sheriff makes sure that order returns, more with his calm demeanor than with his revolver.... A few, somewhat stupid women, real, taciturn men—America around 1900 was disorderly, but not a bad country."[16] When the 1939 Errol Flynn western *Dodge City (Herr des Wilden Westens)* was released in West Germany in 1950, some reviewers applauded Flynn's efforts to establish order with his "Colt concessioned by the state."[17] *Dodge City* and *My Darling Clementine* were representative of a specific subgenre, the historical epic that unlike "outlaw westerns" affirmed the just power of the American state. In these "town-tamer" westerns, powerful criminals cause social injustice; the hero defeats them and thus empowers the decent town folk, bringing progress to the frontier.[18] An East German reviewer did not accept this message and criticized *Dodge City* for not portraying the true social conditions during the colonization of the American West and for promoting the dangerous lesson that "real men" exist only where fights, shootings, and lootings take place.[19] West German authorities, on the other hand, bought the message. In 1954, West German Protestant Film Commissioner Werner Hess found western films generally much less dangerous than gangster movies, because in contrast to gangster films, westerns did not urge the viewer to identify with the criminal. West Germans had begun to successfully moralize westerns and in doing so focused on the "town tamers" that featured a righteous hero. These West German assessments of westerns echoed with American Robert Warshow's defense of the genre (published both in the United States and in Germany in 1954), in which he claimed that in contrast to brutal gangster films, westerns did not feature irresponsible violence, but rather a hero who refrained from violence until all other means were exhausted in his fight against evil.[20]

The image of strong, yet restrained masculinity that commentators found in these westerns was particularly appealing as West Germans were struggling to portray the new army as nonaggressive, antitotalitarian, and staffed by male "citizens in uniform." It is perhaps no coincidence that West German reviewers of the "town tamers" explicitly referred to their judicious use of weapons. And in 1953, West German commentators interpreted both *High Noon* and *Shane*, two westerns that found critical acclaim around the world, as representations of such a restrained hero. One West German paper twice repeated a quote from *Shane* that likely had special resonance in the context of West German debates over rearmament: "A weapon is as good or bad as the man who uses it."[21] While East German authorities did not share such positive views of westerns, attacks on these films became a less potent weapon in the Cold War battle. Soon however, the uneasiness that American young rebel movies caused in both Germanies provided East German officials with new material.

THE WILD ONE AND WEST GERMAN YOUTH RIOTS

In 1955, West German reviewers of the Marlon Brando movie *The Wild One*, connected male unruliness to gender upheavals in the United States and identified it with working-class behavior. The West German distributor encouraged movie theater owners to make Brando and his rebellious image central to their advertising campaigns with slogans such as "Marlon Brando, Racing Rebel in the Rush of his Drives." While many posters showed Brando in leather jacket and jeans on his motorbike, some featured him with the young main female character, his love interest in the movie. In one he was grabbing her blouse; others featured their faces, she with a worried expression on one side of the image, Brando staring straight ahead on the other. None promised the visual unity of a taller man protecting a smaller woman that was the convention for so many posters in this period.[22] Since the early 1950s, West German reports had combined references to Brando's refusals to wear a suit—a symbolic rejection of bourgeois values—with treatments of his (sexual) success with American women. "His popularity is not astonishing," explained one article, because the American woman, "who is the most spoiled woman in the world—and who so often and with such pleasure stresses that she reigns over her man, does not hide anymore that her heart and her senses react most strongly to the brutal 'Gorilla sex appeal.'"[23] In *The Wild One*, which depicted a gang of white bikers terrorizing a small American town, Brando was a "hero with sex appeal, whom women allow to beat them up."[24] Thus, West German commentators portrayed American women as victims of men and saw female-induced brutality at the center of American male hyperaggression. This imagery drew on Weimar and Nazi views of overly strong American women. But unlike the "girl" of the 1920s, these women were not simply frigid. Instead they lived out masochist pleasures to compensate for the power they had over men. A movie like *The Wild One* was of course successful among both adolescents and adults in the United States and abroad, because it depicted a rebellious and lively youth culture and also raised moral objections against it.[25] Most West German reviewers ignored this mixed message, praised the movie as a realistic depiction of American conditions and used it as an opportunity to assert differences between West Germany and the United States.

One West German reviewer, however, warned in 1955 that *The Wild One* would become an ideal for many German adolescents.[26] Soon several incidents seemed to prove him correct. In June 1955 a West Berlin gang with heavy motorbikes, among them at least one young woman, frequently drove to a cafe called Big Window on the river Havel in the outskirts of West Berlin. They shocked patrons through "provocative skinny-dipping" and noisiness. In clear allusion to the American example, they called themselves "The Wild Ones of the Big Window," while a West Berlin newspaper report referred to them as "Marlon Brandos."[27]

The connections between American movies and adolescent misbehavior became more worrisome in the course of 1956. That summer, a gang of young men that the media called *Totenkopfbande* ("skull and crossbones"

Figs. 7 and 8.   West German advertising for *The Wild One* with Marlon Brando, 1955. Courtesy Stiftung Deutsche Kinemathek, Schriftgutarchiv.

gang, thus allegedly using a symbol from *The Wild One*) would regularly meet in the no-parking zone in front of a bar in the West Berlin neighborhood of Wedding on Thursday nights. "Skull and Crossbones," or "Death Head," was a symbol used by an infamous SS unit, but also by oppositional youth groups of the 1940s known as Edelweiß-Pirates. It is not clear whether the Wedding youths themselves adopted it, or whether the West German press assigned it to them. In any case, the SPD member of the West Berlin parliament who discussed the influence of *The Wild One* on the gang referred to the American example and did not mention any possible connections to German traditions.[28] Disturbed by the noise of the gang's motorbikes, people living in the neighborhood repeatedly called the police. Confrontations between the adolescents and the police usually followed and attracted a growing audience. On July 12, 1956, for example, about two hundred adolescents gathered in front of the bar, and by 9 P.M. the numbers of spectators had swollen to about five thousand adults and adolescents. Adolescents prevented cars from passing, and the police had difficulty reestablishing public order. When the same scenes repeated themselves a week later, the police turned to stronger means and used water hoses to disperse the crowd.[29]

Disturbances recurred and spread to other cities. West Berlin saw by far the highest number of incidents. In the period from April to September, the West Berlin police alone counted thirty-six riots and arrested 309 male participants. Riots reached their peak in the summer and fall of 1956. There were at least eighty-one riots in all of West Germany from March 1956 to March 1957 and at least nineteen more by the end of 1958. In the aftermath of these events, it became West German consensus that *The Wild One* had in fact started youth riots and that Marlon Brando in his leather jacket was the model for rebellious young men in West Germany, although earlier reviews had referred to biker gangs of unruly youths already in existence.[30]

Riots were generally characterized by confrontations with the police. Some happened at concerts or after movie showings, others came about when mostly male adolescents gathered spontaneously in public spaces. One of the first riots took place during a Hamburg concert by jazz musician Louis Armstrong in October 1955, when adolescents aired their dissatisfaction with the brevity of the concert and the cancellation of a second one. When the police tried to disperse the crowd, some fights ensued. During other the riots, adolescents provoked battles with the police by holding up traffic, "taking over" public places, or hassling passersby. Generally it seems that gatherings became riots, including fights or the destruction of property, when the police or other adults tried actively to rein in adolescents.[31] Police reaction varied. In some cases adolescents were arrested, in others police used their clubs to show adolescents "that authority still exists."[32]

The vast majority of rioters were male. The number of girls was highest, about 12 percent, at disturbances after concerts or movies. Perhaps not surprisingly, reports mostly ignored the young German women present even though they focused heavily on American women as instigators of male rebellion. Most of the rioters were ages sixteen to eighteen and most were apprentices or unskilled laborers of the working class.[33] Even if they were rarely involved in riots, some middle- and upper-class youths certainly admired the working-class adolescents who modeled their behavior on American movies. One middle-class youth reported that he too watched young rebel movies, was fascinated by the rebelliousness of the fast-paced music—even as he found it somewhat "primitive"—and understood why adolescents revolted against the "prescribed tracks."[34]

Much to the concern of many Germans, the riots appeared to be the mere tip of an iceberg: it seemed that, rioting or not, more and more young men were hanging out in the streets, wearing jeans, and publicly listening to the latest American hits on jukeboxes or transistor radios. As in the riots, women played a subordinate role among these groups of young men, whose behavior was characterized by a certain machismo (which the marketers of *The Wild One* had undoubtedly tried to foster). Perhaps less than 10 percent of West German youths initially participated in such forms of behavior in 1955 and 1956, but the American-influenced styles began to spread among adolescents. Nonetheless the public outcry was disproportionate to their numbers.[35]

 In response to the male rebels, West German observers combined pejorative references to American popular culture with an older German bourgeois attitude that associated working-class men with a lack of male respectability. In the 1950s, the press resurrected the term *Halbstarke* ("hooligans," literally, "semistrong"), which had been used for young male working-class delinquents since the second decade of the twentieth century. The tabloids in particular helped to spread the term, and soon respected newspapers and scholarship also discussed riots, as well as more widespread male adolescent mannerisms, as the *Halbstarkenproblem*. Participants of riots had a contradictory attitude toward the term: they spoke of their gatherings as *Halbstarken* meetings, but usually rejected the label for themselves.[36]

The fashions of *Halbstarke* particularly underlined the connection between American movies and German male unruliness. Standard dress for

West German *Halbstarke* was jeans, T-shirts, and short jackets (sometimes made of leather), revealing clear similarities with the male heroes of *The Wild One, Rebel Without a Cause,* and *Blackboard Jungle.* Young males would go to great lengths in order to achieve the right look. Tight pants were a must, and for some it was important to wear the original Levis jeans and not the imitations from the German Woolworth stores. When T-shirts were not yet available in Germany, young men would wear the high backs of undershirts in the front, in order to achieve the high-cut neck. Others wore bright, colorful shirts. Their hair was greased back and combed into ducktail plumes. The money that adolescents had available for their own personal use, though still small sums, was increasing rapidly in the mid-1950s. During these years, the West German economy was growing at a fast pace, and some adolescents may have visibly participated in an expanding consumer culture earlier than their parents. Often the amounts on which they could draw personally were higher for boys than for girls, and higher for apprentices and workers than for high school and university students, who in these years came mostly from the middle and upper classes. These funds certainly helped young rebels to realize their fashion statements.[37]

Commentators increasingly identified *Halbstarke* by their fashions. Some simply referred to them as the "leather jackets," whereas others attacked their "jeans-dressed spiritual life."[38] To many parents, educators, and commentators, these fashions, especially the bright colors, ducktail plumes, and casual posture of the male rebels appeared distinctly unmanly and even feminine.[39] In 1955 and early 1956, most West German observers believed that these styles were restricted to working-class male adolescents—and could be rejected as such.

In this context it is not surprising that West German officials were outraged at the American production *Rebel Without a Cause* with James Dean, which reached Germany in 1956. This movie portrayed white American middle-class youths behaving in ways that West Germans associated with unacceptable working-class styles: in the film, young men from wealthy, white suburbia sported jeans and leather jackets and engaged in dangerous knife fights and deadly car races, thus rebelling against parents and public order.[40] *Rebel* gave a psychological explanation for adolescent misbehavior that many West Germans found unconvincing. James Dean had to rebel, because his weak middle-class father was completely overpowered by his mother and thus could not be an authority or model for his son. Many West German officials in the 1950s who recognized intense social conflict as one reason for the demise of the Weimar Republic did want

Fig. 9. *Halbstarke* with Levi jeans, leather jackets, and attempted ducktail plumes in West Berlin, 1956. Photo: Will McBride, courtesy Bildarchiv Preußischer Kulturbesitz.

to bring down class barriers in West Germany. But West German authorities, if they imagined a society devoid of class hierarchies, certainly did not want to see it symbolized by young middle-class men who, like the adolescents in *Rebel*, wore "working-class" jeans.[41] When it became obvious that not all West German *Halbstarke* were from working-class backgrounds, one West German commentator scoffed at the suggestion that West German *Halbstarke* were possibly prefiguring a classless society, since "respectability, moral behavior, and the educational influence of cultural values" were foreign to them, and their behavior and styles were clearly "at the bottom."[42] West German press commentaries rejected deviations from bourgeois female and male respectability and had particular trouble coming to terms with middle-class adolescent rebels.

State officials echoed such concerns. Adenauer feared "proletarianization" as an *"Verostung"* ("Easternization") of Germans, thus giving such worries an ethnic and political dimension.[43] In 1956, when West German Minister of the Interior Gerhard Schröder urged that adolescents be offered better leisure-time activities, he warned that "in the race with the enormous purchasing power of the mass taste, moral values are threatened." Members of his party, the governing CDU/CSU faction, also called for a stricter youth protection law, and politicians in several West German states, especially in conservative Bavaria, urged strong police action against adolescent rebels. In the trials against rioters, whose actions were by and large harmless, some judges warned that they were a threat to state order and handed down relatively high sentences of up to one year imprisonment.[44]

These West German reactions bore considerable resemblance to American fears about juvenile delinquency, which had reached their peak a little earlier from 1953 to 1956. During these years, a loose conglomeration, including U.S. educators, church groups such as the Catholic Legion of Decency, politicians like FBI director J. Edgar Hoover, and members of the media, claimed that mass culture was at the root of an alleged explosion of adolescent misbehavior. These worries, which were part of an American cultural conservatism that crossed political divides, were even explored in congressional hearings. Separate teenage cultures were indeed developing in the United States as adolescents stayed in school longer and as an entertainment industry catered to their increased purchasing power. These youth cultures were different from the new German one in at least one major point: whereas the automobile played a large role in U.S. adolescent lives, from drive-in theaters to joy rides, few German adolescents had access to cars. U.S. cultural conservatives interpreted the fashions and behavior of American adolescents as a form of juvenile delinquency, and local authorities tried to reign in these new forms of adolescent behavior. In some cities, high school administrators banned "tight blue jeans" and "ducktail haircuts," because they saw, as one magazine reported, a "connection between undisciplined dress and undisciplined behavior."[45] Commentators across the country linked the new fads to lower-class and African American culture and worried that they would lead to "open revolt against society"[46] or to totalitarian seduction. But earlier than Germans, U.S. observers came to believe in the first half of the 1950s, that no class or race was immune to this problem. Some of these U.S. critics would probably have agreed with the dire warnings East Germans voiced about American culture.[47]

BORDER DISPUTES OVER AMERICAN CULTURE

East German authorities successfully played on West German fears of American-led Western self-destruction. Indeed, they directed their own indictments of American popular culture as much at the West as at the East German consumer. "The fatherland of the youth is the German Democratic Republic," read one East German manifesto, "To All of You" *(An Euch Alle)* by the youth organization FDJ in early 1956, "because it is here that the best national traditions and the great cultural heritage of the German people are preserved, cultivated, and made accessible to the working people, and not where American nonculture, nationalist-supremacist race hatred, gangster movies, trash novels, boogie-woogie, etc., are supposed to prepare the adolescents for murder, killings, and war.... We need healthy, courageous, skilled young people who are prepared to work and to defend the fatherland."[48] West Germany here was portrayed as inundated with American popular culture and therefore lacking an authentic national identity. Even as East German leaders sought to further the economic and political power of the working class, they did not shed another tradition—that of seeing working-class cultural styles as negative, especially when they were based on the consumption of "low" culture. Like West German commentaries, East German critiques associated male adolescent rebels with sexually provocative women and provocative fashions. The East German officials implied that these male adolescents' focus on American fashions, and their desires to consume, led them politically astray. East Germans did not explicitly talk about these cultural expressions of Americanized youths as working-class behavior, but by repeatedly linking such adolescent rebels to fascism, they used an indictment that was perhaps even more powerful in the postwar German context.[49]

To the dismay of both East and West German authorities, the West Berlin border theaters were exporting *Halbstarken* styles, along with dances and music rooted in African American culture, into East Germany. In April 1956 the West Berlin youth magazine *Blickpunkt* described afternoon showings in the border theaters, where young East Berliners came straight from school to watch mostly American movies. "The speakers with the music, which was just as 'hot' as the atmosphere, were blaring the syncopated Dixielands a little louder than in other movie theaters. That was necessary," commented the magazine, "because otherwise one would not hear the tune with all the audience's rhythmic stamping of their feet." *Blickpunkt* asked why these movie theaters, with their "cultural aid to the East," catered mainly to an audience of *Halbstarke* and why tax money was spent to "propagate" culture that was controversial even in West Germany.[50]

Internal East Berlin reports estimated in 1956 and 1957 that each day about twenty-six thousand East Berliners went to the movies in the West Berlin border theaters. In certain theaters, East Berlin adolescents made up 90 to 100 percent of the visitors.[51] Moreover, young East German males also listened to American music, wore American fashions, and even rioted. When American jeans were prohibitively expensive because of the high exchange rate for West German D-Marks, East Berliners, for example, would tighten domestic blue or black pants and outfit them with rivets.[52] In reaction, East German authorities either asserted that *Halbstarke* did not exist under socialism, or, if they acknowledged the presence of young rebels, they used the English term "rowdies" rather than *Halbstarke*, thus suggesting that adolescent misbehavior was in fact a foreign import.[53] Like their West German counterparts, East German officials rejected a consumption-oriented masculinity that was apparently fashioned after American imports and that signaled lack of male restraint.

BLACKBOARD JUNGLE, ROCK AROUND THE CLOCK, AND AMERICAN RACE RELATIONS

This East and West German "consensus" about what constituted proper masculinity (and femininity) had racial underpinnings, as became clear in debates over American movies and the American music they imported. Commentators in both states were hostile toward the African American–influenced music styles and dances, like boogie-woogie and rock 'n' roll, that East and West German adolescents copied from American films. These styles posed clear challenges to East and West German gender mores, and both sides labeled them "primitive." Yet, in seeming contradiction, both East and West Germans were at the same time critical of American racism. For example, one East German indictment of American popular culture, *An Euch Alle* (To all of you), criticized boogie-woogie and race hatred in the same sentence.[54] Such a contradiction also became apparent in East and West German reactions to rock 'n' roll and to *Blackboard Jungle*. This American juvenile-delinquency movie, which was released in West Germany in late 1955, depicted American race relations through the story of a white male teacher in an urban high school and introduced the rock 'n' roll hit "Rock Around the Clock."

West German reviewers compared *Rebel* and *Blackboard Jungle* and
stressed that they were much more positively impressed with the latter.[55]
Especially in its depictions of racial tensions and poverty, *Blackboard Jungle* seemed at once more convincing and safely distant to West German
commentators. Some East and West Germans altogether ignored the issue
of race relations in *Blackboard Jungle*, but others used the depiction of
blacks, Puerto Ricans, and various white ethnic groups as an opportunity to
distance themselves from American racism. Thus many West German papers emphasized the restraint and calmness of the unprejudiced white male
teacher and of his hardworking African American student played by Sidney Poitier who together were able to isolate the white troublemaker.[56]

Blackboard Jungle gave a progressive view of race relations, for the
movie undermined the stereotype of the black rapist and his white victim,
when it showed a young white man attacking a white female teacher.
Many West German papers illustrated reviews of *Blackboard Jungle* with
a still photo in which the female teacher, swinging her hips and wearing
high heels, walks by the crowd of male students; about half of these students, all whites, are shouting and whistling, while others, among them the
black student, look on with some boredom.[57]

The movie also shaped West German representations of *Halbstarke*. In
1956 one West German photographer took a picture of a group of young
West German men in short jackets and with longer hair who were leaning
against a fence reminiscent of the one around the school in *Blackboard*.
These young men appeared to be looking with desire and disdain at a
young woman walking by. In contrast to the teacher in *Blackboard*, the
woman did not wear stockings or high heels and her body was covered by
a coat that went well beyond her knees. This German woman was both
modern (as could be seen in her short hairstyle) and respectable.

In the case of *Blackboard Jungle*, by contrast, some West German commentators made the visibly sexual American woman, rather than her male
attackers, into the sexual perpetrator. One paper commented on the "psychological failure...especially of the female teacher who emphasized her sex
appeal too much" and concluded that the movie depicted this as an excuse
for the delinquents.[58] Another one found it "improbable and at least very
reckless...if a cute doll like the new female teacher is exposed to *Halbstarke*."[59] Here again, West Germans tried to disassociate themselves from
sexually expressive American women, while they portrayed these women as
causes of working-class male adolescent upheaval across races. Similarly, a
West German reviewer argued that West German single mothers, who sent
their children to the movies in order to be undisturbed with their lovers at

Fig. 10.   A German *Blackboard Jungle?* The photographer of this 1956 street scene in Germany was clearly influenced by images from the U.S. movie. Courtesy Ullstein Bilderdienst.

home, were responsible for German juvenile delinquency.[60] In these instances, sexually provocative American and German women served as a negative foil and obstacle to male self-restraint—whether in whites or blacks.

Other West German papers and the East German press saw the female teacher more as the innocent victim of the American delinquents. One East German commentator extrapolated that the male delinquents in the movie were all potential murderers prone to violating even motherhood: American delinquents would allegedly kill their own mothers. Both takes on the movie—the teacher as sexual perpetrator and the teacher as innocent victim—reinforced gender ideals of female sexual passivity and male restraint. The film departed from racist American and European stereotypes when it pointed out that both white and black men could achieve this ideal masculinity.[61]

One West German magazine, which did not recommend the movie for adolescents, even tried to "top" the racially liberal message. That this positive development occurs in one of the African American students, the magazine commented in January 1956, "may seem to us in Germany symptomatic for the unused power of other races; as we know, Americans think differently and much less respectfully of the Negroes."[62] Such commentary positioned Germans as antiracists who had overcome their racist, anti-

Semitic past and valued African Americans who allegedly were not yet in the grip of modern materialism. In suggesting an alliance of sorts between Germans and African Americans, it also helped Germans position *themselves* as victims; after displacements, reparations, economic hardship, and fraternization in the aftermath of National Socialism and World War II, many Germans felt victimized by the occupation forces.

Both East and West German papers applauded *Blackboard Jungle* as a realistic depiction of conditions in America and gleefully reported attempts of the U.S. ambassador in Italy, Clare Booth-Luce, to ban *Blackboard Jungle* from the Venice Film Festival. Booth-Luce had announced that the movie would leave a bad impression of U.S. youth and U.S. schools and thus would support the anti-American propaganda of Italian communists. Her action contributed greatly to the attractiveness of the movie, both among adolescents and among adult commentators and officials. Many West Germans expressed satisfaction when one of the West German rating boards recommended the movie as "especially valuable" (but only to people older than sixteen), since this further confirmed that West Germany was indeed more liberal than the United States. In West Germany the film was very successful, the thirteenth most-watched movie of 1956.[63]

Yet, reactions to *Blackboard Jungle* also pointed to the limits of racial liberalism in both Germanies: East and West German calls for racial equality proved compatible with rejections of African American culture. Thus East and West German reviewers of *Blackboard Jungle* reveled in the restrained, "cool" manliness of the hardworking African American student, and yet some reviewers made the fast-paced jazz in the soundtracks of *Blackboard* and *The Wild One* into a symbol of juvenile delinquency. *Blackboard* itself encouraged such an interpretation: in one scene Sidney Poitier asked his fellow black students to stop "jazzing it up," that is to stop inserting African American singing styles, when they are preparing to sing in a school Christmas performance. In late 1955 East and West German commentators did not yet know just what furor rock 'n' roll and *Blackboard Jungle*'s theme song, "Rock Around the Clock," would soon cause, but East German reviewers in particular criticized the "boogie" that male adolescents in *Blackboard Jungle* dance during school breaks. West German reviewers felt that the fast-paced jazz in the soundtrack of *Blackboard* effectively symbolized and illustrated American male delinquency and did not want German adolescents to adopt either the dances or the juvenile misbehavior associated with this music. East and West German commentators thus linked lack of male restraint to music like jazz and dances like the boogie that they recognized as rooted in African American culture.[64]

At a public debate about *Blackboard* in West Berlin, participants found it "courageous" that the movie showed "the dark sides of freedom" and the "return to barbarism and degeneration of mores."[65] One West German paper maintained in its review that juvenile delinquency was in fact an "expression of American civilization."[66] Once again these commentaries used concepts such as degeneration that were rooted in eugenics and that linked deviations from gender norms to racial inferiority. In West Germany in the 1950s, the "dark side" of freedom was signified by lack of male restraint and women's exaggerated sexuality.

East German papers exploited such West German concerns when they hailed *Blackboard Jungle* as a realistic depiction of conditions in both the United States and West Germany. One East German reviewer maintained that juvenile delinquency did not occur in all countries: while *Halbstarke* were a special problem in West Berlin, Moscow did not know such a phenomenon. This was simple deceit, since during these years Soviet papers and officials were attacking the so-called *stilyagi*, young men in adapted zoot suits and young women in short skirts and with bright lipstick, who were dancing to western tunes. In spite of evidence to the contrary, East German authorities also continued to assert that *Halbstarke* did not exist on their own territory.[67]

East and West German visions of racial equality relied on an ideal of male restraint across classes and races. This very ideal allowed East and West German authorities to reject much of African American culture, as became especially clear when Germans tried to come to terms with rock 'n' roll. From September 1956, the East and West German press reported about riots after screenings of the rock 'n' roll movie *Rock Around the Clock* and after rock concerts in the United States and Western European countries. Both sides further emphasized connections between male unruliness and African American culture.[68]

In September 1956, the West German youth magazine *Bravo* announced the arrival of *Rock Around the Clock* in West Germany and explained that the "wild rhythm" of Bill Haley's music, featured in the film, was rooted in the ritual music of "Africa's Negroes." The magazine printed pictures of male English rock fans and reported that they had rioted. Announcing that under the influence of rock 'n' roll, "cool Englishmen" had turned into "white Negroes," *Bravo* labeled rioting as typically black behavior. In the same article, the magazine urged its German audience not to behave like the English. Even as the magazine ostensibly admired rock 'n' roll, *Bravo'* s linkage between rioting Englishmen and "Negroes" warned against rock 'n' roll in racist terms.[69] As they had done earlier with boogie-

Fig. 11. West German advertising for *Rock Around the Clock* with Bill Haley, 1956. Courtesy Bundesarchiv Berlin—Filmarchiv.

woogie, East German commentators assessed rock 'n' roll—in films and elsewhere—using racial undertones similar to West German reactions. East German papers described rock 'n' roll as "decadent," an appeal to "primitive" humans, and a threat to proper values.[70]

Before any of the reports about riots appeared, the West German movie rating board had been outright enthusiastic about the "fun rhythm of rock 'n' roll" and had judged the film to be suitable for adolescents older than ten: "The movie had hardly any plot, but offered fun and entertainment."[71] The West German distributor for *Rock Around the Clock* tried to stir some controversy by giving the movie a German title *Außer Rand und*

Band—"out of control"—that had more rebellious connotations than the American original. Advertisements for the movie promised "By Day and Night—24 Hours of Music," "A Jazz Festival on the Screen," and "Rock and Roll—More than a Jazz Style: A Bacillus among Friends of Hot Music." Some movie posters featured Bill Haley with a curl of hair in his forehead; others showed male and female dancers twisting and jumping. In one a man was holding a woman protectively by the shoulders and kissing her on her hair. None of the posters made any explicit reference to the African American roots of the music or to riots; this promotion campaign clearly sought to portray rock 'n' roll as rebellious, but not too rebellious.[72]

The film became a huge success in West Germany, as in November and December 1956, adolescents in at least four West German cities lived up to the press reports about riots in other countries. In one city, some young men and women marched up and down a main street shouting "Rock around the clock" and "Bill Haley," which caused disbelief and consternation among on-lookers.[73] Reports about such events in the West German press further emphasized the links between American influences and German misbehavior, and East and West German commentators soon worried about gender and racial transgressions on the part of German rock 'n' roll fans.

EAST GERMAN REEVALUATIONS OF YOUNG REBELS

Not everyone, however, was outraged by *Halbstarken* behavior. In the course of 1956, two East German evaluations of West German *Halbstarke* emerged. Some East German officials continued to connect *Halbstarke* and their lack of male restraint to Western militarism and even fascism. But others reevaluated their stance against American popular culture and juvenile behavior; they came to see *Halbstarke* as legitimate resisters against the West German political system and West German rearmament.

This greater tolerance on the part of some East German officials was partially due to the realization that, in the mid-1950s, East Germans were increasingly looking to West Germany for consumer goods. As interrogations of East Germans who were stopped by East German police on their way home from shopping in West Berlin indicated, shoppers described Western goods as more fashionable and cheaper—in spite of prohibitive exchange rates.[74] Especially in the months after the Twentieth Party Congress of the Soviet Communist Party, which had turned against Stalinism in February 1956, the East German communist youth organization FDJ confronted this problem, no longer globally condemning consumers of Western fashions.

These efforts were part of a "thaw" in the Soviet Bloc that had begun after Stalin's death in 1953 and reached its peak in the early fall of 1956 when Polish workers struck and demonstrated and an armed uprising against communist leaders and Soviet control broke out in Hungary. In contrast to their lack of preparation during the crisis in 1953, the party leadership around Ulbricht tried to be ahead of and contain any momentum for reform.[75] In October 1955, the SED Central Committee once again admonished the FDJ for isolating itself too much from the majority of East German youth. Central Committee member Albert Norden urged FDJ leaders not to fill their speeches with "theorems," but to "spice them with jokes" and to be "fun friends" at dance events. Party leader Ulbricht himself declared: "What do we have to lose?" and suggested that *"Halbstarke"* who had authority among other youths might well work together with FDJ members in attracting adolescents. In July 1956 the Central Committee of the SED even announced a fight against "dogmatism," and some party members saw an opportunity to question Ulbricht's leadership. In this context, party leaders pursued a policy with many potential contradictions. They continued to condemn American cultural influences, yet tried to harness Americanized youth cultures for their own purposes.[76]

The very statement by the FDJ leadership that attacked American influences in West Germany in February 1956, *An Euch Alle,* also announced an "open discussion about the ideals of our new life that find their fulfillment in the construction of socialism in the German Democratic Republic." It further declared that there would be open "youth forums" where "representatives of the organization, men and women from public life, and members of the state apparatus will answer openly and clearly any question by young people."[77]

Indeed, the FDJ clearly tried to use consumption in order to attract adolescents in 1956. In the public forums organized by the FDJ, young people asked why fashions in East Germany were not up to Western standards and complained especially that the new tighter pants were not available. The East German state tried to counter such complaints by announcing fashion shows and by opening special clothing stores for teenagers. In May 1956, at a public forum organized by the East Berlin FDJ, adolescents and officials openly discussed why no American movies were shown in the GDR. Adolescents complained that East Germany produced no music films with "hits." They also asked why movies "like *Blackboard Jungle*" were not released in the GDR. Officials blamed this on the U.S. government, which allegedly prohibited the export to East Germany of any movie that found fault with American social conditions. Here America, rather than East Germany, appeared repressive, but FDJ officials felt on the defensive.[78]

Issues of consumption were also at the center of the movie *Eine Berliner Romanze* (Berlin romance), which the East German state film company produced in 1956. In this movie, two West Berlin boys, one called Hans and one called "Lord," pursue the East Berlin girl Uschi on one of her excursions to the Western part of the city. Both boys sport haircuts that resemble ducktail plumes, but the most striking attributes of Lord are his good clothes and his transistor radio, which he buys with money made from shady deals. One East German reviewer commented that both boys tended toward being *Halbstarke,* but he did not see this as a problem since "*Halbstarke* were unpleasant only if they appeared in groups." The reviewer went on to complain that it was too often forgotten that "on their own they were understanding, diligent, boyish, and funny."[79]

However, the East German program brochure for the movie made distinctions between Lord and the hardworking and exploited Hans. The movie sympathized with *Halbstarke,* but at the same time made clear that the desires that Western consumer culture and a capitalist economy raised could lead young men only in two directions: either into crime, as in the case of Lord—who was clearly more Americanized—or into poverty, as in the case of Hans. Uschi ultimately begins a relationship with Hans, and the movie ends with the hope that they will pursue a stable life in the Eastern part of the city, where both will be able to find work. As the brochure emphasized, Uschi, originally blinded by the glamour of the West, chooses Hans "not for his appearance."[80] With this focus on the taming stability of a heterosexual relationship, *Berliner Romanze* proposed a solution to male adolescent misbehavior that over the next years West Germans would also increasingly see as a remedy for their *Halbstarkenproblem.*

At the same time, however, East German indictments of *Halbstarke* continued. Some East German papers criticized the movie for not making clear distinctions between East and West, especially for not successfully countering Uschi's conviction that life in the East was boring. Likewise, earlier accusations that had connected adolescent consumers of American popular culture to fascism, for example in the context of the June 1953 uprising, continued. Thus in September 1956, the East German press claimed that a West Berlin gang of adolescents, who had destroyed some public property and bathed in the nude, had displayed "cowboy movie posters" and "Nazi badges" in their headquarters. The commentator clearly perceived nude bathing as a sexual transgression, which he linked to both American influences and National Socialism.[81]

Yet that very month, in September of 1956, just as the West German *Halbstarken* riots reached a first peak and rock 'n' roll made it into the German consciousness, the FDJ effectively turned this East German logic around. Now, according to the FDJ, not the adolescent *Halbstarke* but their attackers used "old Nazi methods." The statement by the FDJ Central Council identified a so-called *Halbstarken* campaign directed at the West German youth by the "Hitler officers" from the defense ministry and other Bonn ministries. As the FDJ argued, West German authorities were attacking all West German and West Berlin youth "in order to force them into the barracks," that is, into the West German army. The FDJ claimed that the "appearance" of many West German adolescents—who of course drew heavily on American imports—signified that they preferred a life of "personal freedom" to "death on the battlefield."

Since *Halbstarken* behavior was heavily shaped by American examples, it was contradictory that the FDJ used this celebration of (male) resistance for a renewed indictment of American popular culture in West Germany. Whereas earlier statements had claimed that American popular culture directly militarized West German adolescents, East German officials now alleged an even more sophisticated conspiracy: West German authorities first used American culture to corrupt youths into "lasciviousness" and "inhumanity" and then responded by disciplining these adolescents in the military.[82]

Several reports in East German papers hailed fights between West German adolescents and West German police or soldiers as resistance against conscription. In September 1956, the East Berlin paper *Der Morgen* analyzed the youth riots in West Germany as protest "against bad conditions in the workplace" and against "the threat of military drills." Even though the paper commented that their "drive to action" was often misdirected, it clearly evaluated *Halbstarken* behavior as a political act.[83] This constituted a departure from earlier East German official statements that had seen West German *Halbstarke* exclusively as importers of deviance and political unrest into East Germany. The FDJ, with some reservations, validated "proletarian" cultural styles that drew on the consumption of American mass culture as working-class resistance against economic and political oppression in West Germany.

Yet, this stance proved to be problematic for East German authorities. In September of 1956, just as West Germany was experiencing a large number of riots, West German papers also reported riots in East Germany. In Rostock, for example, rioters had gathered in front of a movie theater and threatened policemen; it took the baton-wielding police more than an hour to regain control. Similar reports came out of Halle and East Berlin, and in several East German cities adolescents expressed their enthusiasm for American music by dancing and shouting in the street.[84]

East German officials saw such rioters within East German borders as a threat to state authority, and in October 1956, the FDJ ordered its East Berlin bureau to take special care to prevent "incidents by adolescent rowdies" at the anniversary of the founding of the GDR on October 7.[85] East German authorities used these official celebrations to display East Germany's might and unity. Perhaps ironically, this order was given at the very same meeting during which the FDJ Central Council suggested that West German *Halbstarke* were legitimately resisting West German authorities.

HALBSTARKE AND WEST GERMAN POLITICS

Despite the contradictions and hypocrisy of this stance, the East German reevaluation of *Halbstarken* behavior as an act of political resistance against oppression and rearmament exacerbated fears over *Halbstarke* in West Germany. In this context, some West German commentators, state officials, and politicians, like their East German counterparts, politicized American popular culture and the styles associated with it. At the same time, West Germans struggled over the East German suggestion that *Halbstarken* behavior was politically motivated.

Many West German commentators saw sinister political intentions behind *Halbstarke*. At a time when West Germans were discussing both rearmament and the recent prohibition of the West German communist party KPD by the West German Constitutional Court, some press commentaries and police investigators wondered whether adolescent riots were the result of communist plots.[86] In their most outraged attacks on *Halbstarke*, however, West Germans employed the same logic as many East German indictments of American popular culture: they associated the behavior of *Halbstarke* and their consumption of American popular culture with alleged National Socialist threats. Thus, West German commentator Walter Abendroth, the former cultural editor of the weekly *Die Zeit*, discussed the effects of *Rock Around the Clock*, warning against the "craze" of film and jazz fans and excessive admiration of movie stars. He paralleled adolescents' "fanatic" behavior with that of Nazi followers and asked, "Who knows to what intricacy and audacity these mass highs, like the orgies of jazz fans, could grow, if at the critical moment certain motives were introduced?" Further, Abendroth criticized "primitivism," the "loss of universal, humanistic education," "lack of true religious faith," and "superstitious belief in the healing power of psychoanalysis."[87] Such commentary reiterated fears about the political consequences of a materialist manipulation of youth under consumer capitalism. In espousing a new masculine, yet non-militarist, ideal, West German commentators conflated Nazis and *Halb-starke*, even though there was no evidence that *Halbstarke* were espousing Nazi ideology. Moreover, with their references to "primitivism," West Germans used a vocabulary with a long tradition in eugenics that had become an important part of Nazi racism. In reintroducing such terms in the context of criticizing youth consumption of jazz or rock, which were rooted in African American culture, West German critics of the youth rebellion resurrected racial hierarchies even as they warned against a return to National Socialism.

Another West German commentator combined his critique of the high number of former SS officers who had been appointed to the West German army with a warning that *Halbstarke* on motorbikes, who were beating up soldiers, were a "motorbike-SA." In comparing *Halbstarke* to the Nazi Storm Troopers (SA), which conjured up a link between Nazism and homosexuality, he indicted young rebels as sexual deviants. Such an indictment has to be seen in the context of West German laws and expert opinions (upheld by the Constitutional Court in 1957) that criminalized homosexuality, denied homosexuals the status of victims of National Socialism, and linked male homosexuality explicitly to dangerous aggression in men. This link also served to reject the notion brought forward by the GDR press that the actions of *Halbstarke* constituted legitimate resistance.[88]

In an influential 1956 West German treatment of *Halbstarke*, high school teacher and education expert Hans Muchow contrasted civilized (implicitly white) behavior with three stages of regression into a "wild form." Muchow, who was the first to formulate a comprehensive theory of *Halbstarken* behavior in the 1950s, in a curious way combined biology, genetics, psychology, and political analysis. Clearly he was influenced by the eugenics-based discourse of the Weimar Republic. Thus he argued that the biggest group of *Halbstarke* belonged to an ever-increasing group of "primitives," who could not achieve psychic maturity and, under the conditions of modern society, acted like "wild ones." Biologically incapable of moving beyond menial labor, they took joy in noise and behaved rather cowardly, because they would flee riot scenes as soon as the police arrived. Muchow thus implied that they were unproductive and unmanly.

Muchow identified a second, smaller group of young rebels: they were the "educationally frustrated" from "honorable circles" and "orderly families," whose middle-class affluence was another root of *Halbstarken* behavior. As he explained, these adolescents oscillated between fear and aggression because their parents had fulfilled all their wishes—that is, had let them overconsume—or had not educated them at all. Muchow described both the primitives and the educationally frustrated as adolescents who "did not know what they were doing," in allusion to the German title of *Rebel Without a Cause.*

While Muchow claimed that the "primitives" and the "frustrated" made up the majority of *Halbstarke,* he alleged that a dangerous "avant garde" of "nihilists" led this majority. Muchow maintained that the "nihilists," "like the blonde gang leader in *Blackboard Jungle,*" shaped the style of *Halbstarken* behavior, consciously regressed into the "wild state," took pleasure in dismantling values, and led other adolescents in a fight against the police and against law and order. Muchow's analysis affirmed the notion that German *Halbstarke* were modeling their styles and behavior on American movies and especially on *The Wild One, Blackboard Jungle,* and *Rebel Without a Cause.* American movies provided a vocabulary for Muchow's description of youthful misbehavior as a German and international phenomenon. He combined this with an older vocabulary rooted in eugenics, by making various links between cultural and biological "primitivism" and "decline."

Muchow's theory of *Halbstarke* drew on all existing fears that had shaped the German public debate: fears of working-class upheaval, the adoption of working-class styles by male middle-class youths, and conscious political actions against the state. Muchow stressed that these transgressions were not harmless and warned of parallels between the National Socialist rise to power and *Halbstarken* behavior. While Muchow rejected the notion that youth riots were directed by "political circles," he identified them as a danger to the state. The state had to counter them with strong action, such as using water hoses or, since mandatory military service had become "problematic," introducing mandatory social service of half a year. Other West Germans were less restrained; a minority of press reports and letters to editors demanded military service as a way to educate adolescents. Muchow also recommended more state-directed cultural offerings for the youth. He concluded that "totalitarian systems," including National Socialism and socialist states, with their state youth organizations, more easily tamed such adolescent rebellions.[89]

In this and other arguments, the German Cold War was explicitly part of the discussion. Another educator, Adolf Busemann, pointed to the dangerous implications of *Halbstarken* behavior; he warned that a critique of "the Eastern dictatorship was vain hypocrisy or worse if we do not stop the process of regression into barbarism and brutalization, which is rooted in the abuse of democratic freedom." While Busemann did not employ the word "degeneration," he, like Muchow, expressed fears of biological decline.[90] Implicit in such statements was an ideal West German citizen in uniform who would have to defend Western families and Western culture on three fronts: against the National Socialist past, against the Cold War enemy in the East, and against the allegedly self-destructive exaggeration of freedom associated with American culture.

In this climate it was politically shrewd that in September 1956, Chancellor Konrad Adenauer called attacks and defamations against the West German army shameful and announced that they were the work of *Halbstarke*. The chancellor skillfully associated all opponents of the West German army with unmanly cultural expressions that all political parties rejected in 1956. Like so many other commentators, Adenauer at once delegitimized and politicized *Halbstarken* behavior. Dutifully, both the governing CDU and the opposition party SPD released statements in support of the West German army, and the SPD even warned against a return to the "rowdiness of the 1930s," which had led to the demise of the Weimar Republic.[91] Adenauer's and the SPD's stance further fostered the West German need to search for political motivations behind *Halbstarken* behavior.

WEST GERMAN DEPOLITICIZATION ATTEMPTS

Yet many West Germans tried to counter the notion that *Halbstarke* were engaging in political activities. In one case, an adolescent distributed leaflets stating: "*Halbstarke* are against conscription," and some trial records likewise referred to *Halbstarken* riots as demonstrations against the draft.[92] In spite of Adenauer's accusations, West German papers rarely mentioned such incidents, perhaps because they were rare, or perhaps because they might confirm the East German suggestion that *Halbstarke* were resisting conscription. The West German press also ignored statements by the West Berlin chapter of the SPD youth organization *Die Falken* ("the falcons"), which most clearly formulated a political vision that connected the consumption of American popular culture and styles associated with *Halbstarken* behavior to resistance against conscription. In advertisements to draw in new members in the mid-1950s, *Die Falken* stressed "that life did not entail just work" and that their leisure time cultural offerings included folk dances as well as boogie, classical music as well as cool jazz. Significantly, they declared that for them "all of these issues [including leisure] ... were deeply political questions." Their indictment of conscription culminated in the announcement that "We find it more useful to practice jazz than to march in new uniforms," and they offered assistance to everyone from East and West who resisted conscription.[93] This stance, which turned the consumption of displeasing American popular culture like the boogie into a vehicle for political resistance, contrasted with the position of the main body of the SPD, as well as virtually all other public youth organizations, who were careful to distance themselves from *Halbstarke*. And even within the West Berlin *Falken*, rifts existed between "rock 'n' roll" groups and those who wanted what they saw as intellectual and disciplined political work—and who were increasingly headed by middle- and upper-class male youths.[94]

Male *Halbstarke*, with their spontaneous gatherings and riots and with their public displays of distasteful dances and fashions, certainly ran counter to proper political involvement, which all mainstream parties defined as voting, organized involvement in political parties, and service to the state. Because most of the riots indeed had no clear leadership but happened spontaneously when youths (mostly boys) took theaters apart or rampaged through the streets, one magazine commented somewhat condescendingly that these adolescents had no political agenda. Yet the very same article talked of the "evil power" of *Halbstarke*.[95]

When the West Berlin city parliament debated the youth riots in September 1956, Mayor Franz Amrehn countered assertions that youth riots were politically directed. Instead he described the riots as an international phenomenon and stressed that they also had occurred in the United States and even in East Germany and the Soviet Union. Amrehn emphasized that West Berlin was no "Wild West," and as the main causes for riots, he cited the scarcity of housing and the conditions of the war and postwar years "that had loosened morality." Although Amrehn implied that poverty in the postwar period was one root of unruly youth behavior, he also acknowledged that many youths from "good homes" had been taking part in the riots.[96]

Amrehn and most members of the West Berlin parliament from Christian Democrats to Social Democrats agreed that the police had to step in to guarantee public safety and to preserve the authority of the state. West Berlin officials decided to use more undercover agents, because adolescents were so hostile toward officers in uniform. At the same time Amrehn and his government, like the Bonn government, urged the press not to report on gangs and riots in detail. Moreover, Amrehn and many speakers from various parties also agreed that "positive" youth social work and cultural programs were needed. Clearly they imagined programs that would counter the effects of American consumer culture. The speaker from the

SPD who described West Berlin youth riots as modeled on American examples, especially on *The Wild One,* urged, with applause from both the SPD and CDU, that libraries be used to educate the youth into "valuable and worthy members of our community."[97]

But the West Berlin city government had actually already gone further. The riots in Wedding had apparently stopped when the city government called a meeting with adolescent rioters at the end of July 1956. The *Totenkopfbande* (Skulls and Crossbones gang) that had caused disturbances and public outcries throughout the summer had reportedly brought flowers to Mayor Amrehn and had apologized. The mayor in turn had given the boys a meeting place with a jukebox and had paid out of the city budget for a concert that attracted six thousand adolescents—everyone "who drove motorbikes with racing saddles and wore Texas pants."[98]

In September 1956 the youth magazine *Bravo* applauded the actions of the city government. The magazine explained that rowdies had always existed and attacked those who now wanted to declare a "national emergency." Further, it rejected the notion that everyone "who wore tight jeans, who drove around on scooters or motorbikes with other adolescents, or who behaved a little more provocatively" was a dangerous *Halbstarker.* *Bravo* was a new weekly magazine that the Munich publisher Kindler and Schiermeyer had just introduced in August of 1956. The magazine addressed an adolescent audience with a modern colorful layout including big headlines and many photographs. Aside from movies and movie stars, *Bravo* devoted extensive coverage to popular music, including the latest American imports. Within a year the magazine had a run of two hundred thousand, and by 1960 it had a readership of about 1.6 million per week. *Bravo's* commercial success was inseparable from the success of a commercial youth culture that catered specifically to adolescents and that imported many of its icons from the United States. The magazine became the main source of information on American movie stars and music, but many of its articles also revealed a paternalistic attitude toward adolescents.

In the fall of 1956, *Bravo* urged both *Halbstarke* and the police to calm down. At the same time, the magazine criticized police brutality, asserted that nobody cared about the younger generation, and urged politicians, especially the Minister of the Interior, to do more for youth rather than work against them. *Bravo* told West German authorities to look to West Berlin, where the *Halbstarkenproblem* had allegedly been solved quickly with the help of the mayor and "a first-rate jazz band." *Bravo* clearly pursued a double strategy that was typical of its style—and of many other efforts by the U.S. and West German entertainment industry to sell youth culture to adolescents and adults. On the one hand, the magazine fostered associations between adolescent unruliness and American popular culture. On the other hand, it sought to make youth fashions and music acceptable in an commercialized youth culture and suggested that adolescents were right to attract attention. The magazine even claimed that jazz music, rather than causing adolescent rebelliousness, could in fact be used to curb male over-aggression, and demanded state support for this position.[99]

An earlier attempt by the West Berlin government to cooperate with a commercial movie producer on a film, *Die Halbstarken*, that would speak to the problems of German young rebels had failed. In the spring of 1956, West Berlin city officials, actors, and producers had participated in public meetings in an effort to assure an authentic depiction of adolescents. The movie, a self-conscious West German answer to *The Wild One, Blackboard Jungle*, and *Rebel Without a Cause*, took place in a working-class setting and depicted a gang of juveniles who committed robberies. Only one gang member came from a middle-class family. The West Berlin government withdrew funding for the movie, because it did not show "any positive solutions" to juvenile upheaval. But with the public discussions and a highly publicized search for the actress who would play the main female character, the movie producers were able to gain public attention in East and West, well before the film was released in October 1956. The film, shot in black and white like *Blackboard Jungle*, featured some typical *Halbstarken* behavior and styles, such as a disturbance in a public swimming pool, fast-paced American music, and jeans and short jackets for boys and girls. The film established the star status of Horst Buchholz, who played the gang leader Freddy. Movie posters that showed him throwing a stone certainly fostered his rebellious image. Overall, however, *Die Halbstarken* was hardly representative of 1950s young rebels, since it traced the path of its protagonists into robbery and even murder. Accordingly many West German critics felt that it misrepresented young rebels as criminals.[100]

The movie is noteworthy, because it helped to spread the term *Halbstarke* and because it translated into German terms a trope that characterized German views of American juvenile delinquency. It portrayed a young, sensual German woman, Sissy (Karin Baal) as the evil force behind the male delinquents in the film, and thus took up a phenomenon that West German reviewers of American young rebel movies had identified as a typically American problem. At the end of the movie Sissy exposed her avarice and even shot her lover, the gang leader. The notion that young sexual women instigated male misbehavior would also be part of West German discussions of rock 'n' roll.

Fig. 12. Advertising at a Munich theater for *Die Halbstarken* with Horst Buchholz and Karin Baal, 1956. The film was the West German "answer" to American young rebel movies. Photo: Felicitas Timpe, courtesy Bildarchiv Preußischer Kulturbesitz.

Whereas West German producers and reviewers saw Freddy's character modeled on American examples from *Blackboard Jungle* or *Rebel Without a Cause*, they billed Karin Baal as the German answer to the sexy French actress Marina Vlady.[101] In the minds of many Germans, French women perhaps expressed their sexuality more "normally" than American women who allegedly vacillated between frigidity, oversexualization, sadism, and masochism. In any case, with the help of the West Berlin tabloid *B.Z.*, the West German movie producers conducted a public contest in the spring of 1956 to find "a girl like Marina Vlady, the sweet and sinful innocence from Paris." More than seven hundred girls came to the open auditions. The role of Sissy went to fifteen-year-old Karin Blauermel, soon renamed Karin Baal. As the producers and the press emphasized, she lived with her mother and grandmother in the working-class district Wedding (the same one where the riots were soon to take place).[102] Baal, whose acting career was launched with the film, loomed large in movie posters behind the stone-throwing Buchholz. Perhaps to associate Baal with Asians and a perceived threat from the Bolshevist East, these posters exaggerated her slanted eyes.

In spite or because she was depicted negatively, Baal's tight pants, sweaters, and open hair and bangs became a model for many German girls.[103] Some of these young women also identified with male idols such as James Dean when they purchased short jackets and jeans. One girl remembered that for two years she wore only black sweaters and black jeans (called "*Amibüxen*," "American pants," by distraught mothers). She saw her outfit as a conscious rejection of the petticoats and wide skirts that were in fashion in the mid-1950s.[104]

Overall, the movie furthered the notion that *Halbstarken* behavior was not politically motivated by portraying young rebels as robbers motivated by an evil woman. Increasingly, West German commentators agreed with this evaluation. One paper even suggested that demonstrations against conscription and clashes between adolescents and soldiers were probably nonpolitical and sought to explain them as mere fights over the attention of girls. Nonetheless, the commentator saw a connection with politics: he identified the devaluation of everything military by the occupation forces as the political root of the adolescents' rejection of the West German army. At the same time he criticized East German authorities who interpreted "any bad word directed against a soldier" as protest against the Adenauer government. Another paper echoed such comments and rejected the idea that riots were communist-organized demonstrations against conscription.[105]

In the debates over American cultural influences and *Halbstarke*, East and West German authorities constructed the ideal of a new, self-restrained, postfascist German man not taken over by consumer culture. At the same time, the gender mores authorities formulated were central to linking fascism and American popular culture, and to rejecting both. Distinguishing themselves from fascism was certainly a worthy project for East and West Germans, but it is necessary to look carefully at these attempts to leave the past behind. In connecting deviations from gender norms—lack of male restraint and sexually provocative, emasculating women—to lower-class and African American culture, East and West German officials reinscribed class and racial hierarchies even as they criticized poverty and American racism. Ironically, even though both Germanies were ethnically homogenous as never before, authorities relied on gender norms and negative racial stereotypes to contain rebellious youth behavior and to fight the Cold War battles.

The debates about *Halbstarke* and American influences were a crucial part in the complicated processes of reconstructing Germanness in East and West. East German authorities conflated the consumption of American popular culture with fascism and capitalist militarism, while West Germans conflated it with fascism and Eastern totalitarianism. These moves served related political functions: in their quest for a Germanness untainted by National Socialism, both Germanies connected the threat of fascism to American cultural influences, thus hiding the Third Reich's German origins.

In East and West Germany, authorities translated these visions into public policy: they usually urged youngsters to read good books, go to concerts to hear classical music, watch only movies recommended by state agencies, or take ballroom dance classes. Thus both states politicized culture and for the most part supported cultural forms that did not pose challenges to the gender norms that were central to the reconstruction of German national identities in East and West.[106]

Yet, this logic clearly put West German authorities, who were struggling to build a military and political alliance with the United States, into a more vulnerable position. And to make things worse, West Germans felt threatened by FDJ efforts that, for a time in 1956, seemed to give *Halbstarke* cultural and political legitimacy. In this context many West Germans sought to assure themselves that *Halbstarke* were only a tiny minority, and at the same time rejected *Halbstarken* fashions and mannerisms. In October 1956 the polling institute EMNID published a study of West German and West Berlin adolescents with the rather timely title "How Strong Are the *Halbstarke?*" EMNID asserted that only few *Halbstarke* existed. Reports about EMNID's findings in the West German press revealed that many West Germans saw adolescents' American-influenced cultural styles closely linked to a dangerous lack of political commitment to the West German state. In this atmosphere traditional European dances, with their compatibility with "bourgeois" gender mores, were a symbol of West German political stability. Newspapers distilled the EMNID study as follows: German adolescents respected authority, were satisfied with their work, had no illusions—and liked to dance the waltz.[107]

However, as the 1950s wore on, and as consumption assumed growing importance as a Western weapon in the Cold War, West Germans would have to develop new answers, and a different, consumption-oriented masculinity, in their efforts to find a new, German, way between Eastern totalitarianism and American-led alleged Western self-destruction. Already by the late fall of 1956, the "thaw" in the Soviet Bloc began to dissipate. Soviet troops suppressed the Hungarian uprising in November 1956. At the same time Polish reform efforts were halted, and in East Germany dissenting intellectuals were put on trial. East German officials retreated from their stance that promised an accommodation of *Halbstarken* styles and increasingly reverted to earlier attacks that labeled both young German rebels and American popular culture fascist. West Germans, in turn, would increasingly depoliticize both American imports and *Halbstarken* behavior.

3 Lonely Crowds and Skeptical Generations

Depoliticizing and Repoliticizing Cultural Consumption

In 1956, as youth riots were shaking both Germanies, the West German paper *Hamburger Anzeiger* illustrated an article about the psychology of German adolescent rebels, so-called *Halbstarke*, with stills from the American movie *Rebel Without a Cause*. The three pictures featured James Dean's character in a knife fight with other adolescents, beating his father, and arguing with police; they were juxtaposed with a photo of a presumably German boy and girl innocently enjoying a picnic in a meadow. The accompanying article assured parents that most adolescent crises were "necessary and completely natural" developmental phases. The author cited a psychologist who advised parents to treat their children during these rebellious periods at once with "tolerance and strictness," because otherwise "dangerous derailments" could occur.[1] Similarly contradictory statements could be heard from East Germans. In 1957 an East German commentator reported about East Berlin male adolescents who idly hung out at street corners and who would take their hands out of their pockets only to fix their "James Dean" haircuts. He described these adolescents as "harmless, but endangered."[2] Like his West German counterpart, this journalist suggested that adolescents underwent periods of rebellion that were natural and harmless, but could, under certain conditions, turn dangerous. These more liberal voices that evaluated *Halbstarken* behavior as a natural life stage were in marked contrast to those in both East and West Germany who warned against *Halbstarke* as serious political threats. Interestingly, they agreed with their conservative counterparts on one point: East and West German adolescents, and especially young males, modeled their rebellious behavior on American examples transmitted to Germany via American movies and music.

106

Shifting and contested evaluations of *Halbstarke* were part of important East and West German transformations in the second half of the 1950s. In 1955 and 1956, West Germans, strongly believing in the adverse effects of American cultural influences, found themselves on the defensive against two kinds of East German attacks. First, East German authorities portrayed West Germany and its rebellious adolescents as inundated with American popular culture. They alleged that the consumption of American imports made these adolescents prone to fascist seduction. In 1956 East German officials introduced an idea that worried West Germans perhaps even more: some East German officials proclaimed that through their rioting and their appearance, West German male rebels were in fact resisting the West German government. In the following years, however, East German authorities returned to their earlier stance, namely that adolescent consumption of American popular culture posed a consistent threat to East German socialism. West Germans authorities, on the other hand, increasingly convinced themselves that *Halbstarken* behavior was mostly harmless and nonpolitical and made consumption central to West German identity.

The year 1955 was a turning point, not only because the two Germanies became formally sovereign, because they rearmed, or because the Allies affirmed the division of Germany at the Geneva meeting. It was after 1955 that consumption levels increased at a faster pace in West than in East Germany, and consumption in the two opposing states took on ever more divergent meanings. In West Germany, social scientists, politicians, and the entertainment industry constructed a masculinity compatible with consumption.[3] This required reconfiguring the visions of class and race that had been crucial to conservative reconstruction of Germanness in East and West in the first half of the 1950s.[4] In undertaking their reevaluations of youth behavior, West Germans drew on American cultural imports, like films, and also relied on American social science research. In East Germany, officials attempted for a brief period in the mid-1950s to accommodate Western-influenced youth cultures, but these attempts soon failed and were followed by an increased politicization of adolescents' cultural consumption. These diverging stances—what one might call the ostensible depoliticization of youth cultures in the West and their renewed politicization in the East—shaped national politics in both countries in the later 1950s, affecting reconfigurations of their German past and the Cold War struggles between the two states. East and West Germans continued to invoke American popular culture, but they did so in increasingly different ways.

REBELS WITHOUT A CAUSE? ACCOMMODATING ADOLESCENT
CONSUMPTION IN WEST GERMANY

It was perhaps not by chance that the 1956 West German article describing rebellious youth behavior as a natural developmental phase was accompanied by stills from *Rebel Without a Cause*. For when *Rebel* reached West Germany in late 1955, the film introduced the notion that all adolescents, including those from the middle and upper classes, were prone to disagreeable actions. Depicting white middle-class youths who were rebelling against parental authority and public order, *Rebel* relied heavily on psychology and parental failures to explain adolescent misbehavior across classes. Specifically it showed how weak fathers and overly strong mothers were responsible if such adolescent tendencies went out of bounds.

The West German article that saw adolescent rebelliousness as a natural stage in need of channeling differed considerably from most other West German voices. In the mid-1950s more conservative West German commentators, ranging from movie reviewers to researchers to politicians, evaluated *Halbstarke* as the dangerous product of a working-class atmosphere inhabited by overly aggressive men as well as lascivious and dominant women; commentators considered these men and women overly susceptible to consumer culture and especially to American cultural influences. Initially, such sentiments had shaped most West German reactions to *Rebel*. For example, one guide for educators maintained that the dramatic car race between two boys, during which one was killed, was especially unbearable because of "the female main character (Judy) who with smiling nonchalance gave the starting signal." West German commentators who sought to render *Halbstarke* a working-class phenomenon were outraged that *Rebel* located such deviations from bourgeois gender mores in the middle class.[5]

West German reviewers and officials were particularly annoyed at the psychological explanations that *Rebel Without a Cause* offered for middle-class juvenile rebelliousness; they found the depiction of the weak father, who responded to his wife's every whim, dangerous and unconvincing. Instead they tried to preserve their class-specific paradigm for understanding *Halbstarke*. One reviewer, for example, complained that the film relied exclusively on psychology and therefore portrayed adolescents as "rebels without a cause." Another West German reviewer criticized the focus on psychology in *Rebel* as a typical American weakness; he did so, ironically, in a striking gender imagery that repeated the movie's focus on overbearing mothers: "And thus mother America again presses her sweet little scoundrels and cute murderers to her atomic breast... and shouts to us, who really should be outraged: 'Let them go, for they don't know what they are doing.'"[6] Such imagery echoed an East German poster against rearmament that showed a skeletal woman in a U.S. military uniform and with red fingernails pressing a small man in an old German uniform against her breasts—the German general in turn had his revolver on top of the heads of West German politicians Adenauer and Schumacher.[7] German commentators depicted the American nation as a dangerous mother, but did not yet believe that middle-class mothers were at the root of German juvenile delinquency.

The West German movie rating board decided to prohibit showings of *Rebel* to young people under sixteen because adolescents would experience the adults in the movie "as comical figures" and would be very impressed by "the rebellion against authority, from rowdiness at school to shootings with the police." Therefore the movie would hinder "proper ethical formation."[8] American reviewers had likewise seen the depictions of middle-class juvenile delinquency as dangerous, but in contrast to many West German reviewers they were quite convinced that the destruction of the patriarchal family *across* classes was at the root of the problem. Since the late 1940s, U.S. social scientists had begun to worry about the effects of specialization, bureaucratization, and the rise of a consumption-oriented society on American families. They concluded that under these conditions the authority of American fathers was declining in disturbing ways. Especially white middle-class men were allegedly no longer able to stand up to wives or to children. Juvenile delinquency and homosexual tendencies, as in the interest the boy Plato showed for James Dean's character in *Rebel*, were the result. *Rebel* also followed American social scientists when it suggested that the heterosexual, but basically asexual relationship between the James Dean and Natalie Wood characters was a solution to adolescent misbehavior. West German movie posters underlined this message: Dean held and protected Wood—in marked contrast to his weak father. In its indictment of mothers and its celebration of the patriarchal heterosexual relationship, *Rebel* thus reiterated widely accepted views that permeated U.S. social science discourse and the media in the 1950s.[9]

The psychological focus that *Rebel* suggested was compatible with a reevaluation of mass culture. In the United States, Cold War liberal social scientists increasingly rejected the view of those American "alarmists," that is, cultural conservatives, who saw mass culture as the root of juvenile delinquency. According to these liberal interpretations, psychological formations in families, rather than mass culture, were responsible when adolescent behavior went out of bounds. Mass culture, Cold War liberals argued, could in fact help adolescents channel their rebelliousness and adapt socially.[10]

Over the next few years, the psychological explanations that *Rebel* employed became increasingly accepted also in West Germany. In press and scholarship, more and more voices appeared that saw adolescent rebelliousness across classes in terms similar to those that reshaped American evaluations of juvenile delinquency and consumption. After 1956, West German social researchers including Curt Bondy, Viggo Graf Blücher, and in particular Helmut Schelsky, contributed to these new interpretations of adolescent behavior. In 1956 and 1957, sociologist Schelsky and his disciple Blücher published books and several articles on youth in West German society. During the same period, psychologist Bondy directed his study that dealt specifically with *Halbstarken* riots and was funded by the West German Ministry of the Interior. While these scholars did not form a coherent group, they drew on each other's work and shared important assumptions.[11]

These scholars increasingly moved away from the outright rejection of consumer culture, particularly in the form of American imports, that characterized many East and West German reactions to *Halbstarke*. Instead, they came to see adolescent rebelliousness and consumption as part of a normal life stage, which remained, however, in need of proper channeling. Within this logic, American westerns and young rebel movies, as well as boogie and rock 'n' roll, lost much of the danger that conservative and Marxist critics had posited.

The work of scholars like Bondy, Blücher, and Schelsky is significant not simply because of its focus on youth. In interpreting youth behavior in the context of larger socioeconomic changes that West Germany underwent in the mid-1950s—most significantly the development of a more consumption-oriented society—these commentators, like their American counterparts, engaged in a larger political project. Far from operating at the margins of national politics, as many commentators have assumed, debates about youth were one important site where a Cold War liberal consensus—as one might call it—first took shape.

In the second half of the 1950s, West German Cold War liberals were replacing religiously inspired conservatives in positions of power. The impact of liberalism in postwar Germany was by no means confined to the small Free Democratic Party; rather, in the late 1950s and early 1960s, the whole West German political system underwent an important shift. Despite many differences, the governing Christian Democrats (CDU/CSU) and the opposition Social Democrats (SPD) moved toward a Cold War liberal consensus. And even as the Christian Democrats won the 1957 election with the slogan "No experiments," liberals made themselves increasingly felt within that party. Struggles between CDU liberals, clustered around the champion of the "social market economy," Ludwig Erhard, on the one hand, and the conservatives around Chancellor Konrad Adenauer on the other, increased during the following years. Consequently, extreme conservatives like Family Minister Franz-Josef Wuermeling lost some of their appeal. Wuermeling resigned in 1962 and Erhard replaced Adenauer as chancellor in 1963. The SPD, too, underwent important change. During the second half of the 1950s, the party abandoned Marxism for good, while a new, younger leadership emerged around Willy Brandt. Brandt was West Berlin mayor from 1957 to 1966 and would later became the West German chancellor from 1969 to 1974. In 1960 he modeled his first candidacy for the chancellorship on the youthful image of U.S. president John F. Kennedy, and in 1963 he became party leader. These developments in the West German political landscape paved the way for the Great Coalition of CDU and SPD from 1966 to 1969.

In the late 1950s and 1960s, conservatives did remain vocal in West Germany, especially in discussions about youth, but the power of their perspective was gradually diminished by liberal ideas and liberal policies on culture, society, and politics that officials from CDU and SPD increasingly shared. Although they did not specifically refer to themselves as liberals, but rather positioned themselves as impartial observers, scholars like Blücher, Bondy, and Schelsky contributed to this development.[12]

In coming to terms with the social transformations that the "economic miracle," the rapid economic expansion and increased consumption of the 1950s, brought, these social scientists and other West Germans often looked to the United States for inspiration. In 1956 and 1957, David Riesman's *The Lonely Crowd* became an important reference point for many of these writers and thinkers. Although *The Lonely Crowd* had been hardly noticed in West Germany when it was first published in the United States in 1950, it was translated into German in 1956 and gained prominence in Germany at the exact time that some youths were challenging the existing social system.[13] In his book, Riesman described postwar American society as characterized by economic abundance, mass culture, bureaucratization, permissiveness, and a population of outer-directed personalities. In contrast to the inner-directed personalities of earlier bourgeois societies, who had internalized guidelines of behavior, these outer-directed personalities were yearning for approval from their peers.

In one of the ironic twists of transatlantic interactions, Riesman was actually influenced by the Critical Theory of the German-Jewish members of the Frankfurt School who had emigrated to the United States in the 1930s. Max Horkheimer, Theodor Adorno, Leo Lowenthal, and Herbert Marcuse among others, concluded that mass culture was manipulated from above by a culture industry. It promised only illusory emancipation, contributed to the destruction of the autonomous individual, and was an instrument of authoritarianism in both the United States and fascist regimes. Unlike conservative or other Marxist critics, they denied the existence of a redemptive "high" culture or a "genuine," "authentic" popular culture distinct from mass culture. Riesman took up some of these insights, but softened the critique of consumer capitalism.[14]

Sociologists like Schelsky were certainly no friends of the Marxist Frankfurt School, some of whom had returned to Germany by the 1950s. But Schelsky and others were drawn to Riesman's work for several reasons. West German intellectuals firmly believed that industrialization and the connected developments of increased leisure time and social change had progressed further in the United States. Social research on the United States therefore provided useful models against which they tested West German conditions. Even more importantly, while Riesman had not focused on youth per se, his studies of the effect of consumer culture in America at once explained, affirmed, and, within limits, critiqued a transformation West Germans saw their own country undergoing.[15]

Riesman's terminology and theses, which confirmed the basic stability of a consumption-oriented society while offering some criticisms, proved to be attractive to West Germans. In the mid-1950s West Germans after all found themselves on the defensive on several fronts: against their fascist past, against their present Cold War enemies, and against Western, and especially American-style, consumer culture. Conservative reactions to consumption generally, and to the mid-1950s consumption-oriented youth rebellion in particular, had connected the increasing consumption of (American) popular culture to worrisome materialism, to the destruction of gender mores, and to fascist threats. By contrast, one commentator in the *Frankfurter Allgemeine Zeitung* concluded that, since the *Halbstarken* phenomenon was an international one, "the market economy, Americanism, and too much freedom" were hardly the causes for adolescent rowdiness. A few West German commentators and some voices in the East German press were suggesting in 1956 that young male rebels legitimately resisted the West German government or at least displayed more "civil courage" than their parents.[16] Riesman showed a way out of that impasse.

In 1956 Schelsky and sociologist F. H. Tenbruck, in lengthy reviews of the German edition of *The Lonely Crowd*, stressed that Germans should not merely be astonished or shocked at the American conditions Riesman described. Rather they urged West German readers to see the many parallels to German development. Tenbruck worried that the majority of German readers would use *The Lonely Crowd* to confirm their low opinions of Americans as conformist, lonely, and shallow, since Riesman himself emphasized these qualities in the outer-directed personality. Tenbruck pointed out correctly that Riesman favored what he described as the inner-directed personality types of bourgeois society. At the same time, however, Tenbruck emphasized that neither Riesman nor Tenbruck himself saw the development of a society comprising outer-directed personality types as a bad development.[17]

In particular, these Cold War liberal West German sociologists took up Riesman's conclusion that increased automation and increased leisure time worked together to level class distinctions. In 1952 Schelsky had introduced the concept of a "leveled middle-class society," referring to the decline in status among many refugees in West Germany. But by 1956, he and his disciple Blücher began to relate the concept increasingly to the rise of a consumption-oriented society.[18] This vision of a classless consumerism was an exaggeration in both the American and West German context. Although working-class families reached higher levels of consumption, class-based access to consumer goods did not disappear. In West Germany, Economics Minister Erhard designed policies that were consciously geared to achieve an "elevator effect" where high-income groups would be able to afford things first and only later would the entire society be lifted.[19] Yet the concept of increased consumption as a class leveler was promoted particularly in relation to youth. Blücher reiterated this thesis in the most important West German journal for youth matters, *deutsche jugend*, and described 1950s West Germany as an emerging classless "leisure-time society" where "other-determined" labor was used to acquire the means for a "self-determined" leisure time. He even spoke of the spiritual release of youth.[20]

In their writings, both Schelsky and Blücher acknowledged that 1950s adolescents of all classes were adopting patterns of behavior that had been pioneered by the unorganized proletarian youth of the 1920s. In the foreword to Blücher's 1956 study, Schelsky explained matter-of-factly that one had to come to terms with the fact that an older bourgeois educational attitude *(Bildungshaltung)* had disintegrated. He especially emphasized that the "earlier dualism of an extreme drive to socialize on the one hand" (implicitly among the working class) and of introversion and isolation from parents and peers on the other (implicitly among the middle class) had evolved into new forms of communication that hardly distinguished adolescents from adults or members of the working class from those of the middle class.[21]

These themes of a classless West German society echoed in Schelsky's widely received book *Die skeptische Generation* (The skeptical generation) and also in the writings of the architect of the West German economic miracle, Ludwig Erhard, including his *Wohlstand für alle* (Prosperity for all). Published in 1957, both books became blueprints for changing society and politics in West Germany.[22] Their authors embraced the consumer society that had emerged in West Germany by the mid-1950s. Schelsky again spoke positively of the disappearance of class differences in youth behavior, while Erhard stressed that a growing consumer culture had positive effects because it softened the West German class structure. Moreover, Erhard announced: "Every citizen must be conscious of consumer freedom and the freedom of economic enterprise as basic and inalienable rights, whose violation should be punished as an assault on our social order."[23]

The Social Democrats were slightly more ambivalent about the power of consumption. Their 1959 Godesberg Program, which formalized the SPD's move away from Marxism and its identity as a working-class party to a "people's party," also made access to consumption a central goal. The program acknowledged that income and property were unjustly distributed, but proposed an economy with "high overall productivity" and "broad mass purchasing power" as a solution. Almost echoing Erhard, the SPD declared that "free consumer choice" and "free choice of employment" were the basis of a "social democratic economy."[24]

Cold War liberals thus saw the rise of what they claimed was a classless society as a positive good. In formulating their vision, liberals reworked the charges that both West German conservatives and East German authorities had brought against consumption-oriented and American-influenced youth cultures: charges that adolescent consumption of American movies, fashions, and dances was a dangerous phenomenon; charges that cultural consumption made boys overly aggressive and girls overly sexual; charges that linked adolescent behavior to working-class immorality, racial inferiority, and fascist threats; and finally East German suggestions that adolescent rebels were engaging in political resistance.

Schelsky and Blücher positioned themselves in contrast to conservative and Marxist cultural critics who had bemoaned the adolescents' dependence on movies and their lack of abstinence and proper political involvement. Blücher challenged the idea that movies had an evil impact on adolescents; he also rejected the notion that West German youth was characterized by dance crazes.[25] Cold War liberal social scientists also reevaluated the connection conservatives made between consumption, especially of American popular culture, and the destruction of gender mores. Yet in their need to reevaluate the images of overly aggressive men and overly sexual women that conservatives had drawn, it appears that many liberals were compelled to ignore altogether the gender-specific implications of the transformation they saw their societies undergoing.[26] For example, Schelsky and Blücher agreed with Riesman in postulating that gender roles converged in modern societies. Conservatives had watched this alleged development with much agitation, and Schelsky himself had issued some warnings about the negative social impact of working mothers. Now, however, Blücher and Schelsky, like Riesman, saw the converging of gender roles as a normal, not necessarily negative development. At the same time, Blücher, like most American social scientists, downplayed the gender-specific implications of adolescent experience, although differences between girls and boys were even visible in Blücher's own presentation of evidence. Thus Blücher reported that girls participated less in the informal groups and gangs outside of their homes than boys. Also, he found that girls performed more household chores, but he interpreted this as a mere leftover from preindustrial times.[27]

In fact, it was specifically the behavior of young men (who after all had been at the center of worries about *Halbstarke*) and their needs for aggression and adventure that liberal views of German youth reinterpreted. Some researchers made the consumption of movies and jazz, considered dangerous earlier, into an important part of male adolescent development. Thus in December 1956, the West Berlin newspaper *Der Tag* summarized two psychological studies exploring the effects of movies on young people. Both concluded that a clear connection between movies and delinquency could not be proven. The article quoted one study that even found adventure films important for adolescent development: adult men who were conspicuous in their belligerent behavior and "mannerisms of Indian chiefs" *(Häuptlingallüren)* had never aired these feelings as boys; and westerns, for example, helped boys to live out their aggressions before puberty and thus prevented belligerence in adults.[28] Such a logic associated adolescent overaggression directly with a racial other, American Indians, and at the same time made it part of a normal adolescent life stage. To be sure, the practice of comparing nonwhites to children had a long history in European and American racism.[29] Now, however, American Indians were associated with adolescence and this life stage was seen as positive. The fact that it remained racialized might point to persisting ambivalence toward unruly adolescent behavior. Another commentator suggested that westerns helped men to rebel secretly and in the movie theater. In this vision, westerns were a healthy antidote to the lack of control men experienced in modern life. In giving westerns this psychological function, these West Germans aligned themselves with a view increasingly accepted in the West and promoted, for example, by UNESCO.[30] Consumption of such cultural goods was not a goal in itself, but rather could put men on the right track; it allowed them to ultimately become good fathers, workers, and defenders of the nation.

Cold War liberal scholars and commentators thus disassociated rebellious male adolescent behavior from conservative indictments of racial degeneration and of working-class deviance. At the same time they saw American cultural products, such as westerns and jazz, which East and West German conservatives had connected to adolescent misbehavior and political derailment, not as dangerous, but instead as healthy for West German young males. Psychological concepts were key to this transition. Many psychologists had followed Sigmund Freud in rejecting the concept of degeneration when it was based on notions of immutable biological heredity.[31] Such insights played a crucial role in the development of antiracist discourses. By the 1940s authors who rejected the idea of biologically based hierarchies between different races explained both racism among whites and alleged feelings of inferiority among African Americans in psychological terms. In particular they directed attention to the failings of black and white mothers, who variously frustrated or smothered their children thus causing aggressive behavior. In the process, scholars and popular writers drew up new normative models of adolescent development and parenting, and even affirmed differences, for example, between white Americans and African Americans, in socio-psychological terms. But even as psychology could reaffirm hierarchies, it shifted the terms in which people thought about human differences. In the United States and in Germany, forms of behavior that critics had associated with both the working class and non-German, nonwhite racial groups came to be seen as part of normal adolescent development for all classes or ethnic groups.[32]

"DEPOLITICIZING" *HALBSTARKE* IN WEST GERMANY

Liberal reevaluations of manliness and praise for an allegedly classless West German society of consumers became important building blocks for redefining *Halbstarken* behavior as nonpolitical, and therefore served an important political function. In 1956, for example, one opinion survey found that both sexes were most impressed with realistic movies, but concluded with satisfaction that girls, more so than boys, liked love stories and happy endings. The author of the study located this allegedly "skeptical" behavior of West German male and female adolescents in the context of German history. These healthy West German adolescents were not merely turning against everything traditional as part of a natural developmental stage, they were also overcoming the "atmosphere of inner deception, deceit, and disappointment" of the war and postwar years. In their movie consumption, they were searching for a life that was "authentic—natural—and without illusions."[33] In this case the gender-specific, "realistic" cultural tastes of adolescents set them apart from fascist and totalitarian seduction.

West German Cold War liberals made cultural consumption compatible with a new German identity that they located beyond fascism and totalitarianism, indeed beyond all ideologies. Blücher maintained that the youth did not show any patterns of behavior or thinking that were shaped by ideologies.[34] Schelsky favorably called the West German youth "skeptical" because they had moved beyond the world of ideologies. The SPD likewise understood its new program as "unideological," and in 1960, Erhard, too, urged his fellow CDU members to pursue a social policy beyond any ideology.[35]

To postulate an end of ideologies was likely the Cold War liberals' most powerful move, for several reasons. By celebrating this paradigm, Blücher, Schelsky, and Erhard brought themselves close to the mainstream of Western thought. In these same years, many Western intellectuals, such as Daniel Bell or Raymond Aron, after all were promoting the idea of an end of ideologies. In the German context this perspective helped liberals place themselves in a position superior to both communism and National Socialism. Second, by maintaining that 1950s Germany, like its Western allies, was moving beyond ideologies, Blücher and other Cold War liberals delegitimized any fundamental critique of modern Western societies, be it from the right or from the left. Thus Blücher cited cultural anthropologists, especially Margaret Mead and Ruth Benedict, whose works had been published in West Germany in the early 1950s, and he generally agreed with researchers who had identified the "relativism of cultural norms also of Western culture." Even as they acknowledged it, these thinkers contained the radical potential of this cultural relativism.[36] Finally, drawing parallels to American social developments and reevaluating them as positive, scholars like Blücher, Tenbruck, and most importantly Schelsky, also divorced themselves from the tradition of cultural pessimism common in twentieth-century Germany that had associated modernity with decay. For these West German Cold War liberals, a lot was at stake: they sought to disconnect themselves from Nazism by erasing differences between West Germany and other Western societies and by fully integrating themselves into the fight against communism. In short, Cold War liberals supported the notion that West Germany was participating in the West's fight against totalitarianism.

Significantly, Cold War liberals' insistence on the end of ideologies implied giving culture a new place in West German politics and society: cultural consumption was assigned to a nonpolitical, "private" space. In 1956, one commentator, sociologist Hans Kluth, in *deutsche jugend* denied that all juvenile delinquents, or each and every visitor to a jazz event or "Wild West" film were potentially frightening and dangerous *Halbstarke*. Instead, he described *Halbstarke* as a transhistorical, psychological phenomenon that arose from the clash between drives for attention and action as well as from spiritual and social instability during adolescent development. Kluth asserted that in West Germany in the mid-1950s, adolescents in big cities were deprived of possibilities to fulfill their need for adventure. Their actions had to be seen simply as "action for action's sake." Kluth criticized adults for not being able to tolerate this behavior by controlling and limiting it, but he did not call for strong state action. At the same time, he explicitly contrasted *Halbstarke* of the 1950s with the dangerously politicized youths of the Weimar Republic and National Socialism, whose instability, he said, had been solicited for political purposes, including war and the persecution of Jews.[37]

Similarly, psychologist Bondy made an effort to disassociate adolescent behavior during movie showings, concerts, and riots from both juvenile delinquency and political expression. Bondy, who had requested sociological literature from the U.S. State Department in 1955, stressed that he could not find any political motivation behind *Halbstarken* behavior, but only "pseudo-political connections." For example, Bondy explicitly denied that *Halbstarke* who rioted in a West German city and removed signs from a military drafting agency—and who were thus likely expressing dissatisfaction with conscription—were voicing true political opinions. He even went so far as to reject the behavior of Hamburg *Halbstarke*, who were shouting "rock 'n' roll" and "Russians out"—and thus were turning against West Germany's Cold War enemy—as nonpolitical. The conviction that adolescent rebels lacked any conscious political motivation and were thus really "rebels without a cause" became increasingly widespread and served to depoliticize adolescent behavior.[38]

In *Die skeptische Generation*, Schelsky argued along similar lines and contrasted the "skeptical," depoliticized youth of the 1950s with what he called the "political" youth of the period before 1945.[39] By asserting that his own contemporaries—the parents of 1950s youth—had transformed themselves from a "political" into a skeptical generation as well, Schelsky also whitewashed his own generation's association with Nazism. Schelsky himself had actually assumed his first university position in German-occupied France in the 1940s.[40]

With his references to nonpolitical generations, Schelsky applied a concept that Riesman had developed to the German context. Earlier Schelsky had cited Riesman, maintaining that people who defined themselves mainly through consumption displayed an "often quite useful immunity toward politics."[41] Schelsky now proclaimed German youth to be "nonpolitical democratic" and thus put them at the center of a liberal system. If anything was still German about this youth, it was the fact that this generation was fulfilling its "fate" with special German thoroughness.[42] Thus Schelsky suggested that West Germans were indeed better liberals than West Europeans or Americans, and he abandoned the fight for a special German way between consumerism in the West and socialism in the East. These assessments rested on rendering the German youth rebellion of the 1950s a "private" matter, where rebellious youth behavior became a mere "nonpolitical" expression of style. Schelsky described the postwar generation as one that was tolerant, sober, and successful, and who fled the power of society into the private realm.[43]

The main focus of Schelsky's study was on the so-called *Flakhelfergeneration*, youths who had initially been socialized under the Nazis, but in the last section of his book he explicitly extended his conclusions to the *Halbstarke*. Citing three examples of unruly adolescent behavior in his conclusion, Schelsky referred to the "ecstatic devotion to the lively music of jazz sessions," to certain "acrobatic dissolved" forms of dancing, and the "individual rage" of *Halbstarken* rioters. He thus explicitly connected rebellious behavior to American influences. Yet, unlike conservative commentators, Schelsky did not refer to the challenges these forms of behavior posed to traditional gender roles. In fact, his rhetoric effaced gender and race as central components of the youth rebellion. Further, Schelsky, as Bondy before him, explicitly turned against those who had described this youth behavior as a turn to primitivism. This rhetoric of primitivism and gender upheaval was dominant in conservative East and West German reactions that identified American cultural imports as a political threat. By contrast, Schelsky was able to accommodate cultural styles rooted in African American culture and emphasized that these forms of youth behavior had no significance beyond being an expression of "vitality" in an increasingly technical world. Like Kluth, Bondy, and other Cold War liberals, he stressed that these were neither political challenges nor precursors of political challenges to come.[44] In this logic, being unpolitical indeed meant being normal. Therefore in 1956 and 1957, Blücher, Kluth, Bondy, and Schelsky formulated an assessment of the teenage rebellion that would inform later scholarship on—as well as the memories of—1950s adolescents.

Yet considering the hype that rebellious youths were causing in West Germany during these very years, it is not surprising that liberal interpretations continued to be contested. As Schelsky and Tenbruck had predicted, conservatives drew on Riesman's terminology to "modernize" their critiques of *Halbstarke* and consumer culture and to justify controlling adolescent consumption. One researcher, for example, rejected rock 'n' roll, where young people danced without partners, as a metaphor for the "loneliness" of the individual.[45] Others sought to save the adolescent from "the loneliness in the crowd" and "from drowning his personality in a termite-like collectivism."[46] By drawing on Riesman's terminology, these conservatives again conflated consumption with totalitarian threats.

Cold War liberals took seriously such criticisms of consumer culture. Schelsky himself echoed some worries of cultural conservatives that German adolescents could succumb to vulgar materialism with consumerism as a life goal, or, worse, turn into criminals. In 1955 Schelsky warned of a "consumption terror."[47] And in 1957, he revealed a certain ambivalence, when he evaluated *Halbstarke* as nonpolitical, yet also predicted that they would be the precursors of a "youthful secession against the conformity of modern society."[48] Blücher, following Riesman's descriptions of the other-directed personality, associated the typical behavior of modern adolescents of both genders with qualities stereotypically assigned to femininity, such as "softness" and "lack of consciousness." With such characterizations Blücher, like Riesman and Schelsky, betrayed his satisfaction with the developments that accompanied the rise of a "modern," consumption-oriented society.[49] And in 1963 in his first speech as chancellor to the West German parliament, Erhard responded to critics who bemoaned West Germany's growing materialism by urging his fellow West Germans not to lose track of Christian values.[50] West German Cold War liberals like Schelsky and Erhard thus retained a good amount of hostility toward cultural styles associated with lower-class culture generally and toward

American popular culture specifically. Yet these hostilities were not incompatible with their efforts to depoliticize youth cultures and to celebrate a consumption-oriented West German society.

Defining *Halbstarken* behavior as nonpolitical required two things: it was necessary for West German Cold War liberal commentators to describe adolescent consumption as a matter of personal style, and also to classify unacceptable youth behavior as a private or family problem, for which they sought private solutions. In spite of their efforts to normalize adolescent rebellious behavior, most liberal commentators found that riots, for example, exceeded acceptable limits. With an American-influenced, psychology-informed discourse, West Germans increasingly looked in the family for the roots of exaggerated *Halbstarken* behavior. This increasing focus on the family background of the *Halbstarke* further helped West Germans to transform *Halbstarke* from a political into a psychological and private problem. Importantly, reasserting gender difference was central to Cold War liberal efforts and appeared to explain and resolve the apparent threats posed by youth cultures.[51]

Virtually all liberal commentators agreed that broken homes were the main reason adolescents went beyond their normal needs for adventure. Kluth concluded that adolescents "from inadequate family conditions" were the main participants in *Halbstarken* riots. Many studies on the psychological effects of movies now made "broken homes" rather than movies responsible, if adolescents did not properly contain their needs for adventure and aggression. In an article on movies about juvenile delinquents, including among others *Blackboard Jungle,* one of the promoters of "good" films for West German youth announced that broken homes were the main explanation for adolescent problems. The void left by irresponsible parents could be filled only with difficulties by public officials like the fatherly teacher in *Blackboard.*[52]

Commentators did not make the death of fathers during the war solely responsible for domestic problems; rather they concluded that adolescent development could suffer even in two-parent households. Thus Bondy saw West German society characterized by a collapse of values, where social/class pride (*Standesehre*), national and religious convictions, and moral rules appeared to be empty words to adolescents and adults. In terms that were strikingly similar to Riesman's, Bondy suggested that the present society valued adaptability to reach maximum efficiency and success.[53] In this context, lack of parental guidance in all classes could lead to "excesses." Bondy found that rioting *Halbstarke* came from all classes and that the majority of them did live with two parents; his statistics even showed that they did so in greater numbers than the overall West German adolescent population.[54] In two-parent families, asserted Bondy, mothers' participation in the workforce was one key factor in instability. Another factor, whether mothers worked or not, was, according to Bondy, the diminishing authority of fathers.[55] Interestingly, Bondy here gave the same reasoning for adolescent rebellion that *Rebel Without a Cause* with its weak father figure had suggested earlier and that conservative critics of the movie would not accept for a middle-class setting.

Just as West German liberal scholars had located exaggerated rebellious behavior in the private realm of the family, they also found a private solution to the problem, one that *Rebel* had likewise suggested. Heterosexual relationships of male *Halbstarke* with girls increasingly appeared to solve the problems of male overaggression. In a context where West German social scientists, including Schelsky, and the Constitutional Court, West Germany's highest court, had linked male homosexuality to male overaggression, affirming heterosexuality became especially important. Scholars asserted that, after a stage of male adolescent aggression and search for adventure, young men would settle into calm, monogamous heterosexual relationships. Blücher, for example, stressed that most West German adolescents underwent a development that took them from socializing with their own sex to turning to friendship and usually marriage with the other sex. Bondy found that *Halbstarke* stopped rioting as soon as they had a steady girlfriend.[56]

The affirmation of the nuclear family that *Rebel Without a Cause* had suggested as a solution to the problem of adolescent misbehavior became an increasingly common trope in West Germany. In this context a relationship between two German movie stars took on symbolic importance. Young actress Romy Schneider had risen to prominence playing in *Sissi* (1955) and *Sissi, die junge Kaiserin* (1956), two of the most successful movies of 1956 and 1957. Schneider portrayed the virtuous Bavarian duchess Elizabeth, "Sissi," on her way to marriage with the future Austrian emperor Franz-Josef. The West German press noted with satisfaction that Hollywood sharks tried to attract Schneider, but without success.[57] For them Hollywood was clearly the measure of success, but it also symbolized fears of a certain American cultural imperialism. As long as Schneider was a star, rejoiced one *Spiegel* reader, "We have every reason to be delighted with the good taste of the masses."[58] In late 1956, a romance between Schneider, the symbol of feminine German innocence, and Horst Buchholz, who as the main hero of the West German movie *Die Halbstarken* had become the personification of the West German young male rebel, became the subject of attention. The "good" German Sissi appeared to tame the bad Americanized *Halbstarken*.[59] Properly domesticated, *Halbstarke* could find a home and the right sort of family in the Federal Republic.

And whereas in 1955, reviews of *The Wild One* had focused on the sexual female audience as an instigator of male rebellion, but had not mentioned the relationship Brando's character developed with a "good" waitress, a 1958 West German advice manual on how to treat *The Wild One* in youth groups suggested that they discuss friendship with a girl as a solution to the *Halbstarken* problem and supplement it with discussions about the effects of war, wealth, and the mass media.[60] The psychological reasons (destruction of the patriarchal family) and solutions (affirmation of the heterosexual nuclear family) for adolescent misbehavior that *Rebel Without a Cause* had suggested, became central to assessing, containing, and "depoliticizing" *Halbstarken* behavior in West Germany.

ACCOMMODATING EAST GERMAN *HALBSTARKE*

In 1956 and 1957, some East German portrayals of East German *Halbstarke* similarly employed psychological concepts in coming to terms with East German young rebels. During the "thaw" of 1956, the East German communist youth organization Free German Youth (FDJ) had tried to make adolescent cultural consumption into a means of attracting East German adolescents. Further, in contrast to earlier East German hostility toward *Halbstarke* in East and West, the FDJ had even described West German *Halbstarke* as resisting conscription "through their behavior and appearance" (which drew heavily on American cultural imports). By November 1956, however, the Soviet army suppressed the Hungarian uprising, and trials against some GDR intellectuals stymied many expectations of a cultural and political opening. The position of party leader Ulbricht continued to be somewhat shaky nonetheless—it would take Ulbricht until 1958 to fully consolidate his power—and in this context, some experiments in the cultural sphere were possible.[61]

One of the most important expressions of the openness in East German thinking about cultural consumption and the proper development of socialist personalities was the 1957 DEFA production *Berlin Ecke Schönhauser,* which was conceived in the summer of 1956. In contrast to their earlier movies *Alarm im Zirkus* (1954) and *Berliner Romanze* (1956), the screenwriter Wolfgang Kohlhaase and the director Gerhard Klein of *Berlin Ecke Schönhauser* (Berlin corner Schönhauser) depicted *Halbstarke* not as a problem that arose in capitalist societies and threatened East German socialism from the outside, but as a genuine East German problem. Both the

Fig. 13. *Halbstarke* under state socialism. Still from *Berlin Ecke Schönhauser,* the East German "answer" to Western young rebel movies, 1957. Photo: Siegmar Holstein and Hannes Schneider, DEFA, courtesy Bundesarchiv Berlin—Filmarchiv.

filmmakers and East German reviewers of *Berlin Ecke Schönhauser* freely acknowledged that *Halbstarke* existed also in the Eastern part of the city and in the GDR.[62]

Already during the production of the film, one East German magazine cited an interview with Wolfgang Kohlhaase, who explicitly compared his film with the West German production *Die Halbstarken.* In the article, which was illustrated with stills from both movies, Kohlhaase stressed that in contrast to the gangster story of *Die Halbstarken, Berlin Ecke Schönhauser* was a "social study."[63]

Berlin Ecke Schönhauser was set in the old East Berlin working-class neighborhood Prenzlauer Berg, which, like Friedrichshain and Mitte, was in the mid-1950s a hub for East Berlin *Halbstarke*. The plot centered on a young worker, Dieter, who feels misunderstood by his coworkers, state authorities, and his family. During a fight, Dieter and his friend Kohle have with Karl-Heinz, a delinquent bourgeois East Berlin boy, Kohle hits Karl-Heinz in the head. Believing that they have inadvertently killed Karl-Heinz, Dieter and Kohle flee to West Berlin. There, in a camp for East German refugees, Kohle gets killed. Dieter returns to East Berlin to start a sensible life with his girlfriend Angela who is expecting a baby by him.

East German reviewers focused less on the actual plot of the movie than on the atmosphere in East and West Berlin that it portrayed. The movie showed East Berlin boys and a few girls hanging out in the streets, sporting American fashions like jeans and ducktail plumes, and listening and dancing to fast-paced music. When Dieter asks Angela how men should look she answers, "Like Marlon Brando." In turn Angela, like Sissy in *Die Halbstarken*, wears tight sweaters, capri pants, and a ponytail. Kohle regularly visits West Berlin border theaters to watch American movies. This portrayal of adolescent styles, which showed that East Berlin adolescents had adopted West German and American influences, was indeed much more radical in the East German context than the plot, which predictably supported the notion that West German state authorities were repressive. *Berlin Ecke Schönhauser* was the most open acknowledgment that American cultural imports were attractive also to East German adolescents. It became one of the most-watched movies in East Germany in 1957, and East Berlin *Halbstarke* identified with its actors.[64] As one *Halbstarker* from Friedrichshain remembers, "*Berlin Ecke Schönhauser*, that was us!"[65]

East German reviewers stressed that the movie was realistic and that the *Halbstarke* it portrayed were basically good-natured. They reported that many of the adolescent actors, like most of the youths in *Die Halbstarken*, had been picked right from Berlin streets. One commentary recommended the movie as a thoughtful and realistic depiction of modern youth and contrasted it with American and West German productions that merely depicted adolescents as gangsters. The filmmakers saw the film as an East German response to Italian neorealism. The neorealists focused on the stories of "common" people and saw their own documentary style as an alternative to "commercial," Hollywood-style film. Their films were generally rejected by the East German leadership as inappropriate for inspiring workers in the construction of socialism. In the case of *Berlin Ecke Schönhauser*, during the "thaw" of 1956 and 1957, however, many reviewers were positively impressed with its neorealist style.[66] The daily *Neues Deutschland* urged its readers to take the tram in the evening along the Schönhauser Allee, where they would encounter adolescents exactly like the ones portrayed in the movie—adolescents "who touch up their hair, which is cut like James Dean's, the Hollywood heartthrob."[67]

Berlin Ecke Schönhauser reevaluated the attributes of East and West German *Halbstarke*, most importantly their fashions and consumption of jazz music. In an argument with his brother who is in the police force, Dieter rails against complaints over such styles: "When I stand on the corner I am *halbstark*, when I dance boogie, I am American, and when I don't wear my shirt tucked in, it's politically incorrect."[68] As one reviewer noted, Dieter wore jeans *and* worked hard.[69] Promotions of the movie even featured a jazz trumpeter in front of the shadow of a saxophone and thus made direct allusions to jazz.[70] Also, the *Halbstarken* rowdiness that the movie depicted was similar to incidents reported in the West. In one scene, for example, a group of boys and a girl stood at a street corner listening to a radio. As one brochure for the movie explained, the rhythm of the music makes them adventurous: they throw a stone into a street lamp and thus "commit a little mischief." While some reviewers made connections between the "hot music" and misbehavior, many warned against overdrawn reactions.[71]

East German reviewers took *Berlin Ecke Schönhauser* as an opportunity to discuss the causes of *Halbstarken* behavior, and their explanations were very similar to the liberal views of adolescent development that were spreading in West Germany. Thus one East German reviewer was impressed with how well the movie portrayed "the psychology of the young people."[72] East German explanations ranged from the effects of World War II when many fathers had been killed, to parents who were not paying enough attention to their children, to "the West," which lured weaker characters. While East German reviewers saw parallels between East and West German youth behavior, they did not discuss adolescent rebelliousness as an expression of decadence or as resistance against conscription in either the East or the West. Nor did they discuss girls as instigators of male adolescent rebelliousness. One reviewer pointed out that the seamstress Angela, who is the only girl in a gang of boys and Dieter's girlfriend, is driven into the street by her mother, a widow who wants to be alone with her boyfriend.[73] Even as many East German reviewers made references to the dangerous conditions in West Berlin, they agreed that adolescents' natural need for adventure and bad homes in the East endangered young people. The "home without protectors," according to one reviewer, drove ado-

Fig. 14.   Alienated East German youth? Advertising poster for *Berlin Ecke Schönhauser*, with Ekkehard Schall and Ilse Page, 1957. Courtesy Bundesarchiv Berlin—Filmarchiv.

lescents near desperation. Script writer Kohlhaase himself explained that he had gone through police records of East German rowdies and had found that 70 percent of their behavior was due to failures of parents and educators, especially in the aftermath of the disruptions that the war brought to family life. The movie showed that not just Angela's widowed mother, but also Karl-Heinz's "complete" bourgeois family with two avaricious and negligent parents led their adolescent into delinquency. West Berlin reviewers praised *Berlin Ecke Schönhauser* for locating the social reasons of the *Halbstarkenproblem* in the homes and families of the *Halbstarke* and

agreed with the examples that *Berlin* gave: single mothers, who were sending their daughters into the streets until midnight, in order to be alone
with their lovers, and stepfathers, who drank and beat up their stepsons.
For the West German reviewers, such problems clearly existed across borders: "lack of understanding and love, cold routines, and occasionally abuse
by adults without any scruples" were said to be the enemies of youthful
needs for adventure everywhere.[74] As one solution to these problems, the
film introduced a fatherly, understanding police officer, a "state father" of
sorts, who was trying to prevent adolescents from disturbing the public order too much.[75]

But interestingly, *Berlin Ecke Schönhauser*, like the West German liberal discourse on adolescence, also focused on a heterosexual relationship
to resolve overdrawn East German rebelliousness. As the East German
program flyer said, Dieter's girlfriend Angela was the only one who gave
him support. Dieter returned to East Berlin to "create a meaningful life together with Angela."[76]

With *Berlin Ecke Schönhauser*, the filmmakers and East German reviewers severed the connection that other East German critics had drawn
between American influences, the destruction of gender mores, and German national decay. Instead, the movie and East German reviewers suggested that wearing Western fashions and listening to American music
were mostly harmless aberrations on the road to a restrained heterosexual
socialist German personality.

POLITICIZATION AND REPRESSION IN EAST GERMANY

Yet *Berlin Ecke Schönhauser* marked merely a brief hiatus in East Germany when Western fashion attributes could be retained in the formation
of socialist German personalities. Throughout 1957, rumblings against increased West German and American influences could be heard from East
German party officials, and in the fall of 1957, the SED leadership under
Ulbricht started an outright campaign against "revisionism," which coincided with increased attacks on American cultural imports. By 1958 any leniency toward East or West German *Halbstarke* had all but disappeared.

In July 1957 Alfred Kurella, a staunch Ulbricht supporter who was soon
to be head of the new Commission for Culture in the Central Committee
of the SED, gave a speech in which he warned against the "danger of growing decadent influences." Kurella maintained that in the phase of late capitalism and imperialism—a phase that socialists believed both West Germany and the United States were undergoing—artistic forms as well as

human relations were disintegrating, thus pushing the "animalistic ele-ment" of human existence into the foreground. Kurella criticized those who were celebrating "degeneration" and "disease," and declared that it was the task of socialist culture to "save the cultural and social life of the...nation from this destruction" and to repair and continue the "true national culture."[77] At the very time that West German Cold War liberals made Germanness compatible with the consumption of American cultural products, East German authorities sought to resurrect a Germanness de-void of Western influences and returned to a eugenics-based language to attack deviations from their socialist norms.

The SED Culture Conference in October 1957 warned that during the preceding two years "damaging influences of the Western capitalist non-culture" had "penetrated" East Germany. With the renewed attacks on Western decadent culture and its impact in East Germany, both music and films, in particular if they were American or Western-influenced, came un-der intense scrutiny and criticism. East German officials once again con-nected these forms of cultural consumption to unacceptable resistance against the East German regime.

Not unexpectedly, *Berlin Ecke Schönhauser* came under increasing at-tack in this climate. In spite of his overall positive assessment, the reviewer in *Neues Deutschland* had stressed that the film represented conditions "where we are not." "We" clearly meant the Party and the youth organi-zation FDJ, and the reviewer suggested that the filmmakers' next movie should depict the Party's positive impact.[78] At the 1957 Culture Confer-ence, one speaker, Alexander Abusch, who would succeed Johannes Becher as Culture Minister in 1958, used a direct quote from the end of *Berlin Ecke Schönhauser*, when the fatherly police officer announces in a voice-over: "Where we are not, is our enemy." Abusch warned against taking the fight against dogmatism too far and criticized intellectuals who—allegedly sponsored by West Germans and Americans—had supported the Hungar-ian uprising. At the same time he indicted showings of popular "light" movies in East German movie theaters and expressed outrage against the sales of "light music," including Western hits in East German music stores, and against the "inferior" programs in East German dance halls.[79] In 1958 another cultural official criticized *Berlin Ecke Schönhauser* for focusing exclusively on a minority of youth who were not yet deeply rooted in so-ciety; instead, he insisted, East German movies should portray the major-ity of East German adolescents who were working in factories and doing "honorable service" in the National People's Army.[80] That same year offi-cials reiterated such statements at the Second Film Conference, at which the DEFA directors of *Berlin* and other East German youth films were reprimanded for depicting "abnormal figures" and indulging in Italian neorealism, rather than dealing with such important issues as the new East German army.[81]

In 1958 more and more demands for positive depictions of the National People's Army appeared in the East German press, and in 1959 a number of East German movie productions, portraying honorable East German soldiers defending the East German borders, followed these demands. Moreover, East German productions, like the movie *Reportage 57*, showed the downfall of a capitalist society in West Germany, for which rock 'n' roll was a clear signifier.[82]

At the same time, East German authorities reverted to earlier attacks on what they called rowdies. In contrast to the short period in 1956 when the FDJ had believed West German *Halbstarke* to be resisting West German authorities and especially rearmament, East German officials again charged that West Berlin rowdies came into East Berlin to cause disorder. One internal report did speak about the problems in homes (including statistics on working mothers) and a neglect of adolescents' special needs in puberty that along with Western influences led adolescents into delinquency. It also acknowledged that, since the uprising in Hungary, adolescents resisted state authorities with greater frequency.[83] In public, however, East German officials placed exclusive blame on the impact of Western and American influences from rock 'n' roll to gangster movies and American comic magazines for leading East German adolescents astray.[84]

In alleged self-defense, GDR authorities took measures to curb Western influences on East German youth. Thus in May 1957, the Politburo announced a ban on student travel to West Germany and NATO countries.[85] Restrictive measures against rock 'n' roll and jazz music and fans followed. In such a context, cultural consumption could not be depoliticized.

CULTURAL CONSUMPTION AS A WESTERN COLD WAR WEAPON

In the late 1950s, East and West Germany were embarking on increasingly different political and cultural paths. A certain consensus had existed in 1955 between East and West German conservative authorities, both of whom explicitly politicized cultural consumption and rejected American cultural influences. Whereas East Germans had returned to this stance after a brief period of openness in 1956 and 1957, West German attitudes were increasingly shaped by liberal ideas about adolescent development and cultural consumption. In important ways these ideas also influenced

West German Cold War policies toward East Germany and West German evaluations of East German young rebels.

American sociology had given West Germans tools to formulate a vision that did not see consumption as a political threat, but rather as a means of political stability in a society allegedly increasingly devoid of class and ideological differences. At the same time the American government, and under American pressure the West German government, made consumption into a West German Cold War weapon. The ostensible depoliticization of culture was in fact a new form of politicization.

Since the East German uprising of June 1953, the U.S. government had influenced and funded West German programs to support morale in the East, spending $30 million in the years from 1953 to 1958. The first of these programs, in the summer of 1953 focused on food relief, providing East Germans with food packages they could pick up in West Berlin. The East German leadership responded with a campaign of denunciations of this "Ami bait" and severely restricted traffic to West Berlin. The program succeeded in fostering dissatisfaction among the East German population, but this situation probably helped Ulbricht to consolidate his power in the summer of 1953. In the aftermath of these experiences, both German and American officials strove to avoid public U.S. identification with the programs, a policy adopted in order to avoid offering a basis for "retaliation or reaction" by the Soviet Zone authorities.[86] At the same time program goals expanded to supporting church institutions in the GDR, helping people persecuted there, and "developing a sense of resistance" and fostering "identification with the Free World" among the East German population. While West Germans and Americans sought to avoid an image of American manipulation, which would have met with hostility in both Germanies, large sections of these programs were geared toward drawing East German adolescents into West Berlin and West Germany. Exposing these adolescents to Western consumer goods became one increasingly important focus of such initiatives.[87]

Beginning in the spring of 1955, the West Berlin government, with American financial support, instituted a program to draw East German adolescents into "the island of freedom," West Berlin, where East German authorities could not tightly control entry because of Berlin's special status under Allied rule. East German adolescents could get reimbursement for their travel expenses as well as a per diem paid to their West Berlin escorts from public youth organizations, who likewise received a per diem. Acceptable purposes for visits ranged from "general sightseeing and enjoyment of cultural opportunities including motion pictures," to participation in rallies and organized youth leisure activities, to "brief courses of instruction." Exposure to cultural life in West Berlin was clearly an important objective of these programs, and the per diems included a special allotment for movie tickets and one theater visit. Within a year word had spread in East Germany, and about eight thousand adolescents had visited West Berlin.[88]

In the mid-1950s, the major part of U.S. assistance went into fostering contacts and ties with East German inhabitants and especially adolescents of the ages from fifteen to twenty-five, since even brief visits to West Germany, according to one American official, could alleviate the "feeling of frustration, bitterness, and impotence" that living under an oppressive communist regime created. The American sponsors found it particularly important to reach East German youths, because they were less "immune" than older East Germans to communist indoctrination. Since the East German government made travel in youth groups increasingly difficult, churches and West German groups with contacts in East Germany arranged for letters from relatives, fake or real, to invite individual adolescent visitors to West Germany, where they would stay in youth hostels and be acquainted "with political, cultural, and economic objectives of the free world." In some cases meetings with American families were included, so that East German adolescents learned that Americans were "very nice people." American government officials estimated that in 1955, the trips of about twenty-one thousand East German adolescents had been supported with U.S. funds, and that a total of 120,000 East German adolescents had received travel aid in one form or another.[89] In 1957 almost DM 7 million were spent on youth meetings, DM 357,000 out of the budget of the West German ministry of All-German Affairs, and DM 6.6 million of U.S. funds.[90]

When East Germany imposed tight restrictions on adolescent travel to West Germany in 1957, and the number of East German travelers to West Germany dropped by 80 percent, West German and American officials searched for alternative routes to influence East Germans.[91] Beginning with the Christmas season of 1958, American and German funds (ca. DM 1 million per drive) were allocated and dispensed through the West German Ministry of All-German Affairs to support youth organizations in sending packages to East German adolescents. Youth organizations bought the contents of packages through collective purchasing, but mailed them as if they were individual gifts from private senders. The parcels mostly reached their destinations without being confiscated by East German authorities. In the Christmas season of 1958 about 26,900 gifts were mailed, and a few months later, during the Easter season, an additional 34,430 parcels went to East German adolescents.[92]

The expressed purpose of this program was "not to relieve suffering or provide the necessities of life for needy persons," but to offer "a form of contact with and tangible evidence of interest in individual youths" in East Germany. The organizers believed "that this kind of contact can have maximum impact, if it consists of gifts of items that young people are generally inclined to treasure and ... would otherwise not be able to have." This approach required "less essential and higher quality consumer goods." As possible gift items the organizers suggested clothes, sports equipment, leather bags, and fountain pens, gifts "of substantial value" that "the young person will use or wear with pride and pleasure, which will serve as constant reminder of a friend or friends in the West, and which other young people may see and recognize as gifts from Western friends." West German youth organizations were told to select as recipients of the parcels adolescents who were "open-minded to Western ideology ... whose attitudes leave them open to influence of this kind of contact."[93]

American and West German officials clearly wanted to make these efforts appear to be the actions of private individuals and were especially concerned that their involvement would be found out.[94] If East German authorities reacted with repression, they could be exposed as politicizing a matter of private interaction between East and West German individuals. To further support the notion that the packages to the East were nonideological and nonpolitical, West German and American officials recommended items like pens that were controversial neither in East nor in West Germany, but that were easier to get and of higher quality in the West. Just as the depoliticization of consumption in West German Cold War liberal discourse served political purposes, so did the institution of programs to "privately" expose East German adolescents to Western consumer goods. As West German and American officials ostensibly depoliticized consumer culture, they made it increasingly into a political Cold War weapon.

While Americans and increasingly their West German allies sought to define recreation and consumption as nonideological spaces, they were clearly concerned with what adolescents in East and West consumed and how they spent their leisure time.[95] American officials followed closely the rejection of "Soviet culture" and the popularity of Western culture, including films, dance music, and fashions in East Germany.[96] They were satisfied that the "East German public does not accept crude Soviet propaganda [i.e., films, plays, literature] as entertainment." Increasingly, they registered with interest the popularity of West European and American movies and movie stars as well as of rock 'n' roll among East Berlin students, and of "Western culture, from dance music to films" among the general East German public.[97] One official indeed commented in 1957 that "good films" from the West would help to "keep East Germans in touch with the non-Communist world" and wanted to make such movies more easily available to the East German film purchasing agency. He further suggested "[o]ne of the best ways to resist the Communization of East Germany would appear to be the maintenance of Western tastes among the population."[98]

West German authorities shared such sentiments. Not only did they try to control the quality of movies East Germans saw, but American and West German officials also made sure that East Germans could get access to American and West European movies for the most part only in the West. In order to raise the quality of movies consumed by East German visitors and also to expose them to the shop windows in the center of West Berlin, the Bonn government funded an "All Berlin Cultural Program" beginning in September 1958. This program allowed East Germans to see all movies rated "valuable" and "especially valuable" by the West German rating boards in all West Berlin movie theaters for an exchange rate of one to one (when the regular rate was at least five times higher). West German officials, who did not publicize that West Berlin theaters received full reimbursement for their costs, thus greatly "improved" programs in the so-called border theaters. These theaters were located mostly in the comparatively poor working-class districts that formed the border with East Berlin and had frequently been criticized by East and West Germans for showing mostly B movies. Moreover, much to the satisfaction of West German officials, the new program drew many more East Berliners into the heart of West Berlin and especially to the shop windows of the Kurfürstendamm, where East Germans came to see the West "with new eyes."

The program was a resounding success. In September and October of 1958 alone, 1.27 million East German visitors came. The "valuable" movies popular among them ranged from *Die Trapp-Familie* (the German movie on which *Sound of Music* would be based) to *Blackboard Jungle, Gone with the Wind,* and *Rear Window.* Movie theaters received, according to one West Berlin official, "deeply moving" thank-you notes.[99]

East German authorities watched these developments with some apprehension. Internal reports estimated that the West Berlin theaters that were showing "valuable" movies attracted about 7 million visitors per year and acknowledged that many East Germans combined their visits to movie theaters with shopping in West Berlin. Also officials complained about the lack of entertaining movies in their own territory. In internal reports and in the press, East German officials continued to make American films, including westerns and rock 'n' roll movies, responsible for violence in the East, and complained that some adolescents played hooky in order to go to West Berlin movie theaters, where they could easily be recruited for espionage by Western agents. East German authorities urged schools, parents, and the FDJ to discourage adolescents from going to the movies in West Berlin.[100] East German officials recognized the consumption of Western movies, music, and fashions as a source of resistance against their regime. All attempts to accommodate these phenomena in 1956 and 1957 failed as a conservative party elite opted for repression.

After the curious East and West German consensus on the damaging effects of American popular culture in the first half of the 1950s, the German Cold War battle lines shifted in the following years. In 1955 and 1956 the dominant conservative voices in both Germanies had closely linked American popular culture to German unruliness and had thus suggested that rebellious *Halbstarke* were in fact an American import. Yet by the end of the decade, German Cold War liberals had dramatically widened the definitions of acceptable and even normal adolescent cultural consumption and behavior, especially for young men. This expansion of options for young men depended on the concurrent depoliticization of their actions, which rendered normal adolescent needs for adventure as well as more outrageous forms of behavior like rioting into nonpolitical, psychological, and private phenomena.

In 1959, for example, the semiofficial West Berlin youth magazine *Blickpunkt* illustrated how harmless most *Halbstarke* were: the magazine put on a cartoon that featured a young German man, Felix, in tight jeans, leather jacket, and ducktail plume. Felix's monologue accompanied the drawing. He was lazing around in the morning, had just gotten rid of his latest girlfriend, and was now interested in a "doll" with "enormous proportions," who was accompanying his friend Harry. When Harry and he disagreed over whether the band from the night before had any "drive," Felix got annoyed that Harry's "steady" supported Harry and vowed to entice her away from him, presumably to tame her. The cartoon portrayed Americanized Felix with his American fashions and his use of American words like "drive," "jam," and "fans," not as a political threat, but as simply ridiculous. Yet, it also illustrates another point: the terms of depoliticization in the West insured that the new youth culture came at a price. Misogyny was clearly an ingredient of the new adolescent masculinity that had become acceptable with the psychologizing of youth rebellion. The cartoon painted this misogyny as ridiculous, but normal.[101]

Depoliticization came also at price for East German adolescents. In the second half of the 1950s, West German officials sent back numerous East German adolescents who were trying to move to the West, but who could not prove that they came for political reasons. Girls were sent back more often than boys, because they, even more so than boys, came to the West allegedly only because of family problems. Yet, many boys apparently did not arrive for the right reasons, either. As one official put it, "curiosity, adventurousness, and especially the hopes for a pleasurable and carefree and enjoyable life in the so-called golden West" motivated many East German adolescents to flee the East. In addition, West German officials found that in 1956 more than half of the adolescents who wanted to stay in the West came from "broken homes." West German officials may well have been dissatisfied with the results of their own policies and statements that linked freedom of consumer choice and democracy, but the terms of depoliticization also allowed them to interpret East, like West, German rebelliousness, as a psychological phenomenon.[102]

Depoliticization served important political functions. West German Cold War liberals certainly lost the defensiveness that had characterized conservative West German reactions to both Americanized youth cultures and to East German attacks on West Germany as inundated with American popular culture. When West German Cold War liberals depoliticized consumption and at the same time made it into a political Cold War weapon, they moved away from conservative visions that had seen consumption as a problem linked to working-class immorality and American imports. In stressing that West Germany was in tune with a development of the Western world and evaluating this positively, West German liberals made the consumption of American and African American culture part of a German adolescent life-stage and thus in a sense "Germanized" consumption. East Germans, by contrast, affirmed much narrower visions of acceptable German culture.

4 Jazz and German Respectability

"Jazz music has first of all nothing to do with politics." With these words Reginald Rudorf began his 1964 memoir about his postwar efforts to promote American jazz in East Germany, efforts that ended with Rudorf's arrest in 1957 and his subsequent emigration to West Germany. His statement may come as a surprise from someone who had suffered political persecution in East Germany for promoting jazz. Further, it seems incongruous in the German context where jazz musicians and fans had been the subject of political persecution during the Third Reich, and, after 1945, had been harassed in East Germany and publicly disdained in West Germany. Yet by the 1960s, Rudorf's statement was echoed by many West Germans.[1]

From the 1920s to the 1950s, jazz had many outspoken enemies in Germany. During these years, Europeans usually referred to all American popular music as jazz. Like their counterparts in the United States and elsewhere, German opponents of jazz frequently positioned the music outside the realm of culture; for them everything that "Culture" was supposed to be, jazz was not.[2] Many of these attacks had found their culmination in Nazi attempts to prohibit jazz and in the Nazi persecution of jazz fans. After 1945, when jazz experienced a renaissance in both Germanies, opponents again took up the interlinked notions of sexual transgression and racial decay. They were particularly concerned about the jam sessions that Hot-Clubs put on in East and West German cities in the late 1940s and early 1950s.

In the course of the 1950s, however, many Germans in East and West came to think of jazz as an acceptable musical form. The increasing respectability of jazz was linked to narrowing definitions of jazz and to redefining the meaning of individual jazz styles—from Dixieland to bebop. Moreover, making jazz respectable required controlling the behavior of jazz fans and especially the way they danced. In both Germanies, it was only in the second half of the 1950s that narrower definitions of jazz as different from "lighter" popular hits gained widespread currency. Jazz promoters distinguished between "authentic" jazz on the one hand and "commercial" music and dances like boogie and rock 'n' roll on the other. In West Germany, radio host, writer, and producer Joachim Ernst Berendt became the most influential person to shape positive reevaluations of jazz. In East Germany, Reginald Rudorf, a social scientist, radio host, and writer, led the project of promoting the music.

Efforts to make jazz respectable in Germany had to take into account accusations of gender disarray, racial degeneration, and commercialism that opponents had leveled against the music. East and West German debates about jazz were also always debates about African Americans, their culture, and their history. Certain assumptions about proper masculinity and proper femininity underlay the efforts to make jazz respectable and also related to changing East and West German views of African Americans. In the discourses on American jazz, as in the debates about movies and fashion, East and West Germans negotiated and redefined the relationship between politics and culture.[3]

MAKING JAZZ RESPECTABLE IN WEST GERMANY

In 1950, in his first book on jazz, Joachim Ernst Berendt set out to present jazz and reactions to it with a critical eye toward the present. Berendt was born in 1922. During his youth the Nazis sent his father, a Lutheran minister, to a concentration camp, where he eventually died. An avid jazz fan before 1945, the young Berendt became a radio host for jazz programs in the French Occupation Zone after his return from the Russian front. Well aware that racism had driven antijazz sentiment in Germany and elsewhere ever since jazz had emerged as a set of distinct musical styles in the 1920s, Berendt asked his readers in the introduction to *Der Jazz* (The jazz) to put aside their prejudices and to follow his vindication of the music.[4]

This vindication relied on making jazz into a serious artistic and philosophical enterprise removed from the realm of consumerism and consumer culture. Berendt carefully narrowed the definitions for what he considered "authentic jazz." He claimed that most of what was talked about as jazz was in fact not jazz at all. Jazz, according to Berendt, was not a dance music, and true jazz fans did not dance while listening to the music. Berendt thus disassociated jazz from the dance halls that had characterized the arrival of consumer culture in both Europe and the United States since the late nineteenth century. He also discredited those jazz fans who were dancing and romping around at jam sessions in postwar German Hot-Clubs and other jazz joints. For Berendt, listening to jazz was an intellectual experience, and in his complicated and inaccessible study, he went to great lengths to show that jazz music represented "the essence of the modern age" as well as any twentieth-century philosopher could.[5]

Like many thinkers before him, Berendt asserted that, like modernity, jazz was characterized by an ever increasing androgyny. In the universities, claimed Berendt, women had given up everything that distinguished them from men; in turn, the concept of masculinity had lost much of its former meaning for men. In America androgyny had developed further; there, he said, men even participated in beauty contests. "American life," he explained, "is under the dictatorship of women and is nonetheless shaped by men." Berendt argued that this androgyny found its expression in both jazz and modernist twelve-tone music.

Although he mourned androgyny as a "flight from tension" on the part of modern humanity—thus revealing his own ambivalence about modernity—Berendt, unlike most critics of jazz, did not find the destruction of traditional femininity and masculinity that jazz symbolized a reason to dislike the music. He made clear that jazz could not be rejected simply because it came out of the bars of New Orleans or Chicago; after all, he argued, no one had criticized Euripides because the Greek tragedy had emerged from Dionysian orgies. Berendt thus did not deny the social origins of jazz, but instead argued that jazz, like all "good culture," had transcended those origins. He described the twentieth century as a world in disarray and asserted that jazz grew out of this chaos, but nonetheless had the power to order it. Good jazz, Berendt implied, was not the jazz of the Hot-Club dance sessions, which symbolized gender upheaval in the minds of many East and West Germans.[6]

In a 1952 article for the *Frankfurter Hefte*, Berendt developed his vision of jazz as an important artistic expression in more accessible terms. Using formal analysis, Berendt distinguished a sequence of different jazz styles, from the Dixieland- and Chicago-style of the 1920s, to the swing of the 1930s, and finally to the bebop and cool jazz of the postwar period. He drew on the systematic analysis that Frenchman Hugues Panassié had developed in the 1930s and argued that one jazz style followed the other almost logically.[7] Further, Berendt found parallels between the development of jazz and the trajectory of European music from baroque to classic to Romanticism and the recent modernist music of Stravinsky. In so doing, Berendt validated jazz as a serious artistic tradition, but at the same time made European music the standard against which the "progress" of jazz was to be judged. Ever more emphatically, he asserted that the popular hits and dance music that American and European radio stations were broadcasting were not jazz.

While Berendt acknowledged that jazz musicians had adopted and adapted European harmonies and instruments, he also emphasized the African elements of jazz and stressed that neither jazz music nor African American jazz musicians were "primitive." He explained that European-trained ears had difficulty understanding the African influences, and especially the rhythms of jazz. The New Orleans jazz of the 1920s, for example, did not sound "beautiful according to the sensibility of white man," but it was a truthful and adequate expression of the situation of the oppressed "for whom music is often the most perfect and only possibility to claim freedom and humanity."[8] Berendt believed that whites had the moral responsibility both to feel compassion toward blacks and to try to understand their music, for, as he made clear, whites had caused the plight of African Americans.

Yet Berendt also claimed jazz as a white music. In his interpretation of the 1920s Chicago jazz, which white musicians had developed after listening to black migrants on Chicago's South Side, Berendt focused mostly on Bix (Leon Bismarck) Beiderbecke and his German ancestry. Berendt alleged that the longing of the Beiderbecke family "for the forests of Pomerania" (most of which had become part of Poland after World War II), for "the lakes of Mecklenburg" (which was part of East Germany after World War II) and "for the Prussia of Bismarck" (which had been distinctly authoritarian) had driven Bix "into a romantic state.... out of which the first important white musician grew who could feel compassion for and reshape the melancholy of black music born out of century-long slavery and oppression." It is hard to say whether Berendt consciously drew parallels between the fate of postwar Germans and African Americans as peoples dispersed and displaced, but he certainly took advantage of the German roots of a famous jazz musician to make jazz more acceptable to Germans. Perhaps Berendt's interest in Chicago jazz was merely strategic.

Berendt paid relatively little attention to the big bands of the 1930s and 1940s. He applauded the swinging rhythms and technical perfection of the swing musicians of the 1930s, but he did not spend much time on the mostly white swing big bands who, playing in ballrooms and theaters, had brought black dance band music into the popular mainstream. After World War II, the U.S. Army had spread these rhythms in Germany, and many Germans listened and danced to them enthusiastically. While Americans also continued to dance to swing, a new format for swing concerts in the United States confirmed Berendt's contention that jazz was not a dance music. Since the late 1930s, the orchestras of Benny Goodman and Duke Ellington had given concerts in New York's Carnegie Hall where dancing had been prohibited.[9]

Berendt's real interest was the intellectual jazz of the years after 1945. He explicitly preferred the more Spartan, less danceable music of bebop and cool jazz over earlier styles. Bebop had been developed by black musicians such as Charlie Parker and Dizzy Gillespie in Harlem jazz clubs around 1945. The small bebop combos put much emphasis on the improvising soloist and played a jazz characterized by unusual asymmetric melodies and dense polyrhythms sometimes perceived as nervous. Berendt observed that it was hard "for the uninitiated" to understand this music.

Bebop musicians, according to Berendt, had tried to lift music onto an "absolute sphere" independent of the feelings of the improvising musicians and their audience. In particular, Berendt admired how bebop musicians—ostensibly breaking their link to their audience/consumers—showed open disdain for their audience. Comparing bebop's "critical relationship to time and causality" to that of modernist literature and music, Berendt located bebop as a logical development in responses to modernity and made it into "high" culture. Cool jazz, which was just emerging as a distinct style as Berendt was writing and which he had heard during a trip to the United States, had taken up certain symphonic effects from European classical music. Berendt did not mention this, but explained that cool finally had resolved bebop's imbalances and, together with Stravinsky's music, represented "the human concept of a whole era." Bebop and cool jazz, Berendt's favorite jazz styles, however, were the ones least likely to find an appreciative audience among many Germans.[10]

Concluding that jazz represented the "spiritual state of modern man," Berendt stressed that jazz had gone beyond its African and African American roots to gain appeal around the world. He thus made jazz into a universalizing experience. Perhaps it was not by chance that Berendt seemed to like cool jazz even better than bebop. Played by both black and white musicians, and combining "white" and "black" musical styles, cool jazz quickly became the symbol of successful racial integration. In the aftermath of intense German nationalism prior to 1945 and in the context of West German efforts to erect the Christian West as a cultural and political ideal in the first half of the 1950s, Berendt's stance was in many ways radical. He appreciated the theoretical and musical sophistication of bebop musicians, who considered themselves artists and sought to reject racial stereotypes of black performers. Yet, by focusing on jazz as a "universal" music, Berendt, like many other critics in the United States and elsewhere, could not appreciate the specific political implications that bebop, for example, had in the context of African American struggles against oppression.[11]

Berendt's project, then, was to make jazz respectable as a music originating in black America and as a music that equaled or surpassed European classical music in quality. Validating jazz as the proper musical and intellectual expression of modernity, Berendt uncoupled the associations with primitiveness, feminization, decadence, and racial degeneration that characterized discourses on modernity generally since the nineteenth century and on jazz specifically since the 1920s. At the same time that Berendt valued jazz as an ordering force in modernity, he also reevaluated modernity as not altogether negative.

Perhaps nowhere did Berendt's position crystallize so well as in his 1953 exchange with sociologist/philosopher and Critical Theorist Theodor W. Adorno, a member of the Frankfurt School who had returned to Germany in 1949 from his exile in the United States. In the West German monthly *Merkur*, Berendt defended jazz against Adorno's vehement attacks published in the same journal. The exchange increased Berendt's public visibility in West Germany.

In his article "Perennial Fashion—Jazz," Adorno reiterated arguments against jazz that he had developed since the 1930s and criticized jazz as a standardized music fostering "pseudo-individualization." He characterized jazz as a music where "everything unruly" was "from the very beginning integrated into a strict scheme" and explained that "its rebellious gestures are accompanied by the tendency to blind obeisance." The jazz fan paralleled "the sadomasochist type" in analytical psychology "who chafes against the father figure while secretly admiring him, who seeks to emulate him and in turn derives enjoyment from the subordination he overtly detests." Further, Adorno suggested that African American spirituals "were slave songs and as such combined the lament of bondage with the obsequious affirmation of bondage." In later forms of jazz—Adorno mentioned swing and bebop—this dynamic continued.[12]

Adorno's critique of jazz was striking in that he did not make the music industry, but jazz itself—its African American musicians and the customs associated with the music—responsible for a vicious cycle of meaningless rebellious styles and their immediate containment. Adorno's critique of jazz centered around standardization in the production of popular music, yet in his specific indictments he presented, and rejected, what he saw as typical jazz consumer behavior inescapably produced by the music itself. Adorno maintained that the shocked enemies of jazz had a much better idea of its sexual implications than its apologists. Whereas in his 1936 essay "On Jazz," Adorno had, reluctantly, suggested that jazz had sexually ambiguous implications and thus possibly challenged patriarchal authoritarianism, he abandoned this argument in his 1953 assessment.[13] In his new essay, Adorno did not explicitly spell out his view of truly rebellious masculinity and femininity, but his criticism of jazz implied that he strongly disapproved of the behavior of jazz musicians and fans. Louis Armstrong, according to Adorno, was comparable to one of the great eunuchs of the eighteenth century. Jazz fans followed Armstrong's dangerous example: " 'Give up your masculinity, let yourself be castrated,' the eunuch-like sound of the jazz band both mocks and proclaims, 'and you will be rewarded, accepted into a fraternity which shares the secret of impotence with you.' " Clearly, Adorno had great disdain for these emasculated male fans.[14]

Adorno did not merely criticize the "emasculation" of male jazz fans, but suggested that female fans were even more manipulated than their male counterparts; girls, reported Adorno, had trained themselves to faint when a "crooner" began to sing. Cued in by a light signal, they clapped during radio shows, and they called themselves "jitterbugs"—"bugs which carry out reflex movements" and which were "performers of their own ecstasy." These females appeared to be even more out of touch with their "true" needs than male jazz fans.

In his response to Adorno, Berendt sought to sanitize, desexualize, and decommercialize what he considered true jazz and proper jazz fan behavior. He criticized Adorno for giving the impression that jazz was dance music. Audiences hardly ever danced in any of the well-known jazz joints of America and Europe, he noted. Jazz indeed had always been a music "by few for few."

Berendt reasserted that, from a musicological point of view, one needed to distinguish between authentic jazz on the one hand and popular dance and entertainment music on the other. He went on to show that jazz distinguished itself from popular hits through complex rhythmic variety, unique tones, and, most importantly, improvisation. "True jazz," claimed Berendt, "is the most lively musical expression" of the twentieth century. In fact Berendt reasserted the old high culture/low culture dichotomy and firmly positioned jazz in the realm of high culture. In promoting a narrow definition of jazz that excluded dancing, and in focusing on the technical accomplishments of jazz musicians, Berendt countered assertions by jazz opponents, including Adorno, that jazz caused gender disarray. Berendt thus rejected the notion that anything about jazz was not respectable; his validations focused on improvisation, that is, the unmanipulated aspects of jazz, but also on the respectability of "authentic" jazz musicians and their audience. Berendt thus made jazz compatible with the bourgeois notion of high culture and with a bourgeois gender system.[15]

Berendt and Adorno also sharply disagreed over the political implications of jazz. Even as Adorno acknowledged that European dictators of "both shades" railed against the decadence of jazz, he saw jazz musicians and fans as protofascists. Jazz fans were allegedly prepared to bow down and obey, just as the integration of stumbling movements with the collective "march step" in jazz dancing taught them. Adorno thus drew parallels between their musical and political styles. In typical Cold War fashion, which contrasted one's opponents allegedly ideological stance with one's own objective nonideological position, Adorno spoke of those who championed jazz as an authentic and therefore valuable art form—and who most certainly included Berendt—as "jazz ideologues." He announced that those who believed jazz to be modern art had given themselves up to "barbarism."

Berendt, on the other hand, emphatically asserted that jazz and authoritarianism or dictatorships were incompatible. He reminded Adorno that "for the second time in fifteen years" people in East Germany lived under threats because they liked jazz. The music indeed "immunized" its followers against totalitarianism, and it was not by chance, said Berendt, that the military was hostile toward jazz. In this context, he rejected Adorno's assertion that jazz fans were sadomasochists and scolded Adorno for making African Americans, who had been oppressed by whites, into sadomasochists who were blindly obeying their oppressors. Berendt thus developed a vision of a new restrained masculinity that was at the same time antimilitarist. Both blacks and whites, Berendt implied, could achieve this new masculine ideal through "good" jazz.

Adorno appeared deeply offended by Berendt's assertions and explained that he criticized jazz not for its "wildness, but for its tameness." Moreover he pointed out to Berendt and to the West German public that he, Adorno, was after all the primary author of "the most discussed American book" about racial prejudice, *The Authoritarian Personality*, and that he himself had been a victim of Nazi persecution. Adorno's 1950 study, in which he linked the decline of paternal authority to totalitarian tendencies, had indeed been influential in the United States. Adorno found it "grotesque" that Berendt was trying to protect blacks "against the alleged white feeling of superiority—that of someone who had been persecuted by Hitler." He concluded his response to Berendt with unusually clear words, "Jazz is bad, because it carries the traces of what has been done to the Negroes and about which Berendt is rightly indignant. I do not have any prejudice against Negroes other than that they differ from whites in nothing but their color."[16]

Adorno thus rejected ideas that assumed the biological racial inferiority of blacks, and yet at the same time he erected racial hierarchies with regard to culture: he was unwilling to recognize jazz as a valid cultural and artistic expression and portrayed African American jazz musicians and their fans as culturally inferior. The gender norms that emerged in Adorno's arguments on jazz and his contributions to Critical Theory more generally may help to unravel this apparent paradox.[17] Adorno's vision of resistance to authoritarianism, if resistance was ever possible, clearly did not include the gender transgressions at the center of the jazz experience.

In spite of their differences, Berendt and Adorno in the end shared more than their bitter exchange indicated. Berendt's validations of jazz as noncommercial, antiauthoritarian, modernist art music increasingly relied on a sexual conservatism that was similar to Adorno's. In his 1953 manual for jazz fans, *Jazzbuch*, Berendt described as the emblematic "true" jazz fan, a Catholic priest who was listening to jazz in his remote monastery and for whom jazz was compatible with the writings of Augustine. Further, Berendt made a distinction between the "serious" fans and the so-called "Swing-Heinis"—a term that the Nazis had likewise used in their persecutions of jazz fans. Berendt described "Swing-Heinis" as youths who, with their striped socks, short pants, and long hair, stood in direct opposition to the soldier ideal, and thus implied that jazz fans were male. Berendt urged true jazz fans, who, according to him looked down on "Swing-Heinis" for their wildness and their pursuit of fashion, not to eject them from their circles. Indeed serious, respectable jazz fans should teach these "Swing-Heinis" about the true meaning of the music. These ideas had class implications: Berendt wanted jazz fans to shed styles associated with lower-class culture and to assume a more bourgeois demeanor. Clearly, Berendt's ideas were attractive: his *Jazzbuch*, which contained Berendt's history of jazz as well as short treatments of musical forms, individual musicians, and jazz instruments, sold seventy-five thousand copies within months. Upon its publication, Berendt became the single most powerful jazz critic in West Germany. He also spread jazz music and his ideas through radio and, after 1954, through television programs. Over the next four decades, he would have a deep impact on the European music scene as a writer, producer, and organizer of festivals, who promoted jazz, blues, and "world music."[18]

THE SUCCESS OF JAZZ IN WEST GERMANY

The image of the intellectual male jazz fan whom Berendt championed differed from the fans frequenting the numerous jazz clubs that had formed as so-called Hot-Clubs in big West German cities in the late 1940s and early 1950s. Many jazz clubs ran their own bars with live music, where jazz musicians and jazz fans met, talked, and danced. Particularly popular were their jam sessions. In West Berlin, the "Jazz-Club Berlin" counted six hundred participants, both men and women, and was led by Hans-Wolf Schneider, who was the trombonist of the West Berlin Dixieland band "Spree City Stompers" and the owner of the West Berlin club Eierschale. Club members, many of them students of both genders, had themselves decorated Eierschale, which became the prime meeting spot for club members and those West Berliners who considered themselves bohemians. As West Berlin papers reported, here club members danced in "wild" styles to live music from jazz bands. Many of these clubs were organized in the West German Jazz Federation, which published its own journal *Jazz-Podium* modeled in many ways on the American *Downbeat*.[19]

Many leading members of the jazz clubs grew increasingly dissatisfied with the quality of the music and the behavior of fans at jam sessions; they were also unhappy about the negative reporting in the press.[20] In the early 1950s, the German Jazz Federation started efforts to counter the negative image of jazz with its publications and with lectures. Promoting the image of an "intellectual," nondancing jazz fan was part of its efforts, and the Jazz Federation sponsored Berendt to give lectures on his ideas.[21]

By 1955 the new type of more "intellectual" jazz fans became widely visible in West Germany. For many of them Berendt's *Jazzbuch* became a bible. In West Berlin these "respectable" fans organized in the newly founded New Jazz Circle Berlin. The club held jazz concerts and made sure that information on jazz events was published in the press. Most importantly the club organized regular lectures; here the audience listened intently to recordings, which "jazz experts"—either guest speakers or club members—interpreted. These events at first took place in the basement of a Berlin restaurant, but after the restaurant closed in late 1955, club members found a space in the West Berlin American cultural center *Amerikahaus*, which like many other American cultural centers in West German cities became a meeting place for jazz fans.[22]

New Jazz Circle founder Wolfgang Jänicke demanded serious dedication from members. He insisted that they would forego their membership if they did not attend the lectures regularly. What they heard there was often quite similar to the ideas that Berendt had spread. In 1956, for example, a professor from the Berlin Music Academy spoke about the influences of jazz on modern classical music and vice versa. Members formed subcircles to discuss individual jazz styles from swing to bebop, to cool, to West Coast jazz. Authenticity, a concept that had become so important in distinguishing jazz from commercial music, played a big role also in the jazz clubs. The goal of many club members was to own first editions of records by jazz stars like Louis Armstrong, Bessie Smith, or Charlie Parker.[23] They were thus trying to get these musical performances in their presumably most authentic and least commercialized state. By collecting, these jazz fans were engaging in a form of consumption that had been acceptable for bourgeois men since the nineteenth century, one that was, in Leora Auslander's words, at once "individual," "creative," "authenticity-based," and "order-making."[24] As one West German commentator reported, the record was the "instrument" of the jazz fan. Since records made repeated listening possible, they allowed for a more intellectual jazz experience that was much different from live jazz concerts.[25]

Like Berendt, the New Jazz Circle sought to make jazz respectable by disassociating it from sexuality and juvenile delinquency. In 1957, around two hundred adolescents regularly filled the big hall in the Berlin *Amerikahaus* for lectures organized by the New Jazz Circle. At least 90 percent of them were young men. The *Tagesspiegel* reported that these jazz fans usually came in work or office clothes and rarely wore jeans. The paper remarked that their activities were far different from the disturbances that rowdies were causing in Berlin (and other East and West German cities) during this same period; indeed one could hardly imagine that others of their age would roar, jump on benches, and make loud noise with bells during public "so-called jazz concerts."[26] New Jazz Circle founder Jänicke complained that jazz was unfairly associated with the "degeneration of youth."[27]

According to one statistic, over 50 percent of the largely male membership of the New Jazz Circle were students, civil servants, or white collar workers, and another third were skilled workers and artisans. The great emphasis on respectability may well have discouraged young working-class Berliners from participating in the circle. Opinion surveys conducted for the U.S. government by West German polling institutes suggest that as narrower definitions of jazz prevailed, jazz became increasingly popular among young people from the West German middle and upper classes.[28]

The New Jazz Circle was also much more attractive to men than to women. One reason may have been that in the 1950s young women, frequently kept in their homes by parents and household responsibilities, generally had less leisure time than young men. Yet the particular activities of the club were probably the most important factor in discouraging women from joining. Those young women who went out were often young workers who, even if they knew about the club, may have felt alienated by the intellectual approach to music and by the class composition of the membership. In any case, young women, who were frequently discouraged from purely "intellectual" activities and instead urged to prepare for their future roles as wives and mothers, joined in much lower numbers than men. This audience composition of the New Jazz Circle fit with the target group of educated, young, predominantly male visitors that the American cultural centers attracted—to the satisfaction of U.S. government officials. Yet not all jazz fans adhered to such standards of respectability, nor did all girls dislike jazz, and it seems that the Jazz Club Berlin with its greater focus on live music and dancing attracted more women.[29]

Different types of jazz fans at times listened to the same musicians, albeit very differently. In March 1956 the West Berlin youth magazine *Blickpunkt* (published by the West Berlin association of public youth organizations) criticized the behavior of Lionel Hampton and his audience at a Berlin concert. The audience had "no idea about jazz," yet it was able to influence Hampton's performance negatively. Hampton allegedly turned into a mere "showman" spurred on by the wishes of his noisy audience. Those who knew Hampton from records could, according to *Blickpunkt*, hardly enjoy his performance or the brass players of his "gang" who were rolling around on the stage. The "true enthusiast" did not get to see the "true Lionel Hampton" whose music, according to the article, had almost as many nuances as chamber music. Exactly following Berendt's logic, *Blickpunkt* asserted that Hampton drew his powerful style from his connection with Harlem, the "steamy Negro part of New York," measured Hampton's achievements against European music, and demanded restrained seriousness from his audience.[30]

In spite of the efforts by West German jazz clubs to make the music acceptable, jazz became extremely controversial after 1955 in the wake of the *Halbstarken* rebellion. When West Germans first expressed their outrage over the youth riots that were shaking West German cities in 1955 and 1956, they frequently blamed *Halbstarken* behavior on rock 'n' roll and jazz. Such commentaries saw rock 'n' roll as a form of jazz and they pub-

licly associated *Halbstarke* with the very qualities that opponents had used
to reject jazz: lack of male restraint, female lasciviousness, racial degeneration, and protofascism.[31]

It was in the context of the *Halbstarken* consumption of rock 'n' roll
that West German champions of jazz stepped up their efforts to divorce respectable jazz from nonrespectable commercial dance music. One journal
on youth matters published an article titled "Jazz Is Not for *Halbstarke*."[32]
When debates over adolescent rebels began to shake Germany, jazz clubs
also asserted that they were not *Halbstarke*. The Eierschale, widely regarded as one of the prime jazz clubs of Berlin, required that visitors show
student identification or membership cards of a jazz association, as one paper reported in 1955, in order to keep out *Halbstarke*.[33] Berendt, as the recognized expert on jazz matters, helped their efforts by asserting in the
West German press that rock 'n' roll, which became closely associated with
the *Halbstarken* rebellion, was not jazz.[34] Jazz fans succeeded in establishing that rock 'n' roll was a commercial music with simple rhythms and
tunes distinct from respectable, "high culture" jazz.

Indeed, jazz increasingly seemed a remedy against youthful unruliness.
As one article in *Die Welt* noted, in the context of *Halbstarken* riots, the
work of the "New Jazz Circle" and the "Jazz Club Berlin" could not be underestimated; since they directed adolescent protest into appropriate channels, these clubs were promoting adolescents' well-being and were thus
worthy of state support. After all, the author of the article noted, the jazz
enthusiasm of the youth could not be suppressed. Therefore he recommended that adolescents be guided to express their enthusiasm in an environment where jazz was not simply used to attract customers. Further, he
urged state support for drawing adolescents out of sinister bars and into
state-sponsored jazz cafés; if supported properly, jazz allegedly helped educate adolescents. The article explicitly quoted Adorno's "Perennial Fashion—Jazz" and rejected his thesis that jazz fans were looking mainly for
submission. Quoting New Jazz Circle president Jänicke, the author suggested that young people at the age of sixteen to eighteen recognized the
world of adults as often "false." Boredom with this bureaucratized world
further contributed to their dissatisfaction. Jazz had retained an element of
protest from the time it evolved out of the spirituals and blues of "Negro
slaves," and adolescents responded to this element. The article thus acknowledged that jazz could be a vehicle for protest, but saw that protest as
part of normal psychological adolescent development. The enthusiasm for
jazz was clearly part of a life stage, because, as the author pointed out, the
love of jazz often declined with increasing age.

The article juxtaposed the behavior of jazz fans with the unruliness of *Halbstarke*. In the riots caused by the *Halbstarke*, the author maintained, latent adolescent protest had turned into anarchy. Accompanying the article was the picture of a girl probably dancing rock 'n' roll, who was throwing her partner through the air. Most true jazz fans rejected such displays, the caption claimed, alluding to the clear depiction of gender disarray. In this logic then, which echoed studies on West German youth that social scientists were publishing in these same years, adolescents felt a natural urge to protest against the adult world. This psychological phenomenon could be directed into proper channels by allowing, yet carefully supervising, popular culture consumption.[35]

West German civic leaders began to follow these suggestions. In 1956–57 city officials in the West Berlin borough of Kreuzberg put on ten jazz lectures and one jazz concert as part of their youth protection efforts, which included ballroom dancing lessons with instructions on how to behave toward the other sex, and evening classes where girls were advised on cosmetics and hygiene.[36] Such state-sponsored events marked the growing acceptance of jazz in West Germany, which accelerated over the following years. However, this phenomenon was not merely the result of changing attitudes within West Germany. Indeed, it cannot be fully understood without looking at the battles over jazz in East Germany.

"AUTHENTIC" JAZZ AND POLITICS IN EAST GERMANY

Around 1950, East German authorities, like their Soviet counterparts, had started an outright campaign against jazz, which remained highly controversial in the following years. Not surprisingly, jazz fans in East Germany found it more difficult than West German fans to pursue their interests. Frequently, they smuggled records and Western publications on jazz into the GDR and listened to Western radio stations. Yet some East German voices existed that sought to make jazz officially acceptable.

The most outspoken promoter of jazz music in the GDR was Reginald Rudorf. Born in 1929, Rudorf came from a middle-class family and was a member of the East German SED. By the early 1950s he was teaching social sciences at the University of Leipzig.[37] In August 1952 Rudorf published an article in the East German music journal *Musik und Gesellschaft*, in which he contrasted what he called "authentic" jazz, like blues and Dixieland, with those musical forms, like swing, sweet, and bebop, that the American music industry allegedly produced as part of an American imperialist strategy. In making this distinction between two types of jazz,

Rudorf was carefully walking a line within official East German rhetoric. Since the late 1940s, it was East German policy to emulate Soviet propaganda and vehemently reject or even prohibit jazz as a decadent, commercial music. Rudorf echoed official East German Cold War rhetoric when he claimed that with "inauthentic" jazz, Americans were trying to prepare their own population and especially the people of West Germany and West Berlin for war. In 1954 two articles in the same journal followed in which Rudorf further pursued his validations of "authentic" and rejections of "commercial" jazz.[38]

Rudorf located his arguments in favor of jazz firmly within the official cultural doctrine of the East German SED. After all, the SED's Central Committee had announced its fight against formalism and called for a search for an authentic German national culture in March 1951. In distinguishing between good, authentic jazz on the one hand and commercial dance music and modern jazz on the other, Rudorf employed the official vocabulary and drew heavily on East German musicologist Ernst Hermann Meyer. For example, Rudorf indicted swing music and bebop as "decadent." Further, he frowned upon the rhythmic "excesses" of percussionists or the "atonal" lines in swing. At the same time that he derided certain aspects of jazz, Rudorf stressed that African American folk music, including some forms of jazz, could fruitfully stimulate the development of a new "clean" German dance music. Rudorf followed a logic that jazz fans in the Soviet Union had employed with varying success since the 1930s.[39]

In his rejections of musical forms like swing and boogie, Rudorf linked the absence of male and female respectability to threats against proper German national identity. For example, he turned against the American swing big bands, consisting mostly of white musicians, that had brought black dance hall music into the popular mainstream. Asserting that commercialized jazz undermined German respectability and "proper taste," Rudorf spoke of "orgies" that the "boogie-woogie cult" caused in West Germany and Berlin; he announced that these were intended "to barbarize the youth, to divide the unity of German culture and finally to influence the music production of the GDR." Rudorf alluded to the allegedly sexualizing effects of American music and equated it with pornography. He thus warned against the dangers that popular jazz posed in terms that linked German national identity to respectable gender mores.

Rudorf considered these commercial forms of jazz to be attacks on female respectability in particular. Thus he compared American-imported jazz dancing to women's wrestling contests, which were a popular object of East German scorn. The photographs that accompanied the 1952 article juxtaposed a tightly packed crowd of Americans—women with loose shoulder-length hair and tight dresses and men in suits dancing in front of a big band (labeled "mass jazz in Hollywood")—with a close-up of a blond German girl with braids in the traditional dirndl and a male partner dressed in a white shirt and a traditional vest dancing to Bach's "Peasant Cantata." In 1954, Rudorf even more vividly described what he considered unacceptable behavior on the part of jazz musicians and fans. Certain rhythms and tones led to excesses and "degenerate" dancing, he argued, not just in the United States and West Germany, but also, though to a lesser degree, in East Germany. "The ecstatic jumps of the deplorable brushheads and their *Amizonen*," quipped Rudorf, "are at their worst when the orchestra plays louder, when a saxophone begins to squeak in a vulgar way or when shrill trumpet solos ring." By identifying male jazz fans merely by their bouffant hairstyles and speaking of them derogatorily as "the brushheads," Rudorf associated them with fashion and thus with femininity. Further, with *Amizonen* Rudorf employed a term that West Germans used to refer to German women who were fraternizing with American troops. Rudorf once again portrayed Americanized German women as overly sexual and as masculinized.[40]

East German authorities could only agree with these indictments of American music. But how then could Rudorf argue that some forms of jazz did not pose these threats to proper gender roles and to proper German- ness? Rudorf used the concept of "authentic" jazz, which he positioned clearly beyond the realm of Americanized mass culture. Indeed, he pro- posed that "authentic" jazz could help to counter the dangerous effects of American commercial music in East Germany and elsewhere. He was care- ful to put authentic jazz in the same category as folk music from socialist countries: just as East Germans could learn from the lively music of the Soviet Union and the other people's republics, so too, Rudorf suggested, East Germans could learn from "authentic" jazz. As a positive example of someone who had learned from Soviet music, Rudorf mentioned his Leipzig acquaintance Kurt Henkels and his orchestra. Henkels in fact was playing swing and other jazz rhythms, but Rudorf tried to validate Henkels's efforts without ever mentioning him in the context of jazz.[41]

Rudorf's validation of jazz, like Joachim Ernst Berendt's in West Ger- many, rested on distinguishing authentic from inauthentic music and on separating "authentic" jazz from any associations with decadence or un- bridled sexuality. Yet in spite of similarities in their logic, Berendt and Rudorf came to very different conclusions. Berendt did not see jazz pre- dominantly as a dance music. He particularly valued more "intellectual" and less danceable styles like bebop and cool jazz and argued that black musicians, such as Charlie Parker and Dizzy Gillespie, were important intellectuals. Many West German jazz associations, like the West Berlin New Jazz Circle, followed Berendt's ideas; they rejected dancing and treated jazz as an art music that required theoretical and philosophical education on the part of its listeners.

In contrast to Berendt and many of the West German jazz associations who found bebop and modern jazz most valuable, Rudorf rejected such forms of jazz as "decadent" and as an expression of African American decadence specifically. In 1954 Rudorf explained that the oppression of African Americans had induced a crisis in their culture. Some African American musicians had sold out to the music industry, he argued, while others, "often disconnected from the struggle of their people," had sought refuge in technical experiments. Bebop musicians thought that they were protesting commercialism and artistic oppression when objectively, wrote Rudorf, "they were merely making decadence richer by one form of expression." Rudorf criticized black and white musicians who had created their music in recording studios rather than in dance halls. He particularly disliked Charlie Parker's music because Parker revealed "nihilist tendencies" in his "morbid performances." Further, Rudorf explained, the "cult of technical experiments" continued in cool jazz characterized by atonality and other formal elements "which were adversaries of melody and therefore of music." In modern jazz, he concluded, a unity existed between "decadent form" and "decadent content." Rudorf assured East Germans that such modern jazz was not played in the GDR, but that it existed in West Germany.[42]

Race played a complicated role in Rudorf's criticisms. He certainly did not draw his distinction between good and bad jazz along color lines. Indeed, he saw black musicians as both the greatest traitors and the greatest hope for jazz. Thus he reserved his most scathing critiques for the black bebop musicians and his most celebratory remarks for the black musicians who played spirituals and blues. Yet his indictments of certain forms of jazz dancing as "degenerate" placed Rudorf on a continuum with those who had promoted racial hierarchies that positioned (white/"Aryan") Germans as superior to Jews, blacks, and other groups, like Gypsies. The concept of degeneracy evoked this racial logic, and by using it in the context of dances and music that Rudorf saw rooted in African American culture, he also reasserted racial hierarchies between black Americans who lacked respectability and good white Germans. Finally, in validating authentic jazz, Rudorf used rhetoric that had anti-Semitic undertones: like other East

German officials and intellectuals, he turned against the "cosmopolitan" culture industry and "cosmopolitan" hits.[43]

ORGANIZING EAST GERMAN JAZZ FANS

Rudorf's use of official terminology allowed him to carve a space for jazz in East Germany, and it contributed to the confusion in both his own efforts and in official responses to him. Within his framework of distinguishing authentic from commercial and modern "formalist" jazz, Rudorf was able to broaden the range of officially acceptable tunes. In 1952 he celebrated Dixieland as authentic music for blacks and whites in the American South; he urged that only these forms of jazz be played in the GDR, and he rejected all later jazz styles. Two years later, Rudorf demanded that swing rhythms, too, should be played and broadcast in East Germany. He now suggested, for example, that the music of Benny Goodman and Tommy Dorsey as well as tunes by Duke Ellington and George Gershwin were valuable. Although Rudorf did not elaborate how these musical styles fit with celebrations of the "folk," East German officials followed this lead. When authorities sought to regain approval among their population after the uprising of June 1953, they allowed Rudorf and his friend Heinz Lukasz to produce a series for East German radio that focused on the more traditional forms of Dixieland and Chicago jazz. Under the title *Vom Lebenslauf einer Musik* (On the life of a musical form), the program aired on all East German radio stations from September 1954 to March 1955. Given Soviet and East German rejections of formalism, it is not too surprising that authorities found Dixieland more palatable than the atonal bebop. Horst Lange, a West German jazz expert with a preference for traditional jazz, reported that in a few months more "true jazz" came over the East German radio waves than could be heard in years in the West.[44]

In the same period, from the summer of 1954 and through the spring of 1955, informal jazz clubs sprang up all over the GDR. Many of them were connected to local chapters of the state youth organization FDJ at schools and universities. Rudorf lectured on jazz first in monthly lectures in Leipzig and then all over the GDR. And in early 1955, he and Lukasz were able to invite the West Berlin Spree City Stompers, who played Dixieland and thus in the more traditional vein; the band came to participate in the production of a movie on jazz that Rudorf and Lukasz were making.[45]

In early 1955 Rudorf and Lukasz obtained formal recognition for their own informal Leipzig group from the local FDJ chapter. Rudorf claimed that one of the group's goals was to find a new dance music for Germany, and explained that the group would attack the "cosmopolitan" and "anti-national" intentions of modern American dance music. Yet dancing was clearly neither Rudorf's nor the Leipzig club's priority. The group got together for lectures by Rudorf and for concerts. By suggesting that commercial jazz music, too, needed to be studied carefully, Rudorf may have tried to leave the door open for the music forms that he himself publicly indicted.[46] In the context of a repressive regime, studying the alleged evil of cultural forms that had fallen into disgrace could be one of the few ways to actually consume them, particularly in groups. During their meetings, club members listened to and critiqued studio as well as concert recordings.[47]

Although Rudorf and Lukasz advertised their jazz club as an organization firmly rooted in the political missions of the party and FDJ, their group was actually not very different from its West German counterparts. Almost half of the members were students and like many West German jazz clubs, the group attracted mostly men: of its sixty-two members in 1955 only five were women. Similarly, 90 percent of the audience at lectures organized by the West Berlin New Jazz Circle were male. Close ties to the Leipzig University may have caused this makeup of the club's membership, since Leipzig, like all East German universities, had more male than female students. But it is likely that the activities of the club also implicitly excluded East German women, who, like West German women, were usually discouraged from pursuing purely intellectual matters.[48].

Although the East German label Amiga once again released jazz records after 1954, East German jazz fans relied heavily on informal contacts with West Germans and West Europeans for recordings and information. Both East and West German jazz fans smuggled records and jazz literature into the GDR. After his successes with the radio program and the establishment of the Leipzig club, Rudorf became more audacious and sought to formalize these contacts. Writing to the East German Ministry of Culture in December 1954, he demanded official support for jazz clubs across the GDR, for the scientific study of jazz, and for close ties with West German and European jazz fans. Rudorf indeed portrayed his efforts within the GDR as well as his contacts to West German jazz fans as part of the East and West German fight against "Americanization."[49]

Yet East German officials understandably had some doubts about a stance that sought to turn American jazz against the Americanization of East and West Germany, and they began to use Rudorf's arguments against him. In April 1955 officials of the East German Ministry of Culture, apparently upon receiving Rudorf's request, called a meeting about jazz. The three-hour meeting took place in the office of the Association of German Composers and Musicologists (VdK) and experts from the VdK participated, showing how coordinated the efforts of state functionaries and artists' associations were. At the meeting, Rudorf went so far as to say that the music of American "Negroes," namely jazz, had been influenced by Europe and especially by Germany through the German *Ländler* (slow waltzes) and chorales. To counter the concerns of East German officials, Rudorf again portrayed his efforts on behalf of jazz as part of the search for a German national dance music. Officials, however, were no longer convinced. One of East Germany's foremost music experts, Georg Knepler, acknowledged that "a true folk music of the Negroes" existed; however, it was not up to Germans, but to the American people to "occupy themselves" with it. True to the Stalinist logic that each nation had to find its own way to socialism, Knepler did not want Germans to rely on African American music in their search for a national German revolutionary culture.

The officials also rejected Rudorf's thesis that the fans of "true jazz" were often antifascists, although Rudorf made reference to those jazz fans who had been forced into concentration camps under National Socialism. Neither were officials convinced by Rudorf's assertions that West German jazz fans were adversaries of American fascism and race hatred; nor were officials swayed by Rudorf's suggestion that alliances between East and West German jazz fans were desirable because West German jazz fans worked for an all-German reconciliation and opposed the Paris Treaties, which had paved the way for West Germany's admission to NATO and rearmament and which East Germany was adamantly attacking. Instead the officials indicted Rudorf and jazz fans in Germany and abroad as followers of "cosmopolitan" dance music and "internationalism." Directly linking jazz to unacceptable femininity and masculinity, one official countered Rudorf's suggestion that jazz was the music of the urban proletariat with the assertion that it had emerged from brothels and gangster hangouts.[50]

Perhaps misreading the meeting in the office of the VdK, Rudorf wrote a letter several days later to the Central Council of the FDJ seeking official recognition and support for his contacts with West Germany. He even wanted to send a GDR-delegation to West German jazz festivals and used the same arguments he had brought forward in the meeting: an alliance with West German jazz fans was necessary in fighting rearmament, Americanization, and race hatred.[51]

This letter led officials from the FDJ Central Council to investigate the doings of the Leipzig jazz club. In a report to the Central Council, the head of the Leipzig Youth Club, Helmut Thomas, defended himself for permitting the jazz group in the first place; Thomas said he had hoped that the group would foster "hatred against the imperialists and fascists of America." He denied being familiar with the scholarly questions regarding jazz and had assumed that jazz was a valid topic, because articles and broadcasts about it had appeared in the East German press and on radio.[52]

In the context of East German socialism, the jazz group needed to prove that it fostered both German (socialist) culture and politics. Thomas reported, however, that the political value of the group was rather weak and criticized Rudorf for calling all enemies of jazz "fascists" in a January 1955 lecture in Leipzig. Further, Thomas complained that, although the group had taken a stance against the Paris Treaties and had called on West German friends to do the same, no members had volunteered for the East German KVP. The KVP consisted of police units who were to be the building blocks for East Germany's as yet unofficial army. Thomas and other FDJ officials attacked the jazz group for being too preoccupied with technical, that is, musicological, rather than political matters. Rudorf, according to Thomas, avoided political arguments in order to retain the membership of some "bourgeois" male youths. Their preoccupation with jazz, these official criticisms implied, led the Leipzig jazz fans to neglect their manly duties as citizens and soldiers. Higher FDJ officials consulted with both Erich Honecker, who was just concluding his time as the head of the FDJ, and with officials from the Ministry of Culture. They put pressure on Thomas who agreed to dissolve the group in May 1955. As an alternative, East German officials suggested that the members form a group that would research the folk music of the Soviet Union and the other people's republics.[53]

While the members' lack of commitment to the nascent East German army was clearly a major factor in the officials' decision to dissolve the group, public indictments centered on the rumor that the group had made the American president Eisenhower its honorary member. One FDJ official made this accusation at a FDJ conference in Leipzig and later Erich Honecker repeated it at the Fifth Parliament of the FDJ in May 1955. In fact the group had intended to name some honorary members from outside of the GDR, among them the head of the West German Jazz Federation and two West German jazz critics and members of the West German Communist Party, and some British jazz musicians, but no Americans and certainly not the head of the reigning capitalist superpower.[54]

In those same months of spring 1955, *Musik und Gesellschaft* published articles that demoted Rudorf's theses about jazz. Officials who had been present at the meeting in the VdK office wrote two of these attacks. The authors, Knepler and Ludwig Richard Müller, vehemently rejected Rudorf's suggestion that the enemies of jazz were in fact fascists themselves. According to both authors, any jazz in its present form was the dance music of American imperialism.[55]

Because GDR officials positioned themselves as champions of civil rights in the United States and generally believed in the revolutionary potential of the authentic "folk" music of the oppressed, these attacks on jazz required that it be denied the status of authentic African American music. Müller declared that it did not matter whether jazz contained elements of "Negro folk music"; rather it mattered to what ends jazz was being used. Knepler stressed that East German composers and musicians greatly admired both the cultural creativity of African Americans and the fight for equal rights against the barbarian racial policies of the ruling class in the United States. Indeed, in order to prove that he was not a racist, Knepler acclaimed the work of African American actor and singer Paul Robeson, who during these years, because of his involvement in the U.S. Communist Party, was fighting to retain his U.S. citizenship. At the height of Soviet attacks on jazz, Robeson himself had published an article directed against jazz in the major Soviet music journal in 1949. In words that Rudorf had picked up in his 1952 article on jazz, Robeson argued that spirituals and blues were the only true Negro music in the United States. "Commercial" jazz, whether played by whites or African Americans, "prostituted and ruthlessly perverted the genuine expressions of folk life."[56] Knepler now followed Robeson in refuting Rudorf's thesis that jazz was the music of the Negro proletariat in the American South. Blues and spirituals—which Robeson had sung—were indeed true folk music, according to Knepler, but jazz was not.

Both Müller and Knepler supported this rejection of jazz with references to its sexualizing effects. Knepler spoke of the marks that brothels and gangster hangouts had left on jazz, while Müller was especially worried about the "public display of sexual drives" among jazz fans who danced. To prove his point, Müller listed quotes from Gorki, Sartre, and old German communist Clara Zetkin, who had remarked "In my time one did this in bed." And he linked jazz to "primitive" behavior, explaining in the words of Walter Ulbricht that the " 'ape culture' of decadent jazz" had to be countered with a new, healthy German dance culture.

The two authors also attacked Rudorf's suggestion that authentic jazz music could be distinguished from commercial deviations. Müller denounced the alleged conspiracy of an "aristocracy" of jazz-crazy musicians, radio hosts, music editors, and publishers, who promoted "true" jazz, which, he argued, did not exist. He further indicted "this aristocracy" for looking down on sappy German hits, even though these songs in their harmonics were closer to the German "cultural realm." Knepler explicitly rejected the distinction between true "hot" jazz and false "sweet."[57]

In critiquing all jazz, both Knepler and Müller employed a vocabulary similar to Rudorf's rejections of commercial jazz. Elements of "decadence," lamented Knepler, had intruded into the so-called true jazz. In jazz the "exuberance" of "Negro dances" turned into "hysteria," intense expressiveness "degenerated" into empty clownery. Müller bemoaned the attempts of composers and musicians to satisfy the tastes of "Swing-Heinis" through "sexual groans" and unacceptable "decadent" dances.

Thus, both East German opponents and promoters of jazz relied on the same concepts—like decadence and disdain for a capitalist music industry—in arguments for their respective causes. This overlap undoubtedly contributed to the confusion that characterized official East German attitudes toward jazz in the years after 1955. While many officials sought to root out jazz, others tried to use it to attract young people to the socialist cause. FDJ and Culture Ministry officials had rejected Rudorf's vindication of jazz in the spring and summer of 1955; they prohibited the Leipzig jazz club and stopped Rudorf's and Lukasz's radio programs. However, in February 1956 the FDJ Central Council included a defense of jazz in its manifesto *An Euch Alle*. The council explicitly took "authentic" jazz off the list of detrimental products, from pornographic movies to comics, that West Germany and the United States were allegedly using to destroy the morality of German girls and boys: "Jazz is not the invention of war mongers but an old folk music of oppressed Negroes," the manifesto declared. Relying on Rudorf's differentiation between "true" and "commercial" jazz, the authors suggested jazz fans in the GDR were not yet aware that American imperialism was exporting "false" jazz. The FDJ Central Council recommended that the FDJ give East German jazz fans the opportunity to get to know "true" jazz, so that they could be protected from enemy influences.[58]

In this atmosphere of confusion, more jazz clubs and jazz journals were founded in 1955 all over the GDR. In Halle, for example, a group of jazz fans organized within the FDJ group of the university in early 1955. Under the leadership of Siegfried Schmidt, the Halle jazz club began publication of a newsletter in December of 1955. The *Jazz-Journal*, although merely typed and mimeographed, was modeled on magazines like the American *Downbeat* and the West German *Jazz-Podium* and published a mix of jazz history and news about activities of fans at home and abroad. In its first issue, the authors followed Rudorf's lead and carefully distinguished between authentic and commercial jazz.[59]

However, the second and third issues of the *Jazz-Journal*, published in January and February of 1956, contained at first cautious and then more forceful defenses of modern jazz and specifically bebop. The Halle group had sent a jazz combo, the "Hans Buchmann Quintett," to an amateur jazz festival in West Germany, where the quintet won third place and was subsequently invited to appear on a television show with Joachim Ernst Berendt in West Germany. In its February 1956 issue, the *Jazz-Journal* reported that influences on the quintet included bebop. Recently, the journal explained, the quintet had moved toward cool jazz and was developing its own distinctive style. The journal used words that Berendt could have written: "The Buchmann-Quintett plays uncompromised jazz." The members were striving for nothing but "a musical ideal, a true artistic message." Not surprisingly, once the Halle group supported bebop and the idea of artistic autonomy, the FDJ quickly prohibited the *Jazz-Journal*.[60]

In spite of the forced dissolution of his Leipzig group, Rudorf further pursued his activities on behalf of jazz. He continued to lecture in Leipzig and elsewhere, and in early 1956, he and Lukasz even tried to regain official recognition for their group. This time they defined themselves as a group of critics, researchers, and interested listeners whose task was to foster "authentic" jazz and to investigate the "social problematic" as well as the "musical structure" of jazz. This approach brought Rudorf even closer to the jazz clubs in the West, who studied jazz "scientifically," and his efforts to gather official support failed.[61]

However, alongside this failure in 1956, more traditional jazz styles like Dixieland and swing became ever more acceptable and accessible in East Germany, especially after the Twentieth Party Congress of the Soviet Communist Party had called for a fight against dogmatism. Thus the state film company DEFA finally released the long-anticipated film on the history of jazz to which Rudorf and Lukasz had contributed. The film reflected ongoing efforts to navigate between acceptable and unacceptable jazz; it contained examples of Dixieland, but censors had cut all references to modern jazz and all scenes filmed with the West Berlin band Spree City Stompers. That same year an East German publishing company issued a book, *Neger, Jazz, und tiefer Süden* (Negroes, jazz, and the Deep South), that validated spirituals, blues, and jazz musicians like Louis Armstrong and Duke Ellington.[62] In April 1956 the FDJ organized a public meeting in Berlin between members and officials about the topic of jazz. After hearing the demands from the audience, the officials, among them FDJ functionary

Hans Modrow (who would become East German prime minister in late 1989) and composer Hanns Eisler, promised to make jazz more accessible. Whereas East German officials had canceled Rudorf's and Lukasz's radio jazz programs in 1955, they now allowed East German swing and Dixieland bands to play on radio and television. A 1955 article on jazz by a Soviet musicologist that evaluated some jazz positively appeared in *Musik und Gesellschaft* and was echoed in many other East German magazines.[63]

This greater leniency in East Germany occurred in the context of the "thaw" in the Soviet orbit. After the Twentieth Party Congress, the organizing committee for the Sixth World Youth Festival decided to hold it in Moscow during the summer of 1957 and, to demonstrate Soviet openness, included a competition for Soviet and visiting jazz groups. In the spring of 1957, East German authorities held their own contest to determine who would represent the GDR in Moscow. The winner was the "Jazz-Band Halle," a Dixieland orchestra led by Alfons Zschockelt, but bands oriented toward cool and West Coast jazz were also allowed to participate.[64]

Despite this greater openness, SED officials, like their Soviet counterparts, continued to be suspicious of the activities of jazz fans. For one, Rudorf organized jazz concerts with the East German Protestant church. Also Rudorf and Lukazs became more radical in their criticisms of the regime. At the time of the uprising in Hungary in October 1956, they decided to bring forward demands for the freedom of modern art. According to his memoirs, Rudorf announced at a lecture in Dresden that jazz, Picasso, Sartre, Stravinsky, and Beckett would be allowed and accepted in East Germany only if the political foundations of the regime were changed. Apparently Rudorf had come around to Berendt's West German position that jazz was art music; he now demanded freedom for jazz on those grounds. At another lecture, in Munich, Rudorf argued that East German adolescents were expressing their protest against the dogma of Marxism-Leninism through their enthusiasm for jazz.[65]

East German officials, who had put Rudorf under surveillance by the secret police, the *Stasi*, finally decided to take action. At another lecture, Rudorf and Lukasz were beaten up, on the orders of functionaries.[66] Both left for West Germany, with the help of West Berlin Spree City Stomper Hans-Wolf Schneider, but Rudorf soon decided to return to Leipzig. In the GDR, officials increasingly clamped down on jazz clubs, and after another trip to West Germany, Rudorf was arrested in March of 1957. He was tried for slandering the FDJ and the SED in front of Leipzig and Munich audiences. During the trial the judge accused him of having used jazz as a cover for political crimes. Rudorf was sentenced to two years in prison.

Fig. 15. "Serious" fans at a public forum on jazz in East Berlin, April 1956. Drawing: Vontra, reprinted from *B.Z. am Abend*, April 4, 1956.

After a phase of confusion and leniency, East German officials accepted only spirituals, blues, Dixieland, and swing. Faced with the onslaught of rock 'n' roll after 1956, some East German officials found at least some forms of jazz preferable, but many continued to be especially suspicious of efforts to promote more modern jazz. In this increasingly repressive climate, numerous jazz musicians and jazz club members, among them Siegfried Schmidt and Alfons Zschockelt of Halle, left for West Germany. Kurt Henkels followed in 1959. Having served two years in prison, Rudorf also moved to West Germany in 1959, where he worked as a journalist. Now a staunch Western Cold Warrior, he argued that jazz was not political in his memoir on the suppression of jazz in the GDR. But he also became increasingly disenchanted with what he perceived to be West Germans' failure to recognize him as a resister against totalitarian socialism.[67]

JAZZ AS A COLD WAR WEAPON

In the meantime, West German and American press and officials were watching closely what was happening in East Germany. The West German magazine *Der Spiegel*, for example, featured a story on Rudorf's efforts on behalf of jazz in 1955. And both West German papers and dispatches from the American mission in Berlin noted that Rudorf was beaten up and later arrested.[68]

In 1955 and 1956, the American press reported that European audiences from both sides of the Iron Curtain had received American jazz musicians enthusiastically. In November 1955 the *New York Times,* for example, ran the following headline "United States Has Secret Sonic Weapon—Jazz."[69] American magazines likewise reported that Europeans took jazz much more seriously than Americans, studied it carefully, and mostly listened to jazz concerts in a respectable manner.

In this climate, jazz became an attractive American and West German Cold War weapon for several reasons. American psychological studies asserted that jazz was in fact a normal expression of youthful restlessness. Combined with reports about the greater respect Europeans had for jazz, these studies led white Americans to see jazz increasingly as unthreatening inside their country and as an adequate expression of American pluralism abroad. European jazz fans undoubtedly consumed jazz, but with the success of promoters like Berendt and jazz clubs like the New Jazz Circle Berlin, their consumption did not carry negative connotations, such as the idea that consumer culture destroyed gender mores.[70] Undoubtedly well aware of the fact that Europeans saw jazz as an African American music, American authorities tried to use jazz to counter the adverse effects on public opinion abroad that the ongoing violations of African Americans' civil rights had caused—and which they sought to track carefully, for example, in opinion surveys on the case of Emmett Till, an African American boy who had been brutally murdered by whites. Finally, and very importantly, the suppression of jazz in East Germany and other countries of the Warsaw Pact made jazz into an attractive messenger for American democracy. In fact, jazz, like modernism in art and literature, could become part of the anticommunist battle.[71]

After many requests from the field and the positive press reports, the Voice of America introduced a popular jazz program for Soviet youth in late 1955, which was hosted by Willis Conover. Jazz also became an official part of the cultural programs that the United States Information Agency sponsored after 1956. In July 1957 an exhibition "Jazz in USA" opened in the *Amerikahaus,* the American cultural center in Frankfurt. An accompanying catalogue featured articles from West Germany's foremost jazz promoters, among them Dietrich Schulz-Köhn and Joachim-Ernst Berendt.[72]

In January 1958 a month-long photo exhibit on the history of jazz, which was accompanied by lectures concerts and films, opened in the Berlin

Amerikahaus. As one newspaper reported, in spite of the many visitors, the exhibit was characterized by "the silence of a museum." Nobody spoke loudly, and most visitors wandered silently through the exhibit. Especially popular was a booth with music literature where two young men, "who wore their New Jazz Circle Berlin tags" like "medals of honor," answered questions. Most visitors wore a "uniform" of tight pants and oversized sweaters and, as the paper noted, their gender was recognizable only through their haircuts: the "gentlemen" wore their hair combed to the front, the "ladies" combed back. Judging by the description of their fashions, some of the visitors of the exhibit were likely so-called "Exis," young men and women mostly from the middle and upper class who formed a kind of bohème in some West German cities. Such adolescents countered their parents' notions of respectability by engaging in cultural and sometimes also sexual experimentation. Many of them strove for a more "authentic" life and looked for models among French existentialists and the American Beats—both groups that adored jazz. While the German "Exis" encountered some outrage on the part of parents and educators, they never received the same level of public attention as *Halbstarke* or rock 'n' roll fans. The reporter at the Berlin exhibit clearly did not feel threatened by their demeanor, and merely ridiculed those young men who quickly parted their hair again (and thus returned to more traditional hairstyles) before leaving the exhibit. For the time being, the "rebelliousness" of these jazz fans, including their challenges to gender mores, had been safely, and often literally, contained in a museum-like atmosphere.[73]

As jazz was depoliticized, it became an increasingly attractive weapon also for West Germans against both youthful rebelliousness at home and against the Cold War enemies to the East. The dual function of jazz as a tamer of *Halbstarke* and as a representative of Western democracy contributed to its astounding proliferation in West Germany in the second half of the 1950s. Jazz festivals took place in several cities, the Cologne Academy of Music began to teach jazz, a wide array of jazz books appeared, scores of jazz recordings and introductions into jazz were released, and the number of jazz shows on radio and television increased dramatically. The second edition of Berendt's jazz compendium titled *Das große Jazzbuch* came out in 1958 and sold more than two hundred thousand copies. Like local governments in other West German cities, the West Berlin government in 1959 decided to open jazz dance cafes to attract young people.[74] Jazz never appealed to the majority of Germans, and German jazz musicians had difficulty supporting themselves through their music, but in 1957 an opinion survey conducted for USIA (United States Information

Agency) found that West Germans saw jazz more positively than their West European neighbors in France, England, or Italy.[75]

Jazz indeed appeared to be perfect for the new pluralist, postfascist West German society. In spite of evidence that jazz, in its now widely accepted narrow definition, attracted mostly middle- and upper-class youths, one journal announced that the jazz "expert audience" came from all walks of life. In 1958, a Cologne paper explicitly sought to counter remaining "misunderstandings" about jazz, such as the idea that jazz was the same as rock 'n' roll and that "*Halbstarke* were tearing down concert halls" with jazz. The paper published an article by West German jazz expert Dietrich Schulz-Köhn ("Dr. Jazz") who was the host of jazz programs for the WDR (Westdeutscher Rundfunk), the radio station that covered much of Western Germany. Schulz-Köhn had been an avid jazz fan during the Third Reich, had helped many jazz musicians, and had believed that jazz would be an important musical form after the Nazi's "final victory." In his 1958 article, he described jazz as a musical Esperanto but made it clear that one had to learn how to distinguish jazz from bad music. Like other experts, he stressed the specific rhythms and improvisation in jazz, saw close links between jazz and classical music, and reported even that adolescent jazz fans were increasingly buying classical music. Also, he pointed out that neither jazz nor classical music had anything in common with popular hits. Although jazz required a different language to be understood, the present generation was "bilingual" and literate in both classical and jazz music. Within the half century since its inception, jazz, according to Schulz-Köhn, had accomplished astonishing things. The music had overcome all dividing lines: differences in status and education, differences of race, religious denomination, and political conviction, and even the borders between nations and countries. Sensible persons and institutions, such as churches and schools, therefore had integrated jazz into their "intentions." The city of Cologne was about to sponsor six "Jazz Concerts for the Youth" in early 1959. The only boundary that remained was that of age, and Schulz-Köhn predicted optimistically that in the next generation jazz would be a "matter of course." Like many other jazz experts, Schulz-Köhn explicitly rejected the conflation of jazz and rock 'n' roll; he sought to validate jazz as a respectable music that transcended its African American origins. Such affirmations of jazz were part of constructing a society based on bourgeois values in West Germany. Ironically, many of those who were promoting these bourgeois gender and cultural norms claimed to be constructing a raceless and classless society.

Jazz became the appropriate cultural expression for the "end of ideologies" that American, West European, and specifically West German intellectuals were postulating in the second half of the 1950s. Quoting a music professor, Schulz-Köhn interpreted jazz as a music that, when performed perfectly, "carried its meaning and affirmation in itself."[76] According to this logic, jazz ideally had nothing to do with politics and yet, through its "apolitical" privileged place, it could become a political weapon of the West. American and West German authorities tried to avoid any association with the negative stereotypes associated with consumer culture, even as they made consumption increasingly into a Cold War weapon. In this context, jazz appeared to be an ideal vehicle in the cultural and political battles of the Cold War.

Some West German officials certainly grasped this potential. As we have seen, in September 1956, the West Berlin *Tagesspiegel* reported that West German chancellor Konrad Adenauer had denounced those who bad-mouthed the new West German army as *Halbstarke*. The very same article announced that "not Prussian military marches, but symphonic jazz and chamber concerts, and symphonic brass music" would make up most of the repertoire of the new West German army bands.[77] And in August 1958, West German defense minister Franz-Josef Strauß went even further. In response to an inquiry Berendt had made for the West German Jazz Federation, Strauß suggested that he saw jazz positively: "the community-building powers" of jazz converged with the efforts of the West German army. Strauß stressed that he was thinking of "pure jazz" (*Jazz in Reinkultur*), and not of "pseudo-jazz." Within the army several bands were playing jazz in their free time, and Strauß wanted to support them. Moreover Strauß suggested forming a "Head Jazz Band" (*Leit-Jazz-Kapelle*) that would be made up of especially qualified musicians and would lead others into the proper direction. Strauß explicitly used jazz to show that West Germany and the West German army differed from both its German Cold War enemy to the East and from the Third Reich. He criticized the suppression of jazz in totalitarian regimes and explained that with its improvisations and its freedom to have many forms, jazz did not fit into the picture, "according to which the dictatorships of the world want to change the world through brutal force." Thus in Strauß's, as in Schulz-Köhn's logic, jazz came to symbolize the new pluralist society espoused increasingly by West German politicians in the second half of the 1950s.[78]

Strauß's views were widely reported and received with some astonishment. Most baffled was perhaps Berendt himself. In a response, Berendt reiterated that jazz and the military were incompatible. He suggested that Strauß had merely made a shrewd move, and that officers of the West German army, the *Bundeswehr*, would let him talk, but would be careful to enforce their own vision of discipline in the army. Clearly unsure how to assess the situation, he assured his readers that an army band, if it played jazz, could not be a real military band.[79] If Berendt had doubts about West German officials' commitment to jazz, they were not unfounded. When he and his friends established contacts with Polish jazz fans and decided to attend a Polish festival with two jazz bands, the West German Foreign Ministry refused to give any support, for fear of "political difficulties."[80] In his 1958 book, Berendt emphasized again that resistance was characteristic of jazz.[81] Berendt's intentions of constructing a respectable, antiauthoritarian jazz audience certainly ran counter to Strauß's efforts. And yet Berendt's efforts in many ways had made it possible that ostensibly nonpolitical jazz could be put to political uses by the West German state.

In East Germany in the meantime, officials allowed concerts of traditional jazz, but tried to ensure that bands did not play too much Western music. Never again would they prohibit jazz altogether, but they watched closely when jazz fans tried to found formal groups. Official East German suspicions were further fostered by American and West German efforts to make the music into a messenger of liberal democracy and a Cold War weapon in the second half of the 1950s.

These efforts cut across party lines. By the late 1950s, the mayor of West Berlin and emerging national leader of the opposition Social Democrats, Willy Brandt, used the new image of jazz to portray himself as a modern and liberal politician. Brandt had himself photographed with Louis Armstrong by his side—with Armstrong eating German bratwurst.[82]

For East and West German officials, who were trying to make a break with the German past, jazz likely had some attraction because of it roots in African American culture, and perhaps also because many white American jazz musicians were Jewish, although that was not an explicit topic. However, tolerance had clear limits; jazz promoters claimed that jazz had transcended its African American origins. Jazz, in order to be acceptable had to be "deracialized" and even "whitened." Further, in debates over jazz both East and West Germany asserted visions of culture that rendered conservative gender mores and respectable Germanness interdependent. In both countries, jazz also needed to be "desexualized" before it could become respectable.

Nonetheless important differences emerged: On the defensive against Western imports, East German authorities were far more repressive. In this context, jazz fans and officials continued to see jazz as a potential vehicle for political resistance, a possibility that West Germans had successfully contained. Thus in the second half of the 1950s, the two Germanies embarked ever more clearly on separate, yet always related paths—in both the realm of politics and of culture.

5 Presley, Yes—Ulbricht, No?
Rock 'n' Roll and Female Sexuality in the German Cold War

When rock 'n' roll crossed the Atlantic to Germany in the second half of the 1950s, it brought not only rioting young men, but also young women into the public eye. In late 1956, a cartoon in the East Berlin daily, *Berliner Zeitung*, showed a small, emaciated Elvis Presley performing under larger-than-life female legs in front of a crowd of girls much bigger than he was. The girls were throwing off garter belts and bras and licking their thick lips in obvious sexual excitement. The accompanying article identified girls as the main consumers of American "nonculture" and commented that rock 'n' roll appealed to primitive humans. West Germans had similar worries: according to one commentator, female rock 'n' roll fans illustrated the dangerous "sexualization of the fifteen-year-olds."[1]

In a more feverish pitch, such statements employed a rhetoric that East and West German critics had earlier leveled against dances like the boogie and against jazz music. Both East and West German authorities, albeit in increasingly different ways, politicized the actions of female and male rock 'n' roll fans. Three interconnected concerns shaped East and West German reactions to rock 'n' roll: worries about uncontrolled female sexuality and male aggression and perceptions of racial difference. The public behavior of female rock 'n' roll fans at dances and concerts and in the streets challenged the traditional norms of female respectability that authorities in East and West Germany had made central to their respective reconstruction efforts.[2] Commentators worried that such women had a negative impact on young men, making them at once weak and overly aggressive. Thus worries about the actions of female rock 'n' roll fans were intimately linked to concerns about male rebelliousness. At the same time the uproar about rock 'n' roll was in marked contrast to the images of restrained and respectable jazz musicians and fans that East and West German jazz promoters and clubs drew with increasing success by the mid-1950s.

With the advent of rock 'n' roll, girl rebels attracted widespread attention as sexual beings. To be sure, some girls had been taking active part in the *Halbstarken* subcultures that had formed in many working-class neighborhoods in the mid-1950s and that caused much anxiety for East and West Germans. A few girls had joined street gangs in these neighborhoods. While girls undoubtedly had subordinate roles in gangs and riots, they were watched with some admiration by many female contemporaries. The East and West German press, however, had mostly ignored them, and officials had only on occasion referred to their alleged sexual allure, claiming that it encouraged male deviance. Perhaps because of their small numbers, girl members of youth subcultures found it more difficult than their male counterparts to gain public acknowledgment for their actions. This changed with rock 'n' roll.

Rock 'n' roll challenged East and West German constructions of national identity because Germans saw it as a black or black-influenced music that undermined gender norms. In their critiques of rock 'n' roll musicians and fans, commentators reaffirmed the links between consumption, sexuality, and femininity. Many attacks on musicians and fans also employed racial slurs and stereotypes, and it took Germans longer than Americans to see rock 'n' roll as "whitened" music.[3] Because of associations with blackness and unbridled sexuality, rock 'n' roll, like its predecessor jazz, represented a threat in postwar East and West Germany. At first, neither East nor West German officials considered the activities of rock 'n' roll fans harmless; authorities on both sides treated uncontrolled female sexuality as un-German and marked it as unacceptable by associating it with blackness. In the context of the continuing politicization of culture in the postwar period and of the renewed fears concerning consumer culture in the 1950s, many commentators in East and West perceived the behavior of rock 'n' roll fans as an outright youth rebellion. They regarded girls' involvement in rock 'n' roll culture and the connections of rock 'n' roll to black American culture as a threat with political implications worthy of the attention of politicians and youth policies.

However, the story of rock 'n' roll reception, like the story of jazz, is also the story of increasing divergence between the two German states. By the late 1950s, West German authorities were much less threatened by rock 'n' roll fans than their East German counterparts. West German social scientists, the entertainment industry, and officials successfully "tamed" the music, while East German officials openly persecuted rock 'n' roll fans.

Two quite different political and social systems consolidated their power in the second half of the 1950s, and they developed different strategies of containing rebellious youth—and each other. As the fights over rock 'n' roll once again show, issues of consumption were at the heart of the Cold War battle, a battle that now became ever more lopsided. This time, girls and femininity were at the heart of the struggle.

GERMAN REACTIONS TO ELVIS PRESLEY

When the West German weekly *Der Spiegel* ran a cover story on Elvis Presley in December 1956, it described his American fans as girls steeped in "orgiastic hysteria." According to *Der Spiegel*, the American music industry had pushed Presley after "the first symptoms of collective erotic eruptions" appeared, and the magazine even spoke of an "uprising of female teenagers."[4] In late 1956 and 1957, many more West German newspapers reported extensively on American female teenagers who were said to swarm around Presley wherever he showed up and who would even go so far as to tear his clothes off in ecstasy. The West German press thus made a clear connection between rock 'n' roll and white American female sexual "excesses."[5]

Just two months earlier, West German papers had evaluated rock quite differently, namely as instigating male rebellion. In September of 1956, *Der Spiegel* reported in an article on Presley's success that riots had occurred at American rock 'n' roll concerts; here *Der Spiegel* treated Presley's fans as overly aggressive male delinquents and supported these concerns with references to nonwhite cultures and worries about the effectiveness of state power. In racist terms, the magazine warned that American youths at Presley concerts were dancing by themselves "like haunted medicine men of a jungle tribe governed only by music—rock 'n' roll." The term "tribe" was not a German invention, rather *Der Spiegel* adopted it from American reporting and even used a direct quote from *Look* magazine, which had announced, "Going to a rock 'n' roll show is like attending the rites of some obscure tribe whose means of communication are incomprehensible. An adult can actually be frightened."[6] *Der Spiegel* illustrated its article with pictures of two young white men, one of them with a bare torso, the other with a ducktail plume. Both "dancing rock 'n' roll fanatics" were swinging arms and hips in a fashion distinctly different from the European ballroom dances, where the restrained man led his female partner. The article added a punch at the American occupation in Germany when it asserted that American papers reported news from the "rock 'n' roll front" with the same steadiness that German papers "reported violent acts committed by American soldiers in Germany."[7]

This press coverage resonated in both Germanies, where youth riots had shaken several cities since 1955. When *Blackboard Jungle* had brought Bill Haley's song "Rock Around the Clock" to Germany in December 1955—and had implied a connection between the song and the juvenile delinquency shown in the movie—some commentators in Germany, like their American counterparts, had begun to make rock 'n' roll into the culprit that instigated male misbehavior. These fears were exacerbated by the reports of riots after Presley concerts in the United States and violence after showings of the movie *Rock Around the Clock* in London and Oslo in the summer of 1956.[8]

However, in the fall of 1956, the attention German papers gave to Presley's American girl fans transformed the discourse on rock 'n' roll. Rock 'n' roll was now not so much about male overagression as it was about feminized men and overly aggressive women. Also, once German commentators recognized that girls were Presley's most active fans, they began to describe the threat of rock 'n' roll in openly sexual terms. This shift went hand-in-hand with an effort to question Presley's masculinity.

As in the United States, gender ambiguity was one of Presley's outstanding characteristics for German promoters and opponents.[9] The music industry and press commentary worked together to effectively feminize him. In 1956, Presley's American label RCA/Victor decided to market Presley in Germany with the slogan "He walks like Marilyn Monroe but at home he is a model son."[10] Employing a double strategy, the company sought to make Presley outrageous by associating him with the hip-swinging Monroe in public performances, while portraying him as tame and even dutiful in his private life. West and East German papers picked up on press releases from RCA and Presley's West German record company Teldec, which marketed no fewer than thirteen Presley singles under the RCA label in late 1956.[11] However, the German commentators played with RCA's slogan to further underline Presley's outrageous gender ambiguity and not surprisingly, they dropped the line on the "private" model son altogether. An article in a West Berlin paper, for example, announced that Presley was "wiggling his hips like a Marilyn Monroe in men's pants."[12] In another variation on RCA's slogan, an East German commentator quipped that Presley was trying to "compensate for his vocal shortcomings by wildly swinging his hips like Marilyn Monroe."[13] The close association between Monroe, who along with French actresses like Marina Vlady and Brigitte Bardot had become a symbol of female sensuality in Germany, in fact made Presley into a rebel

Fig. 16. "From Dixieland to Kinseyland." Cover photo of Elvis Presley in the West German magazine *Der Spiegel*, December 12, 1956. Reprinted with permission from *Der Spiegel*.

quite different from a predecessor like Marlon Brando. In its cover story in December 1956, *Der Spiegel* reinforced the connection between Presley and open sexuality. The cover photo featured Elvis's lips in a sensual O and was titled "From Dixieland to Kinseyland," thus reminding readers of the worrisome sexual behaviors among Americans that Alfred Kinsey had found and that had been widely reported in West Germany. When describing Presley's concert performances, *Der Spiegel* doubted that Presley's moving hips were alluding to male sexual behavior and instead described his gestures as those of a "talented female striptease dancer."[14] That description had also been used by outraged American commentators, and along with the American expression "Elvis, the Pelvis," it was taken up by the German press.[15]

West German commentators harnessed alleged racial characteristics to criticize Presley and his fans, this time to support the notion of female aggression and male weakness. Some West German reports suggested that Presley's way of moving put not just his male gender, but indeed also his racial origins in doubt. One paper in the West suspected that Presley must have "black blood" in his ancestry if he was moving and singing in this extraordinary fashion.[16] Another article on Presley described rock 'n' roll as a music of "Negro bands" and an authentic emotional outburst "from the deepest rainforest."[17] In a third attack, one West German paper referred to Presley's thick lips as part of the ideal man in the United States. Drawing on a vision of overly strong American women that dated at least from the 1920s, the article also described the United States as a state run by women (*"Frauenstaat Amerika"*).[18] In this last instance, a reference to a stereotypical feature of African Americans, thick lips, was used to underline that in the United States gender norms were turned on their head. Importantly, gender and racial ambiguities on Presley's part elicited gender and racial transgressions on the part of his female fans. Unlike earlier writers who associated rock 'n' roll with male overaggression and blackness, commentators now turned against female aggressiveness; they reported that in the United States Presley's girl fans attacked policemen and exhibited active sexual desire toward this feminized man with "thick lips," which most Germans considered a feature characteristic of blacks. West German commentators conflated male weakness with blackness and linked both to female desire. These associations of blackness both with male overaggression and male weakness reaffirmed Western stereotypes of black men.[19]

East German officials, too, associated the public visibility of girls as consumers of rock 'n' roll with primitiveness and, implicitly, with blackness. The 1956 cartoon in the *Berliner Zeitung* that showed a small, thin Presley in front of a crowd of large girls clearly implied that rock 'n' roll turned gender roles on their head: American girls, who were throwing garterbelts, were sexual aggressors who emasculated men. Their hairstyles marked these girls as possibly black (short, curly dark hair) or white (blond ponytails), but in portraying all of them with stereotypical "Negroid" features (wide noses, thick lips), the cartoon labeled their behavior typically black. The accompanying article, a direct response to the "Dixieland to Kinsey-

Fig. 17. East German cartoon: "Presley and His Followers." Reprinted from *Berliner Zeitung,* December 13, 1956.

land" *Spiegel* story, also put this reversal of gender roles into a racial context: it claimed that girls were the main consumers of rock 'n' roll, described as American "nonculture," and asserted that the music appealed to primitive humans. Even as highlighting American racism was one way to fight the Cold War against the United States and West Germany, East German authorities could not relinquish their own association between female sexual passivity, "civilization," and "whiteness."[20]

Such German statements came at a time when American and German papers and promoters were reporting that Presley had taken rock 'n' roll "out of the category race or rhythm and blues music."[21] Some music promoters had tried to disassociate rock 'n' roll from blackness since the early 1950s, although African Americans were the inventors and performers of rock 'n' roll's "predecessor," rhythm and blues. Alan Freed, a white U.S. radio disk jockey who became famous playing rhythm and blues songs to a mixed-race audience, used the term rock 'n' roll in order to avoid the negative connotation of blackness that rhythm and blues carried for many whites.[22] Ultimately it was white performers, especially Bill Haley and Elvis Presley, who gave rock 'n' roll its broad popularity among white audiences, while they sang numerous songs by black musicians. American critics of rock 'n' roll first focused on the explicitly sexual lyrics ("leer-ics") of rhythm and blues or rock 'n' roll songs. Most of the songs that were marketed to whites featured edited lyrics, but in the mid-1950s many commentators continued to be concerned about the ways in which musicians and fans moved. One paper described Presley as a "Sexhibitionalist" whose obscene performances were designed to arouse the "libidos of little girls."[23] Also, American attacks on rock 'n' roll made frequent allusions to "jungle rhythms," thus linking the music to blackness in a negative fashion, no matter whether whites or blacks performed it.[24]

American rhetoric against rock thus shared many similarities with East and West German attacks. In all three, those who leveled racist attacks against rock 'n' roll were not necessarily in favor of racial segregation, yet they felt threatened by a music and dance styles that they identified as rooted in black culture. Allusions to gender upheaval and alleged racial transgressions reinforced one another to render rock dangerous. One difference between Germany and the United States was that East and West Germans focused more on American women as manipulators, thus drawing on a long tradition in German views of America, whereas U.S. reports mostly considered female rock fans as being manipulated.

EAST AND WEST GERMAN FEMALE ROCK 'N' ROLL "HYSTERICS"

Many West German commentators still hoped, in the spring of 1957, that the American "mass hysteria" around Elvis Presley was a uniquely American phenomenon and would not take hold of Germany. In spite of evidence to the contrary, they juxtaposed the "hysteric" behavior of American teenagers with the "more rational" reactions of German girls. Journalists thus praised German girls who, confronted with the movie *Love Me Tender*, allegedly urged Presley to get rid of his make-up.[25] One West German paper expressed relief that German women, unlike their American contemporaries, would not "melt" when they saw Elvis' wide, soft—and implicitly unmanly—face. German girls did not seem swayed by Presley's eyeliner and his uniquely American eroticism.[26]

However, as other reports indicate, East and West German girls, and boys, also liked rock 'n' roll. By 1956 sales of Presley records were going well, although German radio stations still refused to play the music. Several factors contributed to the success of rock 'n' roll in Germany: the negative reporting in the press, the music programs of AFN, BFN, and Radio Luxemburg that featured rock 'n' roll, the proliferation of juke boxes in soda fountains, and a series of rock 'n' roll movies starring Haley or Presley.[27]

Already in October 1956, a local Berlin newspaper reported that "rock 'n' roll reigned in the Hot-House," a West-Berlin club. As the paper pointed out, girls were the more accomplished rock dancers and preferred to buy their Coke themselves rather than have some guy step on their fashionable shoes. They would even turn their back on a clumsy young man and grab their girlfriend to "rock" on the dance floor! Rock 'n' roll provided for a dramatic loosening of the traditional dance styles where the man led as the woman followed. Consequently, one West German commentary in 1956 described rock 'n' roll dancers as "wild barbarians in ecstasy," and worried that their dancing "degenerated" into "vulgar and erotically expressive movements." Women and men threw each other through the air, and rock 'n' roll dancers often held each other just by the hand and were thus able to individually design their movements. This "open dancing" even made it possible that girls dance with each other in public. Therefore, the dynamic dance style associated with rock 'n' roll appeared to dramatically change gender codes, as girls, in ever greater numbers, forcefully asserted their independence and rejected the male control that older dance styles so effectively symbolized.[28]

This was not the first time that women threw their partners through the air—they had done so earlier when dancing the jitterbug or the boogie. However, the German, like the American, press reported much more extensively about rock 'n' roll than it had about earlier fads, and in spite of some references to earlier dance crazes, for example concerning the Charleston of the 1920s, press reports and promoters treated rock 'n' roll as something new.[29]

Many parents were rather shocked by the reports in the press and by the behavior of their daughters and sons; in response they often prohibited them from listening to rock 'n' roll on the home radio or on one of the newly acquired record players. At times they were more openly racist than published statements and, employing vocabulary from before 1945, rejected rock 'n' roll as "Negro" and even "nigger" music and/or as produced by Jews.[30] At least one outraged father read the label of his son's Fats Domino record and upon finding the name of the (African American) producer Dave Bartholomew exclaimed "Jewish! All made by Jews!"[31] Such open racism on the part of parents—which was no longer acceptable in East or West Germany—contributed to the sense among adolescents that they were engaging in something radical.

The West German youth magazine *Bravo* showed ambivalence toward the black origins of rock 'n' roll, perhaps once again trying to appeal to both adolescents and parents. When advertising the first German rock 'n'

Fig. 18.   Gender upheaval. A German rock 'n' roll girl wearing pants throws her male dance partner through the air, 1957. Courtesy Ullstein Bilderdienst.

Fig. 19.　Dancing rock 'n' roll fans made up in the new fashions, 1957. Courtesy Ullstein Bilderdienst.

roll dance championship, *Bravo* stressed that rock 'n' roll came into existence among "Negroes": "They played it hotter, more convincingly, and danced it better, more freely and more elegantly." *Bravo*'s message was contradictory: comparisons with "Negroes" certainly served to underline the outrageous character of the new musical style, yet some of *Bravo*'s comments valorized black styles exactly because they were outrageous. *Bravo*, after all, urged German boys and girls to try for themselves the dance styles developed by African Americans.[32]

The shocking fashions of female rock 'n' roll fans exacerbated fears in East and West. Their looks signified a loss of femininity to critical contemporaries.[33] A West German critique of an outspoken female Presley fan imagined her this way in 1958: "half-long pants, funny jacket, sauerkraut figure like a toilet brush."[34] Apparently the outraged author considered her to be too slender and with large breasts or a mop of hair. Others commented on the boyish looks of girls with ponytails.[35] In the East, too, young women sported jeans or tight pants and short sweaters, and female ideals were fashioned after Western models. In an East German youth magazine, a report on East German male delinquents featured girls with tight pants and short jackets prominently among boys.[36] East German commentaries on these fashions were often quite hostile: "Female creatures of this kind distinguish themselves from the male beings only in their hair, which is eaten regularly by rats, so that one ultimately doesn't know where these rodents wreak more damage, in or on the heads."[37] Wearing men's clothes in public had formerly been reserved for times of emergency, like the war and the immediate postwar period. With their new fashions, many East and West German girls now directly countered the images of female respectability available to them: the "clean" German woman with her hair in a bun and without makeup that the Nazis had promoted (and that West German cultural conservatives too considered an ideal), or the asexual East German worker/mother.[38]

Boys too encountered hostility for imitating Presley's hairstyle and way of moving. One West German adolescent remembers that he had grown his "Elvis curl" secretly for fear of his parents' reactions—when his father was not looking, the son would quickly shape the longer hair over his forehead into a curl. An East Berlin boy adopted the nickname "Elvis" and tried to copy his idol in both haircut and the way he moved his lips. Dress codes were established at times in East and West Germany. In West Berlin, for example, a school required girls to wear skirts to class, while East German schools prohibited jeans.[39]

In East and West, rock 'n' roll fans, with their behavior and looks, made the consumption of rock 'n' roll into a decidedly public event and thus brought up the bourgeois fears of male delinquency and female prostitution historically associated with the streets. Most worrisome to East and West German officials was that girls now did the same things as boys. Adolescents of both sexes danced during movie showings in West German cities. During screenings of the Presley movie *Love Me Tender*, for example, they stomped their feet rhythmically and let alarm clocks go off. Youths copied their moves from films such as *Rock Around the Clock* and *Love Me Tender*, and in some instances in East and West, they danced afterward in the streets. Much to the horror of their elders, they sometimes also rioted.[40] As one witness of a Munich street scene explained, girls, who were present in lower numbers, were much more conspicuous in their extravagant dress and casual behavior.[41] In West Germany, the "wild dancing" of rock 'n' roll, as boogie before it, was coded as working-class behavior, and commentators emphasized increasingly that "respectable" middle- and upper-class jazz fans rejected the "public displays" of boogie and rock 'n' roll dancing.[42] In East Germany, some state-run clubs where adolescents listened to rock 'n' roll and danced apart gained a bad reputation among the population. In 1957 one Karl-Marx-Stadt club was referred to alternately as "rock 'n' roll hall" or "youth brothel." Some parents refused to allow their daughters to frequent these clubs, while state officials took great pains to remedy the situation.[43]

As more and more female rock 'n' roll fans challenged the East and West German ideals of female (sexual) passivity after 1956, the East and West German press oscillated between ignoring them and raging against them. Thus East and West German papers did not report in 1958 about female rioters at a West Berlin Bill Haley concert, although some pictures in the press clearly identified boys *and* girls throwing chairs.[44] Some state officials considered the girls' actions to be insignificant: the district attorney in Hannover stopped a case against two girls who had been arrested during a riot, because they did not have "the consciousness" to support the crowd of male rioters.[45] At the other extreme, one West German paper mobilized the image of the male delinquent *Halbstarke* against female rock 'n' roll fans. In this incident, a West German girl who had supported Presley was criticized as a "typical female *Halbstarke*," with "an open mane, a face full of pimples, a purple loud mouth, and black eyeliner."[46]

In their most publicized challenges to dominant gender norms, girls had to rely on their role as potential girlfriends and wives. Publicly making Elvis Presley into a male ideal, girls in East and West indeed redefined norms of both masculinity and femininity. One female fan, for example, wrote a letter to the editor of a West German newspaper concerning a negative review of a Presley movie in which she accused the reviewer of being "a fat, old, nasty dwarf, a jealous dog, and an old sack."[47] Also in 1958, girls from a West Berlin fan club from the upper-class district of Wilmersdorf announced that Elvis had more success with girls than his critics.[48] East Berlin girls stated their support for Presley by wearing his name on the back of their jeans.[49] These girls went public with their sexual desire, asserted their right to choose their mates and, constructed Elvis into a "softer, understanding man." Thus they argued against the male machismo prevalent in the *Halbstarken* subcultures as well as against the image of the self-restrained, controlling man portrayed as ideal in East and West Germany, as both states were rearming in the mid-1950s.[50] The spreading of rebellious behavior from the working class to a wider circle of girls from middle- and upper-class neighborhoods certainly threatened ideologies that, in both Germanies, had sought to confine women's sexuality to the sphere of marriage and motherhood.

Fig. 20.   Fans at the Bill Haley concert in West Berlin, October 1958. The concert ended in a riot. Courtesy Ullstein Bilderdienst.

It was exactly this double resistance to bourgeois norms of male and female respectability and the transgression of racial boundaries that made rock 'n' roll an attractive dance style and Elvis an important figure for East and West German girls. In spite of, or perhaps because of, the negative reporting about American and German female rock 'n' roll fans, and in spite of the negative reactions of numerous parents, many German girls made it publicly known that they liked Elvis. In Germany, as in the United States, Presley's girl fans were part of his challenge to respectable masculinity; at the same time their association with blackness through Elvis and rock 'n' roll made their own challenges to norms of female respectability all the more radical. Adopting styles that carried connotations of blackness was a radical act for young women in the German context, where blacks, along with Jews, Gypsies, and Asians, had been portrayed as sexual aggressors under National Socialism and into the postwar years. Their actions challenged certain, state-supported norms and thus positioned them as "bad girls." Young women used that position in interesting ways; they asserted their youthful difference and attempted to recast dominant notions of masculinity and femininity, which were, as we have seen, at the heart of reconstruction in both states. Certainly, conservative reactions in East and West Germany left little doubt that rock 'n' roll fans posed a political threat to the established order.[51]

WEST GERMAN REPRESSION AND EAST GERMAN VACILLATIONS

Female sexual impropriety was a central signifier for the threats that rock 'n' roll posed in West Germany. Indeed, one West German newspaper article saw German girls' admiration for Presley at the root of male *Halbstarken* behavior. Commenting on tumultuous scenes in a Berlin movie theater after a showing of *Love Me Tender* in 1957, the reporter wondered whether *halbstarke* boys would perhaps behave differently, if *halbschwache* (semiweak) girls did not show such preference for guys like Presley.[52] In January 1957 the West German movie rating board (consisting of church and state officials and representatives of the movie industry) mandated cuts from the rock 'n' roll movie *Don't Knock the Rock* before it permitted showings to adolescents younger than sixteen; two scenes that showed "the loose and aggressive flirting of girls" had to be eliminated because the "materialist understanding of life" rampant among adolescents would otherwise be fostered.[53]

Rock 'n' roll became a symbol for the reversal of gender roles at the very time that West Germans were discussing women's social role in the context of a new family law. This law was to legislate spousal property and parental rights. In the discussions, all West German parties affirmed the notion that woman's place was in the home. A cartoon "How to Dance Rock 'n' Roll?" in the West Berlin *Blickpunkt*, the magazine of the semipublic Berlin association of youth organizations *Landesjugendring*, made a direct link between the equal rights debate and rock 'n' roll in December 1956. It showed a boy and a girl dressed in identical T-shirts and tight long pants. The boy was jumping up and kicking the girl right in her stomach. The caption read: "The woman has equal rights, treat her accordingly." In openly misogynist terms, this cartoon made the same arguments that the West German opponents of equal rights were making precisely at this moment. Equal rights for women, like the fashions and individually designed movements of rock 'n' roll dancers (which erased gender differences) would mean a loss of the male protection that was at the center of the reconstructed gender system in West Germany. Although such references to

Die Frau ist gleichberechtigt, behandeln
Sie sie danach!

Fig. 21.
Cartoon "How to
Dance Rock 'n' Roll,"
from a West German
youth magazine. The
caption reads: "The
woman has equal
rights, treat her
accordingly."
Reprinted from
Landesjugendring
Berlin *Blickpunkt*,
no. 59, December
1956; artist unknown.

explicitly political debates became increasingly rare, traditional gender norms remained—relatively unchanged—at the center of mainstream West German reactions to rock 'n' roll.[54]

After the West German parliament had passed a stricter youth protection law in 1957, one member from the CDU/CSU faction, Elisabeth Pitz-Savelsberg, demanded that the new measures be applied to rock 'n' roll. Pitz-Savelsberg had been instrumental in getting the new stricter law through parliament. The new Law for the Protection of Youth in Public raised from sixteen to eighteen the age up to which leisure time activities for youth in bars, dance halls, casinos, and movie theaters were to be regulated. In a 1958 article directed at youth officials in state bureaucracies and private organizations, she described the dangers that the recent West German Bill Haley concerts had revealed. "With his sinister power" and "through his rhythms," Haley had "dissolved all restraint among his audience." Pitz-Savelsberg announced that "rock 'n' roll orgies with Bill Haley or Elvis Presley" belonged into the category of public places that posed dangers to the youth and that the law therefore regulated. She worried about an "overeroticized general atmosphere" and urged that the state be stricter in its youth protection efforts in the public sphere, thus shaping this arena, which was beyond the reach of parents, and aiding them in their education efforts. Authorities and communities were not fulfilling their task to watch out for the common good when they allowed rock 'n' roll "orgies." Instead Pitz-Savelsberg urged that public institutions and companies work together to ensure "cleanliness."[55] Although Pitz-Savelsberg retained the notion of "cleanliness," she omitted terms that had been important in earlier rejections of consumer culture, such as "degenerate" or "primitive," from her attack on rock 'n' roll.

West Germans found themselves particularly on the defensive, when, in 1956 and 1957, some East German voices suggested that American-influenced fashions and styles could be part of the resistance against capitalist regimes and against West German military service. Even during the period of greater flexibility after the Twentieth Party Congress of the Soviet Communist Party, such opinions were hotly contested in East Germany, and as the East German party elite reasserted its authority, any leniency was quickly replaced by the earlier stance that American popular culture posed a consistent threat to socialism. After a brief phase of relaxation, East German authorities reverted to the notion that American commercial music was decadent; rock 'n' roll was a targeted object of their scorn.

East German officials appealed to a petit-bourgeois morality and used the Cold War even more forcefully than their West German counterparts to contain images and behavior perceived as public displays of female sexuality with feminizing effects on men. For example, in 1957 an East German official manual on how the East German soldier was to think and behave made it very clear that knowing how to dance properly and how to resist Western ideology was crucial. The manual also accused the West German government and industrialists, both of whom were labeled fascists, of trying to seduce male West German adolescents with boogie-woogie, rock 'n' roll, pornography, and the busts of female movie stars into the army and into aggression against East Germany and its allies. The manual expressed confidence that, in the long run, East German adolescents would be resilient against these attempts. Nonetheless it reiterated the theme important to both West and East German attacks on American popular culture: the consumption of American culture was connected to female sexual expressiveness, male hyperaggression, and fascist behavior and was therefore incompatible with respectable German femininity and masculinity.[56]

On their own territory, East German officials took an array of measures to curtail the impact of Western influences and specifically of rock 'n' roll. In August 1957 one Culture Ministry official explicitly ordered the state concert agency to prevent the spread of rock 'n' roll because the music and dancing represented a "degeneration" inherent in the American way of life.[57] Also in 1957 the Berlin Haus der Volkskunst offered courses for delegates from all Berlin firms to learn how to distinguish between good and bad dancing and to successfully sponsor dances, so that they would not have to blame the West-Berlin *Halbstarkenproblem* for their failures. That same year Alfred Kurella, the head of the new Culture Commission of the Politbureau and a strong supporter of SED chief Walter Ulbricht, suggested at the SED Culture Conference that more attention be paid to the music and dances of other socialist countries. Boogie and rock 'n' roll would "pale in comparison to the rhythmic and melodic fire of Tadshik, Kasach, or other dances."[58] Some clubs and bars put up signs: "No jeans allowed" or "Dancing apart prohibited."[59] The following year, a new law, the so-called 60:40 clause, ordered that only 40 percent of any public music program, be it on the radio, in juke boxes, or at dance events, could consist of imports from the West. Certification procedures for bands were to insure that they played proper music (preferably no American imports) in a proper fashion (without stressing "hot" rhythms). At a meeting with state officials, however, band leaders made clear that it would be difficult to follow such orders, since audiences demanded Western hits.[60]

Enforcing measures against the spread of rock 'n' roll proved to be difficult. Many of the youth clubs run by the state youth organization continued to tap Western radio stations or used bands and tapes to play almost exclusively Western music. In many cases, sometimes only in the fifteen minutes before closing, visitors were still able to put in a round of "open dancing" that so fundamentally appeared to change gender roles. On the local level, the FDJ indeed advertised its program as distinctly different from "Sunday schools and ballroom dancing." Many East Germans experienced the FDJ dances as quite a contrast to the stiff atmosphere elsewhere, especially in church leisure time offerings.[61]

To counter these problems, officials, after 1958, promoted their own fashion dance, the Lipsi. The dance was a compromise. Its name with the ending "i" had a modern, American ring, and couples danced it to a faster rhythm, but they avoided any of the dangerous "openness" of dancing apart. In spite of enormous propaganda efforts, conducted by the Ministry of Culture, the FDJ, the Association of German Composers and Musicologists (VdK), and the GDR radio stations, the dance had only limited appeal. Instructional movies, public dances, and band contests for the Lipsi failed to convince East Germans to dance to their own, new German dance music that officials had searched for since the early 1950s.[62]

TAMING ROCK 'N' ROLL IN WEST GERMANY

Increasingly both the repressive East German stance and West German conservative attacks on rock 'n' roll diverged from a more lenient West German perspective. In West Germany, attitudes toward rock 'n' roll began to change as Cold War liberal intellectuals, politicians, and the entertainment industry "cooperated" to claim style as a nonpolitical category. After 1957 rock 'n' roll spread in West Germany from working-class adolescents to middle- and upper-class youths.[63] The shift of the working-class styles associated with rock 'n' roll to the middle and upper classes included a transformation—and taming—of these styles. Concurrently the rhetoric against rock 'n' roll in West Germany became milder. Given East and West German authorities' preoccupation with the gender and racial ambiguities imported with rock 'n' roll, the taming of the "threat" of rock 'n' roll in West Germany rested on undermining the racial and gender transgressions in youth styles. As a result, race was effaced from discussions of adolescent behavior.

Liberal critiques of rock 'n' roll relied on psychological explanations to account for the attraction of rock 'n' roll across classes and saw the institution of proper gender roles as a solution to the youth rebellion. As we have seen, psychologist Curt Bondy concluded in his team's study of the *Halbstarkenproblem* that American popular culture could be a part of a normal, rebellious, but nonpolitical life stage for male adolescents, and he interpreted rock 'n' roll in these same terms. Thus he rejected the notion that rock 'n' roll was in fact responsible for the recent youth riots. Rather—at least for boys—the two forms of behavior fulfilled the same needs for psychological and physical release. These findings echoed American commentators, who in assessing the Elvis Presley craze had found that "kids could release their energies while watching him, preventing them from releasing energy in activities that could be harmful."[64] In 1956 at least one German newspaper had already reported this line of argument, but had rejected the notion that rock 'n' roll rhythms helped adolescents gain psychological balance.[65] For Bondy, by contrast, rock 'n' roll consumption did fulfill an important psychological function. At the same time, in his analysis Bondy mostly ignored the female consumers of rock 'n' roll clearly present in his sources. Rather, women became the solution to the problem: Bondy concluded that most boys gave up rioting as soon as they had a steady girlfriend. This assessment was repeated in the West German press.[66]

West German liberals rarely reacted to challenges to gender norms with outright prohibition of cultural products. In contrast to the United States,

Great Britain, and East Germany, where local authorities explicitly prohibited rock 'n' roll concerts and movies, West German authorities avoided
such formal actions—in spite of calls by conservatives like Pitz-Savelsberg.[67]
Here repression was informal. West German state radio simply ignored the
music. The first U.S. rock musician to perform in Germany was Bill Haley
in 1958, and after the riots at his concerts, West Berlin mayor Willy Brandt
announced that such incidents were "embarrassing." Other West Berlin
officials vowed not to allow further rock concerts but announced that they
could not formally ban them. Instead this was accomplished simply by creating prohibitive insurance rates for such events.[68] Discussions in the West
German press after Haley's concerts were notable for affirming the success
of jazz. Time and time again, jazz promoters voiced their contention that
rock was not jazz and that jazz fans did not riot.[69] The riots certainly caused
a stir and even outrage among conservative commentators, but the more
numerous liberal voices saw no fascist or communist threat or any political threat at all.[70]

West German Cold War liberals rendered both riots and rock 'n' roll
into mere cultural styles, which were ultimately nonthreatening, and could
be resolved "privately." Psychologist Klaus Eyferth, a member of Bondy's
team, announced after the Haley riots that they were "attacks against no
one," and simply a wild romping comparable to Karnival. Along similar
lines, a 1958 commentary on Elvis Presley in a West German paper rejected
the notion that his gender ambiguity had any political implications. It described him as "rock 'n' roll idol" for some and as a "singing acrobat of un-
defined gender" for others. The commentary argued what the West German entertainment industry and liberals were promoting: how one
behaved toward Elvis remained "a private matter."[71]

Nevertheless, West German Cold War liberal politicians and social scientists retained hostility toward cultural styles associated with unrespectable
lower-class behavior and specifically toward American popular culture. Yet
these hostilities were not incompatible with their efforts to render youth
cultures nonpolitical and to celebrate a consumption-oriented West German
society. Importantly, reinscribing gender difference was central also to liberal efforts and appeared to resolve the apparent threats posed by youth cultures. While avoiding open prohibition, liberals continued to negatively
portray styles like rock 'n' roll. In the second half of the 1950s, the West
Berlin SPD-run government, for example, continued to promote ballroom
dancing lessons especially in working-class neighborhoods.[72]

The implications of such cultural visions became clear in a 1958 state-
funded film produced specifically for schools and youth groups. *Why Are*

Fig. 22.   "Proper" dancing lessons sponsored by the West Berlin government, 1957. Courtesy Landesbildstelle Berlin.

They Against Us? made use of the new respectability of jazz and modern art in addressing problems of male and female rebelliousness. The movie associated the bad, promiscuous girl (who wore a low neckline) directly with rock 'n' roll. The working-class male hero rejected the "bad" girl, who danced rock 'n' roll in the local soda fountain and who "came on" to boys, for a "good, restrained" middle-class girl who went to museums and jazz concerts (which had recently achieved the status of high culture). The movie was critical of the middle-class father's prejudices against the working-class boy, but as part of legitimizing this critique, the movie makers portrayed "working-class" cultural practices, "public" women, and the consumption of popular culture in very negative terms. The working-class boy, the movie suggested, could raise his status by adopting a bourgeois style of consumption. Thus the classless society that people like Erhard and Schelsky were proclaiming rested to a degree on gender conservatism and bour-

geois values. As in West German social science discourse, youthful rebelliousness in this movie had become a private problem with a private solution—a private solution, however, that needed to be promoted with state
funds.[73]

As rock 'n' roll continued to spread in spite, or because, of these state efforts, the fashion industry and the youth magazine *Bravo*, like their American counterparts, worked to transform the styles that posed challenges to
gender norms.[74] At the same time, the black origins of rock 'n' roll were increasingly effaced from the West German discourses on youth cultures.
Deracialization and sexual containment went hand in hand. For one, Elvis's
induction into the army in 1958 resolved his gender ambiguity. German,
like American, papers adopted a stance toward Elvis that his American
manager Colonel Tom Parker consciously fostered: press releases, photo
opportunities, and interviews showed Presley as a sincere young man serv-
ing his country. *Bravo* celebrated his new respectable appearance with
short hair and no sideburns. When Presley was stationed in West Germany, other commentators soon referred to him as a "tame," yet now
properly masculine, member of the occupying forces. In Germany, as in the
United States, Presley reached a new level of respectability in 1958.[75] Further, West German reviews of *King Creole*, released that same year in Germany, did not even mention that large parts of the movie were set in a
black nightclub.[76] In renditions of Presley's success story, his rise from a
truck driver to millionaire became central, while references to the black
origins of his music all but disappeared. Presley therefore was "whitened"
and masculinized, as his story became compatible with the West German
"economic miracle mentality." While effacing race from discussions signified the greater acceptability of rock 'n' roll, it precluded the acceptance of
African American culture in West Germany.

An increasing focus on a heterosocial realm with clearly defined gender
roles for adolescents appeared to successfully tame the radicalism of the
youth rebellion. The German distributors of Presley's movies and music
consciously exploited and reinforced his attraction for girls, while making
sure that he did not appear overly lacking in respectability. The fact that
Presley was stationed in Germany certainly helped. In 1958, for example,
Starrevue (a 1950s West German *People Magazine* and strong promoter of
Presley since 1956) together with the West German distributor of Presley
movies and Presley's West German label ran a contest for "tea at Elvis's
house." In April 1959 three happy female winners and a female *Starrevue*
reporter had Pepsi with Elvis, in jacket and tie and without sideburns, but
with a carnation in his lapel, at his mansion in Bad Nauheim. The West

German press more generally employed this strategy of showing Elvis as responsible on duty and more casual and admired by girls off duty.[77]

These rock 'n' roll fans were portrayed as typical German "teenagers." This American term had first been used to describe American female Presley fans, but from 1957 onward, "teenagers" increasingly became a label for German girls across classes. For many young German women, the "teenager" carried a much more modern image of femininity, which included greater openness in sexual matters. With her connection to female adolescent consumption, the teenager ran counter to the traditional image of the woman who exerted self-restraint in matters of consumption and sexuality. Initially used as a criticism, but quickly turned into a marketing tool, it carried less rebellious connotations than the term *"Halbstarke."*[78]

In 1958 the West German youth magazine *Bravo* ran the following advertisement: "Moscow—and politics—have lost Ninotscka forever. Silk stockings may be thin, but in the end and above all, they are more attractive than the best of political convictions."[79] This slogan put female fashion at the heart of the "end of ideologies" and suggested West Germany's superiority in the Cold War battle. Like Cold War liberals, the West German fashion industry and some cultural commentators sought to divorce cultural expression from the political realm. The explicit references to the Soviet Union, however, reveal this ostensible depoliticization as a new form of politicization, which pitted West Germany's reconstruction as a liberal haven of consumption against the "politics" of consumer deprivation in the East.

The editors of the youth magazine *Bravo* combined propagating an end of ideology with a rejection of "race hatred." In 1959, for example, teenager advice columnist Steffi rejected the time "of different colored shirts," that is, of street fights by Communist and National Socialist youths in the Weimar Republic. Like many other articles in *Bravo* that reported the commitment of black and white American stars to desegregation, she also turned against "race hatred." What was unusual about the Steffi column, was that she salvaged explicit political meaning for the youth culture. She defined politics as speaking out about freedom and war and claimed that their "bluejeans" prevented "teenagers" of both sexes from violence against people with different political convictions. Not unlike sociologist Schelsky, she concluded that adolescents were in fact less swayed by intolerant ideologies than their predecessors.[80]

In West German rhetoric, the term "teenager" underwent another shift in meaning: by 1959 it could include young men and women, and it now connoted generational difference rather than conflict.[81] This shift was certainly fostered by the systematic marketing of Peter Kraus and Conny Froboess as teenager ideals. Initially, Kraus was sold as the "German Elvis." However, racial ambiguity was not part of his image, and nobody referred to Kraus's thick lips (which he did have). Although Kraus, too, encountered "hysteric teenagers," he was mostly portrayed as a nice German boy, much "more likable in voice and behavior" than the American original. His German covers of American hits were indeed quite tame: Presley's "Jailhouse Rock" became Kraus's *"Hafenrock,"* "Harbor rock."[82] When Kraus was joined by a female mate "Conny," his domestication was almost complete. "Conny and Peter" made movies together and were celebrated as West German rock 'n' roll stars and lively "teenagers."[83] The West German fashion industry used the popularity of "Conny and Peter" to market teenager fashions and claimed to direct the "not so complaisant" wishes of adolescents into "pleasant forms.'[84] "Conny sweaters" for girls as well as "Peter Kraus pulls" (vests) intended for boys stressed different cuts for girls and boys and thus tried to reinstate a larger measure of gender difference.

In the promotion of Froboess and Kraus, traditional gender roles were partially resurrected. Thus Froboess had to be protected from association with too much "sexiness." Froboess's manager/father mobilized the differences between *Halbstarke* and teenagers and criticized Kraus when he allegedly turned too "sexy": "That is something for *Halbstarke* and not for teenagers....If teenager music declines into sex, then [it will do so] without me."[85] On the one hand, the duo was part of a heterosocial teenage world where boys and girls together challenged older norms of respectable dancing or clothing, but on the other hand, they tried to steer away from open challenges to sexual mores.

Newer styles of rock 'n' roll dancing also stressed gender differences, developing from a "wild" style, in which men *and* women threw their partners through the air, to a tamed version in which the male partner hardly moved at all. In 1960 *Bravo* published directions for dancing rock 'n' roll as part of a series on ballroom dancing. The man depicted in the picture, a German singer of sappy songs, Rex Gildo, wore a dark suit and guided Conny Froboess, dressed in a petticoat skirt, while avoiding any excessive movements himself. This style of rock 'n' roll could be safely danced at the private house parties that became the fashion among middle-class youth. Employing the English word "party," Conny and Peter had called for such events in their songs and movies, and German parents and teenagers alike learned to use the same term. The new rock 'n' roll dancing effectively symbolized the ideal female teenager as the acolyte of the controlled and

Fig. 23.   The West German answer to Elvis Presley? "Teenager stars" Conny Froboess and Peter Kraus in a still from the movie *Wenn die Conny mit dem Peter*—"When Conny and Peter," 1958. Courtesy Stiftung Deutsche Kinemathek.

controlling man, avoided allusions to black culture, and made rock 'n' roll compatible with a bourgeois gender system.[86]

Presley's American promoters, consciously trying to attract an older audience, similarly fostered a more respectable image. Upon his release from the army in 1960, Presley no longer performed in live concerts, which had made him so notorious. His first American television appearance after the army was on a Frank Sinatra special where Sinatra—who had attacked Presley's style in the 1950s—and Presley sang each other's songs, culminating in a duet. Presley wore a tuxedo and hardly moved while singing.[87]

While the subversive gender, racial, and class implications of rock 'n' roll consumption lessened, the greater acceptance of rock 'n' roll and sexuality as "private" expressions constituted a widening of options for West German adolescents, especially young women. The tastes of German adolescents changed over the course of the second half of the 1950s. In 1955, before the arrival of rock 'n' roll, only 5 percent of adolescents professed a preference for boogie or jitterbug, but by 1960 almost a third liked American dances. The attempts to tame rock 'n' roll had only limited success. Many young Germans perceived the German rock 'n' roll songs as soft imitations and preferred the American originals, which often were versions whose lyrics and rhythms had already been tamed for a white audience. And fashion makers were hardly able or willing to prevent girls from wearing Peter Kraus vests along with James Dean jackets. Finally, even with their tamed German version of rock, Froboess and Kraus introduced American words such as "baby," "sexy," and "love" into the German vocabulary.[88]

The effect of these developments was contradictory. On the one hand they made public visibility an option for girls across classes. On the other they tamed female behavior that was based on transgressing racial and gender lines. Women were allowed to become visible primarily as potential girlfriends and wives of men. Whereas psychological discourse on male *Halbstarke* suggested that men underwent a normal and rebellious lifestage, girls' participation in consumer culture and their greater "sexiness" was part of their preparation to become the tamers of these young men. For young women, being raucous at rock 'n' roll concerts or taking part in gangs was not considered a normal part of growing up. Female stylishness and even "sexiness" did become acceptable in West Germany, but female rebelliousness did not.

CRACKING DOWN ON ROCK FANS IN EAST GERMANY

In the meantime in 1958 and 1959, East German officials stepped up their propaganda and actions against rock 'n' roll. They considered rock 'n' roll to be such a threat that in 1958 party leader Ulbricht publicly indicted "its noise" as an "expression of impetuosity" reflecting the "anarchism of capitalist society." East German defense minister Willi Stoph supplemented this with warnings echoed in many papers that "rock 'n' roll was a means of seduction to make the youth ripe for atomic war."[89]

In the aftermath of the Haley concert, an organization of artists and intellectuals in East and West Berlin called a meeting in the eastern part of the city at which officials from the GDR Ministry of Culture, the state-owned concert agency, and the State Radio Committee, as well as composers, musicians, writers, scholars, and athletes, discussed and rejected rock 'n' roll. The meeting included West Berliners who also spoke out against rock. Although some East Germans were critical of East German failures to attract adolescents into state-run youth programs, the meeting had another purpose. As with press accounts, it was designed to appeal to conservative critics of American influences and thus to reinforce a consensus on the dangers of rock 'n' roll in East and West. Such a "consensus," however, was increasingly losing its power.[90]

The intensifying East German attacks on rock 'n' roll, in which both Bill Haley and Elvis Presley featured prominently, were part of efforts by East German authorities to accelerate their country's socialist development. They were also part of Ulbricht's ongoing efforts to consolidate his power. In July 1958 the Fifth Party Congress of the SED opened with the slogan: "Socialism wins." Party leaders declared that the GDR had reached a new stage in the development toward communism. They tried to cement this vision by issuing "Ten Principles of Socialist Ethics and Morality," which urged GDR citizens to work for "the international solidarity of the working class," to defend their fatherland, work for socialism, and show a socialist work discipline. The principles also asked citizens to raise their children "in the spirit of peace and socialism into educated humans with a strong character and a steeled body" and to live a clean life, respecting their families. "Private" matters, including family life, were to be subordinated to the goals of socialism.[91]

The main economic task for the GDR would be to demonstrate socialism's superiority over capitalism and to overtake the Federal Republic in per capita consumption by 1961. The party congress was followed in 1959 by a "Seven-Year Plan" designed to achieve and outdo Western production levels. At the same time, SED leaders and the East German press viciously attacked the 1959 Godesberg Programme of the West German SPD, among other things, for its "Erhardism," its "bourgeois ideology," and for its claims to "free consumer choice" at a time when West Germany would allegedly experience "consumer renunciation." The West may well have forced the competition over consumption onto the East German socialists, but it was able to do so because socialists had a commitment to the welfare of their people.[92]

With regard to cultural policy, the 1958 SED Party Congress made clear that its goal was the "construction of a socialist national culture" tied closely to the implementation of the economic goals and the emergence of a "new socialist human being." Other conferences were designed to reinforce this message. In January 1959 a dance music conference organized by the Ministry of Culture, the State Radio Committee, and the German Association of Composers had declared that "dance music was to aid in educating people in the socialist way." According to participants, entertainment was important, but Western hits should be rejected. In April 1959 at the First Bitterfeld Conference, party functionaries and writers urged workers to become active producers of culture. Writers and artists in turn were to have closer contact with the workers. One goal was to raise the general level of education and culture; another was to put the experiences of workers at the center of cultural production. Representations of the construction of the socialist human being, however, could only include conflicts between the individual and others if they were shown to be successfully resolved under socialism. The economic and cultural policies of 1958 and 1959 were a sign that Ulbricht and his supporters were consolidating their hold on power in the aftermath of the quashed uprisings in Hungary and Poland. By the late 1950s they were clearly implementing an *Erziehungsdiktatur,* an educational dictatorship.[93]

These developments coincided with renewed tensions in the Cold War battles between East and West Germany and the Soviet Union and the United States. In 1957 the Bonn government demanded nuclear weapons for West German forces under NATO control. East Germany in the meantime was fortifying its western border. In November 1958 Khruschev issued an ultimatum regarding the future status of Berlin, threatening to cut Western access to the Western part of the city. This second Berlin crisis, during which the Western allies made it increasingly clear that they were not willing to give up West Berlin, lasted until the construction of the Berlin Wall in August 1961.[94]

East German attacks on rock 'n' roll music and fans were part of the mission to consolidate socialism and to expose the evil powers of the Cold War enemies—West Germany and the United States. East German leaders found the issue important enough for high-ranking party officials to participate in the attacks. As Ulbricht put it at Bitterfeld, it was "not enough to reject the capitalist decadence with words, to fight against pulp fiction and petit bourgeois habits, to speak out against 'hot music' and the ecstatic 'singing' of someone like Presley. We have to offer something better."[95] The efforts to provide something better spawned research, publications, and even public events. Their purpose was, however, limited to criticizing Western hits, providing dance lessons, and promoting the Lipsi. Local East

German officials, emboldened by the words of their leadership, in turn took stricter action against East German rock 'n' roll fans.

In 1959 groups of adolescents in several East German cities gave their admiration of rock 'n' roll and Elvis Presley an explicitly political twist. In two Leipzig suburbs, for example, groups gathered in the streets shouting "We want no Lipsi and we want no Ado [sic] Koll, instead we want Elvis Presley and his rock 'n' roll." (Alo Koll was a Leipzig bandleader heavily promoted by authorities.) Then they apparently marched downtown expressing their disdain for the East German leadership. One of them shouted "Long live Walter Ulbricht and the Eastern Zone [East Germany]"; the chorus answered *"Pfui, Pfui, Pfui"* (the equivalent of booing). This was followed by "Long live Elvis Presley"; this time the crowd responded with an enthusiastic "Yes, Yes, Yes."[96]

The Leipzig demonstration was no isolated incident. In late November 1959, a similar demonstration took place in Dresden. According to a police report, about eighty adolescents roamed city streets shouting "We want our old Kaiser Wilhelm, we want no Pieck, Grotewohl, and Ulbricht. We want rock 'n' roll."[97] In other cities, adolescents followed such statements with warnings that "a new June 17"—referring to the June 1953 uprising in East Germany—was about to happen. By late 1959 reports on juvenile delinquency recorded the formation of groups of "Presley-admirers" in at least thirteen East German cities and towns.[98]

In the atmosphere of attacks against rock 'n' roll that had sharpened since 1958, local officials took strict action against fans who voiced their preferences for the music publicly. Officials were not ready to accept either demands for Elvis or attacks on Ulbricht. It is not entirely clear whether the public expressions in favor of rock 'n' roll really increased in 1959, or whether GDR authorities just paid more attention, but probably adolescents were driven to more public statements in favor of rock 'n' roll by the 60:40 clause, the public attacks officials made against the music, and the propaganda to promote the Lipsi.

Another development that may have incensed adolescents was the formation of security groups in FDJ clubs. The Sixth Parliament of the FDJ had just approved the formation of *Ordnungsgruppen*—security groups—in May 1959; these groups, comprising reliable FDJ members older than sixteen, were to enforce order during events in the state-run youth clubs and "to extinguish the remainders of the capitalist way of life among adolescents, including rowdies, drinking, obnoxious behavior toward their elders, reading smut, etc." The function of these security groups was similar to Hitler Youth patrols during the Third Reich. They were to ensure that

Fig. 24.   Lacking Respectability: East German caricature of rock 'n' roll dancers, 1959. Reprinted from *Junge Generation* 13, no. 4, February 1959.

adolescents danced properly and not apart, that the correct music was played, and that the clubs did not tap into Western radio stations. Local officials indeed banned rock 'n' roll dancers from club premises.[99]

In the summer and fall of 1959, the police and courts cracked down on adolescent rock 'n' roll fans with arrests and convictions. The psychological interpretation that saw male adolescent rebelliousness as a sign of normal development was rejected by East German authorities. In this context, rock 'n' roll fans remained a threat to the gender and political order under socialism. The district court in Leipzig alone convicted fifteen demonstrators to jail sentences of six months to four and a half years.[100] Fifteen of the eighty participants in the Dresden demonstration were put in jail.[101] Likewise in the fall of 1959, the Gera police arrested two members of a so-called Presley-Group, which apparently held meetings in apartments and allegedly distributed literature against the leading functionaries of the GDR and the Soviet Union.[102]

In Erfurt the police arrested ten male members of a gang whose idol was Elvis Presley; prosecutors initiated court proceedings against thirteen members for rapes, prostitution, and pimping. A police report claimed the group included forty-six young men and twenty-five young women from fifteen to twenty years old. Their leader was a young man of seventeen whom the others called Presley and who had spent time in West Berlin where he allegedly maintained contacts to West German *Halbstarke*. Some of the other members also had connections with West Germany. In 1958 and 1959, they had allegedly met in specific Erfurt streets and in the state youth club, smashed windows, caused small riots, grabbed the breasts of women and girls, and even committed rapes. When the apartments of some of the members were searched, the police claimed to have found pictures of "sex-bombs" (very sexy women) clipped from newspapers, 24 fascist texts, 12 pictures of Elvis Presley, 93 pictures and postcards from the West, 33 Western newspapers, 358 western and romance novels, and 45 nude photos.[103]

It was apparently after the events in Leipzig, Erfurt, and Gera that SED officials in the highest positions of authority paid increased attention to the issue of rowdies within the GDR. In mid-November 1959, the director of the Department of Security at the Central Committee of the SED, Walter Borning, sent a letter to Erich Honecker, who at the time was a member of the Secretariat of the Central Committee, probably the most powerful organ in the party structure. Borning claimed that the number of groups of organized rowdies who were committing acts of instigation, robberies, thefts, and other crimes had recently increased; he listed a number of examples ranging from attacks on members of police and party to the infractions of the Gera Presley-Group. Overall, Presley admirers made up only a small portion of Borning's letter.[104]

The Secretariat of the Central Committee of the SED was so concerned about such events that it gathered information on the scope of demonstrations and on juvenile delinquency more generally. A report submitted to the secretariat in December 1959, covered incidents ranging from rock 'n' roll protests to robberies to illegal trips to West Germany—such trips required special permission. The document echoed Borning in concluding that the number of reports according to which adolescents were forming gangs and committing crimes had indeed increased. Often these adolescents met in the state-run youth clubs. In at least thirteen East German cities and towns, "Presley admirers," aged sixteen to twenty-one, had formed gangs of fifteen to twenty, among them girls; these gangs combined demands for rock 'n' roll with "outrageous instigation" against GDR leaders. To add insult to injury, they were telling local FDJ leaders that, were rock 'n' roll permitted, they would participate in the activities of the organization. Even though the report listed many crimes where rock 'n' roll played no obvious role, including theft or sabotage, it concluded that "rock 'n' roll admirers" made up most of the juvenile delinquents.[105]

Girls appeared in the report in two roles: as instigators of rebelliousness and as victims. Thus the report noted with an exclamation mark that girls had been among the demonstrators across the GDR, and a group in Magdeburg was allegedly directed by a West German girl from Wiesbaden. At the same time, the report accused members of Presley groups of committing rapes.[106] These attempts to link rock 'n' roll and sexual transgressions had a longer tradition in East Germany. A 1957 East Berlin report on juvenile delinquency had likewise made the "rock 'n' roll atmosphere" caused by the United States responsible for rowdiness, the formation of cliques, rape, and "perverted behavior" in the East.[107] When East German officials attacked rock 'n' roll publicly, they drew heavily on the notion of female sexual impropriety, especially on the part of Western women, and linked it to male rebelliousness and political deviance. An East German flyer about the dangers of Western immorality featured a picture of The Boogie Club, a West Berlin dance hall. On both sides of the club entrance were large signs, each illustrated with a girl in capri pants and a tight T-shirt. East German officials portrayed such clubs as hotbeds of conspiracies to organize provocations in the East.[108]

The 1959 report for the secretariat concluded that the leaders and administrators of the FDJ were still reacting quite improperly in the face of Western influences and juvenile delinquency: they did not take the phenomenon seriously because it concerned a relatively small portion of the East German youth, nor did they recognize that it was through rowdies that the enemy was trying to denounce the socialist system. Cooperation between FDJ leadership and local institutions was also lacking.[109]

In response, the Secretariat of the Central Committee approved a number of measures. The formation of FDJ security groups was to be sped up and these groups were to enforce order during events in the state-run youth clubs. Party administrators were to examine all youth clubs, in order to find out what kinds of adolescents were frequenting them. Finally the secretariat recommended that other state institutions, including the police, the Interior Ministry, and the Ministry for People's Education, take measures to better detect and act upon rowdy behavior.[110]

Such measures were clearly geared toward rock 'n' roll fans, although the accusations about the prominence of these fans among juvenile delinquents were not born out by the incidents enumerated in the 1959 report. Of the infractions listed in the report, only a small percentage was committed by rock fans, and they did not commit the most serious crimes.[111] Rock 'n' roll fans also made up only a small portion of the delinquents listed in a second report about adolescent gangs that was compiled just a few days later. At the same time the accusations leveled against "Presley admirers" became sharper. The Gera Presley-Club mentioned by Borning in November was now said to be directed from West Berlin and to have committed assaults and rapes.[112] It seems that, contrary to evidence, SED leaders were convincing themselves of the evil sexual and political power of rock fans and of their manipulation by the West.

This conviction became apparent in two letters that Paul Verner drafted in December 1959. At the time Verner served as a member of the Secretariat of the Central Committee and head of its Department for West German Affairs. He was also a staunch Ulbricht supporter. In a letter to the party chief, Verner reiterated the measures to be taken and announced that the Central Council of the FDJ had already been informed. In a second letter, to the SED functionaries responsible for youth matters in all districts, Verner outlined these same measures. He also suggested that FDJ organizations in companies were to form groups with police that were to conduct patrols evenings and nights, thus ensuring safety and order in the cities. In both documents Verner described the formation of gangs as part of the psychological warfare of the Bonn government.[113]

Such pronouncements were fueled by a 1958 article in a French publication that appeared to confirm the worries of East German authorities. The periodical *General Military Review* (which, published in Paris, was close to NATO strategists) reprinted an excerpt on "psychological tension" from a book by French author Charles Montirian. The author propagated the idea that youthful Western popular music, transmitted by Western radio stations, was a more productive technique against the communist adversary than McCarthyism. Soviet leaders had recognized this and thus tried to ban such music. The "civilized countries" in turn should not reject their "means of seduction" that made it possible to maintain human contact with an enemy. "Every time a rock 'n' roll or a calypso impresses itself into a communist consciousness, it serves to eliminate something else and this something else will always be something ideological." American music, in other words, could bring about an end of ideologies east of the Iron Curtain.[114]

Some U.S. State Department officials apparently also believed in the power of rock 'n' roll. In 1958 they planned to sponsor a group of American disk jockeys who were to promote American popular music in Europe. When other disk jockeys and senators voiced complaints that such events would enable communists to set off riots and thus would tarnish the reputation of the United States, the State Department withdrew its support. Ultimately the department was mollified when the disk jockeys promised that no rock 'n' roll would be played and that their events would be restricted to U.S. military bases. Unlike jazz, rock 'n' roll was not a music the U.S. government was ready to promote in the late 1950s.[115]

While the SED leaders found some ammunition for the psychological warfare argument in the NATO-paper and also in the West German and American policies that were to expose East Germans to Western consumer culture, most of their claims about Western intentions required purposeful misreadings of the statements of West German leaders and of evidence they had collected about East German youth protests. Verner asserted that an investigation into recent examples of rowdy behavior had shown that many of the gangs were being directly or indirectly organized from West Berlin and West Germany. The reports on which Verner based his assertions revealed contacts with West Germany in the form of pulp fiction or photos of stars that East German adolescents had received, but the reports did not give evidence that the East German "Presley-admirers" were organized from the West. Nonetheless, Verner claimed to find proof for his assertions in a speech that the West German minister for inner German affairs, Ernst Lemmer (CDU), had given in West Berlin where he had urged German youth to stay alert in the face of the communist threat and the division of Germany.[116]

One aspect of psychological warfare, according to East German reports, was to drive West German adolescents into the Cold War battle. After the 1958 West Berlin Haley concert, the official FDJ newspaper, *Junge Welt*, claimed that West German defense minister Franz-Josef Strauß himself had ordered the rock 'n' roll concerts to make adolescents "soft"; in fact he had carefully timed the events to coincide with the draft deadline of the West German army. As evidence the paper marshaled Strauß's statements about jazz as a music for the West German army.[117] During the 1960 Culture Conference of the SED, Alfred Kurella mocked Strauß's statement about the "community building powers of jazz" and announced "one knew what sort of communities were formed during rock 'n' roll orgies," paying no heed to the fact that "orgies" was a term that West German conservative critics of rock 'n' roll had likewise employed. According to Kurella, such "killers" were allegedly needed for the war against the GDR for which the West German Bundeswehr was preparing.[118] Even as East Germany itself was rearming, East German authorities continued to link antimilitarism and allusions to improper sex to attack their West German enemies.

East German authorities also used these links to repress Americanized youth cultures within their own borders. They believed that Western psychological warfare was successful in East Germany. In May 1960 a report drafted for the Department for Youth Affairs of the Central Committee assessed the measures against juvenile delinquency. It found that in spite of numerous public forums with adolescents, parents, and educators, juvenile delinquency was 61.4 percent higher in 1959 than in 1950, despite an overall decline in crime. The reason was that the "West German imperialists and militarists over the previous years had increased their efforts to bring the youth of the GDR under their influence." They were making use of a range of "means of seduction" including music, pulp fiction, and fashions. Quoting the 1958 article in *General Military Review,* the report asserted that the West was exploiting the natural interests of adolescents for dancing and hits. The enemy had succeeded in penetrating all classes of adolescents, especially by means of Radio Luxemburg to which numerous East German adolescents were sending letters, thirty per day in the District of Halle alone. Further, the report described West German fan clubs for music and film stars, with which thousands of East German adolescents had contact via mail, as undercover organizations of Western agents. In a paranoid tone, the report was particularly concerned that enemy activities were not restricted to ideological manipulation, but were also designed "to establish firm organizational forms." Echoing a concern earlier reports on juvenile delinquency had raised, the report also worried about the influence of West German adolescents who had moved to the GDR. According to the report, almost five thousand West German adolescents had come for the first time or had returned to the GDR in 1959. "Not just a few" of them were allegedly spreading Western ideology and played an active role among rowdies and gangs; some were even working directly for the "class enemy." Officials employed this language to make clear that in East Germany the proper class had assumed power. It is of course ironic that East German officials were at the same time railing against styles that had first been adopted by working-class youth.[119]

In the eyes of the SED, the personal was clearly political. The fight against rowdies, Verner suggested, must not focus on simply breaking up

gangs with the help of state institutions, but instead required a strengthening of the ideological and political work among the youth. The party administration, urged Verner, had to grasp that the organization of rowdies
and gangs was "a form of class struggle of the West German imperialists
against the GDR." The party needed to create clarity "concerning the close
connection between personal life and social development" under GDR socialism.[120]

This vision of the personal as political justified measures that infringed
on the privacy of East German citizens. Youth magazines repeatedly urged
adolescents to wear the blue uniform shirts of the FDJ. Also, East German
authorities were tracking mail. According to the 1960 report, 160 to 200
letters from the District of Halle were going to clubs in West Germany
each day and about forty letters were moving the other way. Authorities
also attacked informal youth groups. In 1959 alone, the security groups,
police, and courts apparently disbanded 250 "gangs" with 2,200 members.
Allegedly, these gangs committed generally violent crimes, including attacks on functionaries, resistance against state authority, rapes, and brawls,
and their appearance in public disturbed order and safety. Characteristic of
all gangs was, the report claimed, their Western orientation, which manifested itself in gang names, in their clothing, in contacts to West Germany
and West Berlin, in the exchange of pulp fiction, in listening to Western radio stations in groups, in a cult of Western pop and movie stars, and in increasing contacts with Western agents.[121]

After a brief hiatus in 1956 and 1957, East German authorities made
drawing young people away from Western influences integral to the con-
solidation of socialism. In both the press and at conferences, East German
youth officials reported about cases of East German male youths for whom
shedding blue jeans and learning to dance properly was key to their con-
version to the socialist cause. In these statements it appeared that the attempts to persuade and educate adolescents through personal conversations and attractive youth programs were extraordinarily successful.[122]
Internal reports, however, found deficiencies in the socialist education and
in the fight against the "bourgeois ideology and way of life among seg-
ments of the youth": creators of fashion in the GDR did not yet fully appreciate that adolescents wanted to be dressed stylishly. Nor did the GDR
produce enough attractive hits or exploit the enthusiasm for jazz among
youth.[123] Despite their efforts, East German authorities were unable to
halt the spread of rock 'n' roll or even to ban it completely from state-run
youth clubs. As they continuously complained, East German adolescents
maintained connections with West German rock fans, still listened to

Western radio stations, especially AFN and Radio Luxemburg, and continued to visit West Berlin to buy jeans, go to the movies, or consume rock 'n'
roll. Some youth club administrators decided it was better to let adolescents dance apart than to lose them altogether.[124]

Time and time again the press and SED leaders turned explicitly against
the psychologizing and depoliticizing of music consumption in the West.
After the riots at the West Berlin Bill Haley concert in late October 1958,
an East Berlin paper announced on its front page that it was pure coincidence that Social Democrat West Berlin mayor Willy Brandt and the
Christian Democrat Ernst Lemmer were not at the event. One photo
showed a young man in jeans and zippered jacket, another Brandt and
Lemmer in suits. All three clapped and had their legs spread apart. As the
caption commented, Brandt and Lemmer usually showed their "connection to the people" at events similar to the rock concert with a posture similar to rock fans. Both their posture and their politics were *halbstark*. An
article in the same paper criticized Brandt for simply seeing the riot as an
"expression of the youthful drive for action."[125] In 1961 an instructional
leaflet sent by the Central Committee to all SED district offices repeated
these worries, revealing once again the degree to which party leaders at the
highest level were concerned about the political power of rock 'n' roll. The
authors rejected the Western notion that dance music helped adolescents
"to live out their needs freely"; instead, the music of Bill Haley educated
NATO soldiers without a conscience who followed orders willingly.[126]

The leaflet also attacked "teenager music," citing the lyrics of a West
Conny Froboess song, "Mister Music." These reiterated that youth culture
was at the center of the "end of ideologies": "Kids, would it be wonderful,
if in this world, all humans would understand one another and cooperate as
the youth does. For we happily leave behind politics; music connects us
near and far. Hey, Mister Music, play rock 'n' roll." The SED leaflet argued
that such music seduced adolescents to rise up against the older generation,
while ignoring the true causes of their dissatisfaction. Like many other
statements, it made rock consumption into a political issue. The publication
revealed the hollowness and repressiveness of East German policies. It rejected the argument, apparently made by some adolescents, that Western
dance music should be allowed in the GDR, since it was also broadcast by
the GDR radio station directed at West Germans. As the leaflet announced,
taping these broadcasts was not allowed in East Germany, because such
music was designed to attract West Germans but did not fit with the stage
of social development and the cultural revolution in the GDR.[127]

COLD WAR BATTLES

In West Germany the ostensible "depoliticization" of consumer culture generally and of teenager styles specifically was interrelated with the ongoing politicization of these phenomena in East Germany. Youthful expressiveness became in fact part of West German Cold War liberal identity. In marked contrast to the statements of East German leaders, the chief of staff of the West German army, Adolf Heusinger, announced in 1959 that rock 'n' roll and juvenile delinquency were different things and warned against condemning "all signs of youthful frolicking." Revealing some ambivalence toward rock 'n' roll, Heusinger explained that such "excesses" were largely the fault of grown-ups and not a problem within the West German army. Yet he welcomed "modern forms of social life appropriate for adolescents, including the enjoyment of modern art."[128] In the early 1950s, West Germans had exhibited a contradictory stance of being openly hostile toward American culture, while opting for Western integration; by 1959, West Germans mobilized American culture as part of that integration.

The distance between the attitudes of East and West German government officials was clear: the West German youth magazine *Twen*, which—with a jazz trumpet as its symbol—treated matters of premarital sex positively for boys *and* girls after 1959, was attacked, not by West German state authorities, but by the Catholic church and the SED.[129]

West German authorities treated style as a nonpolitical category, yet politicized that very step in the Cold War context. In 1959 West German papers, as well as the *New York Times*, registered with some disdain the convictions of outspoken Elvis Presley fans in East Germany. And in 1962 a review of an East German dictionary openly mocked the entry that considered rock 'n' roll a political threat.[130] West Germans now attacked East German repression on different grounds: East German authorities violated the private sphere, overreacted to matters of style, and therefore oppressed their own citizens. Properly tamed and contained, consumer culture had become a West German weapon in the Cold War battle.

Epilogue: Building Walls

The reconfiguration of culture and politics that emerged in West Germany in the second half of the 1950s has had indelible effects on the way the 1950s have been remembered. Although it is difficult to reconstruct exactly how *Halbstarke* or rock 'n' roll girls in the 1950s thought about their actions, it is unquestionable that their styles, often influenced by American cultural imports, were subversive, because they conflicted strongly with the gender mores and racial norms propagated by parents and state officials in East and West Germany. It is due largely to a liberal vision of politics that defined popular culture and female sexuality as non-political matters that the radicalism of the 1950s rebellion and specifically the voices of girls in it were lost. This has affected popular memory as well as scholarship on East and West Germany in the 1950s. In both cases, boys have usually been represented as expressing an understandable youthful drive for adventure against social conformity. Girls have often been rendered "harmless" teenagers in petticoat skirts confined within their rooms. Rather than interrogating how this conclusion came about, scholarship on the 1950s youth rebellion has followed the notion that the actions of young East and West German rebels, and especially of girls, consistently lacked political significance.

Ultimately, adolescents of the 1950s may have structured their own life stories accordingly. In the 1950s, West German adolescents likely did not worry whether their actions were political or not. Later, when they constructed their life stories, for example in oral histories, a narrow understanding of politics in West Germany may have prevented them from recognizing as political their informal and public resistance to the gender, racial, and sexual norms that in fact had been at the center of political reconstruction in both Germanies. *Halbstarke* or rock 'n' roll girls may not

206

have thought of their actions as political, but if we define as political all acts designed to effect larger social changes, they were indeed political.[1]

The memories of East German adolescents—and the meanings of their actions in a repressive regime—have been more complicated than those of West Germans. In a recent oral history, East Berliner Wolfgang Hille remembered his involvement in the case of a fellow student who had been expelled from his East Berlin high school in the late 1950s for wearing jeans. Hille saw the expulsion and his own involvement as justified, because "everyone knew that this was a political action." In another oral history, Dietmar Iser, who considers himself a former East Berlin *Halbstarker*, described his and his fellows' actions—which included wearing jeans and fighting with policemen—as nonpolitical.[2] For adolescents confronted with a regime that politicized their behavior so explicitly, this may have been a radical and strategic move. However, in a context where West German liberals increasingly succeeded in interpreting adolescent male rebelliousness as nonpolitical *and* normal, it is not surprising that Iser's view has been taken at face value. In the end, it has become the prevailing view; not only most East and West German *Halbstarke* of the 1950s, but also most scholars since have ignored the political significance of those cultural choices.

This epilogue provides an opportunity to do three things: to sum up how the conviction that young rebels were nonpolitical, which has so deeply shaped memories and assessments of 1950s adolescents, came about in West Germany in response to and in contrast to the politicization of youth in East Germany; to explore how the varying efforts of East and West Germans to come to terms with American-influenced youth cultures relate to another round of youth rebellions in the late 1960s; and to propose how this investigation of Cold War politics and American culture in a divided Germany can help conceive frameworks for a comparative history of the GDR and FRG.

DIVERGING PATHS INTO THE 1960S

In the first half of the 1950s, East German suggestions that West Germany was being overrun by American culture put West German authorities on the defensive, as West Germans juggled their three-fold battle against fascism, East Germany and communism, and American-style consumer culture. In this context officials and educators were deeply worried, for example, by the youth riots of 1955 and 1956. Like their East German counterparts, West German authorities, in this period, explicitly politicized consumption; both sides had linked rebellious youth and their admiration for American popular culture to dangerous transgressions of gender norms, to lower-class immorality, and to fascist threats. Moreover, both sides often used racial stereotypes in attacking any attraction to African American-influenced popular culture. As the West German political and intellectual climate changed, however, this curious consensus largely disintegrated.

By the end of the 1950s, West German Cold War liberals increasingly replaced the religiously inspired conservatives who had seen consumption as a terrible threat. These liberals widened the definitions of acceptable adolescent behavior and of acceptable American imports. Drawing on a liberal social science discourse, they considered adolescent rebelliousness to be a life stage and a nonpolitical phenomenon. In 1959, for example, one commentator called the youth rebellion of the previous years a "rebellion against the unknown."[3] Both male aggression and female sexual expressiveness became less threatening—as did the U.S. movies and music that critics had associated with adolescent misbehavior. Cold War liberals successfully countered East German attacks that had mobilized the ambivalence and even hostility toward America on both sides of the Iron Curtain.

As West German authorities ostensibly "depoliticized" consumption, they made it increasingly into a Cold War weapon, with help from their American allies. In the second half of the 1950s, programs to send parcels of Western consumer goods to East German adolescents (ostensibly from private senders) were part of these efforts, as were attempts to draw East Germans to the movie theaters in the central shopping district of West Berlin. West Germans, like Americans, increasingly equated consumption with democracy. In this climate, consumption in fact remained politicized, if on a different terrain. For the West German authorities of the 1960s, leisure and pleasure were not what would destroy the West; instead, enjoyed in good measure they would actually be a key weapon against the East—exposing economic inferiority and lack of democratic choice.

East German authorities, in the meantime, continued to politicize the consumption of American culture. When officials built the Berlin Wall in August of 1961, they sought to halt more than the drain of workers that was debilitating their economy. Just as importantly, they hoped to stop the influx of West European and especially American cultural products into East Germany with the "antifascist protection dam." In the weeks after building the wall, East German newspapers rejoiced that the much-maligned West Berlin border movie theaters, which had catered to East Berlin adolescents since they opened in the early 1950s, would finally have to close.

To defuse dissatisfaction among the East German population after the installation of the Wall and to draw East Germans to socialism, East German authorities resorted to the same "recipe" that they had employed after the June 1953 uprising and after Khruschev's attacks on Stalinism in 1956: they were somewhat more lenient in the arena of entertainment. Authorities in East Berlin ordered movie theaters to provide "especially interesting" programs and urged restaurants and party organizations to offer more dance events.[4]

Newspapers were full of stories about adolescents who, finally protected from the cultural imperialism of the United States and West Germany, were converting to the socialist cause. The press and youth officials focused heavily on transforming the boys and girls who had frequented bars and dance halls in West Berlin. Some concessions to faster rhythms were necessary, yet East German officials did not endorse rock 'n' roll. Within a week of the Wall's being erected, the East German press reported that state-run youth clubs had turned boys in blue jeans into respectable young men wearing suits and dancing with girls in fashionable dresses. An internal report, however, revealed that these former *Grenzgänger*—transgressors of the border—were people who had transgressed more than the border between sectors in Berlin. According to the report they were young men and women hostile toward the state, who continued to cause riots and "striptease scenes" in some East Berlin youth clubs. Clearly, East German authorities perceived these sexual transgressions as political expressions directed against their state.[5]

Since there were no longer any escape routes for East Germans to the West, the space to maneuver was more limited than in the earlier crisis in 1953–54 or 1956–57. In September 1961 the FDJ started a country-wide campaign against listening or watching "NATO stations"—that is against Western radio and television and the news and culture they carried. FDJ members went so as far as to cut down antennas that were pointing West, though such actions could not completely block the radio waves and television shows that brought the latest West European and American hits and fashions into East Germany. The FDJ leadership also issued directives to its members to beat up "rowdies" before turning them over to the police.[6]

When East Berlin jazz fans founded a jazz club at the Humboldt University in the fall of 1961, authorities were highly alarmed. As part of their agenda, the jazz fans tried to abolish the 60:40 rule that restricted how much music imported from the West could be played at concerts and on the radio. Officials of the FDJ Central Committee claimed that such jazz associations were founded by West German agents and urged local FDJ functionaries to be aware "of the political background of a strengthened jazz movement." Present-day jazz, these officials said, was shaped by commercialism and imperialist ideologies and was thus part of "decadent trends of bourgeois ideology." Well aware of arguments that claimed jazz was the authentic music of blacks in the United States, East German authorities tried to avoid provoking public debates and suggested that jazz fans pursue their interests in "authentic" folk music in existing, carefully supervised dance and music groups. At the same time, they permitted a series of jazz concerts.[7] In the aftermath of the wall, East German party and youth leaders combined some leniency with severe repression.

By contrast, in West Germany, government officials adopted the psychological paradigms of social scientists—both U.S. and West German—to take the edge off adolescent rebelliousness. In 1962, the West Berlin Minister for Youth Affairs, Ella Kay, assessed the 1956 youth riots that East and West Germans had blamed on American popular culture. "It is not easy for adults," said Kay, "to accept that youngsters lean toward rebellion, and that is a step toward adulthood...." Kay thus agreed with wider definitions of acceptable behavior, especially for young men. Such assessments rendered "normal" adolescent needs for adventure as well as more outrageous behavior, like rioting, into mere sociological and psychological, rather than political, phenomena. Kay went on to claim that the Berlin government had learned from the "incidents" and had started bikers' groups and craft shops. She now concluded that the rioters, who caused so many worries in the mid-1950s, had all been decent boys.[8]

West German state officials felt that adolescents' consumption required proper channeling. Kay was particularly proud of three state-sponsored youth dance cafes that had contributed to "fulfilling justified wishes." In these venues, officials offered what they called jazz rather than rock 'n' roll. While West Germans deemed rock 'n' roll largely unthreatening by the late 1950s, jazz carried more positive connotations of youthfulness, proper restraint, and "high" culture. Indeed West German politicians, including such diverse figures as Franz-Josef Strauß and Willy Brandt, viewed it as the proper musical form for a modern liberal democracy. By 1964 the West German Goethe-Institute—designed to represent German culture abroad—was sending West German jazz bands to several Asian countries.[9]

At the end of April 1960, Minister Kay herself opened the first West Berlin dance cafe, called Jazz-Saloon, and served nonalcoholic drinks and beer to adolescents in the club. Among the musicians performing live music was one band, the Johannes Rediske Quartett, that, in the early 1950s, had performed in the notorious jam sessions of the West Berlin club Badewanne. But the meanings of jazz had since changed: by using the word jazz

Fig. 25. Opening of the state-sponsored West Berlin Jazz Saloon, April 1960. The poster announcing the event features a trumpet and a bustier. Courtesy Landesbildstelle Berlin.

in the name and offerings of the club, West Berlin officials tried to show that their club was at once modern, open, and respectable.

West Berlin officials were satisfied that such jazz clubs fulfilled their educational mission. While posters advertising the club displayed a bustier—a symbol of female sexiness—pictures in the press revealed a "respectable" audience: young women in skirts and sweaters and young men in suits.

One commentator reported that pants for young women and jeans for young men were not "desirable."[10] As one social worker concluded, these clubs educated young people not with "the sledge-hammer, but with the jazz trumpet." Most visitors of the jazz cafes came because of the "hot rhythms," the social worker reported; in the clubs, they were able to "move freely" and were valuing this freedom highly, as they allegedly learned to obey "unwritten laws." Such dance cafes thus were part of West German efforts to defuse the 1950s youth rebellion, but they also provided adolescents with the opportunity to listen to "hot," if not too hot, American music in a safe environment. In West Germany, definitions of acceptable adolescent behavior had clearly widened.[11]

Such liberal efforts avoided the eugenics-based rhetoric of primitivism and gender upheaval that East and West German conservatives had used to mark young male rioters and female rock 'n' roll fans as transgressors of gender and racial boundaries and as a political threat. Nonetheless, Cold War liberals, too, retained hostility toward cultural styles like rock 'n' roll, which they associated with a lack of male and female respectability. Indeed, reinscribing gender differences, for example, in the clothing styles of adolescents, was central also to liberal attempts to resolve any threats posed by rebellious adolescents. With the state-sponsored dance cafes, West Berlin officials fostered the "private" solution to overly rebellious behavior—a solution that liberal psychologists and sociologists had also proposed: stable heterosexual relations among adolescents. The club provided a space where both sexes could get together—and would be properly socialized.

A 1960 West Berlin government report on the "situation" of youth located such efforts explicitly in the liberal ideas of scholars like West German Helmut Schelsky and American David Riesman who had confirmed the basic stability of consumption-oriented societies. The report spoke of a "skeptical generation" growing up in an "other-directed" consumer society. Adolescents had been freed from the social constraints of the bourgeois production-oriented society. This transformation, however, left adolescents without firm rules of conduct. In strong contrast to the West German politicians and educators of the early 1950s who had firmly believed that nuclear families of female homeworkers and male breadwinners would prevent juvenile misbehavior, the report maintained that the family alone was unable to solve these problems. In this context, the report claimed, state youth agencies had to fulfill their prime task in the realm of leisure and consumption: to teach adolescents "how to evaluate critically the offerings of the consumer and entertainment industries and how to use them in a meaningful manner." Both the dance clubs and film clubs that the West

Berlin government supported were attempts to fulfill these goals. In this vision, state youth officials, as agents of the expanding welfare state, were to educate adolescents into sensible consumers.[12]

Such state intervention revealed persisting ambivalence toward consumer culture. Throughout the 1960s, many West German conservatives and Cold War liberals alike continued to worry that advertising and consumer culture manipulated German adolescents. Conservatives often rejected consumer culture altogether and argued that the East German enemy was much more successful in containing it than the West. By contrast, Cold War liberals were considerably more tolerant and tried to shape youths into "thinking consumers." In the mid-1960s West German sociologists confirmed that consumer culture was not threatening the stability of the state. According to Walter Jaide, adolescents made use of the offerings of consumer culture, without rejecting "timeless bourgeois conditions" in politics, religion, lifestyle, or attitudes toward work, family, and leisure time.[13] Viggo Graf Blücher built on Schelsky's and his own findings from the 1950s; in 1966 he spoke of an "unprejudiced, ingenious generation." Like Schelsky's "skeptical generation," this generation of adolescents was, at least under favorable economic conditions, resilient to both National Socialism and communism.[14]

It was an "achievement" of West German Cold War liberals from the late 1950s onward to push the issues of popular culture and sexuality into arenas defined as nonpolitical. The redefinition of consumption was an important part in a West German "end of ideologies" paradigm, with which West German Cold War liberals sought to integrate themselves into the alliance of Western societies on the one hand, and to divorce themselves from the Weimar and Nazi past on the other. This shift took place in the context of sustained economic growth. Cold War liberals defined as private and nonpolitical the family, "normal" heterosexuality, and the realm of culture (including both consumer and "high" culture).

Yet these Cold War liberal interpretations were full of contradictions. On the one hand they saw cultural products, such as music or movies, as commodities whose very availability was central to liberal democracy. On the other hand, Cold War liberals, like conservatives and East German socialists, worried about what values specific products fostered. In this context, jazz with its connotations of respectability was preferable to rock 'n' roll. Youthful expressiveness became part of West German Cold War liberal identity, and yet liberals very much worried about families that failed to guide adolescents properly. Cold War liberals denied the political significance of male aggression, and assigned the resolution of adolescent transgressions to the private sphere even as they used state funds to foster this vision. Thus Cold War liberals sought to accommodate heterogeneity, to a degree, in the non-political realm by making it into a matter of style. At the same time, they feared that adolescents were not actively engaged in politics, for example, when on visits to West Berlin they showed more interest in dance clubs than the Wall or the political situation of the divided city.[15] Cold War liberals had a narrower definition of politics than West German conservatives or East German socialists and rejected the heterogeneity expressed in the new youth cultures, and elsewhere, as a basis for political expression.

The logic of depoliticization also continued to shape West German views of East Germany in important ways. It meant that East German adolescents who used their public displays of American-influenced fashions and music to provoke and resist East German authorities could not count on West German official support. Even as East German authorities reacted with repression to adolescent consumption of U.S. imports, West Germans interpreted *Halbstarken* behavior East of the Iron Curtain in the same terms as they did in the West. They used psychological, family-centered explanations to deny any political significance of *Halbstarken* behavior in the East. In 1963 a West German government report on film in East Germany appeared in a series designed to inform the West German public about East Germany and to preserve the "German conscience of unity." It criticized East Germany for presenting Western influences as a crucial cause of East German juvenile misbehavior. At the same time, however, the report, like many West German reviewers, commended the 1957 East German movie *Berlin Ecke Schönhauser* for locating the roots of *Halbstarken* behavior in the East correctly as "lack of understanding on the part of the parents, unhealthy conditions in their homes." The report did not consider the FDJ's or the party's authoritarianism an important motivation for East German *Halbstarke*.[16] Another West German government report on resistance in East Germany did not even mention the sanctions that some East German adolescents encountered.[17] These had ranged from being expelled from school for wearing jeans to prison time for shouting anti-Ulbricht and pro-Presley slogans. West German officials, influenced by American officials and social scientists, sought to foster Western tastes in the East German population, and they sometimes complained when East German authorities suppressed such efforts. Nevertheless they usually defined adolescents who experienced state repression when publicly displaying these tastes as rebels without a legitimate cause.

By the mid-1960s the United States was beginning to lose its status as the source of the most controversial cultural imports in East and West Germany. On both sides of the wall, parents, educators, and party and state officials no longer worried about rock 'n' roll, but about so-called beat music that was produced by British bands such as the Beatles and the Rolling Stones. Many people in East and West were outraged by the long hair styles and loose clothing of male and female beat fans, but reactions in East and West usually followed the different attitudes toward consumption established by the late 1950s.[18]

Throughout the 1960s, and beyond, East German party and youth leaders would continue on their zigzag course. Large numbers of East German adolescents continued to listen to Western music and many East German musicians modeled their own music on these Western imports. In response, East German authorities campaigned repeatedly against listening to Western radio stations like Radio Luxemburg and tried to control the music bands played. Policies remained somewhat unpredictable. Adolescents and artists at times made astonishing gains, only to be persecuted a few months later.

In 1962 Walter Ulbricht announced economic measures that moved the GDR away from central planning. With the drain of workers to the West closed off by the Wall, leaders were willing to undertake some reforms. Alongside demands for individual initiative and decisiveness in the workplace, Ulbricht and the SED provided some openings in the cultural sphere. In a 1963 Youth Communiqué, the SED Politbureau renounced the use of force and admonishments; rather, it made suggestions that sounded similar to the insights of liberal Western social scientists and the entertainment industry: "It is especially important to awaken fun and engagement, so that the boys and girls organize and spend their leisure time mostly by themselves." Leisure time was now a space distinct from the political sphere. "Which tact or rhythm the youth selects is up to it," the Politbureau announced, but concluded, "The main thing is, it remains tactful!"[19] These statements, along with the continuing attacks on the "psychological warfare" of the West, showed how difficult it was for the SED leadership to find a balance between its own calls for self-definition and its demands for constant commitment to the socialist system.

Officials, adolescents, and the producers of movies, music, concerts, and literature made use of these openings after 1962. Adolescents and even party leaders danced the twist, while rock and beat bands sprang up all over the GDR. Movies such as *Das Kaninchen bin ich* (The rabbit is me), *Denk bloß nicht ich heule* (Don't think I'm crying), or *Berlin um die Ecke* (Berlin around the corner, made by the same writer and director as *Berlin Ecke Schönhauser*) once again took up the issue of adolescent alienation under socialism. In 1963 authorities even allowed the first release of an American western, *The Magnificent Seven*, with Horst Buchholz in a starring role. Two years later, the state-owned record company issued an album by the Beatles, while press reports claimed that beat, like jazz earlier, was a protest music in the West.[20]

Soon, however, this youth culture began to escape the control of SED and FDJ. By 1964 Erich Honecker, now in charge of security matters in the Central Committee and the second man behind Ulbricht, and Honecker's supporters attempted to reign in the new openness. In the summer of 1965, the press railed against the gender transgressions beat fans committed. After riots at a 1965 Rolling Stones concert in West Berlin, *Neues Deutschland*, for example, reprinted descriptions from the West German tabloid *Bild-Zeitung*, of girls who threw off their underwear in ecstasy. The East and West German press employed the same images they had used against Elvis Presley in 1956.[21] By the fall of 1965 East German officials withdrew the licenses for GDR beat bands and stopped an FDJ guitar contest when too many of the entries showed American and British influences. Perhaps in reference to the enthusiastic reception of *The Magnificent Seven*, Leipzig SED leaders attacked "American nonculture" among adolescents, including an alleged "Texas ideology" and "ranger behavior." In October the police arrested participants in a so-called "beat demonstration" in Leipzig, where twenty-five hundred fans protested repressive measures. After this event the FDJ endorsed actions where classmates cut the long hair of their peers. Some beat fans were sentenced to prison or forced labor.[22]

In December 1965, the infamous Eleventh Plenum of the SED Central Committee widened the crackdown into a general clear-cutting *(Kahlschlag)*. Honecker gave a speech, in which he accused movies, television shows, and literary works of enhancing brutality and sexual drives and complained that citizens were not defending the GDR against "American immorality and decadence." Instead of Elvis Presley or Bill Haley, the main objects of scorn were now the Beatles and Rolling Stones, who allegedly contributed to the "moral disintegration" of East Germany and who were apparently closely associated with the United States in spite of their British origins. Leaders once again saw transgressions of gender and sexual norms as a threat to socialism.[23]

While the outrage vented at the Plenum drew on old tropes, including attacks on Western psychological warfare, decadence, and primitivism, it also had a new quality. The party and FDJ leadership made less use of the term "degenerate" and instead railed against "skepticism," which "questions everything," against "objectivism," "which positions itself between two fronts" and against the "bourgeois theories of a loneliness of man." These were facile attacks on the ideas of a "skeptical generation," an "end of ideology," and the "loneliness of the crowd" that West German and American Cold War liberals, such as Schelsky and Riesman, had introduced in their efforts to come to terms with consumer culture. Honecker's staunch supporter Paul Fröhlich, a member of the Politbureau, made this explicit when he claimed that the "skepticism of the youth, which is in full force in the West and is spread with clear intentions, for example by Professor Schelsky, who has been exposed as a fascist ideologue" had taken root also among East German writers and adolescents.[24] In the weeks before the Plenum, Schelsky had come under attack in West Germany for a Nazi pamphlet he had written during the Third Reich.[25] Fröhlich exploited this to make links between adolescent consumption of Western popular culture, imperialism, fascism, and intellectuals who were critical of the regime. Party leaders rejected the calls for self-definition that some of them had endorsed earlier as foreign-produced and dangerous. Instead, they recommended raising the East German youth's class consciousness through ideological education. In the wake of the Eleventh Plenum, party leaders prohibited numerous movies, including those that showed adolescent alienation, and cracked down on singers and writers.[26]

The contradictory behavior of the East German regime that engaged with the West in a battle over consumption and at the same time attacked Western culture was not simply the result of a failure of socialist production to fulfill a population's consumer desires. Rather it had deep ideological roots. The study of psychology, which played such an important role in making consumer culture both understandable and acceptable in West Germany in the 1950s, was long repressed in East Germany. In West Germany, psychological models of adolescent development assigned consumption an increasingly important function, although this embrace coexisted with uneasiness about consumer culture. In East Germany, the focus on the individual in psychology—and on individual satisfaction in consumer culture—remained suspect for a long time. In 1966 the SED leadership authorized a new Central Institute for Youth Research in which researchers investigated the attitudes of young men with long hair. Contrary to characterization in the public denunciations of beat fans, these young men were not socially deviant high school dropouts of minor intelligence. Nor were they fully committed to the goals of socialism. Another study found that declining numbers of adolescents opposed listening to Western radio stations. Needless to say, such complex findings could not be made public.[27] The regime encouraged its citizens to formulate their identities primarily as workers, soldiers, socialists, and antifascists, but such allegiances were increasingly undercut and consumer culture played an important role in this subversion. Not until the early 1980s did the regime begin to admit as much. By that time GDR researchers had assimilated the teachings of Western psychology and publicly presented concepts of individuality that rejected the forms of identification the regime had sought to encourage and even impose.[28]

"1968" IN EAST AND WEST

The diverging paths of the two Germanies also meant that a new round of youth rebellions in the late 1960s took a different form in each state. Whereas students were the driving forces behind West German radicalism in the 1960s, they were less likely to rebel in the East German regime. Under state socialism, numerous children of workers were able to obtain higher education, and they felt gratitude toward a system that had provided them with new opportunities, even as it successfully educated them into political conformity. In East Germany, it was young workers who were most likely to air their dissatisfaction with the regime. This became clear during the protests in the aftermath of the Prague Spring. In August 1968, Soviet troops suppressed the reform movement in Czechoslovakia, while East German units participated by securing the border. Some young East Germans, among them more workers than students, distributed leaflets in support of Czechoslovak reforms, voiced protests during dance events, or made their opposition known by playing Western hits in informal gatherings. In response, the East German leadership blamed enemy activities, including the distribution of Western music, for an alleged "depoliticization" among both Czechoslovak and East German youth. Depoliticization in this view was a successful Western attack on socialism.[29] In spite of some evidence of upheaval, the late 1960s constituted less of a rupture in East than in West Germany.

In the West, the student rebels of the late 1960s were challenging the depoliticization of youth cultures. Here, we cannot understand the upheaval of the late 1960s without grasping the particular dynamics of containing the youth rebellion of the 1950s. Male *Halbstarke* and female rock 'n' roll fans of the 1950s participated in a rebellion with clear political implications. Depoliticization did not defuse the rebellion completely. The rebels of the 1960s were not the *Halbstarke* of the 1950s. Nonetheless, a connection exists. In West Germany, as in the United States, the 1950s youth cultures raised expectations for individual expression and sexual openness among young men and women, and some of them expressed these expectations in explicitly political terms in the 1960s.[30]

The late 1960s saw another wave of transfers across the Atlantic. Members of the new radical movements in West Germany demanded personal and political transformations, and in doing so they frequently drew on models from the American counter culture and student rebellion. In both the United States and in West Germany, these movements were greatly varied and often divided, and in the context of this study, I can address only some common themes.[31]

It is as a reaction to both conservatism and Cold War liberalism that the radicalism of the 1960s and 1970s can best be understood. The Cold War liberal consensus that emerged in the late 1950s and early 1960s in West Germany found its most powerful expression in the "Great Coalition" between Christian and Social Democrats after 1966. While this Cold War liberalism began to dominate the political culture and the press, it coexisted with conservatism on the political scene, in educational institutions, and in family life.

The attempt to connect the personal and the political was a challenge to conservatism and Cold War liberalism leveled by student rebels, members of the counter culture, and feminists of the 1960s.[32] For example, Manfred Weißleder, the founder of the Hamburg Star-Club, where the Beatles performed in front of working- and middle-class audiences in the early 1960s, made music and fashions into a distinctly political expression. In his *Star-Club-News*, conceived as an alternative to *Bravo*, Weißleder announced in 1964 that "every sober person preferred a Beatle-hairstyle over the military cut of our recent history." He attacked as hypocrites those who were claiming to advocate freedom while prescribing the correct taste in music and hairstyles.[33] Two years later, counter culture member Dieter Kunzelmann claimed in a widely quoted provocative statement, "I have orgasm problems, and I demand that society take notice."[34] And by the early 1970s, feminists made sexuality a public and political issue, for example in the abortion campaign and in discussions of vaginal orgasm.[35]

These rebels were accused at the time (and since) of turning their backs on politics, but that analysis is hardly convincing.[36] It is not clear whether Kunzelmann's statement about his orgasm problems was meant to be sarcastic, but it certainly entailed a public demand for pleasure. In any case, it has become widely quoted, because it represented a rejection of both conservatism and Cold War liberalism. On the one hand, male and female radicals attacked what they saw as their parents' conservatism. Numerous autobiographical accounts confirm that they focused on conservative gender norms, and in particular on the emotionally removed and authoritarian fathers whose behavior they interpreted as a failure to work through the Nazi past.[37] Conservatives, in turn, did not reject the idea that the personal is political. Rather it was *the contents of the personal,* that is, the demand for open enjoyment and sexual expression made into a public demand, that was unsettling to parents and conservatives more generally.[38]

On the other hand, statements such as Kunzelmann's also undermined the conceptions of politics and sexuality that were central to Cold War liberalism. They sought to weaken or destroy the division of public and private that is one of liberalism's central tenets.[39] The student movement, and later the feminist movement, were at once narcissistic and interested in developing fundamental democratic forms toward self-determination. Members tried to develop interpersonal and sexual relations unencumbered by traditional social restrictions and made these part of their critique of the overall political and economic system of the Federal Republic.[40] The efforts to make the personal political manifested themselves in the new forms of organizing and living that members of the counter culture and student rebellion turned to; some of them joined communes in the 1960s and many others became involved in the squatters' movement of the 1970s. They saw the creation of new living conditions as central to political struggle.[41] The radicalism of the sixties and seventies might be read as a response to several developments: conservative values, the expectations that consumer culture and psychology raised, and the depoliticization of these issues in Cold War liberalism.

Moreover, radicals rejected both conservatives' and Cold War liberals' efforts to separate themselves from the Nazi past. The popular notion that nobody talked about National Socialism in the 1950s is not correct; both conservatives and Cold War liberals in fact did, but in ways that often precluded a careful engagement with that history. Conservatives made links between American-style consumer culture and fascism, whereas Cold War liberals claimed West Germany had undergone a thorough social and political transformation so that the threat of Nazism no longer existed. Radicals read both attitudes as a form of denial.[42]

The sixties radicals employed the language of psychology differently than Cold War liberals had. In 1969 the radical writer Bernhard Vesper aimed psychological concepts at both the dominant culture and the dogmatism of the Marxist-Leninist members of the student movement. He complained, "Sublimating the drives: that is working for later enjoyment ... That's the kind of shit we are trained into, and we have to find our way back to total irresponsibility first, just to save ourselves."[43] The works of philosophers Herbert Marcuse and Wilhelm Reich, which drew on psychology in constructing a leftist critique of capitalist societies, were crucial in helping radicals make this connection between sexual expression and political transformation. Using psychological language, while arguing for personal emancipation as a political act, would be a central feature of texts for the "new subjectivity" in the 1970s, including Peter Schneider's *Lenz* (1973) and Verena Stefan's *Shedding* (1975).

Radicals also recognized the centrality of consumption (and the "culture industry") for Cold War liberalism. It is probably not by chance that early antiauthoritarians made themselves first heard at a convention of West German advertisers in 1964 where they attacked the advertisers as "soul massagers," or manipulators of psyches.[44] Attacks on department stores, which were the beginning of the turn to violent action for some radical groups in the late 1960s, also make some sense in this context. As Detlev Siegfried has observed, radicals took up worries about the manipulative power of the organized entertainment industry that characterized conservative cultural pessimism, but they did so as part of a very different political agenda. This also explains why many of them were attracted to the Critical Theory of the Frankfurt School, especially of Marcuse and Theodor Adorno, whose leftist analysis linked consumerism to dangerous militarism and protofascism.[45]

Like other radicals, West German women's liberationists attacked consumer culture. In 1972 the group *Brot und Rosen*—modeled on the American Bread and Roses—wrote "Our bodies are being used, in order to sell products with which men make millions."[46] German women, like their American counterparts, argued that women were nothing but commodities and objects for men.[47] Women combined the language of Marxist critiques of commodification through consumer culture (commodities) and of psychology (objects) to describe their oppression by men. The attacks on consumer culture made sense to radicals, in part because the entertainment industry and advertisers had in fact actively participated in the process of depoliticization that assigned sexuality to a "private" arena and that meant nonetheless that sexuality needed to be regulated. Feminists, in contrast to male radicals, recognized the gender dynamic in this, and rebelled against the new strains that the sexual revolution put on women.

The radicalism of the 1960s also entailed rejecting high modernism, which was part of portraying West Germany as liberal.[48] As Hans Magnus Enzensberger observed, by the late 1960s buying what was formerly degenerate art (under the Nazis, but also in the minds of Christian conservatives) was a way to separate oneself from National Socialism. Enzensberger criticized "[a] form of antifascism which satisfies itself with having better taste than the Nazis, and which manifests its democratic mentality by buying what the former called 'degenerate': pictures on which nothing can be recognized and poems with nothing in them."[49] Jazz had of course likewise been called degenerate under the Nazis and had become respectable as an "art music" in the 1950s. Certainly, modernism has not been associated simply with one political ideology, whether conservatism or Cold War liberalism. However, Cold War liberals tried to give modern art and music a specific political meaning, using them as symbols of freedom, progress, and prosperity in the West and thus setting themselves apart from totalitarian regimes. Enzensberger exposed the postwar prominence of modern art for what it was: among other things, a form of consumption with political purposes.

Sixties radicalism in West Germany, as elsewhere in the West, was a response to both conservatism and liberalism. Not surprisingly, many of the intellectuals and politicians, who had driven the depoliticization process, were deeply disturbed by the events of the late 1960s, but nonetheless tried to maintain their logic. Others, however, began to see youth as an engine for a democratization of West German society. Reactions to the upheaval ranged from outrage and repression, to limited enthusiasm for reform, to further efforts at depoliticization.

The ambivalence about consumption that existed on both sides of the Iron Curtain would continue to shape the Cold War between the two Germanies over the following decades. Providing access to Western currency, consumer goods, and Western culture would be a central part of West German *Ostpolitik* from the 1970s onward, but many West Germans remained doubtful that such transfers enhanced political opposition to the East German regime. Over the years the GDR would allow homegrown rock music and even increased imports of Western records and stars, including a concert with American Bruce Springsteen in 1988. The inconsistency of East German official actions, driven by a constant fear that the Western imports would lead citizens politically astray, ultimately contributed to authorities' loss of legitimacy. Ambivalence about consumption also manifested itself in demeaning remarks, coming from both East and West, about East Germans who were allegedly interested only in purchasing bananas and not in fighting for freedom after the fall of the Wall in 1989.[50] What the developments of the 1950s and since suggest is that American culture, and consumption in general, have no transhistorical, stable meaning, either antithetical to freedom or bolstering freedom and democracy. We need to ask what sort of politics a focus on consumption, and specific goods, enable at specific moments.[51] A comparative history of the two Germanies has much to offer in this process.

TOWARD A COMPARATIVE HISTORY OF THE TWO GERMANIES

In this book I have tried to elucidate differences and continuities between the two German states during the formative years of the Cold War. In the last few years, German historians have focused much of their attention on developing analytical categories with which to understand the history of the German Democratic Republic. Not nearly as much energy has been devoted to doing the same for West Germany. Perhaps more disturbing, historians of West Germany and of East Germany frequently work with vastly different concepts. Research on West Germany has often focused on issues of "modernization" and "Americanization"; that is, on processes of social and political transformation in the aftermath of National Socialism and under the influence of the Western Allies.[52] The concepts with the most allure for East German historians center on a structural analysis of state socialism. Terms now employed in histories of the GDR include *"durchherrschte Gesellschaft,"*—a society in the firm grip of the government (Kocka/Lüdtke), and *"politische Gesellschaft,"*—political and politicized society (Schroeder), and even "total discursive system" (Bathrick).[53]

Each set of concepts has potential problems. Modernization theories, which were themselves closely tied to the Western Cold War liberalism of the 1950s and 1960s, posit a necessary connection between consumer capitalism, economic prosperity, and political democracy. But as scholars have shown, modernization, like "Americanization," is useful as a term only if it is severed from such prescribed outcomes and more complex meanings of modernity are explored.[54] The second set of terms, those employed for the history of the GDR, all testify to the notion that concepts central to liberal democracies were undermined under state socialism. There was no proper separation of society and government, no autonomy of social, cultural, and economic processes, and no proper division of public and private.[55] Implicitly these concepts cast the West as an ideal case against which state socialism is to be judged. They also imply close parallels between state socialism and the Third Reich and therefore affirm the totalitarianism paradigm.[56]

It is useful to focus on some of the similarities between the West German liberal democracy and East German state socialism in order to test these concepts. The exploration of changing reactions to American-influenced adolescent rebels reveals that there was no neat separation of state and society, in either the West German liberal democracy or under the more authoritarian East German state socialism.[57] Similarities existed between West German conservatives and East German socialists. Neither group believed in a clear separation of public and private, and both considered the personal political. Such similarities are perhaps not so disturbing, since most of us believe that West Germany overcame the conservative 1950s. But the development of more liberal West German attitudes toward adolescent behavior also illustrates the permeability of public and private in a liberal democracy. The division of public and private in liberal democracies—and the relative autonomy of culture and politics—is tethered to visions of "normality." As West German educators, social scientists, and politicians redefined adolescent rebelliousness as normal, they also redefined it as a nonpolitical phenomenon, something that belonged in a realm of psychology and culture and could be resolved there. Visions of normality defined the boundaries within which something could be considered psychological and therefore nonpolitical. Moreover, West German authorities clearly politicized culture as a Cold War weapon, even if they sought to define it as an apolitical space. The efforts to regulate youth cultures in the two Germanies make clear that it is historically inaccurate to distinguish between a nonpolitical West German and a political East German society, and a term like "political society" thus has little potential for instructive comparisons.

This exploration of East and West German encounters with American popular culture also reveals other continuities. It shows how closely intertwined hostilities toward black culture and the rejection of female sexual expressiveness were in both East and West Germany. Indeed, reactions to American popular culture afford us with one important entree into understanding of German racialist concepts after World War II. These concepts were not merely leftovers of fascist times. Even as West Germany underwent a liberal transformation and as East Germany reasserted Stalinism, there were continuities and similarities. In both cases, gender conservatism continued to set limits on tolerance toward cultural and ethnic difference. West German officials, for example, did not embrace those African American cultural styles publicly connected with sexual expressiveness—even when the press had "deracialized" and "whitened" these styles, as in the case of rock 'n' roll.

This legacy raises questions for further research. For example, although we know that adolescent consumers challenged the racial hierarchies and gender norms established by state authorities, we should not conclude that these adolescents were also automatically successful antiracists. In other words, just because the actions of adolescent consumers were politically meaningful does not mean that the political effect of their actions was always or only antiracist. We need more research on how investments in black culture and identifications with African Americans were used by political activists in the 1950s and 1960s.[58] In 1969, for example, a West German feminist announced that "women are the Negroes of all people."[59] With this type of self-conscious identification with African Americans, some German radicals nonetheless produced new forms of marginalization for blacks. Her statement elided both the situation of black women and the possibility that white women could be oppressors. Such problems ought to be tackled not just with regard to German attitudes toward African Americans. We need to ask further questions about how the consumption of minority cultures by ethnic Germans affects attitudes about citizenship and political participation for members of minorities. The alleged depoliticization of culture in Cold War liberalism might be part of new strategies of exclusion, in both Germany and the United States. Personal self-styling or even the self-representation of the nation could be associated with minority cultures—for example those of African Americans or of the German working classes; but those statements would not necessarily translate into political power for such minorities. In other words, we should pursue historically specific analysis of the processes of desire, identification, exoticization, and also objectification involved in these interactions. Certainly, such issues need to be considered when we explore the mechanisms by which East and West Germans have constructed their ethnic "others," from foreign workers since the 1960s to people seeking political asylum in the 1990s.

In writing the histories of the two Germanies, we need to employ concepts that make meaningful comparisons possible, concepts that allow us to think about fundamental differences between the two Cold War enemies as well as similarities between them. It is for this reason that more flexible categories such as "identity," "norms," and "normality" have been at the center of this comparative history of the two Germanies. An inquiry into the formation of identities has to treat them as constantly constructed and reconstructed; it also has to investigate how identities are tied to contested understandings of difference, especially along the lines of gender, race, class, nation, age, and sexuality.[60] Careful attention to the processes of defining and resisting social and cultural norms has facilitated this and other projects that compare the two Germanies.[61]

But constructions of identities also need to be explored in tandem with institutions, in this case to investigate through which channels various German authorities enforced changing norms and how adolescents contested their actions.[62] Recognizing the complicated ways that cultural consumption took place in and affected the public sphere allows us to examine the centrality of (re)constructions of personal identities to state politics. And it is here that we most clearly see differences between the two states. East German elites made many efforts to reject and punish adolescents who openly consumed American imports. Since there was no relative autonomy of state and economy, or of state and party, authorities had the power to curtail American music imports and to use party and cultural organizations affiliated with party and state to control what adolescents consumed. Yet authorities were never completely successful, either before or after the Wall. Even within the state/party-run institutions, there were always adolescents and sometimes educators who sought to increase the range of cultural forms and behavior deemed acceptable. In particular much confusion existed over what constituted "authentic" and appropriate working-class culture, and at times this confusion provided openings for jazz, beat, or even American-influenced fashions. The East German regime was often chaotic and control never complete.

In West Germany, most of the time, what was considered "normal" could be renegotiated more easily than in East Germany. For example, there was a greater variety of expert opinions, which could be exchanged in public and which could change policy decisions. Such variety and change were institutionally anchored. The economy was relatively independent from state institutions. It created and appealed to consumer tastes, and adolescent rebelliousness, within limits, became something companies sold. At the same time, youth identities were most certainly not created in an autonomous private space. There was state intervention, for example, in the rating of movies, or in state youth programs that were to redirect adolescent behavior. Thus the state, often through collaboration with semiprivate organizations, could be promoting a narrow definition of the normal yet allow the persistence of other forms of behavior. At the same time, the state would disallow these behaviors as a source of political action. It was important for Cold War liberal social scientists and politicians to assure themselves that adolescent rebels did not pose political challenges. But there was no order, as in East Germany, from a state culture ministry official to prevent the spread of rock 'n' roll.

In this context the concept of a "society in the grip of the government" might after all be useful. While there is of course no society completely autonomous from the state in the West, it is important to distinguish between the different degrees to which societies have been held in the grip of governments, for example, to account for the different ways in which au-

Fig. 26. Combining an American ducktail plume and the blue shirt of the Communist FDJ at an official demonstration in the East German city Halle, 1961. Courtesy Landesbildstelle Berlin.

thorities in East and West sought to enforce their political visions through youth policies. In the end, East German state socialism was considerably more repressive than the West German liberal democracy.

The history of debates over young rebels in East and West Germany in the 1950s moves us away from the notion that a monolithic Stalinist dictatorship existed alongside a uniformly conservative market democracy. On both sides of the Iron Curtain there were numerous ruptures and changes that deserve further investigation in more detailed institutional and local studies. We should not search only for "the limits of dictatorship" in the East, but should also investigate the limits of liberal democracy in the West.[63] The challenge for a comparative history of the two Cold War Germanies, then, is to hold the similarities and differences between the systems in tension, in order to critically engage the histories of both.

Cultural debates, and more specifically the debates over American culture, were major sites for the construction of identities in the two German states. In the East and West German conflicts over American influences, we can see how the two states tried to lay claim to a German identity in the aftermath of National Socialism and in the face of the Cold War. Moreover, we can trace in these debates how the two crystallized as separate entities. Most importantly, debates over American influences were located in everyday life *and* on the political stage, and it is in the intersections between the two that we can trace the changing cultural politics of national reconstruction and the German Cold War.

Notes

INTRODUCTION

1. Reconstruction has been used mostly to describe West Germany after 1945, but it is a useful concept for both Germanies. Sheehan, "National History," 170, has warned against treating the two Germanies as if they had two separate histories, "joined only at their beginning and their end." See also Kleßmann, "Verflechtung und Abgrenzung." Throughout, translations from the German are my own, unless noted otherwise.

2. On culture as a site for the construction of national identities and nationalisms, see especially Anderson, *Imagined Communities*.

3. Fehrenbach, "German Discourses," 132; Hansen, "Early Silent Cinema."

4. For the history of these connections, see especially Carter, *How German Is She?*; de Grazia, "Introduction"; Auslander, "Gendering"; Huyssen, *After the Great Divide*; Bowlby, *Just Looking*; Elaine May, *Homeward Bound*; Petro, *Joyless Streets*; Roberts, *Civilization Without Sexes*.

5. Naimark, *The Russians in Germany*, 125–28; Fehrenbach, *Cinema in Democratizing Germany*; Moeller, *Protecting Motherhood*; Kühne, "'...aus diesem Krieg.'" On the problem of masculinity after war experiences, see especially Jeffords, *Remasculinization*; Higonnet et al., *Behind the Lines*; Domansky, "Militarization and Reproduction."

6. Naimark, *The Russians in Germany*, 104; Becker, *German Youth*; Kramer, "'Law-Abiding Germans.'"

7. On gender and German reconstruction, see also Carter, *How German Is She?*; Einhorn, *Cinderella Goes to Market*; Fehrenbach, *Cinema in Democratizing Germany*; Gerhard, "'Lösung' der Frauenfrage"; Grossmann, *Reforming Sex*; Heineman, "The Hour of the Woman"; Merkel, *...und Du*; Höhn, "Frau im Haus"; Moeller, *Protecting Motherhood*.

8. For West Germany, see especially Moeller, *Protecting Motherhood*; for East Germany, see Gerhard, "'Lösung' der Frauenfrage."

9. Gerhard, "'Lösung' der Frauenfrage."

10. Merkel, "Leitbilder."

11. On the new role of fathers in postwar Germany, see Fehrenbach, "Rehabilitating the Fatherland"; Moeller, "The Last Soldiers"; Heineman, *What Difference*; Biess, "'Pioneers of a New Germany.'"

12. Harsh, "Society, the State and Abortion."

13. Fehrenbach, *Cinema in Democratizing Germany*; Merkel, *...und Du*; Heineman, "Hour of the Woman"; Moeller, "The Homosexual Man."

14. Merkel, "Leitbilder," 363; Domansky, "Militarization and Reproduction."

15. On frequent German conflations of the United States with fascism, see Diner, *America*.

16. Exceptions include Stern, *The Whitewashing of the Yellow Badge*; Posner, "Afro-America"; Fehrenbach, "Rehabilitating Fatherland." On the taboo of using race as an analytical category in postwar Germany, see Adelson, *Making Bodies*.

17. For overviews on German racism, see Burleigh and Wippermann, *The Racial State*; Gilman, *On Blackness*; Grimm and Hermand, *Blacks and German Culture*; Mosse, *Toward the Final Solution*; Peukert, *Inside Nazi Germany*; Weindling, *Health, Race, and German Politics*.

18. See Iliffe, *Tanganyika Under German Rule*.

19. See Mosse, *Toward the Final Solution*, 175–76; Marks, "Black Watch"; Peukert, *Inside Nazi Germany*, 217; Bock, *Zwangssterilisation*; Pommerin, *Sterilisierung der Rheinlandbastarde*.

20. See Pence, "The 'Fräuleins'"; Höhn, "GIs"; Fehrenbach, "Rehabilitating the Fatherland"; Posner, "Afro-America."

21. "Außer Rand und Band," *Beratungsdienst Jugend und Film* (November 1956): BVII. Georg Knepler, "Jazz und die Volkmusik," *Musik und Gesellschaft* 5 (June 1955): 181–83; Ludwig Richard Müller, "Dekadenz und lebensfroher Neubeginn," *Musik und Gesellschaft* 5 (April 1955): 114–17; "Bericht über die Privattanzschulen," n.d. (ca. 1954), LAB (STA) Rep. 121, Nr. 162.

22. On the history of eugenics, see Kevles, *In the Name of Eugenics*; Mosse, *Toward the Final Solution*; Weindling, *Health, Race, and German Politics*; Grossmann, *Reforming Sex*. On the significance of psychology in antiracist discourse, see especially Barkan, *The Retreat of Scientific Racism*; Feldstein, *Raising Citizens*.

23. On the complicated relationship between race and gender under National Socialism, see, for example, Bock, "Antinatalism"; Marion Kaplan, *Between Dignity and Despair*.

24. Scholars of racism and colonialism are pointing to the complicated intersections of gender, race, and class in nineteenth- and twentieth-century discourses of civilization and nationhood. See, for example, Bederman, *Manliness and Civilization*; Carby, *Reconstructing Womanhood*; Gilman, *Difference and Pathology*; Ware, *Beyond the Pale*; Burton, *Burdens of History*.

25. See Geyer, "The Stigma of Violence."

26. Popular culture and especially such commercialized products like rock 'n' roll have been investigated within the framework of cultural studies, most

notably in scholarship that grew out of the Centre for Contemporary Cultural Studies at Birmingham. See, for example, Hall and Jefferson, *Resistance Through Rituals;* Hebdige, *Subculture;* McRobbie, *Feminism and Youth Culture.* Szemere, "Bandits," has pointed out that, while this work has enabled a critique of liberal capitalism, few scholars have as of yet tried to apply the frameworks developed in this scholarship to the study of the countries that used to be east of the Iron Curtain. See also Bennett, "Putting Policy into Cultural Studies"; During, *The Cultural Studies Reader;* Frow, *Cultural Studies;* Storey, *Cultural Studies.*

27. Hermand, *Kultur im Wiederaufbau,* 294–95, 357–63. For the United States, Lipsitz, *Class and Culture,* 218, has argued that if one defines politics as the social struggle for a good life, rock'n'roll songs "represented politics of the highest order."

28. Ryback, *Rock Around the Bloc,* 34. This is in marked contrast to Ryback's interpretation of the 1960s and recent assertions that rock music was important in the political transformations that led to the demise of socialism in 1989. See Ramet, *Social Currents;* Wicke, "The Times." On the complex meanings of rock in East Germany, see also Rauhut, *Beat* and *Schalmei;* Wierling, "Jugend als innerer Feind"; Mählert and Stephan, *Blaue Hemden.*

29. These interpretations follow Schelsky, *Die skeptische Generation.* See, for example, Blücher, *Die Generation der Unbefangenen.*

30. Maase, *Bravo Amerika,* 12–13. See also Dorner, "Halbstark"; Brauer, "Schaukeln und Wälzen"; Grotum, *Die Halbstarken.*

31. A consensus is emerging among scholars of West Germany that the years after 1956 saw important social and political transformations. See Doering-Manteuffel, "Deutsche Zeitgeschichte"; Erker, "Zeitgeschichte als Sozialgeschichte." On Cold War liberalism in the United States, see Corber, *In the Name of National Security;* Feldstein, *Raising Citizens.*

32. Important exceptions exist: Carter, "Alice in the Consumer Wonderland"; Bertram and Krüger, "Vom Backfisch zum Teenager"; Delille and Grohn, *Perlonzeit.* Maase, *Bravo Amerika,* mentions girls, but ultimately does not see them as important agents of change.

33. For a treatment celebrating the stabilizing American impact (stable families, revived democracies, improved national sentiments) in postwar Europe, see Duignan and Gann, *The Rebirth of the West.* For a much more nuanced treatment that focuses on American economic hegemony, see Berghahn, *The Americanisation of West German Industry.*

34. See Tomlinson, *Cultural Imperialism.* Examples include Mattelart, Delcourt, and Mattelart, *International Image Markets;* Herbert Schiller, *Mass Communications;* Tunstall, *The Media Are American.*

35. On the complex meanings of American culture in postwar Europe, see Kuisel, *Seducing the French;* Pells, *Not Like Us;* Kristin Ross, *Fast Cars, Clean Bodies;* Wagnleitner, *Coca-Colonization and Cold War;* Willett, *The Americanization.* For critiques of the concept of Americanization, see Doering-Manteuffel, "Dimensionen von Amerikanisierung"; Fehrenbach and Poiger,

"Americanization Reconsidered"; Jarausch and Siegrist, *Amerikanisierung und Sowjetisierung;* Lüdtke, Marßolek, and von Saldern, *Amerikanisierung;* Maase, *Bravo Amerika,* 21–40; Morley and Robins, *Spaces of Identity;* Sywottek, "The Americanization of Everyday Life?"

36. Compare Nolan, "America in the German Imagination"; Ermarth, "Introduction."

37. Saunders, *Hollywood in Berlin.*

38. Ibid., 93–116.

39. National Motion Picture Law quoted in Fehrenbach, *Cinema in Democratizing Germany,* 32.

40. Saunders, *Hollywood in Berlin,* 29–30.

41. German Appeal Board for movie censorship on the film *King of the Circus,* quoted in Saunders, *Hollywood in Berlin,* 99. See also Fehrenbach, "German Discourses."

42. Saunders, *Hollywood in Berlin,* 132–33; Frame, "Gretchen, Girl, Garconne?" 27; also Nolan, *Visions of Modernity,* 109, 120–27; von Saldern, "Überfremdungsängste."

43. Adolph Halfeld, *Amerika und der Amerikanismus* (1927), 214, quoted in Nolan, *Visions of Modernity,* 127; Alfred Rosenberg, *Mythos des 20. Jahrhunderts* (1930), quoted in Gassert, *Amerika im Dritten Reich,* 101.

44. Grossmann, "Girlkultur"; Jelavich, *Berlin Cabaret,* 175–86.

45. Grossmann, "The New Woman"; Petro, *Joyless Streets,* 109.

46. Jelavich, *Berlin Cabaret,* 175–86.

47. Bodek, *Proletarian Performance,* 28–31.

48. Tower, "'Ultramodern,'" 90.

49. Fritz Giese, *Girlkultur,* 105.

50. Count Harry Kessler, *Tagebücher 1918–1937* (1961), 458, quoted in Jelavich, *Berlin Cabaret,* 171.

51. Kater, *Different Drummers,* 1–16; Partsch, "Hannibal," 105–16.

52. Giese, *Girlkultur,* 30–35.

53. Oscar Bie, in *Berliner Börsen-Kurier,* May 26, 1925, and January 4, 1926, quoted in Jelavich, *Berlin Cabaret,* 171.

54. Jelavich, *Berlin Cabaret,* 170–71.

55. Hermand, "Artificial Atavism," 68.

56. Giese, *Girlkultur,* 64; Kater, *Different Drummers,* 18–19; Jelavich, *Berlin Cabaret,* 170–75; Nenno, "Femininity," 145–61. On Giese, see Gassert, *Amerika,* 71–72.

57. Domansky, "Militarization and Reproduction," 430–31; Gilman, "Sexology."

58. Dikötter, "Race Culture," 468.

59. See Dickinson, *German Child Welfare,* 143–44; Grossmann, *Reforming Sex;* Weindling, *Health, Race, and German Politics.*

60. Nordau, *Degeneration;* Mosse, *Toward the Final Solution,* 83–87.

61. On the different meaning assigned to the term, see also Pick, *Faces of Degeneration;* Chamberlin and Gilman, *Degeneration.* On biology-based lan-

guage in critiques of mass culture, see also von Saldern, "Überfremdungsängste."

62. Giese, *Girlkultur*, 66–78, 141–42.

63. Compare Leonard, *Jazz and the White Americans*, chap. 2.

64. Fritz Lenz, "Die krankhaften Erbanlagen" (1927), quoted in Kater, *Different Drummers*, 20.

65. *Volkswille*, March 14, 1920, quoted in von Saldern, "Überfremdungsängste," 220.

66. Adolf Halfeld, *Amerika*, quoted in Diner, *America*, 74; Richard H. Stein, "Auslandspropaganda" (1927), quoted in Kater, *Different Drummers*, 19; J. Gigler, "Der Verfall der Musik" (1925), quoted in Kater, "The Jazz Experience," 153; Alfred Heuss quoted in Kater, *Different Drummers*, 22.

67. Günter Dehn, *Proletarische Jugend* (1929), quoted in Peukert, *The Weimar Republic*, 178; Kater, *Different Drummers*, 22.

68. See von Saldern, "Überfremdungsängste"; Kater, *Different Drummers*, 32; Frame, "Gretchen, Girl, Garconne," 31. On efforts to regulate youth, see for example, Harvey, *Youth and the Welfare State*; Linton, "Who Has the Youth"; Peukert, *Grenzen der Sozialdisziplinierung*.

69. Kater, *Different Drummers*, 20–21; von Saldern, "Überfremdungsängste"; on Ford, see Starr, *Red and Hot*, 100–101.

70. Richard Eichenauer in *Musik und Rasse* (1932), quoted in Meyer, "A Musical Facade," 171.

71. *Mitteilungen des Kampfbundes für deutsche Kultur* 1 (1929), quoted in Kater, "The Jazz Experience," 156.

72. "Jugend und Sexualität" (1929), and Dr. J. F., "Die Ehe ein Jazz" (1929), both quoted in Dickinson, *German Child Welfare*, 149. More generally see Dickinson, 148–50.

73. Nolan, *Visions of Modernity*, 121; Petro, *Joyless Streets*, 130–39. On the complicated relationship of the German Left to American popular culture, see for example, Petro; Hansen, "Of Mice and Ducks"; von Saldern, "Überfremdungsängste."

74. Jelavich, *Berlin Cabaret*, 216.

75. Theodor Wiesengrund-Adorno, "Kleiner Zitatenschatz" (1932), quoted in Kater, "The Jazz Experience," 158.

76. K. Heilbutt, quoted in Abrams, *Workers' Culture*, 181. See also Bodek, *Proletarian Performance*, 41–43, 55.

77. Kater, *Different Drummers*, 17; Saunders, *Hollywood in Berlin*, 12; Kaes, "Literary Intellectuals"; Partsch, "Hannibal"; Tower, "'Ultramodern'"; Starr, *Red and Hot*, chaps. 3–4.

78. Hans Siemsen, "Jazz-Band" (1921), quoted in Jelavich, *Berlin Cabaret*, 170.

79. Starr, *Red and Hot*, 61–62; Bodek, *Proletarian Performance*, 99–125; Jelavich, *Berlin Cabaret*, chap. 7.

80. Starr, *Red and Hot*, chaps. 5–10.

81. Saunders, *Hollywood in Berlin*, 222–23; Kater, "The Jazz Experience," 154; Jelavich, *Berlin Cabaret*, 175; Kater, *Different Drummers*, 19.

82. Schäfer, "Amerikanismus," 199–215; Gassert, *Amerika im Dritten Reich*, 164–82; Fehrenbach, *Cinema in Democratizing Germany*, 44–47; Herf, *Reactionary Modernism*.

83. Rentschler, "German Feature Films," 257–66; Rentschler, *The Ministry of Illusion*; Linda Schulte-Sasse, *Entertaining the Third Reich*; de Grazia, "Mass Culture and Sovereignty."

84. See Kater, "Forbidden Fruit?" 11–43; Kater, *Different Drummers*, 170; Gassert, *Amerika im Dritten Reich*, 357–59.

85. Jelavich, *Berlin Cabaret*, 250–57; title page of *Die Dame* reprinted in Burleigh and Wippermann, *The Racial State*, 245.

86. "Noch immer *Girlkultur* in Deutschland?" *Völkische Frauenzeitung*, December 1, 1935; W. Hanke to Propaganda Ministry, March 31, 1939, both quoted in Jelavich, *Berlin Cabaret*, 252.

87. Anonymous letter to Joseph Goebbels, Easter 1939, quoted in Kater, "Forbidden Fruit?" 17.

88. Steinweis, *Art, Ideology and Economics*.

89. Eric Rentschler, "The Elemental, the Ornamental, the Instrumental," summarized in Fehrenbach, *Cinema in Democratizing Germany*, 47–48; Rentschler, *Ministry of Illusion*.

90. Domansky, "Militarization and Reproduction"; Weindling, *Health, Race, and German Politics*.

91. See Meyer, "A Musical Facade for the Third Reich."

92. Kater, "Forbidden Fruit?" 15.

93. Ibid., 19–20. On the functioning of the chamber system, see Steinweis, *Art, Ideology and Economics*.

94. Pohl, " 'Schräge Vögel,' " 249; Kater, *Different Drummers*, 153; Steinweis, *Art, Ideology and Economics*, 166–67.

95. Report by the Reich Youth Leadership, September 1942, quoted in Burleigh and Wippermann, *The Racial State*, 221–22, and in Pohl, " 'Schräge Vögel,' " 243.

96. "Das gesunde Volksempfinden ist gegen Dad und Jo," *Hamburger Gaunachrichten*, October 1941, quoted in Pohl, " 'Schräge Vögel,' " 253–54.

97. Excerpt from circular of the Reichsführer SS and Chief of the German Police Heinrich Himmler, October 25, 1944, concerning "the fight against youth cliques," reprinted in Burleigh and Wippermann, *The Racial State*, 237–39.

98. Kater, *Different Drummers*, 153–62, 177–201.

99. Pohl, " 'Schräge Vögel,' " 244.

100. See Peukert, *Inside Nazi Germany*, 145–66; Burleigh and Wippermann, *The Racial State*, 222–24.

101. Burleigh and Wippermann, *The Racial State*, 224–26; Dickinson, *The Politics of German Child Welfare*, 237–38.

102. On this effort, see Gassert, *Amerika im Dritten Reich*, 352–69.

103. Goebbels on December 16, 1941, quoted in Gassert, *Amerika im Dritten Reich*, 354.

104. Der Reichsführer SS, SS Hauptamt (ed.), "Amerikanismus—eine Weltgefahr," Berlin, n.d. [1943], quoted in Gassert, *Amerika im Dritten Reich*, 355–57.

105. Diner, *America in the Eyes of the Germans*, 110–11; Gassert, *Amerika im Dritten Reich*, 366–68. On the success of anti-Soviet propaganda, see also Grossmann, "A Question of Silence," 33–52; Naimark, *The Russians in Germany*.

CHAPTER 1

1. Bednarik, *Der junge Arbeiter*. For reviews, see Hans Scholle, "Der junge Arbeiter von heute—ein neuer Typ," *Die berufsbildende Schule* 6 (1954): 125–27; "Schlurfe im Dschungel," *Der Spiegel*, no. 31 (1953), 32–33. Bednarik was Viennese, but believed that his findings were applicable beyond Austria. West German commentators agreed.

2. See for example, "So sieht die faschistische Brut der Adenauer, Ollenhauer, Kaiser und Reuter aus!" *Neues Deutschland*, June 21, 1953.

3. See statistics in Guback, *The International Film Industry*, 47. American films were important, although they did not constitute the majority of top-grossing productions. For lists of top-grossing productions in West Germany, see Sigl, Schneider, and Tornow, *Jede Menge Kohle?*

4. For American movies released in East Germany, see Kersten, *Das Filmwesen*, 360–61.

5. Naimark, *The Russians in Germany*, 421–23.

6. On the formation of the two Germanies in the context of the Cold War, see for example, Snell, *Wartime Origins*; Loth, *Die Teilung der Welt*; Harrell, *Berlin*; Diefendorf, Frohn, and Rupieper, *American Policy*; Gimbel, *The American Occupation*; Schwartz, *America's Germany*; Boehling, *A Question of Priorities*; Rupieper, *Die Wurzeln*; Turner, *Reconstruction*; Naimark, *The Russians in Germany*; Kleßmann, *Die doppelte Staatsgründung*; Staritz, *Die Gründung der DDR*.

7. Höhn, "GIs," 15–16; Gimbel, *The American Occupation*; Nelson, *Defenders or Intruders?*; Pells, *Not Like Us*.

8. See for example, Fehrenbach, *Cinema in Democratizing Germany*, chap. 3; Tröger, "Between Rape and Prostitution"; Heineman, "Hour of the Woman"; Grossmann, "A Question of Silence."

9. See Goedde, "From Villains to Victims"; Höhn, "GIs," 135–38; Heineman, "Hour of the Woman," 381.

10. Höhn, "GIs," especially chaps. 3, 5.

11. Naimark, *The Russians in Germany*, chap. 2; Grossmann, "A Question of Silence."

12. Frank Biess has employed this term for East Germany. See Biess, " 'Pioneers of a New Germany.' " On this concept in the West German context, see the Discussion Forum, "The 'Remasculinization' of Germany in the 1950s."

13. Naimark, *The Russians in Germany*, 133.

14. See Pike, *The Politics of Culture;* Jäger, *Kultur und Politik,* chap. 1; Emmerich, *Kleine Literaturgeschichte der DDR,* chap. 3; Naimark, *The Russians in Germany,* 398.

15. On reeducation, see Tent, *Mission on the Rhine;* Roy Willis, *The French in Germany;* Pronay and Wilson, *The Political Re-education of Germany.*

16. See Ermarth, "Introduction"; Schwartz, "Reeducation and Democracy; Pells, *Not Like Us,* 40–52.

17. See Robin, *The Barbed-Wire College;* Fehrenbach, *Cinema in Democratizing Germany;* Schildt, "Die USA als 'Kulturnation.' " On hostilities toward jazz and American cultural policies, see Levine, "Jazz and American Culture"; Leonard, *Jazz and the White Americans;* Panish, *The Color of Jazz.*

18. See especially HICOG survey 181 "The America House Reevaluated: A Study of the Effectiveness of the U.S. Information Centers in West Germany," July 17, 1953, reel 8, frames 5052–59, Merritt Collection On Public Opinion in Germany. See also Rupieper, *Die Wurzeln,* 151; Schildt, "Die USA als 'Kulturnation,' " 261.

19. On the GYA program, see Rupieper, *Die Wurzeln,* 156–62.

20. See Guback, "Shaping the Film Business," 255–66; Fehrenbach, *Cinema in Democratizing Germany,* chap. 2.

21. On May, see Hohendahl, "Von der Rothaut."

22. See Jäschke, "Produktionsentwicklungen"; interview with Wolfgang Hille.

23. See Lange, *Jazz in Deutschland* (1966), 119, 151–52; Kater, *Different Drummers,* 203.

24. Lange, *Jazz in Deutschland* (1966), 153–68; Karl-Heinz Drechsel, insert for *Jazz in Deutschland,* 3–4; Höhne, *Jazz in der DDR,* 21–32; Ruebe, " 'Wir wollten einfach FREUNDE sein...,' " 58–60; Mählert and Stephan, *Blaue Hemden,* 46–47.

25. See Lange, *Jazz in Deutschland* (1966), 119, 151–52; Kater, *Different Drummers,* 203.

26. Paul Höfer in *Aufbau* (May 1946), quoted in Ryback, *Rock Around the Bloc,* 12.

27. Josef Marein, "Tanzmusik so oder so? Jazz—eine Kulturschande?" *Hörzu,* no. 44 (1947).

28. Naimark, *The Russians in Germany,* 410–13.

29. Ibid., 103.

30. Posters published by Amt für Information, Berlin and the Landesregierung Thüringen in 1950. See *Magazin,* 14–15.

31. "Bekenntis und Verpflichtung," *Neues Deutschland,* September 5, 1948, reprinted in Schubbe, *Dokumente,* 91–94, 92.

32. Naimark, *The Russians in Germany,* 434.

33. Speech by Anton Ackermann at the First Central Cultural Conference of the SED, Berlin May 5–8, 1948, reprinted in Schubbe, *Dokumente,* 84–90.

34. See Pike, *The Politics of Culture,* 393–536; Erbe, *Die verfemte Moderne,* 55–59; Naimark, *The Russians in Germany,* 134, 415–16; Lange, *Jazz in*

Deutschland (1966), 164. On Zhdanov's campaign, see Starr, *Red and Hot,* chap. 10; Ryback, *Rock Around the Bloc,* 8–9; Stites, *Russian Popular Culture,* 116–22.

35. See Starr, *Red and Hot,* chaps. 5, 8, 10. On the concept of cosmopolitanism and its relation to anti-Semitism in the Soviet Union and the GDR from the late 1940s to the early 1950s, see Pike, *The Politics of Culture,* 467–72, 560–74. On East German attempts to come to terms with Nazi anti-Semitism, see Timm, "Der 9. November 1938," 246–62. On postwar East German anti-Semitism, see Herf, "East German Communists," 627–61, and Herf, *Divided Memory.* On Communist fears of a "Jewish-cosmopolitan conspiracy" in the 1920s, see Mosse, *Toward the Final Solution,* 187.

36. Harsh, "Society, the State and Abortion." On the problems of attracting the intelligentsia, see also Naimark, *The Russians in Germany,* 401–2.

37. See Fehrenbach, *Cinema in Democratizing Germany;* Maria Mitchell, "Materialism and Secularism"; Dickfeldt, *Jugendschutz als Jugendzensur;* Dickinson, *The Politics of German Child Welfare;* Kleßmann, *Zwei Staaten.*

38. Robert Brüntrop, "Jugendschutz—Herzanliegen unseres Volkes." *Ruf ins Volk* 3 (Dec. 1951), 3.

39. Roseman, "The Organic Society."

40. Brüntrop, "Jugendschutz," 3.

41. Rothe/Becker/Zimmermann/Seidel, *Jugendschutz und Öffentlichkeit* (1953), quoted in Dickfeldt, *Jugendschutz als Jugendzensur,* 114.

42. Hans Seidel, "Was will das neue Jugendschutzgesetz?" (1952), quoted in Dickfeldt, *Jugendschutz als Jugendzensur,* 116; Seidel's article was also widely distributed as a brochure.

43. See Dickfeldt, *Jugendschutz als Jugendzensur,* 144–60; Jäschke, "Produktionsentwicklungen"; "Mit Schmökergrab und Kabarett," *Der Tag,* September 14, 1953.

44. The law was called "Law for the Protection of the Youth in Public," and regulated not only dancing, but also movies, variety shows, gambling, and the consumption of tobacco and alcohol.

45. Hans Engelbach, "Entwurf eines Gesetzes zum Schutze der Jugend in der Öffentlichkeit," (1949), LAB Rep. 13, Acc. 1046, No. 18. Material used to publicize the new youth protection law also focused on the dangers dancing and public dance halls posed for girls. See the flyer by Aktion Jugendschutz, *Was will das neue Jugendschutzgesetz?* (Hamm: Hoheneck-Verlag, 1952), LAB Rep. 13, Acc. 1046, No. 18; "So jung und schon . . ." *Illus,* January 20, 1952. See also "Louise Hartung, Bericht von der Arbeitstagung über das Gesetz zum Schutze der Jugend in der Öffentlichkeit," *Der Rundbrief* 2 (November 1952): 8, LAB Rep. 13, Acc. 1227, No. 88; "Da muß doch an der Leitung etwas nicht in Ordnung sein," *Blickpunkt,* no. 13 (1952); "Die Berliner Jugendgerichtshilfe im Jahre 1955," *Der Rundbrief* 6 (April 1956): 50–60, LAB Rep. 13, Acc. 1022, No. 7.

46. On Gladow, see Heimann, "Das Überleben organisieren"; Gladow's story has been fictionalized in a novel by Erich Loest, *Die Westmark fällt*

weiter, and a film by Thomas Brasch. See also the screenplay and documents in Brasch, *Engel aus Eisen.*

47. See "Höhepunkte im Gladowprozess," *Berliner Zeitung,* March 28, 1950; also "Der vollendete Gangster," *Kurier,* March 28, 1950; "Der nervöse Revolverheld," *Kurier,* March 29, 1950.

48. "Villa mit Panzerjalousien," *Tägliche Rundschau,* April 1, 1950.

49. See, for example, "Berlin ist nicht Chikago," *Neues Deutschland,* April 9, 1950; "Entgleiste Jugend," *Abend,* April 11, 1950.

50. "Die Beweisnahme ist zu Ende," *Tägliche Rundschau,* April 4, 1950; "Villa mit Panzerjalousien," *Tägliche Rundschau,* April 1, 1950; Alice Stettiner, "Amerikanische Kulturbarbarei bedroht unsere Jugend," *Neues Deutschland,* April 4, 1950; Carl Corvus, "Werner Gladow und die Verbrecher-Romantik," *Tagesspiegel,* April 2, 1950.

51. "Die Beweisnahme ist zu Ende," *Tägliche Rundschau,* April 1, 1950.

52. Rudolf Hirsch, "Gladows Vorbilder: Wildwest und Gestapo," *Tägliche Rundschau,* March 31, 1950.

53. Gladow committed his last murder three days after his eighteenth birthday, which made it possible to try him as an adult. See "War der Bandenchef erwachsen?" *Der Tag,* April 1, 1950.

54. Kiebitz, "Ein Psychiater und sein Kommissar," *Berliner Zeitung,* April 1, 1950. See also "Ich riss die Pistolen heraus," *Telegraf,* March 31, 1950.

55. Kiebitz, "Ein Psychiater und sein Kommissar," *Berliner Zeitung,* April 1, 1950.

56. Ibid.; "Krach im Gladow-Prozess," *Telegraf,* April 1, 1950.

57. Slotkin, *Gunfighter Nation,* 293–303, 379. The literature on American westerns also includes, among many others: Lenihan, *Showdown;* Lee Mitchell, *Westerns;* Tompkins, *West of Everything.*

58. See "Dreifache Todesstrafe für Gladow," *Neues Deutschland,* April 4, 1950; "Berlin ist nicht Chikago," *Neues Deutschland,* April 9, 1950; "Der Fall Gladow," *National-Zeitung,* April 12, 1950.

59. "Lehren aus dem Gladow-Prozess," *Tägliche Rundschau,* April 6, 1950.

60. "Der Fall Gladow," *National-Zeitung,* April 12, 1950.

61. "Lehren aus dem Gladow-Prozess"; Stettiner, "Amerikanische Kulturbarbarei bedroht unsere Jugend," *Neues Deutschland,* April 4, 1950.

62. "Lehren aus dem Gladow-Prozess."

63. See Guback, "Shaping the Film Business," 255–66, and Guback, *The International Film Industry,* 47.

64. "Wild-West-Jubiläum," *Film-Dienst* 4, November 9, 1951; "Der 200. Wildwest-Film in Deutschland," *Film-Dienst* 6, April 10, 1953.

65. E. Werner, "Untersuchungen über die Idealbildung," *Bildung und Erziehung* 5, no. 7 (1952): 485–98.

66. See the introduction and answers by court officials in Lavies, *Film und Jugendkriminalität.*

67. See "Gladows Wildwest-Methoden," *Telegraf am Morgen,* March 30, 1950; Stückrath, "Der Überfall der Ogalalla auf die Jugend," *Westermanns*

Pädagogische Beiträge 4 (1952): 220–22. On the problem of race and American imperialism in U.S. westerns, see Engelhardt, "Ambush at Kamikaze Pass."

68. Stückrath, "Der Überfall der Ogalalla."

69. Ibid.

70. "Das Filmwesen in der DDR," *Der Augenzeuge* (Berlin, 1952), LAB LAZ 3196.

71. HICOG officer Oscar Martay quoted in Fehrenbach, *Cinema in Democratizing Germany*, 239.

72. On the festival, see Fehrenbach, *Cinema in Democratizing Germany*, 234–53.

73. Carlbergh and Völckers, "Bericht für den Herrn Regierenden Bürgermeister," December 31, 1954; "Protokoll über die Besprechung in der Frage der Neuregelung der Sondervorstellungen für Ostbesucher (Grenztheater)," February 18, 1955, both LAB Rep. 2, Acc. 1636, No. 2163.

74. MPEA official at special meeting of the MPEA Board of Directors, June 7, 1951, quoted in Guback, "Shaping the Film Business," 266–67.

75. "Westfilm in amerikanischer Versklavung," *Der Morgen*, May 30, 1953; "Kein Mangel an Romantik," *Neue Zeit*, July 24, 1963.

76. Lange, *Jazz in Deutschland* (1966), 146, 151–52.

77. "K.o. durch Töne," *Berliner Montag*, October 31, 1949. See also "Es plätschert weiter," *Der Tag*, December 18, 1949; "Ostzonen-Jazz siegte," *Neue Zeitung*, March 7, 1950; "...bei dunklen Musikanten im Titania-Palast," *Abend*, September 3, 1952.

78. See Berendt, *Das Jazzbuch*, 203–5; Bednarik, *Der junge Arbeiter*, 86–91; Rudorf, *Nie wieder links*, 55–57; "An die jungen Modeherren," *Blickpunkt* no. 21 (1951); Gerd Scharnhorst, "Schräge Musik ist noch kein Jazz," *Die Welt*, March 6, 1955; Glaser, *Kulturgeschichte der Bundesrepublik*, 1:222–23.

79. "Badewanne," *Berliner Wirtschaftsblatt*, May 5, 1951; "Das beste Boogie-Paar," *Telegraf*, October 10, 1952; "Abends schnell mal in die Badewanne," *Nacht-Depesche*, September 30, 1952; "Untergetaucht in der Badewanne," *Der Abend*, April 22, 1953.

80. "Die Erwachsenen sind schuld," *Die Zeit*, January 10, 1952.

81. See "Montmatre in Berlin," *Tagesspiegel*, July 10, 1949; "Ein Abend bei Bohemiens," *Tagesspiegel*, August 6, 1949.

82. See A. Gügler, *Euer Sohn in der Entwicklungskrise* (Stuttgart, 1952), 32–48, reprinted in Kuhnert and Ackermann, "Jenseits von Lust und Liebe?" 50.

83. For an attempt to counter such concerns, see Twittenhoff, *Jugend und Jazz*.

84. Hans Engelbach, "Entwurf eines Gesetzes zum Schutze der Jugend in der Öffentlichkeit," n.d. (1949), LAB Rep. 13, Acc. 1046, No. 18. See also "Wilde in der Badewanne," *N.Z. am Montag*, August 22, 1949; "So jung und schon..." *Illus*, January 20, 1952; "Weil's so schön war," *Blickpunkt* no. 14 (1953); Erna Maraun, "Schutzaufsichtshelfer diskutieren über 'Jugend und Tanz,'" *Der Rundbrief* 5 (March 1955): 23–24, LAB Rep. 13, Acc. 1022, No. 6.

85. "K.o. durch Töne," *Berliner Montag*, October 31, 1949.

86. Wolfgang Menge, "Wenn der Club wach wird...," *Die Zeit,* December 4, 1952.

87. "Nihilismus mit Boogie Woogie in der Badewanne," *Neues Deutschland,* September 7, 1949.

88. East German music professor Ernst Meyer, quoted in Ryback, *Rock Around the Bloc,* 12.

89. Kurt Hager in the East German monthly *Einheit* (1950), quoted in Ryback, *Rock Around the Bloc,* 9.

90. See Ernst Hermann Meyer, *Musik im Zeitgeschehen* (Berlin, 1952), quoted in Rauhut, *Beat,* 19; "In welcher Richtung muß sich unsere Musikkultur entwickeln?" *Neues Deutschland,* January 31, 1952; Reginald Rudolf (*sic*), "Für eine frohe, ausdrucksvolle Tanzmusik," *Musik und Gesellschaft* 2 (August 1952): 247–52; and the positive assessment of Rudorf's article in Notowicz to Uszkoreit, November 3, 1952, BArch P DR1, No. 243.

91. Starr, *Red and Hot,* 215. HA Jugendhilfe und Jugenderziehung, "Entwurf: Präambel 'Verordnung zum Schutze der Kinder und der Jugendlichen,'" Berlin, February 18, 1952, LAB (STA) Rep. 120, No. 2614; "Bericht über die Privattanzschulen," n.d. (ca. 1954), LAB (STA) Rep. 121, No. 162.

92. Alexander Abusch, "Aktuelle Fragen unserer Kulturpolitik," *Neues Deutschland,* June 14, 1950.

93. See for example, Erbe, *Die verfemte Moderne;* Emmerich, *Kleine Literaturgeschichte der DDR;* Jäger, *Kultur und Politik,* chap. 2.

94. Karl-Heinz Drechsel, inserts for *Jazz in Deutschland,* first and second CD; Noglik, "Hürdenlauf zum freien Spiel," 205–21, 207–9; Informationsbüro West Berlin, "Keine Lizenz für Tanzorchester mit amerikanischen Namen," February 4, 1952, BArch K ZSG 120.

95. See "Erster Schritt zur neuen Tanzmusik," *National-Zeitung,* December 23, 1952; Rudorf, *Jazz in der Zone,* 19–32.

96. See "Darf ich bitten—mir in die Tanzstunde zu folgen," *Blickpunkt* no. 6 (1952): 14.

97. Quote from "Zusammenstellung der Erfahrungsberichte der Bezirke für den Monat September 1951," Rundschreiben des Hauptjugendamtes Berlin, November 22, 1951, LAB Rep. 13, Acc. 992, No. 3.

98. For West Berlin, see "Jugend und Musik," *Der Rundbrief* 3 (February 1953): 37; Amt für Jugendförderung, "Protolkoll über die Arbeitsbesprechung," November 20, 1953, LAB Rep. 13, Acc. 1046, No. 11. See also interview with Susanne Quandt. For East Berlin, see Ruth Hoelzel, "Operative Arbeit der Jugendhilfe zur Verhütung der Jugendgefährdung," Berlin, n.d. (1954), LAB (STA) Rep. 119, No. 22.

99. Erna Maraun, "Schutzaufsichtshelfer diskutieren über 'Jugend und Tanz,'" *Der Rundbrief* 5 (March 1955): 23–24, LAB Rep. 13, Acc. 1022, No. 6.

100. Hans-Dieter Wehowski, "Nicht nur Jazzfreunde," *Der Rundbrief* 4 (February 1954): 25, LAB Rep. 13, Acc. 1022, No. 6.

101. See Uebel, *Viel Vergnügen,* 132; interview with Brigitte Lohmeier. The Resi reopened in 1951.

102. Osnabrück church message quoted in Fehrenbach, "The Fight for the 'Christian West,'" 46–47.

103. Quoted in Brüntrop, "Jugendschutz—Herzanliegen unseres Volkes."

104. Franz-Josef Wuermeling, "Das muß geschehen!" *Kirchen-Zeitung*, December 6, 1953, quoted in Grotum, *Die Halbstarken*, 68.

105. Newman to McCloy, March 19, 1951, quoted in Rupieper, *Die Wurzeln*, 168–69. The U.S. government and the U.S. entertainment industry were thus often at odds. See also Fehrenbach, *Cinema in Democratizing Germany*, chap. 2.

106. See Hagen, *DDR—Juni '53*, especially 59–70.

107. Ibid., 104–23. On the uprising, see also Bust-Bartel, "Der Arbeiteraufstand"; Baring, *Uprising in East Germany*; Diedrich, *Der 17. Juni 1953*; Fricke and Spittmann-Ruhle, *Der 17. Juni 1953*; Glaeßner, "Mutmaßungen"; Kowaczuk, Mitter, and Wolle, *Der Tag X*; Mitter and Wolle, *Untergang auf Raten*, chap. 1.

108. For critiques of these stances, see Glaeßner, "Mutmaßungen," 192–94; Bust-Bartel, "Der Arbeiteraufstand."

109. "Augenzeugen berichten," *Junge Welt*, June 19, 1953; "So sieht die faschistische Brut der Adenauer, Ollenhauer, Kaiser und Reuter aus!" *Neues Deutschland*, June 21, 1953.

110. Speech by Otto Grotewohl, June 26, 1953, quoted in Glaeßner, "Mutmaßungen," 192. See also "Alle Kraft für die geduldige Aufklärung der Jugend," *Junge Welt*, June 24, 1953; Wolfgang Neuhaus, "Das hatte mit dem Arbeiter nichts gemein," *Junge Welt*, June 25, 1953.

111. Reprints appeared in *Freiheit* (Halle); "So hausten sie—die Provokateure," *Junge Welt*, June 23, 1953; "Über die Lage und die unmittelbaren Aufgaben der Partei," *Junge Generation* 7, no. 12 (1953): 9–12; Ausschuß für Deutsche Einheit, *Wer zog die Drähte?* My thanks to Herr Czihak of the Landesarchiv Berlin (Außenstelle Breite Straße) for lending me the latter.

112. See "'Tag X'—Made in USA," *Junge Welt*, July 1, 1953.

113. "Augenzeugen berichten," *Junge Welt*, June 19, 1953.

114. Eissler, *Arbeiterparteien und Homosexuellenfrage*, 23–30; Stümke and Finkler, *Rosa Winkel*, 119–43; Bodek, *Proletarian Performance*; Moeller, "The Homosexual Man," 257.

115. Compare Hagen, *DDR—Juni '53*, 84–93; "Bericht über die Tätigkeit der ABV vom 19.06.53, 18 Uhr," Berlin, June 20, 1953, LAB (STA) Rep. 303/26, No. 072; Präsidium der Volkspolizei Berlin, Abteilung K-Leitung, "Zahl der festgenommenen Personen vom 17.06.1953. Massnahmen zum Putschversuch am 17. Juni 1953," Berlin, June 18, 1953, LAB (STA) Rep. 303/26, No. 072.

116. Polit-Abteilung, "Einschätzing der Briefe von verletzten Genossen an ihre Angehörigen," Berlin, June 20, 1953, LAB (STA) Rep. 303/26, No. 072.

117. Präsidium der Volkspolizei in Berlin, Abteilung K, "Zusätzlicher Quartalsbericht über die Vorkommnisse vom 17.-30.06.1953," Berlin, July 15, 1953, LAB (STA) Rep. 303/26, No. 072.

118. Party leaders who were removed included, among others, Rudolf Herrnstadt, the chief editor of *Neues Deutschland*, and the Minister of State

Security, Wilhelm Zaisser. See Baring, *Uprising in East Germany*, 102–9; Hagen, *DDR—Juni '53*, 174–81.

119. "Der Aufstand im Juni. Ein dokumentarischer Bericht (II)," *Monat* 6 (Oct. 1953): 45–66.

120. "Steine gegen Panzer," *Die Welt*, June 17, 1954; Ernst-Otto Maetzke, "Als Steine gegen Panzer flogen," *Die Zeit*, June 15, 1963.

121. See Baring, *Uprising in East Germany*, 98–102.

122. "Genosse Roesky zur Kenntnisnahme," November 17, 1953, LAB (STA) Rep. 121, No. 162.

123. Heinz Baeker, "Die Durchführung von Tanzabenden—ureigenste Angelegenheit der FDJ," and "Freund, kannst du linksherum tanzen?" *Junge Generation* 7, no. 14 (1953): 14–15, 23.

124. "Bei uns ist 3x in der Woche Tanz," *Junge Generation* 7, no. 17 (1953): 19; Mählert and Stephan, *Blaue Hemden*, 100.

125. SAPMO-BArch, ZPA, NL 90/516, reprinted in Mählert and Stephan, *Blaue Hemden*, 98–100.

126. See "Tanzmusik," *Neues Leben*, no. 10 (1954): 18–21.

127. See Rudorf, *Jazz in der Zone*; Ryback, *Rock Around the Bloc*, 15.

128. "Verordnung des Ministerrats der DDR zum Schutze der Jugend," *Gesetzblatt der DDR*, Teil 1, No. 80, September 29, 1955.

129. Bednarik, *Der junge Arbeiter*; Hans Bunk, "Im Zeichen des Zorro," *Lebendige Erziehung* 4, no. 14 (1955): 319–21; Klaus-Dieter Hartmann, "Buch und Filminteressen und finanzielle Lage Jugendlicher mit Volksschulbildung," *Pädagogische Rundschau* 11 (Oct. 1956): 22–29.

130. Bednarik, *Der junge Arbeiter*, 41–91; "Schlurfe im Dschungel," *Der Spiegel*, no. 31 (1953): 32–33.

131. Völckers, "Aktennotiz," November 21, 1954, LAB Rep. 2, Acc. 1636, No. 2163.

132. See chart in Kersten, *Das Filmwesen*, 360–61.

133. Carlbergh to movie theaters, March 31, 1955, LAB Rep. 2, Acc. 1636, No. 2163. See also Carlbergh to Wiener Lichtspiele, April 7, 1955, LAB Rep. 2, Acc. 1636, No. 2163.

134. Völckers to Amrehn, December 5, 1955, LAB Rep. 2, Acc. 1636, No. 2163.

135. For the German movie industry, see Fehrenbach, *Cinema in Democratizing Germany*.

136. Kater, *Different Drummers*, 88, 183–84.

137. "Musik aber keine music," *Abend*, June 2, 1949.

138. Margot Hielscher, "Nach einer Idee von mir," *Lübecker Freie Presse*, June 14, 1949; "…und die Musik spielt dazu!" *Die Welt*, June 8, 1949; "Es ist noch nicht lange her," *Telegraf*, April 13, 1949.

139. "Der versöhnende Jazz," *Telegraf*, June 3, 1949.

140. "Fräulein, pardon!" *National-Zeitung*, June 3, 1949; "Talmi-Alltag und Räuberpistole," *Neues Deutschland*, June 9, 1949; "…und die Musik spielt dazu!" *Die Welt*, June 8, 1949. The movie introduced tropes that would

become part of the *Heimatfilme* of the 1950s. On this successful West German genre see Fehrenbach, *Cinema in Democratizing Germany,* 148–68.

CHAPTER 2

1. *Abgeordnetenhaus von Berlin: Stenographische Berichte: 2. Wahlperiode* (Berlin, 1956), 42d Session, September 20, 1956, 522, (hereafter cited as *Abgh. Berlin*).

2. Hans Heinrich Muchow, "Zur Psychologie und Pädagogik der 'Halbstarken,'" *Unsere Jugend* 8, pt. 1 (Sep. 1956): 388–94; pt. 2 (Oct. 1956): 442–49; pt. 3 (Nov. 1956): 486–91.

3. *The Wild One* (U.S.A., 1954; German: *Der Wilde*); *Rebel Without a Cause* (U.S.A., 1955; German: *. . . denn sie wissen nicht, was sie tun*); *Blackboard Jungle* (U.S.A., 1955; German: *Saat der Gewalt*); *Rock Around the Clock* (U.S.A., 1956; German: *Außer Rand und Band*).

4. On American juvenile delinquency debates, see Doherty, *Teenagers and Teenpics*; Gilbert, *A Cycle of Outrage*; Cohen, "The Delinquents." For a polemic treatment of American teenage culture, see Lewis, *The Road*.

5. See Grotum, *Die Halbstarken,* 44.

6. On the political battles over West German rearmament, see Abenheim, *Reforging the Iron Cross*; Ulrich Albrecht, *Die Wiederaufrüstung*; Cioc, *Pax Atomica*; Doering-Manteuffel, *Die Bundesrepublik,* 73–77; Harder and Wiggershaus, *Tradition und Reform*; Large, *Germans to the Front.* On East Germany, see Thoß, "Volksarmee schaffen." On masculinity and the Wehrmacht in the Third Reich, see Bartov, *Hitler's Army.*

7. On West German youth cultures and American cultural influences in the second half of the 1950s, see especially Maase, *Bravo Amerika*; Heinz-Hermann Krüger, "*Die Elvis-Tolle*"; Grotum, *Die Halbstarken*; Bloemeke, *Roll over Beethoven*; Rauhut, *Beat*, chap. 1.

8. On Schelsky's concept, see Moeller, *Protecting Motherhood,* 119–20; also chap. 3 of this volume.

9. See *Verhandlungen des deutschen Bundestages: 2. Wahlperiode: Stenographische Berichte* (Bonn, 1955) (hereafter cited as *VDBT*), vol. 26, 92d and 93d Session, June 27 and 28, 1955, 5213–20, 5223–302; especially statements by Defense Minister Theodor Blank and by Erich Ollenhauer (SPD), Fritz Erler (SPD), Hasso von Manteuffel (FDP). For further statements by West German politicians against German militarism and for rearmament, see Harder und Wiggershaus, *Tradition und Reform,* 11–39.

10. See *VDBT,* 93d Session, June 28, 1955.

11. Advertisements for the *Bundeswehr* in *Der Spiegel*, nos. 30 and 31, 1956; *VDBT*, 93d Session, June 28, 1955, 5228.

12. *VDBT*, 93rd Session, June 28, 1955, 5230.

13. Domansky, "Militarization and Reproduction"; Moeller, "'The Last Soldiers'"; Biess, "Survivors of Totalitarianism."

14. Wierling, "Mission to Happiness."

15. See Biess, " 'Pioneers of a New Germany.' "

16. "Unordnung," *Welt am Sonntag,* November 6, 1949. See also *"Faust-recht der Prärie,"* Neue Zeitung, November 6, 1949.

17. "*Herr des Wilden Westens* in zwölf Theatern," *Telegraf,* April 9, 1950. The movie also received negative reviews. See "Die Leinwand wird wild," *Nachtexpreß,* April 12, 1950.

18. See Slotkin, *Gunfighter Nation,* 291, 397.

19. "*Herr des Wilden Westens* amerikanisch," *Neues Deutschland,* April 11, 1950.

20. "Ist der Wildwestfilm keine Gefahr?" *Junge Stimme* (Nov. 1954): 1–2; "Der Wildwestfilm ist besser als sein Ruf," *Darmstädter Echo,* May 1, 1954. A translation of Warshow's piece was published in West Germany: Warshow, "Helden aus dem Goldenen Westen," *Der Monat* 6 (March 1954): 639–47.

21. Quotation from "Neu auf der Leinwand," *Telegraf,* October 24, 1953; *"Mein großer Freund Shane," Telegraf,* November 2, 1953. For other positive reviews of *Shane (Mein großer Freund Shane),* see *Neue Zeitung,* October 25, 1953; *Spandauer Volksblatt,* October 25, 1953; of *High Noon (Zwölf Uhr Mit-tags),* "Außenseiter gehen ihren Weg," *Abend,* January 15, 1953; Günter Ebert, "Kammerspiel und Angstschweiß," *Das neue Wort,* April 11, 1953.

22. Advertising for *Der Wilde,* Deutsche Kinemathek, Berlin.

23. This indictment appeared in a review of *A Streetcar Named Desire* in West Germany: "Der 'Gorilla-Typ' triumphiert," *B.Z.,* January 8, 1954. The article used the American term "sex appeal."

24. "*Der Wilde* mit Pferdestärken," *Montagsecho,* April 12, 1955.

25. See Gilbert, *A Cycle of Outrage,* 64, 182–83.

26. "*Der Wilde,*" *Kurier,* April 13, 1955. Other reviews drew parallels to German biker gangs: "*Der Wilde,*" *Abend,* January 21, 1955; "Das ist *Der Wilde,*" *Montagsecho,* March 7, 1955.

27. "Die Berliner Jugendgerichtshilfe im Jahre 1955," *Der Rundbrief* 6, no. 4/5 (1956), Rep. 13, Acc. 1022, No. 7; "Hoher Anteil der Verkehrsdelikte an der Jugendkriminalität," *Tagesspiegel,* August 19, 1956. See also Curt Bondy et al., *Jugendliche stören die Ordnung,* 9, who describe this incident as the beginning of youth riots.

28. See Peukert, *Inside Nazi Germany,* 154; Dr. Stein, *Abgh. Berlin,* 42d Session, September 20, 1956, 522.

29. See "Neue Krawalle am Wedding," *Telegraf,* July 13, 1956; *Berlin. Chronik der Jahre 1955–1956* (1971), 552–53.

30. Grotum, *Die Halbstarken,* 79–80, 231–33; minutes of the West Berlin Ausschuß für Jugend, October 5, 1956, LAB Rep. 2, Acc. 1949, No. 2508.

31. Grotum, *Die Halbstarken,* 87, 141–42.

32. The head of the Braunschweig police quoted in Grotum, *Die Halb-starken,* 99.

33. Grotum, *Die Halbstarken,* 113–15.

34. Interview with Achim Schreiber, quoted in Maase, *Bravo Amerika,* 273; Grotum, *Die Halbstarken,* 118.

35. See Maase, *Bravo Amerika*; Grotum, *Die Halbstarken*, 194–99.

36. Peukert, "Die 'Halbstarken'"; Grotum, *Die Halbstarken*, 110–11.

37. See Sträter, "'Das konnte,'" 152; Maase, *Bravo Amerika*, 77–79; Grotum, *Die Halbstarken*, 72–73, 125–28. On the development of consumption in 1950s Germany, see Mooser, *Arbeiterleben*; Wildt, *Am Beginn der 'Konsumgesellschaft'*; Schildt and Sywottek, "'Reconstruction' and 'Modernization'"; Schildt, *Moderne Zeiten*.

38. See *7 Uhr Blatt*, October 7, 1956; Bondy et al., *Jugendliche stören die Ordnung*, 28.

39. Maase, *Bravo Amerika*, 120–31; Grotum, *Die Halbstarken*, 202.

40. See Karena Niehoff, "*...denn sie wissen nicht, was sie tun*," *Tagesspiegel*, April 1, 1956; Arbeitsausschuß der FSK (Freiwillige Selbstkontrolle der Filmwirtschaft), "Jugendprotokoll: Denn sie wissen nicht, was sie tun..." January 19, 1956, LBS; "*...denn sie wissen nicht, was sie tun*," *Beratungsdienst Jugend und Film* (August 1956).

41. For a critique of the effacement of class differences in *Rebel*, see Martin Rupert, "*... denn sie wissen nicht, was sie tun*," *Frankfurter Allgemeine Zeitung*, March 31, 1956.

42. Stephan Roth, "Die ratlosen Ganzschwachen," *Die Zeit*, April 11, 1957.

43. Konrad Adenauer, *Memoirs, 1945–53*, quoted in Carter, *How German Is She?* 30.

44. *VDBT*, 166th Session, October 25, 1956, 9175; Grotum, *Die Halbstarken*, 172–80.

45. *Cosmopolitan* (Nov. 1957), quoted in Gilbert, *A Cycle of Outrage*, 16.

46. Mawry M. Travis to Senate Subcommittee, quoted in Gilbert, *A Cycle of Outrage*, 18.

47. Gilbert, *A Cycle of Outrage*, 40, 74–76.

48. *An Euch alle*, 5.

49. For an expression of this logic, see also the movie *Alarm im Zirkus* (GDR, 1954).

50. Werner Berger, "Schmarren für die Freiheit," *Blickpunkt*, April 1956. For East German worries, see Referat Film, "Plan 1956," Berlin, December 12, 1955, LAB (STA) Rep. 121, No. 225; *An Euch Alle*.

51. Abteilung Geldumlauf, Berliner Zahlungsverein, "Analyse des Besuches von Westberliner Kinos durch Bewohner unseres Wirtschaftsgebietes," April 16, 1956; "Analyse des Besuches von westberliner (sic) Lichtspieltheatern durch Bewohner unseres Währungsgebietes," May 17, 1957, both LAB (STA) Rep. 121, No. 156. Both reports also expressed concerns about the economic impact of these numbers.

52. Interviews with Peter Dannemann and Dietmar Iser; "Protokoll über einen Erfahrungsaustausch über die Arbeit der Jugendklubs in der DDR," 1960, JA-IzJ A6724.

53. On East German rowdies, see "Protokoll der Sitzung des Zentralrats der FDJ," September 19, 1956, JA-IzJ, 2608; Mählert and Stephan, *Blaue Hemden*, 109.

54. *An Euch alle*, 5.

55. See, for example, "... *denn sie wissen nicht, was sie tun,*" *Frankfurter Allgemeine Zeitung,* March 31, 1956; "... *denn sie wissen nicht, was sie tun,*" *Beratungsdienst Jugend und Film* (August 1956).

56. Fried Maximilian, "Die Saat der Gewalt," *Film, Bild, Ton* 5 (1955/56). The author of "Die Saat der Gewalt," *Abend,* December 2, 1955, saw the presence of many races in the United States as the root of juvenile misbehavior, yet agreed with others who endorsed the progressive view of American race relations.

57. "Die Saat der Diplomatie," *Telegraf,* November 5, 1955; "Diskussion um die Zensur—vorerst platonisch," *Mannheimer Morgen,* November 12, 1955; "Die Saat der Gewalt," *Abend,* November 3, 1955. On the cultural and political impact of the stereotypes of the black rapist and his white female victim in both the United States and Europe, see for example, Vron Ware, "Moments of Danger."

58. "*Saat der Gewalt,*" *Tagesspiegel,* December 4, 1955.

59. Werner Fiedler, "Brutalität—besonders wertvoll?" *Der Tag,* December 2, 1955. See also "Der Dompteur der Klasse," *Telegraf,* December 2, 1955; "Verfälschte Erziehungsprobleme," *Film, Bild, Ton* 5 (1955/56).

60. Erich Richter, "Wenn die Umwelt versagt," *Blickpunkt* (March 1956). For the connections between "racial liberalism" and "sexual conservatism" in the 1950s in the United States, see Feldstein, *Raising Citizens.*

61. See "Halbstarke und Spießer in den USA," *Berliner Zeitung,* December 12, 1955; "Ein richtiger Direks fehlt," *Depesche,* December 8, 1955; "Die Saat der Gewalt," *Abend,* November 3, 1955; "Wen verwirrte *Saat der Gewalt?*" *National-Zeitung,* January 19, 1956.

62. "Wir und der Film: *Saat der Gewalt,*" *Jugendruf* (January 1956): 20.

63. Bloemeke, *Roll over Beethoven,* 59; "'Besonders wertvoll,'" *Der Tag,* October 28, 1955; "Die Saat der Diplomatie," *Telegraf,* November 5, 1955; "Amerikanische Schultragödie," *Wirtschaftszeitung,* November 5, 1955; "Wen verwirrte *Saat der Gewalt?*" *National-Zeitung,* January 19, 1956; "Halbstarke und Spiesser in den USA," *Berliner Zeitung,* December 12, 1955; Sigl, Schneider, and Tornow, *Jede Menge Kohle?* 130.

64. On *The Wild One* soundtrack, see "Das ist *Der Wilde,*" *Montagsecho,* March 7, 1955; "*Der Wilde* mit Pferdestärken," *Montagsecho,* April 12, 1955. For West German reactions to the *Blackboard Jungle* soundtrack, see "Die Saat der Gewalt," *Abend,* December 2, 1956; *Spandauer Volksblatt,* December 4, 1955; for East German reactions, see "Halbstarke und Spießer in den USA," *Berliner Zeitung,* December 12, 1955; "Wen verwirrte *Saat der Gewalt?*" *National-Zeitung,* January 19, 1956.

65. "Schattenseiten der Freiheit," *Kurier,* December 3, 1955.

66. "Amerikanische Schultragödie," *Wirtschaftszeitung,* November 5, 1955.

67. "Die kühne Attacke derer vom Telegraf," *B.Z. am Abend,* November 21, 1955. On *stilyagi,* see Stites, *Russian Popular Culture,* 124–27.

68. See for example, "Die Königin greift ein," *Spandauer Volksblatt,* September 19, 1956; report about riots abroad in *National-Zeitung,* September 28, 1956.

69. "Die ganze Welt rockt und rollt," *Bravo,* September 30, 1956.

70. See for example, "Appell an den Urmenschen," *Berliner Zeitung,* December 13, 1956.

71. FSK, "Jugendprotokoll: *Außer Rand und Band,"* July 6, 1956, LBS.

72. Advertising for *Außer Rand und Band,* Schriftgut 1124, BArch FAB.

73. Sigl, Schneider, and Tornow, *Jede Menge Kohle,* 131; Grotum, *Die Halbstarken,* 81; Maase, *Bravo Amerika,* 96.

74. Roesler, "Privater Konsum."

75. On the 1956 events, see Mitter and Wolle, *Untergang auf Raten,* chap. 2.

76. Albert Norden and Walter Ulbricht in "Protokoll der 25. Tagung des Zentralkomitees der SED," October 24–27, 1955, quoted in Mählert and Stephan, *Blaue Hemden,* 110–11; *Dokumente der SED,* vol. 6, quoted in Dietrich Staritz, *Geschichte der DDR, 1949–85* (1985), 108.

77. *An Euch alle;* also Mählert and Stephan, *Blaue Hemden,* 112–16.

78. See FDJ-Kreisleitung Prenzlauer Berg, "Wocheneinschätzung," February 25, 1956, and June 12, 1956, JA-IzJ AB338; "Warum laufen in der DDR keine amerikanischen Filme?" *Neues Deutschland,* May 26, 1956; Mählert and Stephan, *Blaue Hemden,* 115.

79. "Berlin—aus der Nähe gesehen," *Berliner Zeitung,* May 20, 1956.

80. Program brochure for *Eine Berliner Romanze, Progress Film-Illustrierte,* no. 66, 1956, LBS.

81. See Martin Schulz, *"Eine Berliner Romanze," B.Z. am Abend,* May 23, 1956; Günter Stahnke, *"Eine Berliner Romanze," Junge Welt,* May 18, 1956; "Gangsterliteratur und Naziorden," *Berliner Zeitung,* September 16, 1956.

82. Sekretariat des Zentralrats der FDJ, "Stellungnahme," supplement 1 to "Protokoll," Berlin, September 19, 1956, JA-IzJ 2608. This statement on "the events among parts of the youth in West Germany and West Berlin" was to be published in the FDJ newspaper *Junge Welt* and to be distributed to youth organizations in the West.

83. "Bonner Vergehen an der Jugend," *Der Morgen,* September 14, 1956. See also "Nato-Soldaten unbeliebt," *Neues Deutschland,* September 19, 1956.

84. "Halbstarke prügeln Volkspolizisten," *Nachtdepesche,* October 2, 1956; "Jugendkrawalle in der Zone," *Telegraf,* October 3, 1956; *Die Zeit,* October 18, 1956, quoted in Mählert, *Blaue Hemden,* 109.

85. See "Protokoll der Sitzung des Zentralrats," September 19, 1956, JA-IzJ 2608. These anniversaries would remain occasions for protest. In the fall of 1989 the East German opposition staged demonstrations around that date.

86. Grotum, *Die Halbstarken,* 182.

87. Walter Abendroth, "Das große Kopfschütteln über die Jugend," *Die Zeit,* September 27, 1956. See also Grotum, *Die Halbstarken,* 157–60, 174–75.

88. "Geprügelte Soldaten," *Rheinischer Merkur,* October 12, 1956. See Moeller, "The Homosexual Man."

89. Muchow, "Zur Psychologie und Pädagogik"; Grotum, *Die Halbstarken,* 186. Many German researchers of youth would use Muchow's thesis as a starting point. See for example Bondy et al., *Jugendliche stören die Ordnung;* Schelsky, *Die skeptische Generation;* Kaiser, *Randalierende Jugend.*

90. Adolf Busemann, "Verwilderung und Verrohung," *Unsere Jugend* 8 (April 1956); 159–68, 168.

91. See "Ausrüstung für sechs deutsche Divisionen," *Tagesspiegel*, September 12, 1956; Hans-Georg Hermann, "Die 'Lümmels' des Herrn Bundeskanzler," *Die andere Zeitung*, September 27, 1956. On the SPD stance, see Dietrich Schwarzkopf, "Der Bürger und die Bundeswehr," *Tagesspiegel*, September 12, 1956. Compare also Grotum, *Die Halbstarken*, 128–30; Maase, *Bravo Amerika*, 128–31.

92. Kaiser, *Randalierende Jugend*, 197–98; Grotum, *Die Halbstarken*, 129–30.

93. See the brochures distributed by the West Berlin Senator für Jugend und Sport, *Du und Deine Freizeit* (Berlin, n.d., ca. 1956); and *Wohin? Freizeitfibel für die Schulabgänger 1957* (Berlin, 1957).

94. See Max Jäger, "Es ging nicht nur um Pin-up-Girls," *Blickpunkt* (March 1956); "Kein Allheilmittel," *Blickpunkt* (August 1956); " 'Rock 'n' Roll' und Krawalle," *Blickpunkt* (December 1956). On *Falken* ambivalence toward consumption, see Lindemann and Schultz, *Die Falken in Berlin*.

95. W. Born, "Die böse Macht der Halbstarken," *Wochenend*, no. 13, 1956.

96. *Abgh. Berlin*, 42d Session, September 20, 1956, 517–23; "Parlaments-Debatte über Jugendkrawalle," *Tagesspiegel*, September 21, 1956; minutes of the West Berlin Ausschuß für Jugend, September 28, 1956, LAB Rep. 2, Acc. 1949, No. 2508.

97. *Abgh. Berlin*, 42d Session, September 20, 1956, 522; minutes of the West Berlin Ausschuß für Jugend, September 28, 1956, LAB Rep. 2, Acc. 1949, No. 2508.

98. *Hannoversche Presse*, July 28–29, 1956, quoted in Grotum, *Die Halbstarken*, 83.

99. "Halbstarke und Polizisten herhören," *Bravo*, September 16, 1956. On *Bravo*'s success and strategies, see especially Maase, *Bravo Amerika*, 104–11; for the United States, see Gilbert, *A Cycle of Outrage*, chaps. 10, 11.

100. *Die Halbstarken* (FRG, 1956). For reports, see "Man nennt sie 'Halbstarke,' " *Tagesspiegel*, April 17, 1956; "Wir sind keine Halbstarken," *Die Welt*, April 15, 1956; "Der große Unterschied," *Neues Deutschland*, April 17, 1956; "Sie sind besser als ihr Ruf," *Blickpunkt*, no. 52 (May 1956): 2–4; "Gutwillige Erwachsene stören nur," *Die Welt*, July 28, 1956; "Die Halbstarken," *Beratungsdienst Jugend und Film* (October 1956); " ...fehlt ihnen der Halt?" *Blickpunkt*, no. 57 (October 1956): 4–5; Jüngling, "Halbstarke."

101. "Gutwillige Erwachsene stören nur," *Die Welt*, July 28, 1956; Karena Niehoff, "Die Halbstarken," *Tagesspiegel*, October 7, 1956, 4; "Die Halbstarken," *Spiegel*, no. 42, 1956.

102. "B.Z. sucht... eine Marina Vlady," *B.Z.*, March 23, 1956; " 'Fertig zur Aufnahme!'," *B.Z.*, April 14, 1956; "Achtung, jetzt kommt die Diva!" *Brigitte*, no. 20 (1956).

103. Bertram and Krüger, "Vom Backfisch zum Teenager," 93–94; Dietz, "Sozius-Miezen," 32–34.

104. Delille and Grohn, "Fräulein Grünschnabel"; Dietz, "Sozius-Miezen," 34; "Amibüxen," in Glaser, *Kulturgeschichte*, 2:240.

105. Dietrich Schwarzkopf, "Der Bürger und die Bundeswehr," *Tagesspiegel,* September 12, 1956; *Hannoversche Presse,* August 16, 1956, cited in Grotum, *Die Halbstarken,* 164.

106. For West Germany, see brochures *Du und Deine Freizeit; Wohin?;* for East Germany, see *An Euch alle.*

107. Fröhner, *Wie stark.* For reviews, see "Wie ist die deutsche Jugend?" *Die Zeit,* October 18, 1956; "Die Eltern und Bismarck sind ihr Vorbild," *Der Tag,* October 13, 1956; also Grotum, *Die Halbstarken,* 168.

CHAPTER 3

1. Wolf Schirrmacher, "Jugend in Licht und Schatten," *Hamburger Anzeiger,* June 17, 1956.

2. Horst Knietzsch, "Wo wir nicht sind…," *Neues Deutschland,* September 3, 1957.

3. Kopstein, *Politics of Economic Decline;* Mooser, *Arbeiterleben;* Schildt, *Moderne Zeiten.* Theorists and historians have asserted that in the 1950s a new, masculine, subject of consumption was conceived. See Fraser, "What's Critical About Critical Theory?"; Maase, *Bravo Amerika;* Ehrenreich, *The Hearts of Men.*

4. Conservative in this sense then does not refer merely to a conservative tradition in West German politics but to a cultural vision that shaped East and West German reconstruction in the first half of the 1950s and that relied on rejecting foreign and American influences. Thus I refer to East German authorities espousing such visions often as conservative, although they considered themselves Marxists and communists.

5. "… *denn sie wissen nicht, was sie tun,*" *Beratungsdienst Jugend und Film* (August 1956).

6. See Karena Niehoff, "… *denn sie wissen nicht, was sie tun,*" *Tagesspiegel,* April 1, 1956; Martin Rupert, "… *denn sie wissen nicht, was sie tun,*" *Frankfurter Allgemeine Zeitung,* March 31, 1956.

7. "Conspiracy Against Germany," September 1951, reprinted in *Magazin,* cover, 15.

8. Arbeitsausschuß der FSK, "Jugendprotokoll: Denn sie wissen nicht, was sie tun…," January 19, 1956, LBS.

9. See for example, U.S. reviews in the *New Yorker,* November 5, 1955; *Time,* November 28, 1955. For readings of *Rebel* in the American context, see Biskind, *Seeing Is Believing,* 200–217; Doherty, *Teenagers and Teenpics.* On the social science discourse, see Gilbert, *A Cycle of Outrage,* esp. chaps. 8, 11; Breines, *Young, White, and Miserable,* chap. 1; Andrew Ross, *No Respect,* chap. 2; Feldstein, *Raising Citizens.*

10. Andrew Ross, *No Respect,* chap. 2.

11. Blücher, *Freizeit*; Bondy et al., *Jugendliche stören die Ordnung*; Schelsky, *Die skeptische Generation*.

12. Cold War liberal intellectuals had direct connections with the government: Schelsky was advisor to the family ministry, and Bondy's study made explicit policy recommendations. On postwar German liberalism, see Jarausch and Jones, "German Liberalism Reconsidered"; Conradt, "From Output Orientation"; Theo Schiller, "Parteienentwicklung." On Erhard's views of U.S. capitalism, see Berghahn, *The Americanization*. Also on Erhard, see Carter, "Alice," and Carter, *How German Is She?* chap. 1; Nicholls, *Freedom with Responsibility*. Schildt, *Moderne Zeiten*, 346–50, calls Schelsky a "'modern' conservative."

13. Riesman, *Die Einsame Masse*. See also Schildt and Sywottek, "'Reconstruction' and 'Modernization,'" 439, n. 123.

14. See Jay, *The Dialectical Imagination*, chap. 6.

15. On Riesman as representative of an American Cold War liberal position, see Andrew Ross, *No Respect*, chap. 3.

16. See, for example, Harry Pross's articles in *Frankfurter Allgemeine*, September 29, 1956, cited in Grotum, *Die Halbstarken*, 155, and in von Wensierski, "Die Anderen," 107–8; P. Merseburger, in a series of articles "Rebellen ohne Ziel," in *Hannoversche Presse* in August 1956, cited in Grotum, *Die Halbstarken*, 170.

17. Schelsky's introduction to Riesman, *Die Einsame Masse*; Helmut Schelsky, "Im Spiegel des Amerikaners," *Wort und Wahrheit* 11 (1956): 363–74; F. H. Tenbruck, "David Riesman: Kritik und Würdigung," *Jahrbuch für Amerikastudien* 2 (1957): 213–30.

18. Schelsky, *Wandlungen*. Blücher, *Freizeit*, 11–13, 118–24. See also Braun, "Helmut Schelskys Konzept"; Moeller, *Protecting Motherhood*; Schäfers, "Helmut Schelskys Jugendsoziologie."

19. Schildt and Sywottek, "'Reconstruction' and 'Modernization,'" 426–29.

20. Viggo Graf Blücher, "Jugend auf dem Weg zur Selbstbestimmung," *deutsche jugend* 4, no. 6 (June 1956): 260–65.

21. Schelsky, foreword for Blücher, *Freizeit*, v–vii.

22. Erhard, *Wohlstand für alle*; Schelsky, *Die skeptische Generation*, 5, claimed to analyze the West German adolescent from 1945 to 1955. He indeed drew occasionally on empirical research from this period, but in the context of this study, his work is more interesting as a blueprint for West German society.

23. Erhard, *Wohlstand für alle*, quoted in Victoria de Grazia, "Empowering Women," 283.

24. *Grundsatzprogramm der Sozialdemokratischen Partei Deutschlands* (Godesberger Programm).

25. Schelsky, foreword for Blücher, *Freizeit*, v–vii. Blücher, *Freizeit*, 31; Grotum, *Die Halbstarken*, 149.

26. Blücher, *Freizeit*, 100. For an exploration of this contradiction between gender-specific experiences in the United States and scholars' assertions that gender roles were converging, see Breines, *Young, White, and Miserable*, 57.

27. Blücher, *Freizeit*.

28. "Keine Angst vor Abenteuern?" *Der Tag,* December 9, 1956. On the effect of westerns, the article used a direct quote from Krause-Ablaß, "Entwicklungspsychologische Gesichtspunkte," 55. See also "Auf die richtige Auswahl kommt es an," *Wiesbadener Kurier,* November 3, 1956; "Der Film ist nicht an allem schuld," *Schwäbische Landeszeitung,* November 15, 1956.

29. On this history of racism see, for example, McClintock, *Imperial Leather.*

30. "Pferde, Pioniere und Pistolen," *Stuttgarter Nachrichten,* September 11, 1953.

31. On Freud's rejection of degeneration, see Gilman, "Sexology."

32. On psychology and antiracism, see Feldstein, *Raising Citizens;* Gilbert, *A Cycle of Outrage.* On appropriations of blackness as central to constructions of white masculinity in nineteenth- and twentieth-century America, see Lott, "White Like Me."

33. F. J. Gehrmann, "Illusion nicht gefragt," *Bremer Nachrichten,* September 22, 1956; "Junge Menschen bevorzugen Lebensechtheit," *Kurier,* September 8, 1956.

34. Blücher, *Freizeit,* 118–24.

35. Schelsky, *Die skeptische Generation,* 84–95. For Erhard, see his speech at the April 1960 CDU convention, "Wirtschaftspolitik als Teil der Gesellschaftspolitik," reprinted in Hohmann, *Ludwig Erhard,* 607–23, 614.

36. See Blücher, *Freizeit,* 124. On Schelsky's reception of cultural anthropology, which most certainly influenced Blücher, see Messelken, "Schelsky und die Kulturanthropologie."

37. Heinz Kluth, "Die 'Halbstarken'—Legende oder Wirklichkeit?" *deutsche jugend* 4 (November 1956): 495. See also, "Sind die 'Halbstarken' wirklich so stark?" *Der Tag,* September 18, 1956; "Halbstarke—was tun?" *Telegraf,* September 21, 1956.

38. Bondy et al., *Jugendliche stören die Ordnung;* Henry Kellermann to Curt Bondy, November 29, 1955, RG 59 511.622—2955, Box 2186, NA.

39. Schelsky, *Die skeptische Generation,* 66–84. This was picked up as a positive trait of the West German youth by reviewers. See "Die junge Generation," *Wirtschaftszeitung,* December 7, 1957; Hans Kudszus, "Eine Generation wird besichtigt," *Tagesspiegel,* March 30, 1958.

40. Schelsky, *Die skeptische Generation,* 456. Moeller, *Protecting Motherhood,* 191, has correctly called Schelsky "a sociologist for all seasons." Schelsky had assumed his first university position during the Third Reich. In the first half of the 1950s, he made a name for himself with his sociology of the family that promoted the role of a female homeworker and a male breadwinner and a treatise against Kinsey. Also he served on an advisory board to conservative Family Minister Wuermeling. On Schelsky, see also Lepsius, "Die Entwicklung der Soziologie," 38–39; Glaser, *Kulturgeschichte,* 195–96; Moeller, "The Homosexual Man."

41. Schelsky, "Im Spiegel des Amerikaners," 370.

42. Schelsky, *Die skeptische Generation*, 493. As Schelsky and some of his reviewers emphasized, this postwar West German youth was only the German version of a generation that consolidated Western industrial societies everywhere. Schelsky, *Die skeptische Generation*, 493; Hans Kudszus, "Eine Generation wird besichtigt," *Tagesspiegel*, March 30, 1958.

43. Schelsky, *Die skeptische Generation*, 488. This summary was picked up by Hans Kudszus, "Eine Generation wird besichtigt," *Tagesspiegel*, March 30, 1958; Friedrich Herzog, "*Die skeptische Generation*," *Der Tag*, February 7, 1958.

44. Schelsky, *Die skeptische Generation*, 494–97.

45. Kaiser, *Randalierende Jugend*, 203.

46. See "Die heutige Jugendgefährdung und ihre Überwindung," *Beiträge zum Jugendschutz*, no. 5 (1959): 15, quoted in Dickfeldt, *Jugendschutz als Jugendzensur*, 114.

47. Schelsky, "Beruf und Freizeit als Erziehungsziele in der modernen Gesellschaft," (1955), cited in Schildt and Sywottek, " 'Reconstruction' and 'Modernization,' " 426.

48. Schelsky, *Die skeptische Generation*, 494–97.

49. Blücher, *Freizeit*; Schelsky, *Die skeptische Generation*, 88–90. On Riesman and other American sociologists who assigned traditionally feminine qualities to the other-directed personality, see Breines, *Young, White, and Miserable*, 31.

50. See Erhard, "Politik der Mitte und der Verständigung," speech to the West German Bundestag, October 18, 1963, reprinted in Hohmann, *Ludwig Erhard*, 814–46.

51. On the use of psychology as central to postwar American Cold War liberalism, see Corber, *In the Name of National Security*; Feldstein, *Raising Citizens*, chaps. 3, 4. On the triumph of psychology in West Germany, see also Dickinson, *The Politics of German Child Welfare*, 257–61.

52. Fritz Kempe, "Erziehung der Erzieher—durch den Film," *Film-Telegramm* (February 1956). See also reports on psychological studies in "Keine Angst vor Abenteuern?" *Der Tag*, December 9, 1956.

53. Bondy et al., *Jugendliche stören die Ordnung*, 80–81.

54. Ibid., 54–55. According to Bondy et al., 74.1 percent of rioters lived with both parents in contrast to 63 percent of all West German adolescents. See also Grotum, *Die Halbstarken*, 119–21.

55. Bondy et al., *Jugendliche stören die Ordnung*, 76–77.

56. Ibid., 86–89, 92; Blücher, *Freizeit*; "Totenkopf bürgerlich," *Revue*, no. 19, 1962; Bals, *Halbstarke unter sich*, 146. For Schelsky's views that recognized sexuality as a cultural construct and yet viewed homosexuality as the expression of an abnormal society, see especially his *Soziologie der Sexualität*. See also Moeller, "The Homosexual Man." For a similar logic in the United States, see D'Emilio, *Sexual Politics*; Corber, *National Security*.

57. "Romy Schneider: Die Tochter-Gesellschaft," *Der Spiegel*, March 7, 1956, 35; Sigl, Schneider, and Tornow, *Jede Menge Kohle?* 130–31.

58. Karl Wahl, letter to the editor, *Der Spiegel*, March 21, 1956, 3.

59. See cover of *Bravo*, December 30, 1956.

60. See flyer, *Der Wilde* (1958), LBS.

61. See Mitter and Wolle, *Untergang auf Raten*, chap. 2. See also calls for a more creative and tolerant atmosphere in East German movie production and distribution in "Über Kirchturmperspektiven und Filmgouvernanten," *Deutsche Filmkunst* 4 (July 1956): 193–94.

62. For detailed readings, see Feinstein, "The Triumph of the Ordinary," chap. 2; Jüngling, "Halbstarke."

63. "Zwei Filme—ein Problem," n. p. info., File 1450, Schriftgut, BArch-FAB.

64. Kersten, *Das Filmwesen*, 297; Feinstein, "The Triumph of the Ordinary," 64.

65. Interview with Dietmar Iser.

66. Wolfgang Joho, "Nachkriegsjugend vor der Kamera," *Sonntag*, September 9, 1957. See also Feinstein, "The Triumph of the Ordinary," 67–68.

67. Horst Knietzsch, "Wo wir nicht sind...," *Neues Deutschland*, September 3, 1957; "*Berlin Ecke Schönhauser*," *B.Z. am Abend*, September 2, 1957.

68. See also Schenk, "Jugendfilm in der DDR," 23.

69. "*Berlin Ecke Schönhauser*," *B.Z. am Abend*, September 2, 1957.

70. "*Berlin Ecke Schönhauser*," *Defa-Heft*, no. 13 (1957), LBS.

71. See "*Berlin Ecke Schönhauser*," *Progress Film Programm*, no. 75 (1957), LBS; Horst Knietzsch, "Wo wir nicht sind...," *Neues Deutschland*, September 3, 1957.

72. "Die sich auf der Straße treffen," *Neue Zeit*, September 3, 1957.

73. "*Berlin Ecke Schönhauser*," *Sächsisches Tageblatt*, August 31, 1957.

74. "Unter den Torbögen Ostberlins," *Die Welt*, September 7, 1957.

75. See "*Berlin Ecke Schönhauser*," *B.Z. am Abend*, September 2, 1957; "*Berlin Ecke Schönhauser*," *Sächsisches Tageblatt*, August 31, 1957; "Nachkriegsjugend vor der Kamera," *Sonntag*, September 8, 1957; "Die sich auf der Straße treffen," *Neue Zeit*, September 3, 1957; "Jugend im heutigen Berlin," *Weltbühne*, September 25, 1957.

76. "*Berlin Ecke Schönhauser*," *Defa-Pressedienst*, no. 13 (1957). See also "*Berlin Ecke Schönhauser*," *Progress Film Programm*, no. 57 (1957), LBS.

77. Alfred Kurella, "Einflüsse der Dekadenz," excerpt of speech given in July 1957; for similar arguments, see Alexander Abusch's speech in the 32nd plenum of the Central Committee of the SED in July 1957, "Es gibt nur eine Kulturpolitik," both reprinted in Schubbe, *Dokumente*, 469–72, 473–78.

78. Horst Knietzsch, "Wo wir nicht sind...," *Neues Deutschland*, September 3, 1957.

79. Speech by Alexander Abusch, October 23, 1957, printed in *Dokumente*, 489–95.

80. See remarks by Hermann Schauer, "Die Prager Filmkonferenz und ihre Bedeutung," *Deutsche Filmkunst* 21, no. 2 (1958): 38, quoted in Kersten, *Das Filmwesen*, 94. See also statements made at a party activists' meeting in 1958 cited in Feinstein, "The Triumph of the Ordinary," 76–77.

81. See Schenk, "Jugendfilm in der DDR," 24.

82. See Kersten, *Das Filmwesen*, 105–15. The GDR production *Reportage 57* (1959) drew on negative depictions of *Halbstarke* and rock 'n' roll in West Berlin in its critiques of the West.

83. Ständige Kommission für Jugendfragen, Stadtverordnetenversammlung Gross-Berlin, "Bericht über die Jugendkriminalität," October 10, 1957; see also, report of East Berlin Police to Ständige Kommission für Jugendfragen, October 1, 1958; "Entwurf: Fragen der Verbesserung der Familienerziehung," n.d., ca. 1958, all LAB (STA) Rep. 119, No. 22; report by Werner Zschelle in the materials for the youth protection conference Leipzig, June 17–19, 1958, in *Richtige Jugendförderung ist der beste Jugendschutz* (n.d.), JA-IzB B2668.

84. See *Neues Deutschland* cited in U.S. Mission Berlin, Despatch 379, December 10, 1957, RG 59, 762b.00/12–1057, NA; U.S. Mission Berlin, Despatch 388, December 16, 1957, RG 59, 762b.00/12–1667, NA.

85. See U.S. Mission Berlin, Despatch 45, July 15, 1957, RG 59, 762b.00/7–1557, NA.

86. Ostermann, "Keeping the Pot Simmering"; American Embassy Bonn, Despatch 664, October 22, 1956, RG 59, 511.62b/10–2256, NA.

87. See American Embassy Bonn, Despatch 1784, March 31, 1958, RG 59, 511.62b/3–3158, NA, and Despatches 644 and 645, October 23, 1959, RG 59, 511.62B/1–2359, NA. On consumption and U.S. Cold War policies, see Elaine May, *Homeward Bound*; Hixon, *Parting the Curtain*. On the United States Information Agency, see Thomson and Laves, *Cultural Relations*.

88. American Embassy Bonn, Despatch 2486, May 23, 1955, RG 59, 511.62b/5–2355; Despatch 491, September 20, 1956, RG 59, 511.62b/9–2056; U.S. Mission Berlin, Despatch 11, July 6, 1955 RG 59, 511.62b/7–655, all NA.

89. American Embassy Bonn, Despatch 664, October 22, 1956, RG 59, 511.62b/10–2256, NA.

90. American Embassy Bonn, Despatch 1782, March 28, 1958, RG 59, 511.62b/3–2858, NA. East German authorities instituted similar programs, through which they drew about sixty thousand West German adolescents into East Germany in 1955 and 1956. American Embassy Bonn, Despatch 1782, March 28, 1958, RG 59, 511.62b/3–2858, NA.

91. For statistics on travel between East and West Germany, see American Embassy Bonn, Despatch 743, November 7, 1958, RG 59, 511.62b/11–758, NA.

92. See American Embassy Bonn, Despatches 644 and 645, October 23, 1959, RG 59, 511.62b/1–2359, NA.

93. See American Embassy Bonn, Despatch 961, December 19, 1958, RG 59, 511.62b/12–1958, NA.

94. For American worries about an East German newspaper report, see U.S. Mission Berlin, Despatch 603, February 26, 1959, RG 59, 511.62b/2–2659, NA.

95. See for example, U.S. Mission Berlin, Despatch 1002, June 30, 1955, RG 59, 862b.46/6–3055, NA.

96. See U.S. Mission Berlin, Despatch 197, September 24, 1957, RG 59, 511.62b/9–2457, NA.

97. U.S. Mission Berlin, Despatch 1044, June 18, 1957, RG 59, 762b.00/6–1857; U.S Mission Berlin Despatch 197, September 24, 1957, RG 59, 511.62b/9–2457, NA.

98. John Y. Millar, Acting Chief, Eastern Affairs Division, U.S. Mission Berlin, Despatch 199, September 25, 1957, RG 59, 862b.452/9–2567, NA.

99. See "Bericht über Erfahrungen und Ergebnisse der Maßnahmen zur Förderung des Gesamtberliner Kulturlebens," November 18, 1958; Senator für Volksbildung to the Bundesminister für gesamtdeutsche Fragen, Berlin, December 8, 1958; Dr. Antoine to the Bundesminister für gesamtdeutsche Fragen, March 12, 1959; all in LAB Rep. 7, Acc. 2186, No. 53.

100. Referat Film, "Streng Vertraulich," Berlin, April 16, 1959; Berliner Zahlungsverkehr, "Analyse des Besuches des Lichtspieltheater," (n.d., received by Magistrat February 25, 1960), both in LAB (STA) Rep. 121, No. 156; "Das Kino an der Grenze," *B.Z. am Abend*, September 3, 1959.

101. *Blickpunkt* (Sep. 1959), reprinted in Lindemann and Schultz, *Die Falken in Berlin*, 148. On misogyny in *Halbstarken* subcultures, see Kuhnert and Ackermann, "Jenseits von Lust und Liebe?"

102. Werner Statenschulte, "Der goldene Westen lockte," *Die Welt*, March 28, 1957.

CHAPTER 4

1. Rudorf, *Jazz in der Zone*, 9. In 1966 West German Horst Lange announced that Germans had dragged jazz, often unnecessarily, into politics: see Lange, *Jazz in Deutschland*, (1966).

2. Levine, "Jazz and American Culture." On American hostilities toward jazz, see Levine; Leonard, *Jazz and the White Americans*.

3. My analysis does not focus on whether the different evaluations of jazz that emerged in the course of the 1950s were sound in musicological terms. Rather I examine what cultural and political work these evaluations did in the German context. Gabbard, "The Jazz Canon and Its Consequences," has urged scholars to address the function of jazz in the larger culture. For the United States, see also Panish, *The Color of Jazz*.

4. Berendt, *Der Jazz*. For biographical information about Berendt, see Kater, *Different Drummers*, 96, 208–9; and Berendt's autobiography, *Das Leben—ein Klang*.

5. Berendt, *Der Jazz*, 7, 90. For dance halls and consumer culture, see Abrams, *Workers' Culture*; Stansell, *City of Women*; Peiss, *Cheap Amusements*; Haxthausen and Suhr, *Berlin, Culture and Metropolis*.

6. Berendt, *Der Jazz*, 59–61, 83–84, 90.

7. Berendt, "Zum Thema Jazz," *Frankfurter Hefte* 7 (Oct. 1952): 768–79, and Berendt, *Das Leben—ein Klang*, 318; Panassié, *Le Jazz Hot*. On the evolution of American criticism, see Gennari, "Jazz Criticism." Compare also, Hodier, *Jazz*.

8. Berendt, "Zum Thema Jazz," 775–76.

9. Leonard, *Jazz and the White Americans*, 143.

10. On the relationship of swing and bebop, see DeVeaux, "Emergence of the Jazz Concert," and DeVeaux, *The Birth of Bebop*; Erenberg, "Things to Come." On cool jazz, see also Gennari, "Jazz Criticism."

11. See also his report on his trip to the United States: Berendt, "Americana: Erlebnisse und Gedanken von einer US-Reise," *Melos* 18 (March 1951): 78–82. On the problems of constructing jazz as a universal experience and challenges to this view, see DeVeaux, "Constructing the Jazz Tradition"; Gennari, "Jazz Criticism"; Panish, *The Color of Jazz*. The most famous challenge to this position is LeRoi Jones (Amiri Baraka), *Blues People*.

12. Theodor W. Adorno, "Jazz: Zeitlose Mode," *Merkur* 7 (1953): 537–48; a slightly revised version is translated as "Perennial Fashion—Jazz" in Adorno, *Prisms*, 120–32. With a few alterations, quotations are from the English translation. Compare also Adorno's "On Jazz"; Berendt, *Das Leben—ein Klang*, 314. For Adorno and jazz, see Hansen, "Of Mice and Ducks"; Gracyk, "Jazz"; Jay, *The Dialectical Imagination*, chap. 6.

13. On the earlier essay, see Jay, *The Dialectical Imagination*, 185–87; Hansen, "Of Mice and Ducks," 49.

14. Adorno, "Perennial Fashion—Jazz." For readings that interpret Adorno's use of castration as reinscribing a patriarchal model, see Huyssen, "Mass Culture as Woman"; Wilke, "Torn Halves."

15. Joachim-Ernst Berendt, "Für und wider den Jazz," *Merkur* 7 (1953): 887–90.

16. Theodor W. Adorno, response to Berendt in *Merkur* 7 (1953): 890–93.

17. For the function that gender had in Adorno's analysis of racial prejudice, see Feldstein, *Raising Citizens*, chap. 2.

18. Berendt, *Das Jazzbuch*, 202–6; Berendt, *Das Leben—ein Klang*.

19. See "Eierschale," November 22, 1954; "Thingstätte der Berliner Bohemiens," *Die Welt*, September 19, 1955; H. W. Corten, "Kann der Jazz unserer Jugend schaden?" *Die Welt*, July 21, 1957. On jazz clubs in the early 1950s, see Lange, *Jazz in Deutschland* (1966); Kater, *Different Drummers*; Ralph Willett, *The Americanization*, 86–98.

20. See Gunnar Woyth, "Jazz-Krise! Krise-Jazz!" *Nacht-Depesche*, October 15, 1953; "Jazz-Fans, die nicht tanzen wollen," *Depesche*, January 14, 1954; Gerd Scharnhorst, "Schräge Musik ist noch kein Jazz," *Die Welt*, March 6, 1955.

21. Lange, *Jazz in Deutschland* (1966).

22. See "Drei Jahre NJCB," *Volksblatt*, April 27, 1958. On jazz fans, see also Maase, *Bravo Amerika*, 179–85.

23. See Peter Pfirrmann, "Jazz ohne Rabatz," *Telegraf*, December 20, 1956; "Jazz-Freunde ohne Klamauk," *Tagesspiegel*, June 16, 1957.

24. Auslander, "The Gendering," 86.

25. "Jazz-Freunde ohne Klamauk," *Tagesspiegel*, June 16, 1957.

26. Ibid. See also Peter Pfirrmann, "Jazz ohne Rabatz," *Telegraf*, December 20, 1956.

27. "Jazz-Freunde ohne Klamauk," *Tagesspiegel,* June 16, 1957.

28. See, for example, USIA, Office Of Research, Public Opinion Barometer Reports, Barometer Surveys XX.9 and XX.11, West Germany, May 1957 and October 1958, RG 306, NA. The 1957 survey showed that 24 percent of the upper socioeconomic group, versus 17 percent of all Germans, liked jazz. A year later 29 percent of professionals, versus 11 percent of all Germans, felt that jazz had a positive influence. Not surprisingly, younger people liked it better than the old. Jazz was about equally popular among men and women.

29. "Jazz-Freunde ohne Klamauk," *Tagesspiegel,* June 16, 1957. The observation that jazz clubs were carried by male members of the middle and upper classes is confirmed in Zinnecker, *Jugendkultur,* 160–62; Maase, *Bravo Amerika,* 179; HICOG Survey No. 210, April 15, 1955, reel 9, frames 7066–67, Merritt Collection On Public Opinion in Germany.

30. "Jazz," *Blickpunkt* (March 1956).

31. See, for example, "Viel Lärm um 'Rock 'n' roll,' " *Die Welt,* October 14, 1955.

32. K. Gerhard, "Jazz ist nicht für Halbstarke," *Hessische Jugend* 9, no. 12 (1957): 19–20. See also H. Paechter, "Der Jazz ist respektabel geworden. Virtuosentum und Purismus beherrschen das Feld," *Deutsche Zeitung und Wirtschaftszeitung* 10, no. 81, 1955, 14.

33. "Thingstätte der Berliner Bohemiens," *Die Welt,* September 19, 1955.

34. Joachim Ernst Berendt, "Haleys Musik ist kein Jazz," *Die Welt,* November 8, 1958.

35. H. W. Corten, "Kann der Jazz unserer Jugend schaden?" *Die Welt,* July 21, 1957.

36. Minutes of the 28. Sitzung, Jugendwohlfahrtsausschuß, Bezirksamt Kreuzberg, May 2, 1957, LAB Rep. 206, Acc. 3070, No. 3582.

37. See the autobiography by Rudorf, *Nie wieder links.*

38. Reginald Rudolf *(sic),* "Für eine frohe, ausdrucksvolle Tanzmusik," *Musik und Gesellschaft* 2 (August 1952): 247–52; Reginald Rudorf, "Die Tanzmusik muß neue Wege gehen," *Musik und Gesellschaft* 4, pt. 1 (February 1954): 51–56, pt. 2 (March 1954): 92–95. For similar arguments, see Hermann Meyer, *Musik im Zeitgeschehen* (Berlin, 1952), quoted in Rauhut, *Beat,* 19. On the repression of jazz in East Germany and in the Soviet Union, see Rauhut, *Beat;* Rudorf, *Jazz in der Zone;* Höhne, *Jazz in der DDR;* Starr, *Red and Hot;* Ryback, *Rock Around the Bloc,* 14–16.

39. Rudolf *(sic),* "Für eine frohe, ausdrucksvolle Tanzmusik," and Rudorf, "Die Tanzmusik."

40. Rudolf *(sic),* "Für eine frohe, ausdrucksvolle Tanzmusik," and Rudorf, "Die Tanzmusik."

41. Rudolf *(sic),* "Für eine frohe, ausdrucksvolle Tanzmusik," and Rudorf, "Die Tanzmusik." On Kurt Henkels, see also Rudorf, *Jazz in der Zone,* 37–39.

42. Rudolf, "Die Tanzmusik." See also Rudorf, *Jazz in der Zone,* 43–44.

43. Rudolf *(sic),* "Für eine frohe, ausdrucksvolle Tanzmusik"; Rudorf, "Die Tanzmusik." See also "Die Arbeitsprinzipien der Interessengemeinschaft,"

Leipzig, n.d. (ca. 1955), JA-IzJ A392. My thanks to Raelynn Hillhouse for pointing me to this file.

44. Rudorf, *Jazz in der Zone;* Lange, *Jazz in Deutschland* (1966).

45. See Rudorf and Lukasz, letter to the Zentralrat der FDJ, Kulturabteilung, April 12, 1955; copy of letter, Thomas to Abteilung Kultur, Zentralrat der FDJ, May 10, 1955, both JA-IzJ A392; Rudorf, *Jazz in der Zone.*

46. See for example "Die Arbeitsprinzipien der Interessengemeinschaft," Leipzig, n.d. (ca. 1955), JA-IzJ A392.

47. See Rudorf to Knoblauch, 1. Sekretär der FDJ-Bezirksleitung, January 11, 1955; Sekretariat, "Abschrift," Leipzig, January 26, 1956, which includes a list of members and programs of their weekly meetings from February to April 1955; "Die Arbeitsprinzipien der Interessengemeinschaft," Leipzig, n.d. (ca. 1955), all JA-IzJ A392.

48. Compare Sekretariat, "Abschrift," Leipzig, January 26, 1956, which includes an address list of sixty-five members, JA-IzJ A392. According to official East German statistics for 1955–56, 30 percent of all students were women in 1956; in academic positions the number of women was 14.4 percent. See *Jahrbuch der Deutschen Demokratischen Republik* (1956), 216.

49. See Rudorf, *Jazz in der Zone,* 53–57; Rudorf and Lukasz to Becker, December 29, 1956, BArch P DR 1, No. 243 (the file contains Rudorf's cover letter to Becher, but not the full text of their request). See also "Jazzdiskussion," April 7, 1955, Berlin; Rudorf and Lukasz, letter to the Zentralrat der FDJ, Kulturabteilung, April 12, 1955, both JA-IzJ A392; Georg Knepler, "Jazz und die Volksmusik" *Musik und Gesellschaft* 5 (June 1956): 181–83.

50. "Jazzdiskussion," April 7, 1955, Berlin, JA-IzJ A392.

51. Rudorf and Lukasz, letter to the Zentralrat der FDJ, Kulturabteilung, April 12, 1955, JA-IzJ A392.

52. Copy of letter, Thomas to Abteilung Kultur, Zentralrat der FDJ, May 10, 1955, JA-IzJ A392.

53. Ibid.; also, Kurt Knoblauch, FDJ Bezirksleitung Leipzig, to FDJ-Zentralrat, August 3, 1955; Lamberz, FDJ-Zentralrat, to Knoblauch, January 1, 1956; Rudorf, Lukasz, and Thomas to Karl Namokel, FDJ Zentralrat, December 27, 1955, all JA-IzJ A392.

54. See Lamberz, FDJ-Zentralrat, to Knoblauch, FDJ-Bezirksleitung Leipzig, June 16, 1955; Rudorf, Lukasz, Thomas to Karl Namokel, FDJ Zentralrat, December 27, 1955; "Wie das Gesetz es befahl," *Junge Welt,* no. 114, 1955.

55. Ludwig Richard Müller, "Dekadenz und lebensfroher Neubeginn" *Musik und Gesellschaft* 5 (April 1955): 114–17; Knepler, "Jazz und die Volksmusik."

56. Paul Robeson, "Pesni moega naroda," *Sovetskaia muzyka* (July 1949), quoted in Starr, *Red and Hot,* 221–22. On Robeson, see Duberman, *Paul Robeson.*

57. This distinction had actually first been introduced by Hugues Panassié. See Gennari, "Jazz Criticism." Rudorf adopted it from leftist American jazz critic Sidney Finkelstein.

58. *An Euch alle*, 26.

59. See *Jazz-Journal* 1 (Dec. 1955), JA-IzJ A392.

60. See *Jazz-Journal* 2 (Jan. 1956) and 3 (Feb. 1956); Karl-Heinz Symann, Hot-Club Düsseldorf to Siegfried Schmidt, Halle, January 18, 1956; Friedrich, FDJ, Halle to FDJ-Central Council, January 26, 1956; Rudorf and Lukasz to Karl Namokel, March 12, 1956, all JA-IzJ A392.

61. See Rudorf and Lukasz to Rainer Zimpel, FDJ Bezirksleitung Leipzig, January 4, 1956, JA-IzJ A392.

62. Bartsch, *Neger, Jazz und tiefer Süden*.

63. See Rudorf, *Jazz in der Zone*, 71–79; Noglik, "Hürdenlauf," 209; V. Konen "Legende und Wahrheit über den Jazz," *Musik und Gesellschaft* 5 (Dec. 1955): 391–96, reprinted from *Sovetskaia muzyka* (Sep. 1955).

64. Starr, *Red and Hot*, 249–50; Karl-Heinz Drechsel, insert for *Jazz in Deutschland*, 4th CD (Berlin, no date).

65. Rudorf, *Jazz in der Zone*, 90–100.

66. Ibid., 116–25; Höhne, *Jazz in der DDR*, 28; "Die Tätigkeit des Ministeriums für Kultur, insbesondere der HA Musik auf dem Gebiete des Jazz," n.d. (ca. Sep. 1957), BArch P DR1 No. 243.

67. See Rudorf, *Jazz in der Zone*, 116–25.

68. "Gefahr für den Stehgeiger," *Der Spiegel*, October 26, 1955; *Tagesspiegel*, April 10, 1957, "Zonen-Jazzexperte in Ungenade," *Der Tag*, February 24, 1957; "Prügel für Jazzanhänger," *SBZ-Archiv* 8, April 25, 1957; U.S. Mission Berlin, Despatch 983, May 7, 1957; RG 59, 762b.00/5–757; Despatch 388, December 16, 1957, RG 59, 762.00/12–1657; Despatch 489, January 31, 1958, RG 59, 762b.00/1–3158; Despatch 575, March 10, 1958, RG 59, 762.00/3–1058, NA.

69. The subtitle was "Europe Falls Captive as Crowds Riot to Hear Dixieland," *New York Times*, November 6, 1955, quoted in Levine, "Jazz and American Culture," 17. See also "They Cross the Iron Curtain to Hear American Jazz," *U.S. News and World Report*, December 2, 1955; "Jazzing Up Germany," *Newsweek*, March 12, 1956; "Jazz in the Cold War," *Commonweal*, December 16, 1955; USIA Special Reports, "Jazz Has Firm Foothold in the USSR," 1957, RG 306, NA.

70. Such studies were Aaron H. Esman, "Jazz—A Study in Cultural Conflict," *The American Imago* 8 (June 1951): 219–26; Norman M. Margolis, "A Theory on the Psychology of Jazz," *The American Imago* 11 (fall 1954): 263–91. On the connection between European esteem for jazz and its acceptance among white Americans, see Levine, "Jazz and American Culture"; Leonard, *Jazz and the White Americans*; Gennari, "Jazz Criticism."

71. See Dudziak, "Desegregation." On the links drawn between modernist culture and anticommunism, see Pells, *Not Like Us*, 74; Guilbaut, *How New York*.

72. See Starr, *Red and Hot*, 243–44; Thomson and Laves, *Cultural Relations*, 123; Olaf Hudtwalker, "Jazz in USA," *Jazz Podium* 6 (July 1957), 13.

73. "Man müßte die Waldbühne heizen," *Kurier*, January 9, 1958. On "Exis" see Maase, *Bravo Amerika*; Heinz-Hermann Krüger, "Exis habe ich keine gesehen."

74. See Horst Koegler, "Jazz—theoretisch," *Der Monat* 12 (Oct. 1959): 58–64; Berendt, *The New Jazz Book*. See also Maase, *Bravo Amerika*, 179–85.

75. USIA, Office of Research, PMS-18, "West European Reactions to Jazz," 1957, RG 306, NA.

76. Dietrich Schulz-Köhn, "Der Jazz—Marotte oder Musik," *Kölnische Rundschau*, December 14, 1958. On Schulz-Köhn's activities during the Third Reich see Kater, *Different Drummers*.

77. "Ausrüstung für sechs deutsche Divisionen," *Tagesspiegel*, September 12, 1956.

78. See " Bundeswehr pflegt reinen Jazz," *Tagesspiegel*, August 8, 1958, quoted in Rauhut, *Beat*, 21; "Jazz-Begeisterung in der Truppe," *Die Welt*, August 9, 1958. Busch and Wiehr, "Jugend im Film," have observed that in the second half of the 1950s listening to jazz became "worthy of a good citizen."

79. Joachim E. Berendt, "Jazz auf dem Kasernenhof," *Die Welt*, August 23, 1958.

80. Berendt, *Das Leben—ein Klang*, 315–17.

81. Berendt, *The New Jazz Book*.

82. See Domentat, *Coca-Cola*, 199.

CHAPTER 5

1. "Appell an den Urmenschen," *Berliner Zeitung*, December 13, 1956; H. Heigert, "Ein neuer Typ wird produziert: Der Teenager," in *deutsche jugend*, no. 3 (1959), quoted in Bertram and Krüger, "Vom Backfisch zum Teenager," 94.

2. I focus especially on how young women entered the public through their consumption of rock 'n' roll. For the United States this has been suggested by Echols, "We Gotta Get out of this Place." On the attraction of rock 'n' roll for teenage girls in the United States and Britain, see also Breines, *Young, White and Miserable*, 151–66; Ehrenreich, Hess, and Jacobs, *Re-making Love*. For West Germany, see also Carter, "Alice"; Delille and Grohn, *Perlonzeit*.

3. Erd, "Musikalische Praxis." On rock 'n' roll in 1950s Germany, see also Maase, *Bravo Amerika*; Rauhut, *Beat*; Bloemeke, *Roll over Beethoven*; Ryback, *Rock Around the Bloc*. For the transgressions of racial boundaries in rock 'n' roll in the United States and Britain, see especially Marcus, *Mystery Train*; Lipsitz, *Class and Culture*; Martin and Segrave, *Anti-Rock*; Friedlander, *Rock and Roll*.

4. "Elvis, the Pelvis," *Der Spiegel*, December 12, 1956.

5. For treatments of American girls tearing Presley's clothes off or girls fainting in hysteria, see Manfred George, " Liebesbriefe an einen Toten," *Tagesspiegel*, September 15, 1956; "Der Casanova am Klavier," *Hamburger Abendblatt*, October 6, 1956; "Das Phänomen Elvis Presley," *Telegraf*, October 11, 1956; "Rock and Roll," *Badische Neue Nachrichten*, August 22, 1956; "Der Gorilla mit der Gitarre," *Depesche*, January 11, 1957; "Idol der Mädchen," *Telegraf*, February 9, 1957; "Über Geschmack läßt sich streiten," *Spandauer Volksblatt*, March 22, 1957; "New York empfindet anders als Berlin,"

Telegraf, May 26, 1957; "Ein Gesicht in der Menge," *B.Z.,* October 31, 1957. The West German youth magazine *Bravo* also reported about Elvis's female American fans: "Schwarm von Millionen," *Bravo,* December 2, 1956; "Mädchen schreien für Elvis," *Bravo,* December 9, 1956. Hysteria has historically been described as a female disease. See Showalter, *The Female Malady.*

6. *Look* magazine quoted in "Rock 'n' Roll: Pros 'n' Cons," *Variety,* June 13, 1956, 51, 58.

7. "Der Über-Rhythmus," *Der Spiegel,* September 26, 1956.

8. Ibid. On riots, see "Die Königin greift ein," *Spandauer Volksblatt,* September 19, 1956; "Die ganze Welt rockt und rollt," *Bravo,* September 30, 1956; report about riots abroad in *National-Zeitung,* September 28, 1956; "Rock 'n' Roll Irrsinn," *Neues Deutschland,* November 14, 1956; "Tarzan auf dem Tanzboden," *Frankfurter Rundschau,* September 30, 1956.

9. On Elvis's challenge to respectable manhood, see Simels, *Gender Chameleons,* 14–16. For a reading of Elvis as a female impersonator, see Garber, *Vested Interests,* 365–74. She asserts that Elvis's racial crossover was read as a "crossover move in gender terms: a move from hypermale to hyperfemale," 367. See also Guralnick, *Last Train.*

10. "Deutsche Pitch for Elvis," *Variety,* October 24, 1956; "Elvis, the Pelvis," *Der Spiegel,* December 12, 1956; "Gold aus heißer Kehle," *Beratungsdienst Jugend und Film* (February 1958). My thanks to Mark Cooper for first pointing me to RCA's marketing strategy.

11. Bloemeke, *Roll over Beethoven,* 100.

12. Ker Robertson, "Elvis Presley, Idol von Millionen von Backfischen und bestürzendes Symptom unserer Zeit," *Depesche,* January 18, 1957.

13. Werner Micke, "Philosophie des Stumpfsinns," *Junge Welt,* February 5, 1957, quoted in Rauhut, *Beat,* 31.

14. "Elvis, the Pelvis," *Der Spiegel,* December 12, 1956.

15. For U.S. reporting, see the *New York Daily Mirror,* quoted in Simels, *Gender Chameleons,* 16; "Rock 'n' Roll: Pros 'n' Cons," *Variety,* June 13, 1956, 51, 58; Martin and Segrave, *Anti-Rock,* 60, 62.

16. To explain Elvis's musical style, Manfred George asserted that at some point in Elvis's ancestry "black blood" must have entered his family. He also mentioned that music of the African jungle had been brought over by slaves forced to leave their homes, who today counted "15 million citizens working for their full emancipation," *Tagesspiegel,* February 7, 1957.

17. "Der Casanova am Klavier," *Hamburger Abendblatt,* October 6, 1956.

18. " 'Rock ans Roll': öffentliches Ärgernis," *Badische Neue Nachrichten,* August 22, 1956.

19. See "Elvis, the Pelvis," *Der Spiegel,* December 12, 1956.

20. "Appell an den Urmenschen," *Berliner Zeitung,* December 13, 1956, was a direct response to the December 12, 1956 article in *Der Spiegel.*

21. " 'God-Loving' Jelly-Kneed 'Kid': Parker on Presley," *Variety,* October 24, 1956. See also caption "Black Music Became White," in "Der Über-Rhythmus," *Der Spiegel,* September 26, 1956.

22. Martin and Segrave, *Anti-Rock,* 95. See also Trent Hill, "The Enemy Within."

23. *Mirror-News,* quoted in Martin and Segrave, *Anti-Rock,* 62.

24. See examples in Martin and Segrave, *Anti-Rock,* 52–53.

25. "Nun ja, man lacht." *B.Z.,* April 15, 1957. See also "Zwischenrufe: So ein Himbeerbubi!" *Der Tag,* April 13, 1957; "Ade, Du Himbeerbubi," *Berliner Morgenpost,* April 13, 1957; "New York empfindet anders als Berlin," *Telegraf,* May 26, 1957.

26. "Pulverdampf und heiße Lieder," *Die Welt,* April 13, 1957; "Nun ja, man lacht," *B.Z.,* April 15, 1957.

27. "Elvis, the Pelvis," *Der Spiegel,* December 12, 1956; Bloemeke, *Roll over Beethoven,* 40, 89–90. For adolescents' demands for "hot" American music on German radio stations, see Grotum, *Die Halbstarken,* 167–68.

28. "Waden aus Gummi rollen im Hot-House," *Depesche,* October 23, 1956; "Außer Rand und Band," *Beratungsdienst Jugend und Film* (November 1956): BVII. See also "Bravo sucht den deutschen Meister im 'Rock and Roll,' " *Bravo,* November 13, 1956; "Selbstmördern empfohlen," *Junge Welt* (June 1957). For an exploration of youth dancing as space for female display/victimization as well as for female pleasure, see Frith and McRobbie, "Rock and Sexuality."

29. See Alfred Baresel, "Rock 'n' Roll von allen Seiten betrachtet," *Telegraf,* January 4, 1957.

30. Klaus Theweleit quoted in Bloemeke, *Roll over Beethoven,* 120.

31. Bloemeke, *Roll over Beethoven,* 120.

32. "Wer wird deutscher Meister im Rock 'n' Roll?" *Bravo,* December 9, 1956.

33. See pictures of rock 'n' roll dancers in *Bravo,* November 13, 1956. See also the description of female Elvis fans in tight jeans *("engbehoste Verehrerinnen"),* "Unsere Meinung," *Die Welt,* October 5, 1958. For an insightful treatment of fashion as part of a larger struggle for political and social power, see Roberts, "Samson and Delilah."

34. *Nürnberger Nachrichten,* February 7, 1958.

35. West German commentary quoted in Lamprecht, *Teenager und Manager,* 14.

36. See "Jugend zwischen 18 und 22 Uhr," *Junge Generation* 12, no. 1 (1958): 17–22.

37. East German press quoted in "Alter Feind—neu entdeckt," *Kölnische Rundschau,* August 6, 1958; also "Enge Pullis als Klassenfeind," *Der Tag,* May 9, 1958. One official report complained that even when members of a state youth club put up a portrait of the Russian cosmonaut Gagarin, they contrasted it with a picture of a "lightly clad" girl from a West German magazine. See "Einschätzung der Entwicklung der Jugendclubs," August 8, 1961, LAB (STA) Rep. 121, No. 62.

38. See "Sollen Schulmädchen Hosen tragen?" *Spandauer Volksblatt,* November 6, 1957. For images of women under National Socialism, see Wittrock, *Weiblichkeitsmythen.*

39. Heinz-Hermann Krüger, *"Die Elvis-Tolle"*; Czak, "Spitzname: Elvis"; Carter, "Alice," 201; interview with Wolfgang Hille.

40. "Mein Leben ist der Rhythmus," *Berliner Morgenpost*, November 1, 1958; report on a showing of *Love Me Tender, Beratungsdienst Jugend und Film* 2 (March 1957), BVIII; also the report on a West Berlin showing of *Loving You* in "Gold aus heißer Kehle," *Beratungsdienst Jugend und Film* 3 (February 1958): BII. For East Germany, see Hentschel, Abteilung Kultur, Rat der Stadt Halle to Folkmann, Referat Musik, Ministerium für Kultur, September 24, 1957, BArch P DR1, No. 243; "Protokoll über einen Erfahrungsaustausch über die Arbeit der Jugendklubs in der DDR," 1960, JA-IzJ A6724; cited hereafter as "Erfahrungsaustausch," 1960, JA-IzJ A6724.

41. "Außer Rand und Band 2. Teil," *Beratungsdienst Jugend und Film* 2 (January 1957).

42. See "Kann der Jazz unserer Jugend schaden?" *Die Welt*, July 21, 1957. In 1956 and 1957 rock 'n' roll was often not clearly differentiated from boogie-woogie.

43. "Erfahrungsaustausch," 1960, JA-IzJ A6724. Rolf Lindner, "Straße," 193, has made clear that definitions of deviance have been gender-specific.

44. "Der Sportpalast-ein Hexenkessel," *Spandauer Volksblatt*, October 28, 1958; "Tumulte im Sportpalast," *Telegraf*, Oktober 28, 1958. See also photographs that show girls next to boys throwing chairs, "Wer hat schuld an Rock-'n'Roll-Krawallen?" *Die Welt*, November 8, 1958. For oral histories about girls' participation in riots, see also Bertram and Krüger, "Vom Backfisch zum Teenager."

45. District Attorney for Hannover, quoted in Grotum, *Die Halbstarken*, 113.

46. *Nürnberger Nachrichten*, February 7, 1958. See also the description of a female "*halbstarker* Teenager" in blue jeans and sweater in "Mit Caterina Valente in die Scala," *Mannheimer Morgen*, January 18, 1957.

47. *Nürnberger Nachrichten*, February 7, 1958.

48. Letter to the editor, "Elvis Presley Club," Berlin Wilmersdorf, *Tagesspiegel*, February 2, 1958.

49. "Elvis Presley und die schauen Puppen," *Berliner Zeitung*, August 8, 1958.

50. For a similar analysis of the meaning of rock stars for girls, see Frith and McRobbie, "Rock and Sexuality." Maase, *Bravo Amerika*, 132–35, has raised the possibility that girls' ideals may have contributed to the development of a masculinity that did not rely on the soldier ideal. However, his analysis that girls' admiration for Presley and other stars was an exercise in female slave behavior overestimates the degree to which these girls were relying on approval from men for their self-definition.

51. See Burleigh and Wippermann, *The Racial State*. In the postwar years rapists among the occupation forces were most frequently described as black Americans in the West and as Mongolians in the East. See Grossmann, "A Question of Silence," 47–48.

52. "Pulverdampf und heiße Lieder," *Kurier*, April 13, 1957. See also H. Heigert, "Ein neuer Typ wird produziert: Der Teenager," in *deutsche jugend*,

no. 3 (1959), quoted in Kuhnert and Ackermann, "Jenseits von Lust und Liebe," 94.

53. Arbeitsausschuß der FSK, "Jugendprotokoll: *Außer Rand und Band, 2. Teil*," February 1, 1957, LBS. A minority on the board wanted to ban the movie altogether for youths younger than sixteen because it would foster "loose behavior and propensity for hysteric mass behavior."

54. "Wie tanzt man Rock 'n' Roll," *Blickpunkt* (December 1956): 24. For a discussion of the debates erupting around the new family law, see Moeller, *Protecting Motherhood,* chap. 6.

55. Elisabeth Pitz-Savelsberg, "Das Wächteramt des Staates," *Ruf in Volk* 12 (1958): 89–91. See also her comments in the minutes of the "Studienkonferenz der Bundesarbeitsstelle Aktion Jugendschutz, 'Jugendschutz und Familie,'" November 17, 1958, BArch K B153/2479. On the law, see Dickfeldt, *Jugendschutz als Jugendzensur,* 137.

56. Prötsch, *So müssen unsere Soldaten sein.*

57. Dr. Uszukoreit to state concert agency (Deutsche Konzert- und Gastspieldirektion), August 21, 1957, BArch P DR1, No. 243.

58. Letter from Berliner Haus der Volkskunst, October 1, 1957, LAB (STA) Rep. 121, No. 162. Kurella quoted in "Kreuzzug gegen Rock 'n' Roll," *Frankfurter Rundschau,* November 11, 1957.

59. "Erfahrungsaustausch," 1960, JA-IzJ A6724.

60. "Anordnung über die Programmgestaltung bei Unterhaltungs- und Tanzmusik," January 2, 1958, reprinted in Schubbe, *Dokumente,* 515. Economic considerations likewise played a role: East Germany was paying DM 2 million per year for the rights to perform Western music. See "Protokoll zur Aussprache mit den Institutionen und Kapellenleitern," March 11, 1958, LAB (STA) Rep. 121, No. 230. On protests to certification, see "Erfahrungsaustausch," 1960, JA-IzJ A6724.

61. See Gerlinde Irmscher, "Der Westen im Ost-Alltag"; "Einschätzung der Entwicklung der Jugendclubs," August 8, 1961, LAB (STA) Rep. 121, No. 62; interviews with Hannelore Diehl, Sigrid Tönnies, Margot Hamm, Günter Schmidt. Especially popular was Radio Luxemburg: see "Erfahrungsaustausch," 1960, JA-IzJ A6724.

62. See Rauhut, *Beat,* 40–41; Ryback, *Rock Around the Bloc,* 29.

63. See Maase, *Bravo Amerika.*

64. "Eggheads Bleat about Presley and 'The Beat' in 'Conversation' Piece," *Variety,* November 14, 1956, 53–54.

65. "'Rock and Roll' rollt durch Europa," *Spandauer Volksblatt,* October 14, 1956.

66. Bondy et al., *Jugendliche stören die Ordnung,* 53.

67. On the measures taken in the United States and Great Britain, see Martin and Segrave, *Anti-Rock,* 27–39.

68. "Kripo-Sonderstab greift ein," *Telegraf,* October 28, 1958; "Kripo spürt die Rädelsführer auf," *Berliner Morgenpost,* October 30, 1958.

69. "Nie wieder Jazz im Berliner Sportpalast," *Depesche,* October 28, 1958; Joachim Ernst Berendt, "Haleys Musik ist kein Jazz," *Die Welt,* November 8, 1958.

70. Gösta von Uexhüll, "Zu wild oder nicht wild genug," *Die Welt,* November 8, 1958; "Nachgesang zum zerschlagenen Mobiliar," *Die Zeit,* January 2, 1959.

71. Klaus Eyferth, "Es reicht nicht zu Revolutionen," *Die Welt,* November 8, 1958; "Gold aus heißer Kehle," *Kasseler Post,* May 21, 1958.

72. See interview with Susanne Quandt, who attended one of these courses in 1958.

73. Mohrhof, *Warum sind sie gegen uns?*

74. Compare Gilbert, *A Cycle of Outrage,* chaps. 10, 12.

75. *Bravo,* no. 12, 1958, quoted in Maase, *Bravo Amerika,* 168; "I Like Elvis," *Abend,* October 10, 1958.

76. See, for example, reviews in *Telegraf, Kurier,* and *Die Welt,* all November 1, 1958.

77. Bloemeke, *Roll over Beethoven,* 92–96, quotes the memoirs of the reporter Eva Windmöller.

78. In 1956 German papers were still educating the public that "teenager" meant *Backfisch.* See "Das Phänomen Elvis Presley," *Telegraf,* October 11, 1956; "Das Phänomen Elvis Presley," *Spandauer Volksblatt,* October 12, 1956; "Teenager," *Blickpunkt,* no. 48/49 (1956), 21. *Der Spiegel* in its December 1956 feature on Elvis switched between *"Backfisch"* and "teenager." See "Elvis, the Pelvis," *Der Spiegel,* December 12, 1956. See also the West German dictionary *Der große Herder,* v. 8, (1956), quoted in Maase, *Bravo Amerika,* 162; "Woran starb der Backfisch?" *Quick,* no. 15, 1959, reprinted in *Perlonzeit,* 18–19; "Der (Teenager)-Spleen," *Blickpunkt* (February 1960): 17. On teenager culture, see Maase, *Bravo Amerika,* 158–75; Bertram und Krüger, "Vom Backfisch zum Teenager"; Foitzik, *Vom Trümmerkind zum Teenager;* Lindner, "Teenager."

79. *Bravo,* no. 4, 1958, quoted in Carter, "Alice," 209.

80. *Bravo,* no. 15, 1959, quoted in Maase, *Bravo Amerika,* 144. The author of these columns was a retired male teacher.

81. See Lamprecht, *Teenager and Manager,* 33.

82. "Vom Spieltrieb besessen," *Telegraf,* July 11, 1957; Bloemeke, *Roll over Beethoven,* 127. Erd, "Musikalische Praxis und sozialer Protest," sees Kraus, in contrast to Presley, as whitened in the German context.

83. *"Wenn die Conny mit dem Peter: Teenager-Melodie," Illustrierte Film-Bühne,* no. 4618, n.d., BArch FAB.

84. Interview with teenager fashion producer quoted in Lamprecht, *Teenager und Manager,* 9.

85. Quoted in Lamprecht, *Teenager und Manager,* 107. See also Maase, *Bravo Amerika,* 169.

86. See "Bravo sucht den deutschen Meister im 'Rock and Roll,'" *Bravo,* November 13, 1956; "Erlaubt ist, was gefällt," *Bravo,* no. 6, 1960; interview with Renate Ebert.

87. Martin and Segrave, *Anti-Rock*, 67–68.

88. Zinnecker, *Jugendkultur*, 208, 212; Grotum, *Die Halbstarken*, 214, 219; Maase, *Bravo Amerika*, 164. See also oral history with Klaus Woldeck, quoted in Maase, *Bravo Amerika*, 169, and interviews with Susanne Quandt and Dietmar Iser.

89. Stoph and Ulbricht quoted in Lamprecht, *Teenager und Manager*, 87. See also Zentralinstitut für Lehrerweiterbildung, "Anleitung der Zirkelleiter zum Thema 'Jugendschutz in der DDR,'" September 6, 1957, LAB (STA) Rep. 119, No. 22; "Bill Haley und die NATO," and "Orgie der amerikanischen Unkultur," *Neues Deutschland*, October 31, 1958; "Jugend wird systematisch vergiftet," *Neues Deutschland*, November 2, 1958; "7000 Rowdys 'in Aktion,'" *B.Z. am Abend*, October 28, 1958.

90. On the meeting, see Rauhut, *Beat*, 31–32.

91. See *Für den Sieg der sozialistischen Revolution*, 14–16.

92. See East German commentaries in *Der Godesberger Parteitag*.

93. On the so-called *Bitterfelder Weg*, see Jäger, *Kultur und Politik*, 87–117. On the dance music conference, see Rauhut, *Beat*, 38–39. On the concept "educational dictatorship," see Wierling, "Jugend als innerer Feind."

94. On these developments, see for example Lemke, *Die Berlinkrise*; Fulcher, "Walling In and Walling Out"; Cioc, *Pax Atomica*.

95. Walter Ulbricht, "Fragen der Entwicklung der sozialistischen Literatur und Kunst," (1959), quoted in Rauhut, *Beat*, 37.

96. "Leipziger Jugendliche riefen 'Pfui,'" *Die Welt*, November 3, 1959; Abteilung Organisation Instrukteure, "Vorlage an das Sekretariat," December 4, 1959, Ba SAPMO DY30/IV 2/16/230 (hereafter cited as "Vorlage").

97. Abteilung Organisation to Arbeitsgruppe Jugendfragen, November 30, 1959; Verner to Ulbricht, December 7, 1959, both Ba SAPMO DY30/IV 2/16/230.

98. "Vorlage."

99. Resolution of the Sixth FDJ Parliament quoted in Mählert and Stephan, *Blaue Hemden*, 131; Czak, "Spitzname: Elvis."

100. "Leipziger Jugendliche riefen 'Pfui'," *Die Welt*, November 3, 1959. On the events of the late 1950s and early 1960s, see also Fulbrook, *Anatomy of a Dictatorship*, 163–65.

101. Abteilung Organisation to Arbeitsgruppe Jugendfragen, November 30, 1959, Ba SAPMO DY30/IV 2/16/230.

102. Abteilung Sicherheitsfragen to Honecker, November 11, 1959, Ba SAPMO DY30/IV 2/16/230.

103. HV Deutsche Volkspolizei, Operativstab, Rapport No. 343, December 10, 1959, Ba SAPMO DY30/IV 2/16/230.

104. Abteilung Sicherheitsfragen to Honecker, November 11, 1959, Ba SAPMO DY30/IV 2/16/230.

105. "Vorlage."

106. Ibid.

107. The 1957 report argued that missing sexual education along with the bad moral influences from the West were responsible: Ständige Kommission

für Jugendfragen, Stadtverordnetenversammlung Gross-Berlin, "Bericht über die Jugendkriminalität," October 10, 1957, LAB (STA) Rep. 119, No. 22.

108. Picture Material published by the Zentralrat der FDJ and distributed "to enlighten youths about hardship and demoralization in West Germany," 1958, LAB (STA) Rep. 121, No. 230.

109. "Vorlage."

110. Ibid.; Verner to Ulbricht, December 7, 1959, Ba SAPMO DY30/IV 2/16/230.

111. "Vorlage."

112. Abteilung Organisation Instrukteure, "Weitere Beispiele zur Banden-tätigkeit in der DDR," December 5, 1959, Ba SAPMO DY30/IV 2/16/230.

113. Verner to Ulbricht, December 7, 1959; Verner to 2. Sekretär der Bezirks-leitung, December 8, 1959, both Ba SAPMO DY30/IV 2/16/230.

114. See quotations and analysis of the excerpts from Charles Montirian, *La paix révolutionaire riposte à la subversion* (Paris, 1958), reprinted in *General Military Review* (1958) and quoted in Rauhut, *Beat*, 21.

115. Martin and Segrave, *Anti-Rock*, 82; Shaw, *Rockin' 50s*, 239.

116. Verner to 2. Sekretär der Bezirksleitung, December 8, 1959, Ba SAPMO DY30/IV 2/16/230.

117. "Strauß befahl: Jazz und rockt!" *Junge Welt*, no. 22 (November 1958).

118. Alfred Kurella, "Erfahrungen und Probleme der sozialistischen Kul-turarbeit" (1960), quoted in Rauhut, *Beat*, 37.

119. "Entwurf: Betr. Fragen der Jugenderziehung," May, 14, 1960, Ba SAPMO DY30/IV 2/16/230.

120. Verner to 2. Sekretär der Bezirksleitung, December 8, 1959, Ba SAPMO DY30/IV 2/16/230.

121. "Der Spuk im Klubhaus," *Junge Generation* 13 (May 1959): 28–32; "Entwurf: Betr. Fragen der Jugenderziehung," May, 14, 1960, Ba SAPMO DY30/IV 2/16/230.

122. See report from Leipzig in "Erfahrungsaustausch," 1960, JA-IzJ A6724; "Jugend zwischen 18 und 22 Uhr," *Junge Generation* 12, no. 1, 1958, 17–22; "Geständnis eines Rock'n'Roll-Fans," *Junge Generation* 13, May 1959, 32; "Die Bluejeans-Boys und der Jugendklub," *Morgen*, March 7, 1961.

123. "Entwurf: Betr. Fragen der Jugenderziehung," May, 14, 1960, Ba SAPMO DY30/IV 2/16/230

124. Ibid.; "Einschätzung der Abteilung Volksbildung des Magistrats von Groß-Berlin," December 19, 1060, Ba SAPMO DY30/IV 2/16/230; "Er-fahrungsaustausch," 1960, JA-IzJ A6724.

125. "7000 Rowdys 'in Aktion,'" *B.Z. am Abend*, October 28, 1958.

126. "Nato-Politik und Tanzmusik," *Informationsdienst* 48/IV, 1961, reprinted in Rauhut, *Beat*, 23–26.

127. Ibid.

128. Adolf Heusinger, "Jugend und Bundeswehr," January 1959, in Heusinger, *Reden*, 74–78.

129. See "In kleinen Dosen," *Twen* (October 1959): 20.

130. See "Zuchthaus für Presley-Fans," *Depesche,* November 3, 1959; "Presley-Fans hinter Gittern," *Spandauer Volksblatt,* November 3, 1959; "Zuchthaus für Elvis-Presley-Anhänger," *Westdeutsche Allgemeine,* November 3, 1959; "Leipzig Presley Fans Jailed," *New York Times,* November 3, 1959; "'Krieg' mit Rock 'n' Roll," *Abend,* August 16, 1962.

EPILOGUE

1. Compare the oral histories quoted in Heinz-Hermann Krüger, *"Die Elvis-Tolle";* interviews by author.

2. Interviews with Wolfgang Hille, Dietmar Iser.

3. See Ruth Römstedt, "Blue-Jean-Boy und die Filmpoesie von heute," *Kurier,* January 16, 1959.

4. See "'Blutiger Kid' vor leerem Haus," *Neue Zeit,* August 17, 1961. Thieme, Abteilung Kultur, Friedrichshain, "Informationsbericht zu Veranstaltungstätigkeit im Stadtbezirk," August 28, 1961, LAB (STA) Rep. 221, No. 278.

5. See "Am Tag darauf ohne Texashose," *Neues Deutschland,* August 22, 1961; "Heiße Rhythmen waren erster Schritt," *National-Zeitung,* August 27, 1961; "Bericht über Jugendklubs," November 11, 1962, LAB (STA) Rep. 121, No. 62.

6. Charlotte Petersen, FDJ-Bezirksleitung Berlin, "Auf die richtige Welle kommt es an," *Junge Generation* 15, no. 18 (1961): 32–33; Mählert and Stephan, *Blaue Hemden, Rote Fahnen,* 137–41.

7. See Abt. Agit.-Prop., "Einige Bemerkungen zu Frage des Jazz," Berlin, November 29, 1961; "Unser Standpunkt zum Jazz," Berlin, December 7, 1961, both JA-IzJ AB547.

8. "Totenkopf bürgerlich," *Revue,* no. 19, 1962.

9. See Berendt, *Das Leben—ein Klang,* 323.

10. See "Pressekonferenz des Berliner Jugendclub e.V. am 28. April 1960 anläßlich der Eröffnung des 'Jazz-Saloons,'" LAB Rep. 13, Acc. 2285, No. 464; "Ein ganzes Haus für Jugend und Jazz," *Kurier,* April 30, 1960; Horst Sass, "'Jugend-Jazz-Saloon' überfüllt," *Die Welt,* May 2, 1960; *Kurier,* May 24, 1960; "Berliner Geschichten," *IBZ,* June 18, 1960; "Das haben sie nicht in Paris gelernt," *Blickpunkt,* nos. 97/98 (July 1960); Reiner Breitfeldt, "Es sind keine 'müden Senatsschuppen,'" *Blickpunkt,* no. 104 (1961).

11. Herbert Rudershausen, "Jugendpflege in der Bar," *Der Rundbrief* 10, nos. 9/10 (1960). See also *Abgeordnetenhaus von Berlin: Stenographische Berichte,* 61st session, May 4, 1961, 123–24. Berlin officials modeled their club on a similar one in the West German city Mannheim.

12. Senator für Jugend und Sport, "Bericht über die Situation der Berliner Jugend," *Der Rundbrief* 10, nos. 11/12 (1960): 1–24, especially 5–10.

13. Jaide, *Das Verhältnis,* 129. On conservative, liberal, and left attitudes toward youth and consumption in the 1960s, see Siegfried, "Manipulation und Autonomie."

14. Blücher, *Die Generation der Unbefangenen.*

15. On these concerns about political engagement, see Siegfried, "Manipulation und Autonomie."

16. Heinz Kersten, *Das Filmwesen*, 92–93.

17. See Fricke, *Selbstbehauptung*. Most recently, see Kaff, "Gefährliche politische Gegner."

18. On this outrage in West Germany, see Siegfried, "Manipulation und Autonomie"; in East Germany, see Rauhut, *Beat*; Wierling, "Jugend als innerer Feind."

19. Kommuniqué des SED-Politbüros, September 17, 1963, reprinted in excerpts in Mählert and Stephan, *Blaue Hemden*, 150–52.

20. Mählert and Stephan, *Blaue Hemden*, 152–60; Rauhut, *Beat*, chap. 2; "Kein Mangel an Romantik," *Neue Zeit*, July 24, 1963.

21. Rauhut, *Beat*, 117–18.

22. Mählert and Stephan, *Blaue Hemden*, 165–68; Rauhut, *Beat*, chap. 3; Wierling, "Jugend als innerer Feind," and Wierling, "Der Staat, die Jugend und der Westen."

23. "Stenographische Niederschrift," December 15–17, 1965, SAPMO-BArch DY30 IV 2/1 336.

24. Ibid.; Mählert and Stephan, *Blaue Hemden*, 169–72; Rauhut, *Beat*, chap. 3; Agde, *Kahlschlag*.

25. Armin Mohler, "Der nächste 'Nazi' bitte!" *Welt am Sonntag*, December 5, 1965.

26. See Rauhut, *Beat*, 118.

27. Mählert and Stephan, *Blaue Hemden*, 183–87; Rauhut, *Beat*, 212–16.

28. Maier, *Dissolution*, especially 34–39; Kapferer, "Die Psychologie in der DDR"; Friedrich, *Jugend und Jugendforschung*.

29. Johannes Rech used the term "depoliticization" at the Sixth Meeting of the Central Committee, November 28–29, 1968, quoted in Rauhut, *Beat*, 217. See also Rauhut, *Beat*, 217–18; Mählert and Stephan, *Blaue Hemden*, 145, 177–80; Wierling, "Mission to Happiness."

30. I do not agree with Marina Fischer-Kowalski, "Halbstarke 1958, Studenten 1968," that the *Halbstarke* of the 1950s themselves were the student rebels of the late 1960s in West Germany.

31. Pells, *Not Like Us*; Hollander, *Anti-Americanism*.

32. Feminists have claimed, incorrectly, "The "Personal Is Political" as their invention. On the history of the concept see McCormick, *Politics of the Self*; Herzog, "'Pleasure, Sex, and Politics Belong Together.'" On the rebellions of the 1960s, see also Korte, *Eine Gesellschaft im Aufbruch*; Markovits and Gorski, *The German Left*; Bude, *Das Altern einer Generation*; von Dirke, *"All the Power to the Imagination!"*

33. *Star-Club-News*, December 1964, quoted in Siegfried, "Manipulation und Autonomie." See also Articus et al., *Die Beatles in Harburg*.

34. Quoted in McCormick, *Politics of the Self*, 32.

35. On the West German women's movement, see Frevert, *Women*, 287–303. On the connections between 1950s youth cultures and 1960s femi-

nism in the United States, see Breines, *Young, White and Miserable.* For West Germany, see Pallowski, "Wohnen in halben Zimmern."

36. McCormick, *Politics of the Self,* 74–77.

37. See for example Schneider, *Den Kopf verkehrt aufgesetzt,* 32–79.

38. For the vehement conservative response, see Burns and van der Will, *Protest and Democracy,* 100–101.

39. Markovits and Gorski, *The German Left,* 12–13; McCormick, *Politics of the Self,* 6.

40. McCormick, *Politics of the Self,* 56. See also Burns and van der Will, *Protest and Democracy,* chap. 3.

41. McCormick, *Politics of the Self,* 72–74.

42. Ibid., 48–49.

43. Bernhard Vesper, *Die Reise,* quoted in McCormick, *Politics of the Self,* 66.

44. McCormick, *Politics of the Self,* 43; Kraushaar, "Chronologie der Studentenbewegung," 257–58.

45. Siegfried, "Manipulation und Autonomie"; Kemper, "Der Rock."

46. Cited in Stefan, "Kakophonie," 8. Stefan proudly asserts that such sentences could earlier be read only in the texts of the American women's movement.

47. Karin Schraber-Klebert, "Die kulturelle Situation der Frau," *Kursbuch* 17 (June 1969), abbreviated version reprinted in Anders, *Autonome Frauen,* 52–75, 54.

48. Huyssen, "Mapping the Postmodern," in Huyssen, *After the Great Divide,* 178–221. McCormick, *Politics of the Self,* 42–45, 52.

49. Hans Magnus Enzensberger, "Commonplaces on the Newest Literature," quoted in McCormick, *Politics of the Self,* 53.

50. On rock in the GDR, see Rauhut, *Schalmei and Lederjacke;* on consumption and the end of the Cold War, see especially Maier, *Dissolution;* Kopstein, *Politics of Economic Decline.*

51. See de Grazia, *The Sex of Things,* especially, 2, 227.

52. It is partially for this reason that Konrad Jarausch and Hannes Siegrist sought to test the concept of "Sovieticization" and use it alongside "Americanization" in order to facilitate comparisons between the two states. See Jarausch and Siegrist, *Amerikanisierung und Sowjetisierung.*

53. Lüdtke, "Helden der Arbeit"; Kocka, "Eine durchherrschte Gesellschaft"; Schröder, "Einleitung"; Bathrick, *The Powers of Speech,* 16.

54. In the postwar German context, see Moeller, "Introduction"; and Schildt and Sywottek, "'Reconstruction' and 'Modernization.'"

55. On this problem, see also Jessen, "Die Gesellschaft im Staatssozialismus"; Maier, *Dissolution,* 36, 45.

56. Critiques of the totalitarianism paradigm for an understanding of East German history include Kershaw, "Totalitarianism Revisited"; Jessen, "Die Gesellschaft im Staatssozialismus"; Bessel and Jessen, "Einleitung."

57. On the blurry boundaries of state and society in postwar West Germany, see for example, Moeller, *Protecting Motherhood;* Fehrenbach, *Cinema in De-*

mocratizing Germany. For critical explorations of categories central to liberalism, see for example, Mehta, "Liberal Strategies of Exclusion"; Calhoun, *Habermas and the Public Sphere.*

58. For similar questions in the United States, see Breines, "Postwar Girls' Dark Others."

59. Schraber-Klebert, "Die Kulturelle Situation."

60. See Hall, "The Question of Cultural Identity"; Appiah and Gates, *Identities.*

61. See Heineman, *What Difference;* Wierling, "Mission to Happiness"; Pence, "From Rations to Fashions." Mary Fulbrook's inquiry into an "anatomy of modes of political culture" may also be promising for a comparative history of the two postwar German states. See Fulbrook, *Anatomy of a Dictatorship.*

62. These questions are compatible with approaches Robert G. Moeller has outlined in his "Introduction." See also Eley, "Introduction"; Maier, *Dissolution.*

63. "Limits of dictatorship" refers to Bessel and Jessen, *Grenzen der Diktatur.*

Bibliography

ARCHIVAL SOURCES

Bundesarchiv, Abteilungen Potsdam (BArch P)
  DR 1 Ministerium für Kultur
  DR 6 Staatliches Rundfunkkomitee
  DC 4 Amt für Jugendfragen
Bundesarchiv, Filmarchiv, Berlin (BArch FAB)
  Schriftgut
Bundesarchiv, Koblenz (BArch K)
  B137 Gesamtdeutsches Ministerium
  B153 Bundesministerium für Familie und Jugend
  ZSG 120 Presseauschnittssammlung
Jugendarchiv beim Institut für zeitgeschichtliche Jugendforschung, Berlin
(JA-IzJ)
  Abteilung Kultur beim Zentralrat
  Zentralrat, Sekretariat
  Bezirkleitungen der FDJ
  Broschüren
Landesarchiv Berlin, Außenstelle Breite Straße (LAB (STA))
  Rep. 119 Magistrat von Berlin, Amt für Jugendfragen
  Rep. 120 Magistrat von Berlin, Abteilung Volksbildung
  Rep. 121 Magistrat von Berlin, Abteilung Kultur
  Rep. 303/26 Volkspolizei
  ZA Zeitungsausschnittsammlung
Landesarchiv Berlin, Kalckreuthstraße (LAB)
  Rep. 2 Senatskanzlei
  Rep. 7 Senator für Volksbildung
  Rep. 13 Senatsverwaltung für Jugend und Familie

Rep. 15 Senatsverwaltung für Schulwesen
Rep. 206 Bezirksamt Kreuzberg
LAZ-Sammlung

Landesbildstelle Berlin, Pressearchiv (LBS)

Merritt Collection on Public Opinion in Germany, University of Illinois, Urbana

National Archives, Washington, D.C. (NA)
RG 59 State Department Decimal Files

Washington National Records Center, Suitland, Maryland (NA)
RG 306 United States Information Agency:
• Country Project Files for East and West Germany
• Office of Research:
Special Reports
Public Opinion Barometer Reports
Program and Media Studies

Sender Freies Berlin, Pressearchiv

Stiftung Deutsche Kinemathek, Berlin
Schriftgut

Stiftung Parteien und Massenorganisationen beim Bundesarchiv, Berlin (Ba SAPMO)
DY 30/I IV 2/2 Politbüro Sitzungen
DY 30/IV 2/1 Zentralkomitee Sitzungen
DY 30/IV 2/12 Abteilung Sicherheitsfragen
DY 30/IV 2/16 Abteilung Jugend
DY 30/IV 2/9.02 Abteilung Agitation
DY 30/IV 2/9.06 Abteilung Kultur
DY 30/IV 2/2026 Büro Alfred Kurella
NY 4090 Nachlaß Otto Grotewohl
NY 4182 Nachlaß Walter Ulbricht

RECORDED INTERVIEWS

All interviews were conducted by the author in Berlin in January, February, and July 1993. The names of those interviewed have been changed. Recordings and notes are in author's posession.

Peter Dannemann, born 1944
Hannelore Diehl, born 1940
Renate Ebert, born 1942
Klaus Grohmann, born 1934
Margot Hamm, born 1936
Wolfgang Hille, born 1943

Dietmar Iser, born 1943
Brigitte Lohmeier, born 1936
Jutta Nehrlich, born 1934
Karin Neumann, born 1942
Susanne Quandt, born 1942
Günther Schmidt, born 1943
Rudolf Schütz, born 1930
Werner Schumacher, born 1938
Dagmar Sommer, born 1938
Rita Tetzner, born 1935
Sigrid Toennies, born 1932

PERIODICALS

American Imago
Begegnung
Beratungsdienst Jugend und Film
Die berufsbildende Schule
Bildung und Erziehung
Blickpunkt
Bravo
Deutsche Filmkunst
Deutsche Zeitung und Wirtschaftszeitung
deutsche jugend
Film, Bild, Ton
Film-Telegramm
Frankfurter Hefte
Hessische Jugend
Hochland
IBZ
Jahrbuch für Amerikastudien
Jugendruf
Junge Generation
Lebendige Erziehung
Melos
Merkur
Monat
Musik und Gesellschaft
Das neue Wort
Neues Leben
New Yorker
Pädagogische Rundschau
Revue
Ruf ins Volk
Der Rundbrief

SBZ-Archiv
Sonntag
Der Spiegel
Time
Twen
Unsere Jugend
Westermanns Pädagogische Beiträge
Wort und Wahrheit
Die Zeit

NEWSPAPERS

7 Uhr Blatt
Abend
B.Z.
B.Z. am Abend
Badische Neue Nachrichten
Berliner Montag
Berliner Morgenpost
Berliner Wirtschaftsblatt
Berliner Zeitung
Bremer Nachrichten
Die andere Zeitung
Film-Dienst
Frankfurter Allgemeine Zeitung
Hamburger Anzeiger
Junge Welt
Kasseler Post
Kölnische Rundschau
Kurier
Mannheimer Morgen
Montagsecho
Der Morgen
N.Z. am Montag
Nacht-Depesche
National-Zeitung (GDR)
Neue Zeit
Neue Zeitung
Neues Deutschland
New York Times
Nürnberger Nachrichten
Rheinischer Merkur
Sächsisches Tageblatt
Schwäbische Landeszeitung

Spandauer Volksblatt
Stuttgarter Zeitung
Der Tag
Tagesspiegel
Tägliche Rundschau
Telegraf
Variety
Die Welt
Weltbühne
Westdeutsche Allgemeine
Wiesbadener Kurier
Wirtschaftszeitung

BOOKS AND ARTICLES

Abelshauser, Werner. *Die langen fünfziger Jahre: Wirtschaft und Gesellschaft der Bundesrepublik Deutschland, 1949–1966.* Düsseldorf: Schwann, 1987.

Abenheim, Donald. *Reforging the Iron Cross: The Search for Tradition in the West German Armed Forces.* Princeton: Princeton University Press, 1988.

Abgeordnetenhaus von Berlin: Stenographische Berichte. Berlin, 1951ff.

Abrams, Lynn. *Workers' Culture in Imperial Germany: Leisure and Recreation in Rhineland and Westphalia.* London: Routledge, 1992.

Adelson, Leslie A. *Making Bodies, Making History: Feminism and German Identity.* Lincoln: University of Nebraska Press, 1993.

Adorno, Theodor (Wiesengrund-). "Jazz: Zeitlose Mode." *Merkur* 7 (1953): 537–48.

———. "On Jazz." *Discourse* 12 (fall/winter 1989–90): 45–69.

———. *Prisms.* Cambridge, Mass.: MIT Press, 1981.

Agde, Günter, ed. *Kahlschlag: Das 11. Plenum des ZK der SED 1965: Studien und Dokumente.* Berlin: Aufbau, 1991.

Albrecht, Hartmut et al. *Sozialistisches Menschenbild und Filmkunst.* Berlin: Henschel, 1970.

Albrecht, Ulrich. *Die Wiederaufrüstung der Bundesrepublik: Analyse und Dokumentation.* Cologne: Pahl-Rugenstein, 1980.

Altbach, Edith Hoshino et al., eds. *German Feminism: Readings in Politics and Literature.* Albany: State University of New York Press, 1984.

Anders, Ann, ed. *Autonome Frauen: Schlüsseltexte der neuen Frauenbewegung seit 1968.* Frankfurt am Main: Athenäum, 1988.

Anderson, Benedict. *Imagined Communities: Reflections on the Origin and Spread of Nationalism.* Rev. ed. New York: Verso, 1991.

An Euch alle, die Ihr jung seid! Material der 12. Tagung des Zentralrats der Freien Deutschen Jugend vom 3. und 4. Februar 1956. Berlin: n.d.

Appiah, Kwame Anthony, and Henry Louis Gates, eds. *Identities.* Chicago: University of Chicago Press, 1995.

Articus, Rüdiger et al. *Die Beatles in Harburg.* Hamburg: Christians, 1996.

Auslander, Leora. "The Gendering of Consumer Practices in Nineteenth-Century France." In *The Sex of Things: Gender and Consumption in Historical Perspective,* edited by Victoria de Grazia with Ellen Furlough, 79–112. Berkeley: University of California Press, 1996.

Ausschuß für Deutsche Einheit, ed. *Wer zog die Drähte? Der Juni-Putsch 1953 und seine Hintergründe.* Berlin: Junge Welt, 1954.

Bader, Joseph. *Jugend in der Industriekultur: Ihre Verhaltensweisen zwischen Ideologie und Apparatur, 1910, 1933, 1960.* Munich: Manz, 1962.

Baier, Horst, ed. *Helmut Schelsky—ein Soziologe in der Bundesrepublik: Eine Gedächtnisschrift von Freunden, Kollegen, Schülern.* Stuttgart: Ferdinand Enke, 1986.

Bals, Christel. *Halbstarke unter sich.* Cologne: Kiepenheuer & Witsch, 1962.

Bänsch, Dieter, ed. *Die fünfziger Jahre: Beiträge zu Politik und Kultur.* Tübingen: Narr, 1985.

Baring, Arnulf. *Uprising in East Germany: June 17, 1953.* Ithaca, N.Y.: Cornell University Press, 1972.

Barkan, Elazar. *The Retreat of Scientific Racism: Changing Concepts of Race in Britain and the United States Between the World Wars.* New York: Cambridge University Press, 1992.

Barron, Stephanie, ed. *"Degenerate Art": The Fate of the Avant-Garde in Nazi Germany.* New York: Harry N. Abrams, 1991.

Barth, Bernd-Rainer et al., eds. *Wer war wer in der DDR: Ein biographisches Handbuch.* Frankfurt am Main: Fischer Taschenbuch, 1995.

Bartov, Omer. *Hitler's Army: Soldiers, Nazis, and War in the Third Reich.* New York: Oxford University Press, 1991.

Bartsch, Ernst. *Neger, Jazz und tiefer Süden.* Leipzig: F. A. Brockhaus, 1956.

Bathrick, David. *The Powers of Speech: The Politics of Culture in the GDR.* Lincoln: University of Nebraska Press, 1995.

Baumert, Gerhard. *Deutsche Familien nach dem Kriege.* Darmstadt: Eduard Roether, 1954.

———. *Jugend der Nachkriegszeit: Lebensverhältnisse und Reaktionsweisen.* Darmstadt: Eduard Roether, 1952.

Bauschinger, Sigrid, Horst Denkler, and Wilfried Malsch, eds. *Amerika in der deutschen Literatur: Neue Welt—Nordamerika—USA.* Stuttgart: Phillip Reclam jun., 1975.

Becker, Howard. *German Youth: Bond or Free.* London: K. Paul, Trench, Trubner, 1946.

Bederman, Gail. *Manliness and Civilization: A Cultural History of Gender and Race in the United States, 1880–1917.* Chicago: University of Chicago Press, 1995.

Bednarik, Karl. *Der junge Arbeiter von heute: Ein neuer Typ.* Stuttgart: Gustav Klipper, 1953.

Bennett, Tony. "Putting Policy into Cultural Studies." In *Cultural Studies,* edited by Lawrence Grossberg, Cary Nelson, and Paula Treichler, 23–37. New York: Routledge, 1992.

Benz, Wolfgang. *Von der Besatzungsherrschaft zur Bundesrepublik: Stationen einer Staatsgründung, 1946–1949.* Frankfurt am Main: Fischer Taschenbuch, 1984.

———, Günter Plum, and Werner Röder. *Einheit der Nation: Diskussionen und Konzeptionen zur Deutschlandpolitik der großen Parteien seit 1945.* Stuttgart: Frommann Holzboog, 1978.

Benz, Wolfgang, ed. *Die Bundesrepublik Deutschland.* Vol. 3, *Gesellschaft.* Rev. ed. Frankfurt am Main: Fischer Taschenbuch, 1989.

Berendt, Joachim Ernst. *Der Jazz. Eine zeitkritische Studie.* Stuttgart: Deutsche Verlags-Anstalt, 1950.

———. *Das Jazzbuch: Entwicklung und Bedeutung der Jazzmusik.* Frankfurt am Main: Fischer, 1953.

———. *Das Leben—ein Klang: Wege zwischen Jazz und Nada Brahma.* Munich: Droemer Knaur, 1996.

———. *Ein Fenster aus Jazz: Essays, Portraits, Reflexionen.* Frankfurt am Main: Fischer, 1977.

———. *The New Jazz Book: A History and Guide,* trans. Dan Morgenstern. New York: Hill and Wang, 1962.

Berghahn, Volker R. *The Americanisation of West German Industry, 1945–1973.* New York: Cambridge University Press, 1986.

Berlin. Chronik der Jahre 1951–1958. Schriftenreihe zur Berliner Zeitgeschichte. Vols. 5–7. Berlin: Heinz Spitzing, 1968–74.

Berliner Geschichtswerkstatt e.V., ed. *Vom Lagerfeuer zur Musikbox: Jugendkulturen 1900–1960.* Berlin: Elefanten Press, 1985.

Bertram, Christine, and Heinz-Hermann Krüger. "Vom Backfisch zum Teenager—Mädchensozialisation in den 50er Jahren." In *"Die Elvis-Tolle, die hatte ich mir unauffällig wachsen lassen": Lebensgeschichte und jugendliche Alltagskultur in den fünfziger Jahren,* edited by Heinz-Hermann Krüger, 84–101. Opladen: Leske und Budrich, 1985.

Bessel, Richard, and Ralph Jessen, eds. *Die Grenzen der Diktatur: Staat und Gesellschaft in der DDR.* Göttingen: Vandenhoeck und Ruprecht, 1996.

Bessen, Ursula. *Trümmer und Träume: Nachkriegszeit und fünfziger Jahre auf Zelloloid: Deutsche Spielfilme als Zeugnisse ihrer Zeit.* Bochum: Studienverlag Dr. N. Brockmeyer, 1989.

Biess, Frank. " 'Pioneers of a New Germany': Returning POWs from the Soviet Union and the Making of East German Citizens, 1945–1950." *Central European History.* Forthcoming.

———. "Survivors of Totalitarianism: Returning POWs and the Reconstruction of Masculine Citizenship in West Germany, 1945–1955." In *Revisiting the Miracle Years: West German Society from 1949 to 1968,* edited by Hanna Schissler. Princeton: Princeton University Press, 1999. Forthcoming.

Bigsby, C. W. E., ed. *Superculture: American Popular Culture and Europe.* Bowling Green, Ohio: Bowling Green University Popular Press, 1975.

Biskind, Peter. *Seeing Is Believing: How Hollywood Taught Us to Stop Worrying and Love the Fifties.* New York: Pantheon, 1983.

Bloemeke, Rüdiger. *Roll over Beethoven: Wie der Rock 'n' Roll nach Deutsch-land kam.* St. Andrä-Wördern: Hannibal, 1996.

Blücher, Viggo Graf. *Freizeit in der industriellen Gesellschaft: Dargestellt an der jüngeren Generation.* Stuttgart: Ferdinand Enke, 1956.

———. *Die Generation der Unbefangenen: Zur Soziologie der jungen Men-schen heute.* Düsseldorf: Diederichs, 1966.

Bock, Gisela. "Antinatalism, Maternity and Paternity in National Socialist Racism." In *Maternity and Gender Policies: Women and the Rise of the Eu-ropean Welfare States, 1880s–1950s,* edited by Gisela Bock and Pat Thane, 233–55. New York: Routledge, 1991.

———. *Zwangssterilisation im Nationalsozialismus: Studien zur Rassenpoli-tik und Frauenpolitik.* Opladen: Westdeutscher Verlag, 1986.

Bock, Gisela, and Susan James, eds. *Beyond Equality and Difference: Citizen-ship, Feminist Politics, and Female Subjectivity.* New York: Routledge, 1992.

Bock, Gisela, and Pat Thane, eds. *Maternity and Gender Policies: Women and the Rise of the European Welfare States, 1880s–1950s.* New York: Rout-ledge, 1991.

Bodek, Richard. *Proletarian Performance in Weimar Berlin: Agitprop, Chorus, and Brecht.* Columbia, S.C.: Camden House, 1997.

Boehling, Rebecca L. *A Question of Priorities: Democratic Reforms and Eco-nomic Recovery in Postwar Germany: Frankfurt, Munich, and Stuttgart Under U.S. Occupation, 1945–1949.* Providence, R.I.: Berghahn Books, 1996.

Bondy, Curt et al. *Jugendliche stören die Ordnung: Bericht und Stellungnahme zu den Halbstarkenkrawallen.* Munich: Juventa, 1957.

Borneman, John. *Belonging in the Two Berlins: Kin, State, Nation.* New York: Cambridge University Press, 1992.

Bowlby, Rachel. *Just Looking: Consumer Culture in Dreiser, Gissing, and Zola.* New York: Methuen, 1985.

Bradley, John F. N. *War and Peace Since 1945: A History of Soviet-Western Relations.* Boulder, Colo.: Social Science Monographs, 1989.

Brantlinger, Patrick. *Bread and Circuses: Theories of Mass Culture as Social Decay.* Ithaca, N.Y.: Cornell University Press, 1983.

Brasch, Thomas. *Engel aus Eisen: Beschreibung eines Films.* Frankfurt am Main: Suhrkamp, 1981.

Brauer, Andi. "Schaukeln und Wälzen." In *Bikini: Die Fünfziger Jahre: Kalter Krieg und Capri-Sonne,* edited by Eckhard Siepmann, 245–57. Reinbek bei Hamburg: Rowohlt Taschenbuch, 1983.

Braun, Hans. "Helmut Schelskys Konzept einer 'nivellierten Mittelstandsge-sellschaft.' " *Archiv für Sozialgeschichte* 29 (1989): 199–223.

Breazeale, Kenon. "In Spite of Women: *Esquire* Magazine and the Construc-tion of the Male Consumer." *Signs* 20 (Fall 1994): 1–22.

Breines, Wini. "Postwar Girls' Dark Others." In *The Other Fifties: Interrogat-ing Midcentury American Icons,* edited by Joel Foreman, 53–77. Urbana: University of Illinois Press, 1997.

————. *Young, White and Miserable: Growing Up Female in the Fifties.* Boston: Beacon Press, 1992.

Breyvogel, Wilfried, ed. *Piraten, Swings, und Junge Garde: Jugendwiderstand im Nationalsozialismus.* Bonn: Dietz, 1991.

Breyvogel, Wilfried et al., eds. *Land der Hoffnung—Land der Krise: Jugendkulturen im Ruhrgebiet 1900–1987.* Bonn: Dietz, 1987.

Bridenthal, Renate, Atina Grossmann, and Marion Kaplan, eds. *When Biology Became Destiny: Women in Weimar and Nazi Germany.* New York: Monthly Review Press, 1984.

Brooks Higginbotham, Evelyn. "African-American Women's History and the Metalanguage of Race." *Signs* 17 (Winter 1992): 251–74.

Broszat, Martin, ed. *Zäsuren nach 1945: Essays zur Periodisierung der deutschen Nachkriegsgeschichte.* Munich: R. Oldenbourg, 1990.

Broszat, Martin, Klaus-Dietmar Henke, and Hans Woller, eds. *Von Stalingrad zur Währungsreform: Zur Sozialgeschichte des Umbruchs in Deutschland.* 3d ed. Munich: R. Oldenbourg, 1990.

Brubaker, Rogers. *Citizenship and Nationhood in France and Germany.* Cambridge, Mass.: Harvard University Press, 1992.

Buchheim, Hans. *Deutschlandpolitik 1949–1972: Der politisch-diplomatische Prozeß.* Stuttgart: Deutsche Verlags-Anstalt, 1984.

Bude, Heinz. *Das Altern einer Generation: Die Jahrgänge der 1938–48.* Frankfurt am Main: Suhrkamp, 1995.

Bühler, Karl-Werner. *Die Kirchen und die Massenmedien: Intentionen und Institutionen konfessioneller Kulturpolitik in Rundfunk, Fernsehen, Film und Presse nach 1945.* Hamburg: Furche, 1968.

Burleigh, Michael, and Wolfgang Wippermann. *The Racial State: Germany, 1933–1945.* New York: Cambridge University Press, 1991.

Burns, Rob, and Wilfried van der Will, *Protest and Democracy in West Germany: Extra-Parliamentary Opposition and the Democratic Agenda.* New York: St. Martin's Press, 1988.

Burton, Antoinette. *Burdens of History: British Feminists, Indian Women, and Imperial Culture, 1865–1915.* Chapel Hill: University of North Carolina Press, 1994.

Busch, Hans-Martin, and Hartmut Wiehr. "Jugend im Film—Typen und Idole." In *Immer diese Jugend! Ein zeitgeschichtliches Mosaik: 1945 bis heute,* edited by Deutsches Jugendinstitut, 375–88. Munich: Kösel, 1985.

Bust-Bartel, Axel. "Der Arbeiteraufstand am 17. Juni 1953: Ursachen, Verlauf und gesellschaftliche Ziele." *Aus Politik und Zeitgeschichte* (June 1980): 25–54.

Butler, Judith, and Joan Wallach Scott, eds. *Feminists Theorize the Political.* New York: Routledge, 1992.

Byg, Barton. "Generational Conflict and Historical Continuity in GDR Film." In *Framing the Past: The Historiography of German Cinema and Television,* edited by Bruce A. Murray and Christopher J. Wickham, 197–219. Carbondale: Southern Illinois University Press, 1992.

Calhoun, Craig, ed. *Habermas and the Public Sphere.* Cambridge, Mass.: MIT Press, 1992.

Campbell, David. *Writing Security: United States Foreign Policy and the Politics of Identity.* Minneapolis: University of Minnesota Press, 1992.

Canning, Kathleen. "Feminist History After the Linguistic Turn: Historicizing Discourse and Experience." *Signs* 19 (1994): 368–404.

Carby, Hazel. *Reconstrucing Womanhood: The Emergence of the Afro-American Woman Novelist.* New York: Oxford University Press, 1987.

Carter, Erica. "Alice in the Consumer Wonderland: West German Case Studies in Gender and Consumer Culture." In *Gender and Generation,* edited by Angela McRobbie and Mica Nava, 185–214. Basingstoke: Macmillan, 1984.

———. *How German Is She? Postwar West German Reconstruction and the Consuming Woman.* Ann Arbor: University of Michigan Press, 1997.

Cawelti, John. *The Six-Gun Mystique.* 2d ed. Bowling Green, Ohio: Bowling Green State University Popular Press, 1984.

Chamberlin, J. Edward, and Sander L. Gilman, eds. *Degeneration: The Dark Side of Progress.* New York: Columbia University Press, 1985.

Chapple, Steve, and Reebee Garofalo. *Rock 'n' Roll Is Here To Pay: The History and Politics of the Music Industry.* Chicago: Nelson-Hall, 1977.

CheSchahShit: Die sechziger Jahre zwischen Cocktail und Molotow. Berlin: Elefanten Press, 1984.

Chotjewitz, Peter O. *Der Glöckner von Notre Dame und die Madonna der sieben Monde: Kinotransparente der 50er und 60er Jahre.* Frankfurt am Main: Syndikat, 1977.

Cioc, Mark. *Pax Atomica: The Nuclear Defense Debate in West Germany During the Adenauer Era.* New York: Columbia University Press, 1988.

Cohen, Ronald D. "*The Delinquents:* Censorship and Youth Culture in Recent U.S. History." *History of Education Quarterly* 37 (Fall 1997): 251–70.

Collier, James Lincoln. *The Reception of Jazz in America: A New View.* Brooklyn, N.Y.: Institute for Studies in American Music, 1988.

Conradt, David P. "From Output Orientation to Regime Support: Changing German Political Culture." In *Social and Political Structures in West Germany: From Authoritarianism to Postindustrial Democracy,* edited by Ursula Hoffmann-Lange, 127–42. Boulder: Westview, 1991.

Conze, Werner, and M. Reiner Lepsius. *Sozialgeschichte der Bundesrepublik Deutschland: Beiträge zum Kontinuitätsproblem.* Stuttgart: Klett-Cotta, 1983.

Cooper, Frederick, and Ann Laura Stoler, eds. *Tensions of Empire: Colonial Cultures in a Bourgeois World.* Berkeley: University of California Press, 1997.

Corber, Robert J. *In the Name of National Security: Hitchcock, Homophobia, and the Political Construction of Gender in Postwar America.* Durham: Duke University Press, 1993.

Costigliola, Frank. *Awkward Dominion: American Political, Economic, and Cultural Relations with Europe, 1919–1933.* Ithaca, N.Y.: Cornell University Press, 1984.

Culbert, David. "American Film Policy in the Re-education of Germany after 1945." In *The Political Re-education of Germany and Her Allies After World War II,* edited by Nicholas Pronay and Keith Wilson, 173–202. London: Croom Helm, 1985.

Czak, Iris. "Spitzname: Elvis: Interview with Schorsch T." In *Wunderwirtschaft: DDR-Konsumkultur in den 60er Jahren,* edited by Neue Gesellschaft für Bildende Kunst, 194–97. Cologne: Böhlau, 1996.

Dahrendorf, Ralf. *Society and Democracy in Germany.* Garden City, N.Y.: Doubleday, 1967.

De Grazia, Victoria. "Empowering Women as Citizen-Consumers." In *The Sex of Things: Gender and Consumption in Historical Perspective,* edited by Victoria de Grazia with Ellen Furlough, 275–86. Berkeley: University of California Press, 1996.

———. "Introduction." In *The Sex of Things: Gender and Consumption in Historical Perspective,* edited by Victoria de Grazia with Ellen Furlough, 1–24. Berkeley: University of California Press, 1996.

———. "Mass Culture and Sovereignty: The American Challenge to European Cinemas, 1920–1960." *Journal of Modern History* 61 (March 1989): 53–87.

———, ed., with Ellen Furlough. *The Sex of Things: Gender and Consumption in Historical Perspective.* Berkeley: University of California Press, 1996.

De Lauretis, Teresa. "Sexual Indifference and Lesbian Representation." In *Performing Feminisms: Feminist Critical Theory and Theatre,* edited by Sue-Ellen Case, 17–39. Baltimore: Johns Hopkins University Press, 1990.

Delille, Angela, and Andrea Grohn, "Fräulein Grünschnabel: Backfische, Teenager, Frühreife.," In *Perlonzeit: Wie die Frauen ihr Wirtschaftswunder erlebten,* edited by Angela Delille and Andrea Grohn, 48–52. Berlin: Elefanten Press, 1985.

Delille, Angela, and Andrea Grohn, eds. *Blick zurück aufs Glück: Frauenleben und Familienpolitik in den 50er Jahren.* Berlin: Elefanten Press, 1985.

———. *Perlonzeit: Wie die Frauen ihr Wirtschaftswunder erlebten.* Berlin: Elefanten Press, 1985.

D'Emilio, John. *Sexual Politics, Sexual Communities: The Making of a Homosexual Minority in the United States 1940–1970.* Chicago: University of Chicago Press, 1983.

Denning, Michael. "The End of Mass Culture." *ILWCH* 37 (Spring 1990): 4–18.

Deutscher Werkbund e.V. und Württembergischer Kunstverein Stuttgart, eds. *Schock und Schöpfung: Jugendästhetik im 20. Jahrhundert.* Darmstadt: Luchterhand, 1986.

Deutsches Jugendinstitut, ed. *Immer diese Jugend! Ein zeitgeschichtliches Mosaik: 1945 bis heute.* Munich: Kösel, 1985.

DeVeaux, Scott. *The Birth of Bebop: A Social and Musical History.* Berkeley: University of California Press, 1997.

———. "Constructing the Jazz Tradition: Jazz Historiography." *Black American Literature Forum* 25 (Fall 1991): 525–60.

———. "The Emergence of the Jazz Concert, 1935–1945." *American Music* 7 (Spring 1989): 6–29.

Dickfeldt, Lutz. *Jugendschutz als Jugendzensur: Ein Beitrag zur Geschichte und Kritik öffentlicher Bewahrpädagogik.* Bensheim: Päd.-Extra-Buchverlag, 1979.

Dickinson, Edward Ross. *The Politics of German Child Welfare from the Empire to the Federal Republic.* Cambridge, Mass.: Harvard University Press, 1996.

Diedrich, Torsten. *Der 17. Juni 1953 in der DDR: Bewaffnete Gewalt gegen das Volk.* Berlin: Dietz, 1991.

Diefendorf, Jeffry M., Axel Frohn, and Hermann-Josef Rupieper, eds. *American Policy and the Reconstruction of West Germany, 1945–1955.* New York: Cambridge University Press, 1993.

Dietz, Gabriele. "Sozius-Miezen: Halbstarke Mädchen." In *Perlonzeit: Wie die Frauen ihr Wirtschaftswunder erlebten,* edited by Angela Delille and Andrea Grohn, 32–36. Berlin: Elefanten Press, 1985.

Dikötter, Frank. "Race Culture: Recent Perspectives on the History of Eugenics." *American Historical Review* 103 (April 1998): 467–78.

Diner, Dan. *America in the Eyes of the Germans: An Essay on Anti-Americanism,* trans. Allison Brown. Princeton: Markus Wiener, 1996.

Discussion Forum "The 'Remasculinization' of Germany in the 1950s." *Signs* 24 (fall 1998): 101–69.

Doderer, Klaus, ed. *Zwischen Trümmern und Wohlstand: Literatur der Jugend 1945–1960.* Weinheim: Beltz, 1988.

Doering-Manteuffel, Anselm. *Die Bundesrepublik Deutschland in der Ära Adenauer: Außenpolitik und innere Entwicklung, 1949–1963.* Darmstadt: Wissenschaftliche Buchgesellschaft, 1988.

———. "Deutsche Zeitgeschichte nach 1945: Entwicklung und Problemlagen der historischen Forschung zur Nachkriegszeit," *Vierteljahrshefte für Zeitgeschichte* 41 (January 1993): 1–29.

———. "Dimensionen von Amerikanisierung in der deutschen Gesellschaft," *Archiv für Sozialgeschichte* 35 (1995): 1–34.

———. *Katholizismus und Wiederbewaffnung. Die Haltung der deutschen Katholiken gegenüber der Wehrfrage 1948–1955.* Mainz: Matthias Gruenewald, 1981.

Doherty, Thomas. *Teenagers and Teenpics: The Juvenilization of American Movies in the 1950s.* Boston: Unwin Hyman, 1988.

Domansky, Elisabeth. "Militarization and Reproduction in World War I Germany." In *Society, Culture, and the State in Germany, 1870–1930,* edited by Geoff Eley, 427–63. Ann Arbor: University of Michigan Press, 1996.

Domentat, Tamara, ed. *Coca-Cola, Jazz und AFN: Berlin und die Amerikaner.* Berlin: Schwarzkopf und Schwarzkopf, 1995.

Dorner, Rainer. "Halbstark." In *Bikini: Die Fünfziger Jahre: Kalter Krieg und Capri-Sonne,* edited by Eckhard Siepmann, 233–43. Reinbek: Rowohlt Taschenbuch, 1983.

Douglas, Susan J. *Where the Girls Are: Growing Up Female with the Mass Media*. New York: Times Books, 1994.

Dowe, Dieter, ed. *Jugendprotest und Generationenkonflikt in Europa im 20. Jahrhundert*. Bonn: Neue Gesellschaft, 1986.

Dübel, Siegfried. *Deutsche Jugend im Wirkungsfeld sowjetischer Pädagogik*. Bonn: Deutscher Bundes-Verlag, 1953.

Duberman, Martin B. *Paul Robeson*. New York: Knopf, 1988.

Dudziak, Mary. "Desegregation as a Cold War Imperative." *Stanford Law Review* 41 (November 1988): 61–120.

Duignan, Peter, and L. H. Gann. *The Rebirth of the West: The Americanization of the Democratic World, 1945–1958*. Cambridge, Mass.: Blackwell, 1992.

During, Simon, ed. *The Cultural Studies Reader: History, Theory, Practice*. New York: Routledge, 1993.

Echols, Alice. " 'We Gotta Get Out of this Place': Notes Toward a Remapping of the Sixties." *Socialist Review* 22 (April 1992): 9–33.

Ehrenreich, Barbara. *The Hearts of Men: American Dreams and the Flight from Commitment*. Garden City, N.Y.: Doubleday, 1983.

Ehrenreich, Barbara, Elizabeth Hess, and Gloria Jacobs. *Re-making Love: The Feminization of Sex*. Garden City, N.Y.: Doubleday, 1986.

Einhorn, Barbara. *Cinderella Goes to Market: Citizenship, Gender and Women's Movements in East Central Europe*. New York: Verso, 1993.

Eissler, W. U. *Arbeiterparteien und Homosexuellenfrage: Zur Sexualpolitik von SPD und KPD in der Weimarer Republik*. Berlin: R. Winkel, 1980.

Eley, Geoff. "Introduction 1: Is there a History of the Kaiserreich?" In *Society, Culture, and the State in Germany, 1870–1930*, edited by Geoff Eley, 1–42. Ann Arbor: University of Michigan Press, 1996.

———, ed. *Society, Culture, and the State in Germany, 1870–1930*. Ann Arbor: University of Michigan Press, 1996.

Emmerich, Wolfgang. *Kleine Literaturgeschichte der DDR*. Rev. ed. Leipzig: Kiepenheuer, 1996.

Engelhardt, Tom. "Ambush at Kamikaze Pass." In *American Media and Mass Culture: Left Perspectives*, edited by Donald Lazere, 480–98. Berkeley: University of California Press, 1987.

Engelmann, Roger, and Paul Erker. *Annäherung und Abgrenzung: Aspekte deutsch-deutscher Beziehungen 1956–1969*. Munich: R. Oldenbourg, 1993.

Erbe, Günter. *Die verfemte Moderne: Die Auseinandersetzung mit dem "Modernismus" in Kulturpolitik, Literaturwissenschaft und Literatur der DDR*. Opladen: Westdeutscher Verlag, 1993.

Erd, Rainer. "Musikalische Praxis und sozialer Protest: Überlegungen zur Funktion von Rock and Roll, Jazz und Oper." *German Politics and Society*, no. 18 (fall 1989): 18–36.

Erenberg, Lewis A. "Things to Come: Swing Bands, Bebop, and the Rise of the Postwar Jazz Scene." In *Recasting America: Culture and Politics in the Age of the Cold War*, edited by Lary May, 221–45. Chicago: University of Chicago Press, 1989.

Erhard, Ludwig. *Wohlstand für alle.* Düsseldorf: Econ, 1957. English ed.: *Prosperity Through Competition.* New York: Praeger, 1958.

Erker, Paul. "Zeitgeschichte als Sozialgeschichte Forschungsstand und Forschungsdefizite." *Geschichte und Gesellschaft* 19 (1993): 202–38.

Ermarth, Michael, "Introduction." In *America and the Shaping of German Society, 1945–1955,* edited by Michael Ermarth, 1–19. Providence, R.I.: Berg, 1993.

———, ed. *America and the Shaping of German Society 1945–1955.* Providence, R.I.: Berg, 1993.

Euchner, Walter. "Unterdrückte Vergangenheitsbewältigung: Motive der Filmpolitik in der Ära Adenauer." In *Gegen Barbarei: Essays Robert M. W. Kempner zu Ehren,* edited by Rainer Eisfeld and Ingo Müller, 347–59. Frankfurt am Main: Athenäum, 1989.

Evans, Richard, ed. *The German Underworld: Deviants and Outcasts in German History.* New York: Routledge, 1988.

Fehrenbach, Heide. *Cinema in Democratizing Germany: Reconstructing National Identity After Hitler.* Chapel Hill: University of North Carolina Press, 1995.

———. "The Fight for the 'Christian West': German Film Control, the Churches and the Reconstruction of Civil Society in the Early Bonn Republic." *German Studies Review* 14 (February 1991): 39–63.

———. "German Discourses on Cinema, Modernity, and Identity." *German Politics and Society* 13 (winter 1995): 128–39.

———."Rehabilitating Fatherland: Race and German Remasculinization." *Signs* 24 (fall 1998): 107–28.

———, and Uta G. Poiger, "Americanization Reconsidered." In *Transactions, Transgressions, Transformations: American Culture in Western Europe and Japan,* edited by Heide Fehrenbach and Uta Poiger. New York: Berghahn Books, 1999. Forthcoming.

Fehrenbach, Heide, and Uta G. Poiger, eds. *Transactions, Transgressions, Transformations: American Culture in Western Europe and Japan.* Providence: Berghahn Books. Forthcoming.

Feinstein, Joshua Isaac. "The Triumph of the Ordinary: Depictions of Daily Life in the East German Cinema, 1956–1966." Ph.D. diss., Stanford University, 1995.

Feldstein, Ruth S. *Raising Citizens: Black and White Women in American Liberalism, 1930–1965.* Ithaca, N.Y.: Cornell University Press. Forthcoming.

Ferchhoff, Wilfried. *Jugendkulturen im 20. Jahrhundert: Von den sozialmilieuspezifischen Jugendsubkulturen zu den individualitätsbezogenen Jugendkulturen.* Frankfurt am Main: Peter Lang, 1990.

Filmmuseum Potsdam, ed. *Das zweite Leben der Filmstadt Babelsberg: DEFA-Spielfilme, 1946–1992.* Berlin: Henschel, 1994.

Fischer-Kowalski, Marina. "Halbstarke 1958, Studenten 1968: Eine Generation und zwei Rebellionen." In *Kriegskinder, Konsumkinder, Krisenkinder: Zur*

Sozialisationsgeschichte seit dem Zweiten Weltkrieg, edited by Ulf Preuss-Lausitz et al., 53–70. Weinheim: Beltz, 1983.

Foitzik, Doris, ed. *Vom Trümmerkind zum Teenager: Kindheit und Jugend in der Nachkriegszeit.* Bremen: Edition Temmen, 1992.

Foreman, Joel, ed. *The Other Fifties: Interrogating Midcentury American Icons.* Urbana: University of Illinois Press, 1997.

Foschepoth, Josef, ed. *Adenauer und die Deutsche Frage.* Göttingen: Vandenhoeck und Ruprecht, 1988.

Frame, Lynn. "Gretchen, Girl, Garconne? Weimar Science and Popular Culture in Search of the New Woman." In *Women in the Metropolis: Gender and Modernity in Weimar Culture,* edited by Katharina von Ankum, 12–40. Berkeley: University of California Press, 1997.

Franck, Dieter, ed. *Die fünfziger Jahre: Als das Leben wieder anfing.* Munich: Piper, 1981.

Fraser, Nancy. *Unruly Practices: Power, Discourse, and Gender in Contemporary Social Theory.* Minneapolis: University of Minnesota Press, 1989.

Frevert, Ute. "Frauen auf dem Weg zur Gleichberechtigung—Hindernisse, Umleitungen, Einbahnstraßen." In *Zäsuren nach 1945: Essays zur Periodisierung der deutschen Nachkriegsgeschichte,* edited by Martin Broszat, 113–30. Munich: R. Oldenbourg, 1990.

———. *Women in German History: From Bourgeois Emancipation to Sexual Liberation,* trans. Stuart McKinnon-Evans. New York: Berg, 1989.

Fricke, Karl Wilhelm. *Selbstbehauptung und Widerstand in der Sowjetischen Besatzungszone Deutschlands.* Bonn: Deutscher Bundesverlag, 1966.

———, and Ilse Spittmann-Ruhle, eds. *Der 17. Juni 1953: Arbeiterauftand in der DDR.* 2d ed. Cologne: Edition Deutschland Archiv, 1988.

Frieden, Sandra et al., eds. *Gender and German Cinema: Feminist Interventions. Vol. 2. German Film History/German History on Film.* Providence, R.I.: Berg, 1993.

Friedlander, Judith et al., eds. *Women in Culture and Politics: A Century of Change.* Bloomington: Indiana University Press, 1986.

Friedlander, Paul. *Rock and Roll: A Social History.* Boulder, Colo.: Westview, 1996.

Friedrich, Walter. *Jugend und Jugendforschung: Zur Kritik der bürgerlichen Jugendpsychologie und Jugendsoziologie.* Berlin: VEB Deutscher Verlag der Wissenschaften, 1976.

———, and Adolf Kossakowski. *Zur Psychologie des Jugendalters.* Berlin: Volk und Wissen, 1962.

Frith, Simon. *Sound Effects: Youth, Leisure, and the Politics of Rock 'n' Roll.* New York: Pantheon, 1981.

———, and Angela McRobbie. "Rock and Sexuality." In *On Record: Rock, Pop, and the Written Word,* edited by Simon Frith and Andrew Goodwin, 371–89. New York: Pantheon, 1990.

Frith, Simon, and Andrew Goodwin, eds. *On Record: Rock, Pop, and the Written Word.* New York: Pantheon, 1990.

Fritsch-Bournazel, Renata. *Die Sowjetunion und die deutsche Teilung: Die sowjetische Deutschlandpolitik 1945–1979.* Opladen: Westdeutscher Verlag, 1979.

Fröhner, Rolf. *Wie stark sind die Halbstarken?* Bielefeld: Maria von Stackelberg, 1956.

Frow, John. *Cultural Studies and Cultural Value.* Oxford: Clarendon, 1995.

Fulbrook, Mary. *Anatomy of a Dictatorship: Inside the GDR, 1949–1989.* New York: Oxford University Press, 1995.

Fulcher, Kara Stibora. "Walling In and Walling Out: The Politics and Propaganda of the Second Berlin Crisis, 1958–1962." Ph. D. diss. Princeton University, 1997.

Für den Sieg der sozialistischen Revolution auf dem Gebiet der Ideologie und der Kultur. Berlin: Dietz, 1958.

Gabbard, Krin. "The Jazz Canon and Its Consequences." *Annual Review of Jazz Studies* 6 (1993): 65–98.

Gailus, Manfred, ed. *Pöbelexzesse und Volkstumulte in Berlin: Zur Sozialgeschichte der Straße 1830–1980.* Berlin: Europäische Perpektiven, 1984.

Gaines, Jane, and Charlotte Herzog. *Fabrications: Costume and the Female Body.* New York: Routledge, 1990.

Garber, Marjorie, *Vested Interests: Cross-Dressing and Cultural Anxiety.* New York: Routledge, 1992.

Garofalo, Reebee, ed. *Rockin' the Boat: Mass Music and Mass Movements.* Boston: South End Press, 1992.

Gassert, Philipp. *Amerika im Dritten Reich: Ideologie, Propaganda und Volksmeinung, 1933–1945.* Stuttgart: Steiner, 1997.

Gaus, Günter. *Wo Deutschland liegt.* Hamburg: Hoffmann und Campe, 1983.

Gendron, Bernard. "Theodor Adorno Meets the Cadillacs." In *Studies in Entertainment: Critical Approaches to Mass Culture,* edited by Tania Modleski, 18–36. Bloomington: Indiana University Press, 1986.

Gennari, John. "Jazz Criticism: Its Development and Ideologies." *Black American Literature Forum* 25 (fall 1991): 449–523.

Gerhard, Ute. "Die staatlich institutionalisierte 'Lösung' der Frauenfrage: Zur Geschichte der Geschlechterverhältnisse in der DDR." In *Sozialgeschichte der DDR,* edited by Hartmut Kaelble, Jürgen Kocka, and Hartmut Zwahr, 383–403. Stuttgart: Klett-Cotta, 1994.

Geserick, Rolf. *40 Jahre Presse, Rundfunk und Kommunikationspolitik in der DDR.* Munich: Minerva Publikation, 1989.

Gesetzblatt der Deutschen Demokratischen Republik. Berlin, 1949ff.

Geyer, Michael. "The Stigma of Violence, Nationalism, and War in Twentieth-Century Germany." *German Studies Review* 15 (winter 1992): 75–110.

———, and John W. Boyer, eds. *Resistance Against the Third Reich, 1933–1990.* Chicago: University of Chicago Press, 1994.

Giese, Fritz. *Girlkultur: Vergleiche zwischen amerikanischem und europäischem Rhythmus und Lebengefühl.* Munich: Delphin, 1925.

Giese, Hans, and Gunter Schmidt. *Studenten-Sexualität: Verhalten und Einstellung. Eine Umfrage an 12 westdeutschen Universitäten.* Reinbek bei Hamburg: Rowohlt, 1968.

Gilbert, James. *A Cycle of Outrage: America's Reaction to the Juvenile Delinquent in the 1950s.* New York: Oxford University Press, 1986.

Gillis, John R. *Youth and History: Tradition and Change in European Age Relations, 1770-Present.* New York: Academic Press, 1981.

Gilman, Sander L. *Difference and Pathology: Stereotypes of Sexuality, Race, and Madness.* Ithaca, N.Y.: Cornell University Press, 1985.

———. *On Blackness Without Blacks: Essays on the Image of the Black in Germany.* Boston: G.K. Hall, 1982.

———. "Sexology, Psychoanalysis, and Degeneration." In *Difference and Pathology: Stereotypes of Sexuality, Race and Madness,* Sander L. Gilman, 191–216. Ithaca, N.Y.: Cornell University Press, 1985.

Gilroy, Paul. *There Ain't No Black in the Union Jack: The Cultural Politics of Race and Nation.* London: Hutchinson, 1987.

Gimbel, John. *The American Occupation of Germany: Politics and the Military, 1945–1949.* Stanford: Stanford University Press, 1968.

Glaeßner, Gert-Joachim. "Mutmaßungen über einen Arbeiteraufstand: Der 17. Juni 1953." In *Pöbelexzesse und Volkstumulte in Berlin: Zur Sozialgeschichte der Straße 1830–1980,* edited by Manfred Gailus, 169–98. Berlin: Europäische Perpektiven, 1984.

Glaser, Hermann. *Die Kulturgeschichte der Bundesrepublik Deutschland.* 3 vols. Frankfurt am Main: Fischer Taschenbuch, 1990.

———. *The Rubble Years: The Cultural Roots of Postwar Germany.* New York: Paragon House, 1986.

Der Godesberger Parteitag und das Grundsatzprogramm der SPD (Berlin: Dietz, 1960).

Goedde, Petra. "From Villains to Victims: Fraternization and the Feminization of Germany, 1945–47." *Diplomatic History* 23 (winter 1999): 1–20.

Gracyk, Theodore A. "Adorno, Jazz and the Aesthetics of Popular Music." *The Musical Quarterly* 76 (winter 1992): 526–42.

Gransow, Volker. *Kulturpolitik in der DDR.* Berlin: V. Spiess, 1975.

Grimm, Reinhold, and Jost Hermand, eds. *Blacks and German Culture.* Madison: University of Wisconsin Press, 1986.

Grob, Marion. *Das Kleidungsverhalten jugendlicher Protestgruppen in Deutschland im 20. Jahrhundert.* Münster: F. Coppenrath, 1985.

Grossberg, Lawrence, Cary Nelson, and Paula A. Treichler, eds. *Cultural Studies.* New York: Routledge, 1992.

Grossmann, Atina. "*Girlkultur* or Thoroughly Rationalized Female: A New Woman in Weimar Germany?" In *Women in Culture and Politics: A Century of Change,* edited by Judith Friedlander et al., 62–80. Bloomington: Indiana University Press, 1986.

———. "The New Woman and the Rationalization of Sexuality in Weimar Germany." In *Powers of Desire: The Politics of Sexuality,* edited by Ann

Snitow, Christine Stansell, and Sharon Thompson, 153–71. New York: Monthly Review Press, 1983.

———. "A Question of Silence: The Rape of German Women by Occupation Soldiers." In *West Germany under Construction: Politics, Society, and Culture in the Adenauer Era,* edited by Robert G. Moeller, 33–52. Ann Arbor: University of Michigan Press, 1997.

———. *Reforming Sex: The German Movement for Birth Control and Abortion Reform 1920–1950.* New York: Oxford University Press, 1995.

Grotum, Thomas. *Die Halbstarken: Zur Geschichte einer Jugendkultur der 50er Jahre.* Frankfurt am Main: Campus, 1994.

Grundsatzprogramm der Sozialdemokratischen Partei Deutschlands [Godesberger Programm] (Bonn, 1959).

Guback, Thomas H. *The International Film Industry: Western Europe and America Since 1945.* Bloomington: Indiana University Press, 1969.

———. "Shaping the Film Business in Postwar Germany: The Role of the US Film Industry and the US State." In *The Hollywood Film Industry,* edited by Paul Kerr, 245–75. New York: Routledge & Kegan Paul, 1986.

Guilbaut, Serge. *How New York Stole the Idea of Modern Art: Abstract Expressionism, Freedom and the Cold War,* trans. Arthur Goldhammer. Chicago: University of Chicago Press, 1983.

Guralnick, Peter. *Last Train to Memphis: The Rise of Elvis Presley.* Boston: Little, Brown, 1994.

Haensch, Dietrich. *Repressive Familienpolitik: Sexualunterdrückung als Mittel der Politik.* Reinbek: Rowohlt, 1969.

Hagen, Manfred. *DDR—Juni '53: Die erste Volkserhebung im Stalinismus.* Stuttgart: Steiner, 1992.

Hake, Sabine. *The Cinema's Third Machine: Writing on Film in Germany 1907–1933.* Lincoln: University of Nebraska Press, 1993.

Hall, Stuart. "The Question of Cultural Identity." In *Modernity and Its Futures,* edited by Stuart Hall, David Held, and Tony McGrew, 274–316. Cambridge, Engl.: Polity Press, 1992.

Hall, Stuart, David Held, and Tony McGrew, eds. *Modernity and Its Futures.* Cambridge: Polity Press, 1992.

Hall, Stuart, and Tony Jefferson, eds. *Resistance Through Rituals: Youth Subcultures in Post War Britain.* London: Hutchinson, 1976.

Hansen, Miriam. "Early Silent Cinema: Whose Public Sphere?" *New German Critique* 29 (spring/summer 1983): 147–84.

———. "Of Mice and Ducks: Benjamin and Adorno on Disney." *South Atlantic Quarterly* 92 (winter 1993): 27–61.

Harder, Hans-Joachim, und Norbert Wiggershaus, *Tradition und Reform in den Aufbaujahren der Bundeswehr.* Herford: E.S. Mittler & Sohn, 1985.

Harrell, Edward J. *Berlin: Rebirth, Reconstruction and Division 1945–1948: A Study of Allied Cooperation and Conflict.* Ann Arbor: University of Michigan Press, 1981.

Harsh, Donna."Society, the State and Abortion in East Germany, 1950–1972." *American Historical Review* 102 (February 1997): 53–84.

Harvey, Elizabeth. *Youth and the Welfare State in Weimar Germany.* Oxford: Clarendon, 1993.

Haxthausen, Charles W., and Heidrun Suhr, eds. *Berlin, Culture & Metropolis.* Minneapolis: University of Minnesota Press, 1990.

Hebdige, Dick. *Subculture: The Meaning of Style.* London: Methuen, 1979.

———. "Toward a Cartography of Taste 1935–1962." In *Hiding in the Light: On Images and Things,* Dick Hebdige, 45–76. New York: Routledge, 1988.

Heimann, Siegfried. *Die Falken in Berlin: Erziehungsgemeinschaft oder Kampforganisation? Die Jahre 1945–1950.* Berlin: Verlag für Ausbildung und Studium bei der Elefanten-Press, 1990.

———. "Das Überleben organisieren: Berliner Jugend und Jugendbanden in der vierziger Jahren." In *Vom Lagerfeuer zur Musikbox. Jugendkulturen 1900–1960,* edited by Berliner Geschichtswerkstatt e.V., 105–36. Berlin: Elefanten Press, 1985.

Heineman, Elizabeth. "The Hour of the Woman: Memories of Germany's 'Crisis Years' and West German National Identity." *American Historical Review* 101 (April 1996): 354–95.

———. *What Difference Does a Husband Make? Women and Marital Status in Nazi and Postwar Germany.* Berkeley: University of California Press, 1999.

Herbert, Ulrich, and Olaf Groehler. *Zweierlei Bewältigung: Vier Beiträge über den Umgang mit der NS-Vergangenheit in den beiden deutschen Staaten.* Hamburg: Ergebnisse, 1992.

Herbst, Andreas, Winfried Ranke, and Jürgen Winkler. *So funktionierte die DDR.* 3 vols. Reinbek bei Hamburg: Rowohlt Taschenbuch, 1994.

Herf, Jeffrey. *Divided Memory: The Nazi Past in the Two Germanys.* Cambridge, Mass: Harvard University Press, 1997.

———. "East German Communists and the Jewish Question: The Case of Paul Merker." *Journal of Contemporary History* 29 (1994): 627–61.

———. *Reactionary Modernism: Technology, Culture and Politics in Weimar and the Third Reich.* New York: Cambridge University Press, 1984.

Hermand, Jost. "Artificial Atavism: German Expressionism and Blacks." In *Blacks and German Culture,* edited by Reinhold Grimm and Jost Hermand, 65–86. Madison: University of Wisconsin Press, 1986.

———. *Kultur im Wiederaufbau: Die Bundesrepublik Deutschland 1945–1965.* Munich: Nymphenburger, 1986.

Herzog, Dagmar. "'Pleasure, Sex, and Politics Belong Together:' Post-Holocaust Memory and the Sexual Revolution in West Germany," *Critical Inquiry* 24 (winter 1998): 393–444.

Heusinger, Adolf. *Reden 1956–1961.* Boppard am Rhein: Haraldt Boldt, 1961.

Higonnet, Margaret Randolph et al., eds. *Behind the Lines: Gender and the Two World Wars.* New Haven: Yale University Press, 1987.

Hill, Trent. "The Enemy Within: Censorship in Rock Music in the 1950s." *South Atlantic Quarterly* 90 (fall 1991): 675–707.

Hixson, Walter. *Parting the Curtain: Propaganda, Culture, and the Cold War, 1945–61.* New York: St. Martin's, 1997.

Hodier, André. *Jazz: Its Evolution and Its Essence.* New York: Grove Press, 1979.

Hoerning, Erika M. *Zwischen den Fronten: Berliner Grenzgänger und Grenz-händler 1948–1961.* Cologne: Böhlau, 1992.

Hoffmann, Hilmar, and Walter Schubert, eds. *Zwischen Gestern und Morgen: Westdeutscher Nachkriegsfilm, 1946–1962.* Frankfurt am Main: Deutsches Filmmuseum, 1989.

Hoffmann, Julius. *Jugendhilfe in der DDR: Grundlagen, Funktionen und Strukturen.* Munich: Juventa, 1981.

Hoffmann-Lange, Ursula, ed. *Social and Political Structures in West Germany: From Authoritarianism to Postindustrial Democracy.* Boulder, Colo.: Westview, 1991.

Hofmann, Jürgen. *Ein neues Deutschland soll es sein: Zur Frage der Nation in der Geschichte der DDR und der Politik der SED.* Berlin: Dietz, 1989.

Hofner, Karlheinz. *Die Aufrüstung Westdeutschlands: Willensbildung, Entscheidungsprozesse und Spielräume westdeutscher Politik von 1945 bis 1950.* Munich: Ars una, 1990.

Hohendahl, Peter U. "The Displaced Intellectual? Adorno's American Years Revisited." *New German Critique* 56 (1992): 76–100.

———. "Von der Rothaut zum Edelmenschen: Karl Mays Amerikaromane." In *Amerika in der deutschen Literatur: Neue Welt—Nordamerika—USA,* edited by Sigrid Bauschinger, Horst Denkler, and Wilfried Malsch, 229–45. Stuttgart: Phillip Reclam jun., 1975.

Hohmann, Joachim S., ed. *Sexuologie in der DDR.* Berlin: Dietz, 1991.

Hohmann, Karl, ed. *Ludwig Erhard: Gedanken aus fünf Jahrzehnten.* Düsseldorf: Econ, 1988.

Höhn, Maria. "Frau im Haus und Girl im *Spiegel:* Discourse on Women in the Interregnum Period of 1945–1949 and the Question of German Identity." *Central European History* 26 (1993): 57–90.

———. "GIs, Veronikas, and Lucky Strikes: German Reactions to the American Military Presence in Rhineland-Palatinate during the 1950s." Ph.D. diss., University of Pennsylvania, 1995.

Höhne, Bernfried. *Jazz in der DDR.* Frankfurt am Main: Eisenbletter und Naumann, 1991.

Hollander, Paul. *Anti-Americanism: Irrational and Rational.* Rev. ed. New Brunswick: Transaction, 1995.

Horkheimer, Max, and Theodor W. Adorno. *Dialectic of Enlightenment,* trans. John Cumming. New York: Seabury, 1972.

Hübner, Peter. *Konsens, Konflikt und Kompromiß: Soziale Arbeiterinteressen und Sozialpolitik in der SBZ/DDR, 1945–1970.* Berlin: Akademie, 1995.

Huck, Gerhard. *Sozialgeschichte der Freizeit: Untersuchungen zum Wandel der Alltagskultur in Deutschland.* Wuppertal: Hammer, 1980.

Hunt, Lynn, ed. *The New Cultural History*. Berkeley: University of California Press, 1989.

Hussong, Martin. "Jugendzeitschriften von 1945 bis 1960: Phasen, Typen, Tendenzen." In *Zwischen Trümmern und Wohlstand: Literatur der Jugend 1945–1960*, edited by Klaus Doderer, 521–85. Weinheim: Beltz, 1988.

Huyssen, Andreas. *After the Great Divide: Modernism, Mass Culture, Postmodernism*. Bloomington: Indiana University Press, 1986.

Iliffe, John. *Tanganyika Under German Rule, 1905–1912*. New York: Cambridge University Press, 1969.

Ingimundarson, Valur. "The Eisenhower Administration, the Adenauer Government, and the Political Uses of the East German Uprising in 1953." *Diplomatic History* 20 (1996): 381–409.

Irmscher, Gerlinde. "Der Westen im Ost-Alltag." In *Wunderwirtschaft: DDR-Konsumkultur in den 6oer Jahren*, edited by Neue Gesellschaft für Bildende Kunst, 185–93. Cologne: Böhlau, 1996.

Jäger, Manfred. *Kultur und Politik in der DDR 1945–1990*. Cologne: Edition Deutschland Archiv, 1995.

Jahrbuch der Deutschen Demokratischen Republik. Berlin: Verlag Die Wissenschaft, 1956ff.

Jaide, Walter. *Das Verhältnis der Jugend zur Politik: Empirische Untersuchungen zur politischen Anteilnahme und Meinungsbildung junger Menschen der Geburtsjahrgänge 1940–1946*. Neuwied: Luchterhand, 1963.

Jänicke, Martin. *Der dritte Weg: Die antistalinistische Opposition gegen Ulbricht seit 1953*. Cologne: Neuer Deutscher Verlag, 1964.

Jarausch, Konrad H,. and Larry Eugene Jones, "German Liberalism Reconsidered." In *In Search of a Liberal Germany: Studies in the History of German Liberalism from 1789 to the Present*, edited by Konrad Jarausch and Larry Eugene Jones, 1–23. New York: Berg, 1990.

———, eds. *In Search of a Liberal Germany: Studies in the History of German Liberalism from 1789 to the Present*. New York: Berg, 1990.

Jarausch, Konrad H., and Hannes Siegrist, eds. *Amerikanisierung und Sowjetisierung in Deutschland, 1945–1970*. Frankfurt am Main.: Campus, 1997.

Jarvie, Ian. *Hollywood's Overseas Campaign: The North Atlantic Movie Trade, 1920–1950*. New York: Cambridge University Press, 1992.

Jäschke, Petra. "Produktionsentwicklungen und gesellschaftliche Einschätzungen." In *Zwischen Trümmern und Wohlstand: Literatur der Jugend 1945–1960*, edited by Klaus Doderer, 209–520. Weinheim: Beltz, 1988.

Jay, Martin. "Anti-Semitism and the German Left." In *Permanent Exiles: Essays on the Intellectual Migration from Germany to America*, edited by Martin Jay, 79–89. New York: Columbia University Press, 1986.

———. *The Dialectical Imagination: A History of the Frankfurt School and the Institute of Social Research, 1923–1950*. Berkeley: University of California Press, 1996.

———, ed. *Permanent Exiles: Essays on Intellectual Migration from Germany to America*. New York: Columbia University Press, 1986.

Jazz in Deutschland: Aus dem Amiga-Archiv 1947–65. With an introduction by Karl-Heinz Drechsel. Berlin, n.d. 5 compact disks.

Jeffords, Susan. *The Remasculinization of America: Gender and the Vietnam War.* Bloomington: Indiana University Press, 1989.

Jeffreys, Sheila. *Anticlimax: A Feminist Perspective on the Sexual Revolution.* New York: New York University Press, 1991.

Jelavich, Peter. *Berlin Cabaret.* Cambridge, Mass.: Harvard University Press, 1993.

Jessen, Ralph. "Die Gesellschaft im Staatssozialismus: Probleme einer Sozialgeschichte der DDR." *Geschichte und Gesellschaft* 21 (1995): 96–110.

Jones, LeRoi (Amiri Baraka). *Blues People: Negro Music in White America.* New York: Morrow, 1963.

Jones, Steve. *Rock Formation: Music, Technology, and Mass Communication.* Newbury Park: Sage, 1992.

Jüngling, Irina. "Halbstarke vom Wedding und von der Schönhauser." In *Zwischen Bluejeans und Blauhemden: Jugendfilm in Ost und West,* edited by Ingelore König, Dietmar Wiedemann, and Lothar Wolf, 69–75. Berlin: Henschel, 1995.

Kaelble, Hartmut, Jürgen Kocka, and Hartmut Zwahr. *Sozialgeschichte der DDR.* Stuttgart: Klett-Cotta, 1994.

Kaes, Anton. *From Hitler to Heimat: The Return of History as Film.* Cambridge, Mass.: Harvard University Press, 1989.

———. "Literary Intellectuals and the Cinema: Charting a Controversy (1909–1929)." *New German Critique* 40 (1987): 7–33.

Kaff, Brigitte. *"Gefährliche politische Gegner": Widerstand und Verfolgung in der sowjetischen Zone/DDR.* Düsseldorf: Droste, 1995.

Kaiser, Günther. *Randalierende Jugend: Eine soziologische und kriminologische Studie über die sogenannten "Halbstarken."* Heidelberg: Quelle und Meyer, 1959.

Kaminsky, Amy. "Gender, Race, Raza." *Feminist Studies* 20 (spring 1994): 7–31.

Kapferer, Norbert. "Die Psychologie in der DDR im Spannungsfeld von politischer Funktionalisierung und wissenschaftlicher Emanzipation." In *Politik und Gesellschaft in sozialistischen Ländern: Ergebnisse und Probleme der Sozialistischen Länder-Forschung,* edited by Ralf Rytlewski, 77–98. Opladen: Westdeutscher Verlag, 1989.

Kaplan, Alice Yeager. *Reproductions of Banality: Fascism, Literature, and French Intellectual Life.* Minneapolis: University of Minnesota Press, 1986.

Kaplan, Amy, and Donald E. Pease, eds. *Cultures of United States Imperialism.* Durham: Duke University Press, 1993.

Kaplan, Marion A. *Between Dignity and Despair: Jewish Life in Nazi Germany.* New York: Oxford University Press, 1998.

Kater, Michael H. *Different Drummers: Jazz in the Culture of Nazi Germany.* New York: Oxford University Press, 1992.

———. "Forbidden Fruit? Jazz in the Third Reich." *American Historical Review* 94 (February 1989): 11–43.

————. "The Jazz Experience in Weimar Germany." *German History* 6 (1988): 145–58.

Keilhacker, Martin, and Margarete Keilhacker. *Jugend und Spielfilm: Erlebnisweisen und Einflüsse.* Stuttgart: Ernst Klett, 1953.

Kelley, Robin D. "Notes on Deconstructing 'The Folk'. AHR Forum." *American Historical Review* 97 (December 1992): 1400–1408.

Kemper, Peter. " 'Der Rock ist ein Gebrauchswert:' Warum Adorno die Beatles verschmähte." *Merkur* 45, no. 510/11 (1991): 890–902.

Kenez, Peter. *Cinema and Soviet Society, 1917–1953.* New York: Cambridge University Press, 1992.

Kerr, Paul, ed. *The Hollywood Film Industry.* New York: Routledge & Kegan Paul, 1986.

Kershaw, Ian. "Totalitarianism Revisited: Nazism and Stalinism in Comparative Perspective." *Tel Aviver Jahrbuch für Deutsche Geschichte* 3 (1994): 23–40.

Kersten, Heinz. *Das Filmwesen in der Sowjetischen Besatzungszone Deutschlands.* Pt. 1. Bonn: Bundesministerium für Gesamtdeutsche Fragen, 1963.

Kevles, Daniel J. *In the Name of Eugenics: Genetics and the Uses of Human Heredity.* Cambridge, Mass.: Harvard University Press, 1995.

Kidwell, Claudia Brush, and Valerie Steele, eds. *Men and Women: Dressing the Part.* Washington, D.C.: Smithsonian Institution Press, 1989.

Kleßmann, Christoph. *Die doppelte Staatsgründung: Deutsche Geschichte 1945–1955.* 5th ed. Bonn: Bundeszentrale für politische Bildung, 1991.

————. "Verflechtung und Abgrenzung: Aspekte der geteilten und zusammengehörigen deutschen Nachkriegsgeschichte." *Aus Politik und Zeitgeschichte*, nos. 29–30 (July 16, 1993): 30–41.

————. *Zwei Staaten, eine Nation: Deutsche Geschichte 1955–1970.* 2d ed. Bonn: Bundeszentrale für politische Bildung, 1997.

Kluth, Heinz, Ulrich Lohmar, and Rudolf Tartler. *Arbeiterjugend gestern und heute: Sozialwissenschaftliche Untersuchungen.* Heidelberg: Quelle & Meyer, 1955.

Knauer, Wolfram, ed. *Jazz in Deutschland.* Hofheim: Wolke, 1996.

Kniesche, Thomas, W., and Stephen Brockmann, eds. *Dancing on the Volcano: Essays on the Culture of the Weimar Republic.* Columbia, S.C.: Camden House, 1994.

Kocka, Jürgen. "Eine durchherrschte Gesellschaft." In *Sozialgeschichte der DDR,* edited by Hartmut Kaelble, Jürgen Kocka, and Hartmut Zwahr, 547–53. Stuttgart: Klett-Cotta, 1994.

König, Ingelore, Dietmar Wiedemann, and Lothar Wolf, eds. *Zwischen Bluejeans und Blauhemden: Jugendfilm in Ost und West.* Berlin: Henschel, 1995.

Koonz, Claudia. *Mothers in the Fatherland: Women, the Family, and Nazi Politics.* New York: St. Martin's Press, 1987.

Kopstein, Jeffrey. *The Politics of Economic Decline in East Germany, 1945–1989.* Chapel Hill: University of North Carolina Press, 1997.

Korte, Hermann. *Eine Gesellschaft im Aufbruch: Die Bundesrepublik in den sechziger Jahren.* Frankfurt am Main: Suhrkamp, 1987.

Kowaczuk, Ilko-Sascha, Armin Mitter, and Stefan Wolle, eds., *Der Tag X—17. Juni 1953: Die "Innere Staatsgründung" der DDR als Ergebnis der Krise 1952–54.* Berlin: Ch. Links, 1995.

Kramer, Alan. " 'Law-Abiding Germans?' Social Disintegration, Crime, and the Reimposition of Order in Post-War Western Germany, 1945–1949." In *The German Underworld: Deviants and Outcasts in German History,* edited by Richard Evans, 238–61. New York: Routledge, 1988.

Krause-Ablaß, Margarete. "Entwicklungspsychologische Gesichtspunkte und praktische Erfahrungen as Grundlage für die Beurteilung von Filmen für Kinder und Jugendliche." In *Film—jugendpsychologisch betrachtet,* edited by Wissenschaftliches Institut für Jugendfilmfragen München, 48–59. Munich: Ehrenwirth, n.d.

Kraushaar, Wolfgang. "Notizen zu einer Chronologie der Studentenbewegung." In *Was wir wollten, was wir wurden: Studentenrevolte—zehn Jahre danach,* edited by Peter Mosler, 249–95. Reinbek bei Hamburg: Rowohlt, 1977.

Kreimeier, Klaus. *Kino und Filmindustrie in der BRD: Ideologieproduktion und Klassenwirklichkeit nach 1945.* Kronberg: Scriptor, 1973.

Kreuter, Wolfgang, and Joachim Oltmann. "Coca-Cola statt Apfelmost: Kalter Krieg und Amerikanisierung westdeutscher Lebensweise." *Englisch-Amerikanische Studien* 1 (March 1984): 22–35.

Kroes, Rob, and Marten van Rossem, eds. *Anti-Americanism in Europe.* Amsterdam: Free University Press, 1986.

Krüger, Heinz-Hermann. " 'Exis habe ich keine gesehen,'—Auf der Suche nach einer jugendlichen Gegenkultur in den 50er Jahren." In *"Die Elvis-Tolle, die hatte ich mir unauffällig wachsen lassen": Lebensgeschichte und jugendliche Alltagskultur in den fünfziger Jahren,* edited by Heinz-Hermann Krüger, 129–51. Opladen: Leske und Budrich, 1985.

———, and Peter Kuhnert. "Vom Bebop über'n Beat zum Punk: Jugendliche Musikkulturen im Revier nach 1945." In *Land der Hoffnung—Land der Krise: Jugendkulturen im Ruhrgebiet 1900–1987,* edited by Wilfried et al., 200–211. Berlin: J.H.W. Dietz, 1987.

Krüger, Heinz-Hermann, ed. *"Die Elvis-Tolle, die hatte ich mir unauffällig wachsen lassen": Lebensgeschichte und jugendliche Alltagskultur in den fünfziger Jahren.* Opladen: Leske und Budrich, 1985.

Krüger, Winfried. "Jugendzeitschrift Bravo—Anleitung zur Normalität." In *Immer diese Jugend! Ein zeitgeschichtliches Mosaik: 1945 bis heute,* edited by Deutsches Jugendinstitut, 363–74. Munich: Kösel, 1985.

Kühne, Thomas. " '…aus diesem Krieg werden nicht nur harte Männer heimkehren,' Kriegskameradschaft und Männlichkeit im 20. Jahrhundert." In *Männergeschichte—Geschlechtergeschichte: Männlichkeit im Wandel der Moderne,* edited by Thomas Kühne, 174–92. Frankfurt am Main: Campus, 1996.

————, ed. *Männergeschichte—Geschlechtergeschichte: Männlichkeit im Wandel der Moderne.* Frankfurt am Main: Campus, 1996.

Kuhnert, Peter, and Ute Ackermann, "Jenseits von Lust und Liebe? Jugendsexualität in den 50er Jahren." In *"Die Elvis-Tolle, die hatte ich mir unauffällig wachsen lassen": Lebensgeschichte und jugendliche Alltagskultur in den fünfziger Jahren,* edited by Heinz-Hermann Krüger, 43–83. Opladen: Leske und Budrich, 1985.

Kuisel, Richard. *Seducing the French: The Dilemma of Americanization.* Berkeley: University of California Press, 1993.

Lammers, Karl Christian, Axel Schildt, and Detlev Siegfried, eds. *Die sechziger Jahre: Politik, Gesellschaft und Kultur in den beiden deutschen Staaten.* Hamburg:, Christians, 1999. Forthcoming.

Lamprecht, Helmut. *Teenager und Manager.* Rev. ed. Munich: Rütten und Loening, 1965.

Lange, Horst. *Jazz in Deutschland: Die deutsche Jazz-Chronik 1900–1960.* Berlin: Colloquium, 1966. Rev. ed. Hildesheim: G. Olms, 1996.

Laqua, Carsten. *Wie Micky unter die Nazis fiel: Walt Disney und Deutschland.* Reinbek bei Hamburg: Rowohlt Taschenbuch, 1992.

Laqueur, Thomas. *Making Sex: Body and Gender from the Greeks to Freud.* Cambridge, Mass.: Harvard University Press, 1990.

Large, David Clay. *Germans to the Front: West German Rearmament in the Adenauer Era.* Chapel Hill: University of North Carolina Press, 1996.

Lavies, Hanns-Wilhelm. *Film und Jugendkriminalität: Eine Betrachtung zu einer Umfrage an deutschen Jugendgerichten.* Wiesbaden: Schriftenreihe des Deutschen Instituts für Filmkunde, 1954.

Lazere, Donald, ed. *American Media and Mass Culture: Left Perspectives.* Berkeley: University of California Press, 1987.

Leitner, Olaf. *Rockszene DDR: Aspekte einer Massenkultur im Sozialismus.* Reinbek bei Hamburg: Rowohlt Taschenbuch, 1983.

Lemke, Michael. *Die Berlinkrise 1958 bis 1963: Interessen und Handlungsspielräume der SED im Ost-West-Konflikt.* Berlin: Akademie, 1995.

Lenihan, John H. *Showdown: Confronting Modern America in the Western Film.* Urbana: University of Illinois Press, 1980.

Leonard, Neil. *Jazz and the White Americans: The Acceptance of a New Art Form.* Chicago: University of Chicago Press, 1962.

Lepsius, M. Rainer. "Die Entwicklung der Soziologie nach dem zweiten Weltkrieg 1945 bis 1967." In *Deutsche Soziologie seit 1945: Entwicklungsrichtungen und Praxisbezug,* edited by Günther Lüschen, 25–70. Opladen: Westdeutscher Verlag, 1979.

Levine, Lawrence W. "Jazz and American Culture." *Journal of American Folklore* 102 (1989): 6–22.

Lewis, Jon. *The Road to Romance and Ruin: Teen Films and Youth Culture.* New York: Routledge, 1992.

Lhamon, W. T. *Deliberate Speed: The Origins of a Cultural Style in the American 1950s.* Washington: Smithsonian Institution Press, 1990.

Lindemann, Rolf, and Werner Schultz. *Die Falken in Berlin: Geschichte und Erinnerung—Jugendopposition in den fünfziger Jahren.* Berlin: Elefanten, Press, 1987.

Lindenberger, Thomas. "Alltagsgeschichte und ihr möglicher Beitrag zu einer Gesellschaftsgeschichte der DDR." In *Die Grenzen der Diktatur: Staat und Gesellschaft in der DDR,* edited by Richard Bessel and Ralph Jenson. Göttingen: Vandenhoeck und Ruprecht, 1996.

Lindner, Rolf. "Straße—Straßenjunge—Straßenbande: Ein zivilisationstheoretischer Streifzug." *Zeitschrift für Volkskunde* 79 (1983): 192–208.

———. "Teenager—ein amerikanischer Traum." In *Schock und Schöpfung: Jugendästhetik im 20. Jahrhundert,* edited by Deutscher Werkbund e.V. und Württembergischer Kunstverein Stuttgart, 278–83. Darmstadt: Luchterhand, 1986.

Linton, Derek S. *"Who Has the Youth, Has the Future": The Campaign to Save Young Workers in Imperial Germany.* New York: Cambridge University Press, 1991.

Lipsitz, George. *Class and Culture in Cold War America: A Rainbow at Midnight.* South Hadley, Mass.: J. F. Bergin, 1982.

———. *Time Passages: Collective Memory and American Popular Culture.* Minneapolis: University of Minnesota Press, 1990.

Loesch, Hans, and Richard Rathgeber. "Jugendprotest—Widerspruch ja, Widerstand nein." In *Immer diese Jugend! Ein zeitgeschichtliches Mosaik: 1945 bis heute,* edited by Deutsches Jugendinstitut, 433–50. Munich: Kösel, 1985.

Loest, Erich. *Die Westmark fällt weiter.* Halle: Mitteldeutscher Verlag, 1952.

Loth, Wilfried. *Ost-West-Konflikt und deutsche Frage: Historische Ortsbestimmungen.* Munich: Deutscher Taschenbuch Verlag, 1989.

———. *Die Teilung der Welt: Geschichte des Kalten Krieges 1941–1955.* 2d ed. Munich: Deutscher Taschenbuch Verlag, 1980.

Lott, Eric. "White Like Me: Racial Cross Dressing and the Construction of American Whiteness." In *Cultures of United States Imperialism,* edited by Amy Kaplan and Donald E. Pease, 474–96. Durham: Duke University Press, 1993.

Lüdtke, Alf. " 'Helden der Arbeit'—Mühen beim Arbeiten: Zur mißmutigen Loyalität von Industriearbeitern in der DDR." In *Sozialgeschichte der DDR,* edited by Hartmut Kaelble, Jürgen Kocka, and Hartmut Zwahr, 188–213. Stuttgart: Klett-Cotta, 1994.

———, and Peter Becker, eds. *Akten. Eingaben. Schaufenster: Die DDR und ihre Texte: Erkundungen zu Herrschaft und Alltag.* Berlin: Akademie, 1997.

Lüdtke, Alf, Inge Marßolek, and Adelheid von Saldern, eds. *Amerikanisierung: Traum und Alptraum im Deutschland des 20. Jahrhunderts.* Stuttgart: Steiner, 1996.

Ludz, Peter Christian. *Die DDR zwischen Ost und West: Politische Analysen 1961 bis 1976.* Munich: C. H. Beck, 1977.

Luger, Kurt. *Die konsumierte Rebellion: Geschichte der Jugendkultur 1945–1990.* Wien: Österreichischer Kunst- und Kulturverlag, 1991.

Lüschen, Günther. *Deutsche Soziologie seit 1945: Entwicklungsrichtungen und Praxisbezug.* Opladen: Westdeutscher Verlag, 1979.

Lynn, Susan. "Gender and Post–World War II Progressive Politics: A Bridge to Social Activism in the 1960s U.S.A." *Gender and History* 4 (1992): 215–39.

Maase, Kaspar. *Bravo Amerika: Erkundungen zur Jugendkultur der Bundesrepublik in den fünfziger Jahren.* Hamburg: Junius-Verlag, 1992.

Magazin: Mitteilungen des Deutschen Historischen Museums 3, no. 7 (spring 1993). Issue: "The Image of America as the Enemy of the Former GDR."

Mählert, Ulrich, and Gerd-Rüdiger Stephan. *Blaue Hemden, Rote Fahnen: Die Geschichte der Freien Deutschen Jugend.* Opladen: Leske und Budrich, 1996.

Maier, Charles S. *Dissolution: The Crisis of Communism and the End of East Germany.* Princeton: Princeton University Press, 1997.

Marcus, Greil. *Mystery Train: Images of America in Rock 'n' Roll Music.* New York: Dutton, 1982.

Markovits, Andrei, and Philip S. Gorski, *The German Left: Red, Green and Beyond.* New York: Oxford University Press, 1993.

Marks, Sally. "Black Watch on the Rhine: A Study in Propaganda, Prejudice and Prurience." *European Studies Review* 13 (1983): 297–334.

Martin, Linda, and Kerry Segrave. *Anti-Rock: The Opposition to Rock 'n' Roll.* Hamden, Conn.: Archon Books, 1988.

Marwick, Arthur. *Beauty in History: Society, Politics, and Personal Appearance.* London: Thames and Hudson, 1988.

Mattelart, Armand, Xavier Delcourt, and Michele Mattelart. *International Image Markets: In Search of an Alternative Perspective.* London: Comedia, 1984.

May, Elaine Tyler. *Homeward Bound: American Families in the Cold War Era.* New York: Basic Books, 1988.

May, Lary, ed. *Recasting America: Culture and Politics in the Age of Cold War.* Chicago: University of Chicago Press, 1989.

McAlister, Melani. *Staging the American Century: Race, Religion, and Nation in U.S. Representations of the Middle East, 1945–1992.* Berkeley: University of California Press. Forthcoming.

McClintock, Anne. *Imperial Leather: Race, Gender, and Sexuality in the Colonial Conquest.* New York: Routledge, 1995.

McCormick, Richard W. *Politics of the Self: Feminism and the Postmodern in West German Literature and Film.* Princeton: Princeton University Press, 1991.

McRobbie, Angela. *Feminism and Youth Culture: From Jackie to Just Seventeen.* Boston: Unwin Hyman, 1991.

———. "Settling Accounts with Subcultures: A Feminist Critique." In *On Record: Rock, Pop, and the Written Word,* edited by Simon Frith and Andrew Goodwin. New York: Pantheon, 1990.

McRobbie, Angela, and Mica Nava, eds. *Gender and Generation.* Basingstoke: Macmillan, 1984.

Mehta, Uday S. "Liberal Strategies of Exclusion." In *Tensions of Empire: Colonial Cultures in a Bourgeois World*, edited by Frederick Cooper and Ann Laura Stoler, 59–86. Berkeley: University of California Press, 1997.

Merkel, Ina. "Leitbilder und Lebensweisen von Frauen in der DDR." In *Sozialgeschichte der DDR*, edited by Hartmut Kaelble, Jürgen Kocka, and Hartmut Zwahr, 359–82. Stuttgart: Klett-Cotta, 1994.

———. *...und Du, Frau an der Werkbank: Die DDR in den 5oer Jahren.* Berlin: Elefanten Press, 1990.

Merritt, Anna J. and Richard L. Merritt. *Public Opinion in Occupied Germany: The OMGUS Surveys, 1945–1949.* Urbana: University of Illinois Press, 1970.

———. *Public Opinion in Semi-Sovereign Germany: The HICOG Surveys, 1949–1955.* Urbana: University of Illinois Press, 1980.

Messelken, Karlheinz. "Schelsky und die Kulturanthropologie." In *Helmut Schelsky—ein Soziologe in der Bundesrepublik: Eine Gedächtnisschrift von Freunden, Kollegen, Schülern*, edited by Horst Baier, 68–77. Stuttgart: Ferdinand Enke, 1986.

Meuschel, Sigrid. *Legitimation und Parteiherrschaft: Zum Paradox von Stabilität und Revolution in der DDR 1945–1989.* Frankfurt am Main: Suhrkamp, 1992.

———. "Überlegungen zu einer Herrschafts- und Gesellschaftsgeschichte der DDR." *Geschichte und Gesellschaft* 19 (1993): 5–14.

Meyer, Michael. "A Musical Facade for the Third Reich." In *"Degenerate Art": The Fate of the Avant-Garde in Nazi Germany*, edited by Stephanie Barron with contributions from Peter Guenther et al., 171–83. New York: Harry N. Abrams, 1992.

Meyer, Sibylle, and Eva Schulze. " 'Als wir wieder zusammen waren, ging der Krieg im Kleinen weiter': Frauen, Männer, und Familien im Berlin der vierziger Jahre." In *"Wir kriegen jetzt andere Zeiten"—Auf der Suche nach der Erfahrung des Volkes in den nachfaschistischen Ländern*, edited by Lutz Niethammer and Alexander von Plato. Berlin: J. H. W. Dietz, 1985.

Mitchell, Lee Clark. *Westerns: Making the Man in Fiction and Film.* Chicago: University of Chicago Press, 1996.

Mitchell, Maria. "Materialism and Secularism: CDU Politicians and National Socialism, 1945–1949." *Journal of Modern History* 67 (June 1995): 278–308.

Mitscherlich, Alexander. *Society Without the Father: A Contribution to Social Psychology*, trans. Eric Mosbacher. New York: Harcourt, Brace and World, 1969.

Mittag, Detlef R., and Detlef Schade. *Die amerikanische Kaltwelle: Geschichten vom Überleben in der Nachkriegszeit.* Berlin: Arsenal, 1983.

Mitter, Armin, and Stefan Wolle. *Untergang auf Raten: Unbekannte Kapitel der DDR-Geschichte.* Munich: Bertelsmann, 1993.

Modleski, Tania. *Feminism Without Women: Culture and Criticism in a "Postfeminist" Age.* New York: Routledge, 1991.

————, ed. *Studies in Entertainment: Critical Approaches to Mass Culture.* Bloomington: Indiana University Press, 1986.

Moeller, Robert G. " 'The Last Soldiers of the Great War' and Tales of Family Reunions in the Federal Republic of Germany." *Signs* 24 (fall 1998): 129–45.

————. "Introduction: Writing the History of West Germany." In *West Germany Under Construction: Politics, Society, and Culture in the Adenauer Era,* edited by Robert G. Moeller, 1–30. Ann Arbor: University of Michigan Press, 1997.

————. "The Homosexual Man is a 'Man,' the Homosexual Woman is a 'Woman': Sex, Society, and the Law in Postwar West Germany." In *West Germany under Construction: Politics, Society, and Culture in the Adenauer Era,* edited by Robert G. Moeller, 251–84. Ann Arbor: University of Michigan Press, 1997.

————. *Protecting Motherhood: Women and the Family in the Politics of Postwar West Germany.* Berkeley: University of California Press, 1993.

————. "War Stories: The Search for a Usable Past in the Federal Republic of Germany." *American Historical Review* 101 (October 1996): 1008–48.

Moeller, Robert G., ed. *West Germany Under Construction: Politics, Society, and Culture in the Adenauer Era.* Ann Arbor: University of Michigan Press, 1997.

Mohrhof, Siegfried. *Warum sind sie gegen uns?* Seebruck am Chiemsee: Heering-Verlag, 1958.

Mooser, Josef. "Arbeiter, Angestellte und Frauen in der 'nivellierten Mittelstandsgesellschaft': Thesen." In *Modernisierung im Wiederaufbau: Die westdeutsche Gesellschaft der 50er Jahre,* edited by Axel Schildt and Arnold Sywottek. Bonn: J.H.W. Dietz Nachf., 1993.

————. *Arbeiterleben in Deutschland 1900–1970: Klassenlagen, Kultur und Politik.* Frankfurt am Main: Suhrkamp, 1984.

Morgan, Roger. *The United States and West Germany 1945–1973: A Study in Alliance Politics.* New York: Oxford University Press, 1974.

Morley, David, and Kevin Robins, *Spaces of Identity: Global Media, Electronic Landscapes, and Cultural Boundaries.* New York: Routledge, 1995.

Mosler, Peter, ed. *Was wir wollten, was wir wurden: Studentenrevolte—zehn Jahre danach.* Reinbek bei Hamburg: Rowohlt, 1977.

Mosse, George L. *Nationalism and Sexuality: Middle-Class Morality and Sexual Norms in Modern Europe.* Madison: University of Wisconsin Press, 1985.

————. *Toward the Final Solution: A History of European Racism.* Madison: University of Wisconsin Press, 1985.

Muchow, Hans Heinrich. *Sexualreife und Sozialstruktur der Jugend.* Hamburg: Rowohlt Taschenbuch, 1959.

Mukerji, Chandra, and Michael Schudson. *Rethinking Popular Culture: Contemporary Perspectives in Cultural Studies.* Berkeley: University of California Press, 1991.

Murray, Bruce A., and Christopher J. Wickham. *Framing the Past: The Historiography of German Cinema and Television.* Carbondale: Southern Illinois University Press, 1992.

Naimark, Norman M. *The Russians in Germany: A History of the Soviet Zone of Occupation, 1945–1949.* Cambridge, Mass.: Harvard University Press, 1995.

Nelson, Daniel. *Defenders or Intruders? The Dilemmas of U.S. Forces in Germany.* Boulder: Westview, 1987.

Nenno, Nancy. "Femininity, the Primitive and Modern Urban Space: Josphine Baker in Berlin." In *Women in the Metropolis: Gender and Modernity in Weimar Culture,* edited by Katharina von Ankum, 145–61. Berkeley: University of California Press, 1997.

Neue Gesellschaft für Bildende Kunst, ed. *Wunderwirtschaft: DDR-Konsumkultur in den 60er Jahren.* Cologne: Böhlau, 1996.

Nicholls, A. J. *Freedom with Responsibility: The Social Market Economy in Germany, 1918–1963.* Oxford: Clarendon, 1994.

Niethammer, Lutz, and Alexander von Plato, eds. *"Wir kriegen jetzt andere Zeiten"—Auf der Suche nach der Erfahrung des Volkes in den nachfaschistischen Ländern.* Berlin: J. H. W. Dietz Nachf., 1985.

Niethammer, Lutz, Alexander von Plato, and Dorothee Wierling. *Die volkseigene Erfahrung: Eine Archäologie des Lebens in der Industrieprovinz der DDR.* Berlin: Rowohlt, 1991.

Nikles, Bruno W. *Jugendpolitik in der Bundesrepublik Deutschland: Entwicklungen, Merkmale, Orientierungen.* Opladen: Leske und Budrich, 1976.

Ninkovich, Frank. *Germany and the United States: The Transformation of the German Question Since 1945.* Boston: Twayne, 1988.

Noglik, Bert. "Hürdenlauf zum freien Spiel: Ein Rückblick auf den Jazz der DDR." In *Jazz in Deutschland,* edited by Wolfram Knauer, 205–21. Hofheim: Wolke, 1996.

Nolan, Mary. "America in the German Imagination." In *Transactions, Transgressions, Transformations: American Culture in Western Europe and Japan,* edited by Heide Fehrenbach and Uta G. Poiger. New York: Berghahn Books, 1999. Forthcoming.

———. *Visions of Modernity: American Business and the Modernization of Germany.* New York: Oxford University Press, 1994.

Nordau, Max. *Degeneration.* 1895. Reprint, introd. by George Mosse. Lincoln: University of Nebraska Press, 1993.

Oberndörfer, Dieter. *Von der Einsamkeit des Menschen in der modernen amerikanischen Gesellschaft.* Freiburg im Breisgau: Rombach, 1961.

Obertreis, Gesine. *Familienpolitik in der DDR 1945–1980.* Opladen: Leske und Budrich, 1986.

Oosterhuis, Harry, ed. *Homosexuality and Male Bonding in Pre-Nazi Germany: The Youth Movement, the Gay Movement, and Male Bonding Before Hitler's Rise.* New York: Harrington Park Press, 1991.

Ostermann, Christian F. " 'Keeping the Pot Simmering:' The United States and the East German Uprising of 1953." *German Studies Review* 19 (February 1996): 61–89.

Pallowski, Katrin. "Wohnen in halben Zimmern." In *Perlonzeit: Wie die Frauen ihr Wirtschaftswunder erlebten,* edited by Angela Delille and Andrea Grohn, 23–29. Berlin: Elefanten Press, 1985.

Panassié, Hugues. *Le Jazz Hot.* Paris: R.A. Correa, 1934.

Panish, Jon. *The Color of Jazz: Race and Representation in Postwar American Culture.* Jackson: University Press of Mississippi, 1997.

Partsch, Cornelius. "Hannibal ante Portas: Jazz in Weimar." In *Dancing on the Volcano: Essays on the Culture of the Weimar Republic,* edited by Thomas W. Kniesche and Stephen Brockmann, 105–116. Columbia, S.C.: Camden House, 1994.

Pateman, Carole. "Equality, Difference, Subordination: The Politics of Motherhood and Women's Citizenship." In *Beyond Equality and Difference: Citizenship, Feminist Politics, and Female Subjectivity,* edited by Gisela Bock and Susan James, 17–31. New York: Routledge, 1992.

Peiss, Kathy. *Cheap Amusements: Working Women and Leisure in Turn-of-the-Century New York.* Philadelphia: Temple University Press, 1986.

Pells, Richard. *Not Like Us: How Europeans Have Loved, Hated, and Transformed American Culture Since World War II.* New York: Basic Books, 1997.

Pence, Katherine. "The 'Fräuleins' meet the 'Amis': Americanization of German Women in the Reconstruction of the West German State." *Michigan Feminist Studies* 7 (1992–93): 83–108.

———. "From Rations to Fashions: The Gendered Politics of East and West German Consumption, 1945–1961." Ph.D. diss., University of Michigan, 1999.

Peter, Antonio, and Werner Wolf, eds. *Arbeit, Amis, Aufbau: Alltag in Hessen 1949–1955.* Frankfurt am Main: Insel, 1989.

Petersen, Klaus. "The Harmful Publications Young Persons Act of 1926: Literary Censorship and the Politics of Morality in the Weimar Republic." *German Studies Review* 15 (October 1992): 505–23.

Petro, Patrice. *Joyless Streets: Women and Melodramatic Representation in Weimar Germany.* Princeton: Princeton University Press, 1989.

Peukert, Detlev J. K. *Die Edelweisspiraten: Protestbewegungen jugendlicher Arbeiter im Dritten Reich.* Cologne: Bund-Verlag, 1980.

———. *Grenzen der Sozialdisziplinierung: Aufstieg und Krise der deutschen Jugendfürsorge 1878–1932.* Cologne: Bund-Verlag, 1986.

———. "Die 'Halbstarken.' " *Zeitschrift für Pädagogik* 30 (1984): 533–84.

———. *Inside Nazi Germany: Conformity, Opposition, and Racism in Everyday Life,* trans. Richard Deveson. New Haven: Yale University Press, 1987.

———. *Jugend zwischen Krieg und Krise: Lebenswelten von Arbeiterjungen in der Weimarer Republik.* Cologne: Bund-Verlag, 1987.

————. *The Weimar Republic: The Crisis of Classical Modernity*, trans. Richard Deveson. New York: Hill and Wang, 1993.

Pfeil, Elisabeth. *Die 23 jährigen: Eine Generationsuntersuchung am Geburtenjahrgang 1941*. Tübingen: J. C. B. Mohr, 1968.

Pick, Daniel. *Faces of Degeneration: A European Disorder, c. 1848—c. 1918*. New York: University of Cambridge Press, 1989.

Pike, David. *The Politics of Culture in Soviet-Occupied Germany 1945–1949*. Stanford: Stanford University Press, 1992.

Pipping, Knut, Rudolf Abshagen, and Anne-Eva Brauneck. *Gespräche mit der deutschen Jugend: Ein Beitrag zum Autoritätsproblem*. Helsingfors: Centraltyckeriet, 1954.

Pohl, Rainer. "'Schräge Vögel, mausert euch!' Von Renitenz, Übermut und Verfolgung der Hamburger Swings and Pariser Zazous." In *Piraten, Swings, und Junge Garde: Jugendwiderstand im Nationalsozialismus*, edited by Wilfried Breyvogel, 241–70. Bonn: Dietz, 1991.

Pommerin, Reiner. *Sterilisierung der Rheinlandbastarde: Das Schicksal einer farbigen deutschen Minderheit, 1918–1937*. Düsseldorf: Droste, 1979.

————, ed. *The American Impact on Postwar Germany*. Providence, R.I.: Berghahn Books, 1995.

Posner, David. "Afro-America in West German Perspective, 1945–1966." Ph.D. diss., Yale University, 1997.

Preuss-Lausitz, Ulf et al., eds. *Kriegskinder, Konsumkinder, Krisenkinder: Zur Sozialisationsgeschichte seit dem Zweiten Weltkrieg*. Weinheim: Beltz, 1983.

Prinz, Michael, and Rainer Zitelmann, eds. *Nationalsozialismus und Modernisierung*. Darmstadt: Wissenschaftliche Buchgesellschaft, 1991.

Pronay, Nicholas, and Keith Wilson, eds. *The Political Re-education of Germany and Her Allies After World War II*. London: Croom Helm, 1985.

Prötsch, Hannsgerd. *So müssen unsere Soldaten sein: Eine Betrachtung über das politisch-moralische Antlitz der Nationalen Volksarmee der Deutschen Demokratischen Republik*. Berlin: Verlag des Ministeriums für Nationale Verteidigung, 1957.

Prowe, Diethelm. *Weltstadt in Krisen: Berlin, 1949–1958*. New York, De Gruyter, 1973.

Ramet, Sabrina P. *Social Currents in Eastern Europe: The Sources and Meaning of the Great Transformation*. Durham: Duke University Press, 1991.

————, ed. *Rocking the State: Rock Music and Politics in Eastern Europe and Russia*. Boulder, Colo.: Westview, 1994.

Rauhut, Michael. *Beat in der Grauzone: DDR-Rock 1964 bis 1972—Politik und Alltag*. Berlin: Basisdruck, 1993.

————. *Schalmei and Lederjacke: Udo Lindenberg, BAP, Underground: Rock und Politik in den achtziger Jahren*. Berlin: Schwarzkopf & Schwarzkopf, 1996.

Reese, Dagmar. "The BDM Generation: A Female Generation in Transition from Dictatorship to Democracy." In *Generations in Conflict: Youth Revolt and Generation Formation in Germany, 1770–1968*, edited by Mark Roseman, 227–46. New York: Cambridge University Press, 1995.

Reichel-Koss, Ilse, and Ursula Beul, eds. *Ella Kay und das Jugendamt neuer Prägung: Ein Amt, wo Kinder Recht bekommen*. Weinheim: Juventa, 1991.

Rentschler, Eric. "German Feature Films, 1933–1945." *Monatshefte* 82, no. 3 (1990): 257–66.

———."How American Is It? The U.S. as Image and Imaginary in German Film." *German Quarterly* (fall 1984): 603–19.

———. *The Ministry of Illusion: Nazi Cinema and its Afterlife*. Cambridge, Mass.: Harvard University Press, 1996.

Richter, Rolf. *Defa-Spielfilm-Regisseure und ihre Kritiker*. Vols. 1–2. Berlin: Henschel, 1983.

Riesman, David. *The Lonely Crowd: A Study of Changing American Character*. New Haven: Yale University Press, 1950. German: *Die Einsame Masse: Eine Untersuchung der Wandlungen des amerikanischen Charakters*. With an introduction to the German edition by H. Schelsky. Darmstadt: Luchterhand, 1956.

Roberts, Mary Louise. *Civilization Without Sexes: Reconstructing Gender in Postwar France, 1917–1927*. Chicago: University of Chicago Press, 1994.

———. "Samson and Delilah Revisited: The Politics of Women's Fashion in 1920s France." *American Historical Review* 98 (1993): 657–84.

Robin, Ron. *The Barbed-Wire College: Reeducating German POWs in the United States During World War II*. Princeton: Princeton University Press, 1995.

Roblin, Ronald, ed. *The Aesthetics of the Critical Theorists: Studies on Benjamin, Adorno, Marcuse, and Habermas*. Lewiston, N.Y.: Edwin Mellen Press, 1990.

Roediger, David R. *The Wages of Whiteness: Race and the Making of the American Working Class, 1776–1865*. New York: Verso, 1991.

Roesler, Jörg. "Privater Konsum in Ostdeutschland 1950–1960." In *Modernisierung und Wiederaufbau: Die westdeutsche Gesellschaft der 50er Jahre*, edited by Axel Schildt and Arnold Sywottek, 290–303. Bonn: Dietz, 1993.

Rogin, Michael. "Kiss Me Deadly: Communism, Motherhood, and Cold War Movies." *Representations* 6 (spring 1984): 1–36.

Roseman, Mark. "The Organic Society and the 'Massenmenschen': Integrating Young Labour in the Ruhr Mines, 1945–58." In *West Germany Under Construction: Politics, Society, and Culture in the Adenauer Era*, edited by Robert G. Moeller, 287–320. Ann Arbor: University of Michigan Press, 1997.

———, ed. *Generations in Conflict: Youth Revolt and Generation Formation in Germany, 1770–1968*. New York: Cambridge University Press, 1995.

Rosenberg, Emily S. *Spreading the American Dream: American Economic and Cultural Expansion, 1890–1945*. New York: Hill and Wang, 1982.

Ross, Andrew. *No Respect: Intellectuals and Popular Culture*. New York: Routledge, 1989.

Ross, Kristin. *Fast Cars, Clean Bodies: Decolonization and the Reordering of French Culture.* Cambridge, Mass.: MIT Press, 1995.

Rudorf, Reginald. *Jazz in der Zone.* Cologne: Kiepenheuer und Witsch, 1964.

———. *Nie wieder links: Eine deutsche Reportage.* Frankfurt am Main: Ullstein, 1990.

Rupieper, Hermann-Josef. *Die Wurzeln der westdeutschen Nachkriegsdemokratie: Der amerikanische Beitrag 1945–1952.* Opladen: Westdeutscher Verlag, 1993.

Ryback, Timothy W. *Rock Around the Bloc: A History of Rock Music in Eastern Europe and the Soviet Union.* New York: Oxford University Press, 1990.

Rytlewski, Ralf, ed. *Politik und Gesellschaft in Sozialistischen Ländern: Ergebnisse und Probleme der Sozialistischen Länder-Forschung.* Opladen: Westdeutscher Verlag, 1989.

Saunders, Thomas J. *Hollywood in Berlin: American Cinema and Weimar Germany.* Berkeley: University of California Press, 1994.

Schäfer, Hans Dieter. "Amerikanismus im Dritten Reich." In *Nationalsozialismus und Modernisierung,* edited by Michael Prinz and Rainer Zitelmann, 199–215. Darmstadt: Wissenschaftliche Buchgesellschaft, 1991.

———. *Das gespaltene Bewußtsein: Über deutsche Kultur und Lebenswirklichkeit, 1933–1945.* Munich: Carl Hanser, 1981.

Schäfers, Bernhard. "Helmut Schelskys Jugendsoziologie: 'Prinzip Erfahrung' contra Jugendbewegtheit." In *Helmut Schelsky—ein Soziologe in der Bundesrepublik: Eine Gedächtnisschrift von Freunden, Kollegen, Schülern,* edited by Horst Baier, 57–67. Stuttgart: Ferdinand Enke, 1986.

Schelsky, Helmut. *Soziologie der Sexualität: Über die Beziehungen zwischen Geschlecht, Moral und Gesellschaft.* Hamburg: Rowohlt Taschenbuch, 1955.

———. *Die skeptische Generation: Eine Soziologie der deutschen Jugend.* Cologne: Eugen Diederichs, 1957.

———. *Wandlungen der deutschen Familie in der Gegenwart: Darstellung und Deutung einer empirisch-soziologischen Tatbestandsaufnahme.* Dortmund: Ardey, 1953.

Schenk, Ralf. "Jugendfilm in der DDR." In *Zwischen Bluejeans und Blauhemden: Jugendfilm in Ost und West,* edited by Ingelore König, Dietmar Wiedemann, and Lothar Wolf, 21–43. Berlin: Henschel, 1995.

Schildt, Axel. *Moderne Zeiten: Freizeit, Massenmedien, und "Zeitgeist" in der Bundesrepublik der 50er Jahre.* Hamburg: Christians, 1995.

———. "Die USA als 'Kulturnation': Zur Bedeutung der Amerikahäuser in den 1950er Jahren." In *Amerikanisierung: Traum und Alptraum im Deutschland des 20. Jahrhunderts,* edited by Alf Lüdtke, Inge Marßolek, and Adelheid von Saldern, 256–69. Stuttgart: Steiner, 1996.

———, and Arnold Sywottek. "'Reconstruction' and 'Modernization': West German Social History during the 1950s." In *West Germany Under Construction: Politics, Society, and Culture in the Adenauer Era,* edited by Robert G. Moeller, 413–40. Ann Arbor: University of Michigan Press, 1997.

Schildt, Axel, and Arnold Sywottek, eds. *Modernisierung im Wiederaufbau: Die westdeutsche Gesellschaft der 50er Jahre.* Bonn: Dietz, 1993.

Schiller, Herbert I. *Mass Communications and American Empire.* 2d ed. Boulder, Colo.: Westview, 1992.

Schiller, Theo. "Parteienentwicklung: Die Einebnung der politischen Milieus." in *Die fünfziger Jahre: Beiträge zu Politik und Kultur,* edited by Dieter Bänsch, 37–51. Tübingen: Narr, 1985.

Schissler, Hanna, ed. *Revisiting the Miracle Years: West German Society from 1949 to 1968.* Princeton: Princeton University Press, 1999. Forthcoming.

Schmidt, Michael. *Die Falken in Berlin: Antifaschismus und Völkerverständigung: Jugendbewegung durch Gedenkstättenfahrten, 1954–1969.* Berlin: Verlag für Ausbildung und Studium in der Elefanten-Press, 1987.

Schmitt, Heiner. *Kirche und Film: Kirchliche Filmarbeit in Deutschland von ihren Anfängen bis 1945.* Schriften des Bundesarchivs, no. 26. Boppard am Rhein: Harald Boldt, 1979.

Schneider, Michael. *Den Kopf verkehrt aufgesetzt, Oder die melancholische Linke: Aspekte des Kulturzerfalls in den siebziger Jahren.* Darmstadt: Luchterhand, 1981.

Schröder, Klaus. "Einleitung: Die DDR als politische Gesellschaft." In *Geschichte und Transformation des SED-Staates: Beiträge und Analysen,* edited by Klaus Schröder, 11–26. Berlin: Akademie, 1994.

———, ed. *Geschichte und Transformation des SED-Staates: Beiträge und Analysen.* Berlin: Akademie, 1994.

Schubbe, Elimar, ed. *Dokumente zur Kunst-, Literatur- und Kulturpolitik der SED.* Stuttgart: Seewald, 1972.

Schubert, Friedel. *Die Frau in der DDR: Ideologie und konzeptionelle Ausgestaltung ihrer Stellung in Beruf und Familie.* Opladen: Leske und Budrich, 1980.

Schubert, Klaus von. *Wiederbewaffnung und Westintegration: Die innere Auseinandersetzung um die militärische und außenpolitische Orientierung der Bundesrepublik, 1950–1952.* Stuttgart: Deutsche Verlags-Anstalt, 1970.

Schulte-Sasse, Jochen. "Toward a 'Culture' of the Masses: The Socio-Psychological Function of Popular Literature in Germany and the United States, 1880–1920." *New German Critique* 29 (1983): 85–105.

Schulte-Sasse, Linda. *Entertaining the Third Reich: Illusions of Wholeness in Nazi Cinema.* Durham: Duke University Press, 1996.

Schur, Edwin M. *The Americanization of Sex.* Philadelphia: Temple University Press, 1988.

Schwartz, Thomas Alan. *America's Germany: John J. McCloy and the Federal Republic of Germany.* Cambridge, Mass.: Harvard University Press, 1991.

———. "Reeducation and Democracy: The Policies of the United States High Commission in Germany." In *America and the Shaping of German Society, 1945–1955,* edited by Michael Ermarth, 35–59. Providence, R.I.: Berg, 1993.

Scott, Joan Wallach. *Gender and the Politics of History.* New York: Columbia University Press, 1988.

Senator für Jugend und Sport and Landesjugendring Berlin, eds. *Du und Deine Freizeit.* Berlin. n.d.

———. *Wohin? Freizeitfibel für die Schulabgänger 1957.* Berlin, 1957.

Shaw, Arnold. *The Rockin' 50s.* New York: Hawthorn Books, 1974.

Sheehan, James. "National History and National Identity in the New Germany." *German Studies Review* 15 (1992): 163–74.

Showalter, Elaine. *The Female Malady: Women, Madness, and Culture in England, 1830–1980.* New York: Pantheon, 1985.

Siegel, Sandra. "Literature and Degeneration: The Representation of 'Decadence'." In *Degeneration: The Dark Side of Progress,* edited by J. Edward Chamberlin and Sander L. Gilman, 199–219. New York: Columbia University Press, 1985.

Siegfried, Detlef. "Manipulation und Autonomie: Zur Politisierung der populären Jugendkultur in der Bundesrepublik Deutschland, 1960–67." In *Die sechziger Jahre: Politik, Gesellschaft und Kultur in den beiden deutschen Staaten,* edited by Karl Christian Lammers, Axel Schildt, and Detlev Siegfried. Hamburg: Christians, 1999. Forthcoming.

Siegrist, Hannes, Hartmut Kaelble, and Jürgen Kocka, eds. *Europäische Konsumgeschichte: Zur Gesellschafts- und Kulturgeschichte des Konsums (18. bis 20. Jahrhundert).* Frankfurt: Campus, 1997.

Siepmann, Eckhard, ed. *Bikini: Die Fünfziger Jahre: Kalter Krieg und Capri-Sonne.* Reinbek: Rowohlt Taschenbuch, 1983.

Sigl, Klaus, Werner Schneider, and Ingo Tornow, *Jede Menge Kohle? Kunst und Kommerz auf dem deutschen Filmmarkt der Nachkriegszeit: Filmpreise und Kassenerfolge 1949–1985.* Munich: Filmland Presse, 1986.

Simels, Steven. *Gender Chameleons: Androgyny in Rock 'n' Roll.* New York: Arbor House, 1985.

Slotkin, Richard. *Gunfighter Nation: The Myth of the Frontier in Twentieth-Century America.* New York: Athenaum, 1992.

Snell, John L. *Wartime Origins of the East-West Dilemma over Germany.* New Orleans: Hauser, 1959.

Snitow, Ann, Christine Stansell, and Sharon Thompson, eds. *Powers of Desire: The Politics of Sexuality.* New York: Monthly Review Press, 1983.

Special Issue: "The Black Public Sphere," *Public Culture* 7 (fall 1994).

Stacey, Jackie. *Star Gazing: Hollywood Cinema and Female Spectatorship.* New York: Routledge, 1994.

Stansell, Christine. *City of Women: Sex and Class in New York, 1789–1860.* Urbana: University of Illinois, 1986.

Staritz, Dietrich. *Geschichte der DDR.* Rev. ed. Frankfurt am Main: Suhrkamp, 1996. 1st ed. *Geschichte der DDR, 1949–1985.* Frankfurt am Main: Suhrkamp, 1985.

———. *Die Gründung der DDR: Von der sowjetischen Besatzungsherrschaft zum sozialistischen Staat.* 3d ed. Munich: Deutscher Taschenbuch Verlag, 1995.

Starr, S. Frederick. *Red and Hot: The Fate of Jazz in the Soviet Union, 1917–1991.* 2d ed.New York: Limelight Editions, 1994.

Stefan, Verena. "Kakophonie: Vorwort zur Neuausgabe 1994." In *Häutungen,* Verena Stefan. Frankfurt am Main: Fischer Taschenbuch, 1994.

Steininger, Rolf. *Wiederbewaffnung: Die Entscheidung für einen westdeutschen Verteidigungsbeitrag: Adenauer und die Westmächte 1950.* Erlangen: Straube, 1989.

——, ed. *Der Umgang mit dem Holocaust: Europa—USA—Israel.* Wien: Böhlau, 1994.

Steinweis, Alan E. *Art, Ideology, and Economics in Nazi Germany: The Reich Chambers of Music, Theater, and the Visual Arts.* Chapel Hill: University of North Carolina Press, 1993.

Stella, Simonetta Piccone. " 'Rebels Without a Cause': Male Youth in Italy Around 1960." *History Workshop* 38 (1994): 157–78.

Stern, Frank. *The Whitewashing of the Yellow Badge: Antisemitism and Philosemitism in Postwar Germany,* trans. William Templer. New York: Pergamon, 1992.

Stieg, Margaret F. "The 1926 German Law to Protect Youth Against Trash and Dirt: Moral Protectionism in a Democracy." *Central European History* 23 (1990): 22–56.

Stites, Richard. *Russian Popular Culture: Entertainment and Society since 1900.* New York: Cambridge University Press, 1992.

Storey, John. *Cultural Studies and the Study of Popular Cultures: Theories and Methods.* Edinburgh: Edinburgh University Press, 1996.

Sträter, Winfried. " 'Das konnte ein Erwachsener nicht mit ruhigen Augen beobachten:' Die Halbstarken." In *Vom Lagerfeuer zur Musikbox: Jugendkulturen 1900–1960,* edited by Berliner Geschichtswerkstatt e.V., 137–70. Berlin: Elefanten Press, 1985.

Stümke, Hans-Georg, and Rudi Finkler. *Rosa Winkel, Rosa Listen: Homosexuelle und "Gesundes Volksempfinden" von Auschwitz bis heute.* Reinbek bei Hamburg: Rowohlt, 1981.

Sywottek, Arnold. "The Americanization of Everyday Life? Early Trends in Consumer and Leisure-Time Behavior." In *America and the Shaping of German Society 1945–1955,* edited by Michael Ermarth, 132–52. Providence, R.I.: Berg, 1993.

Szemere, Anna. "Bandits, Heroes, the Honest, and the Misled: Exploring the Politics of Representation in the Hungarian Uprising of 1956." In *Cultural Studies,* edited by Lawrence Grossberg, Cary Nelson, and Paula Treichler, 623–39. New York: Routledge, 1992.

Tenbruck, Friedrich H. *Jugend und Gesellschaft: Soziologische Perspektiven.* Freiburg: Rombach, 1962.

Tent, James F. *Mission on the Rhine: Re-education and Denazification in American-occupied Germany.* Chicago: University of Chicago Press, 1982.

Thompson, Kristin. *Exporting Entertainment: America in the World Film Market, 1907–1934.* London: British Film Institute, 1985.

Thomson, Charles A., and Walter H. C. Laves. *Cultural Relations and U.S. Foreign Policy.* Bloomington: Indiana University Press, 1963.

Thoß, Bruno. *"Volksarmee schaffen—ohne Geschrei!" Studien zu den Anfängen einer "verdeckten Aufrüstung" in der SBZ/DDR, 1947–1952*. Munich: R. Oldenbourg, 1994.

Thurnwald, Hilde. *Gegenwartsprobleme Berliner Familien: Eine soziologische Untersuchung von 498 Familien*. Berlin: Weidmannsche Buchhandlung, 1948.

Timm, Angelika. "Der 9. November 1938 in der politischen Kultur der DDR." In *Der Umgang mit dem Holocaust: Europa—USA—Israel*, edited by Rolf Steininger, 246–62. Wien: Böhlau, 1994.

Tomlinson, John. *Cultural Imperialism: A Critical Introduction*. Baltimore: Johns Hopkins University Press, 1991.

Tompkins, Jane. *West of Everything: The Inner Life of Westerns*. New York: Oxford University Press, 1992.

Tower, Beeke Sell. "'Ultramodern and Ultraprimitive:' Shifting Meanings in the Imagery of Americanism in the Art of Weimar Germany." In *Dancing on the Volcano: Essays on the Culture of the Weimar Republic*, edited by Thomas W. Kniesche and Stephen Brockmann, 85–105. Columbia, S.C.: Camden House, 1994.

Traverso, Enzo. *The Marxists and the Jewish Question: The History of a Debate, 1843–1943*. Atlantic Highlands, N.J.: Humanities Press, 1994.

Tröger, Annemarie. "Between Rape and Prostitution: Survival Strategies and Chances of Emancipation for Berlin Women After World War II." In *Women in Culture and Politics: A Century of Change*, edited by Judith Friedlander et al., 97–117. Bloomington: Indiana University Press, 1986.

Trommler, Frank. "Working-Class Culture and Modern Mass Culture Before World War I." *New German Critique* 29 (1983): 57–70.

Tunstall, Jeremy. *The Media are American: Anglo-American Media in the World*. 2d ed. London: Constable, 1994.

Turner, Ian D. *Reconstruction in Post-War Germany: British Occupation Policy and the Western Zones, 1945–55*. New York: Berg, 1989.

Twittenhoff, Wilhelm. *Jugend und Jazz: Ein Beitrag zur Klärung*. Mainz: Verlag Junge Musik B. Schott's Söhne, 1953.

Uebel, Lothar. *Viel Vergnügen: Die Geschichte der Vergnügungsstätten rund um den Kreuzberg und die Hasenheide*. Berlin: Nishen, 1985.

Usborne, Cornelie. *The Politics of the Body in Weimar Germany: Women's Reproductive Rights and Duties*. Ann Arbor: University of Michigan Press, 1992.

Verhandlungen des deutschen Bundestages: Stenographische Berichte. [VDTB]. Bonn, 1950ff.

Vogel, Angela. "Familie." In *Die Bundesrepublik Deutschland*. Vol. 3, *Gesellschaft*, edited by Wolfgang Benz, 35–86. Frankfurt am Main: Fischer Taschenbuch, 1989.

Von Ankum, Katharina, ed. *Women in the Metropolis: Gender and Modernity in Weimar Culture*. Berkeley: University of California Press, 1997.

Von Dirke, Sabine. *"All the Power to the Imagination!" The West German Counterculture from the Student Movement to the Greens*. Lincoln: University of Nebraska Press, 1997.

Von Saldern, Adelheid. "Überfremdungsängste: Gegen die Amerikanisierung der deutschen Kultur in den zwanziger Jahren." In *Amerikanisierung: Traum und Alptraum im Deutschland des 20. Jahrhunderts*, edited by Alf Lüdtke, Inge Marßolek, and Adelheid von Saldern, 256–69. Stuttgart: Steiner, 1996.

Von Wensierski, Hans-Jürgen. "Die Anderen nannten uns 'Halbstarke.' " In *"Die Elvis-Tolle, die hatte ich mir unauffällig wachsen lassen": Lebensgeschichte und jugendliche Alltagskultur in den fünfziger Jahren*, edited by Heinz-Hermann Krüger, 103–28. Opladen: Leske und Budrich, 1985.

Wagnleitner, Reinhold. *Coca-Colonization and Cold War: The Cultural Mission of the United States in Austria after the Second World War*, trans. Diana M. Wolf. Chapel Hill: University of North Carolina Press, 1994.

Ware, Vron. *Beyond the Pale: White Women, Racism and History*. New York: Verso, 1992.

———. "Moments of Danger: Race, Gender, and Memories of Empire," *History and Theory* 31 (1992): 116–37.

Weber, Hermann. *Die DDR 1945–1990*. 2d ed. Munich: R. Oldenbourg, 1993.

Weindling, Paul J. *Health, Race, and German Politics between National Unification and Nazism 1870–1945*. New York: Cambridge University Press, 1989.

Weitz, Eric. *Creating German Communism, 1890–1990: From Popular Protests to Socialist State*. Princeton: Princeton University Press, 1997.

Wendler, Jürgen. *Die Deutschlandpolitik der SED in den Jahren 1952 bis 1958: Publizistisches Erscheinungsbild und Hintergründe der Wiedervereinigungsrhetorik*. Cologne: Böhlau, 1991.

Weyer, Adam, ed. *Reden an die deutsche Jugend im 20. Jahrhundert*. Wuppertal: Jugenddienst Verlag, 1966.

White, Kevin. *The First Sexual Revolution: The Emergence of Male Heterosexuality in Modern America*. New York: New York University Press, 1993.

Wicke, Peter. *Rock Music: Culture, Aesthetics and Sociology*, trans. Rachel Fogg. New York: Cambridge University Press, 1990.

———. " 'The Times They Are A-Changin': Rock Music and Political Change in East Germany." In *Rockin' the Boat: Mass Music and Mass Movements*, edited by Reebee Garofalo, 81–92. Boston: South End Press, 1992.

Wierling, Dorothee. "Jugend als innerer Feind: Konflikte in der Erziehungsdiktatur der sechziger Jahre." In *Sozialgeschichte der DDR*, edited by Hartmut Kälble, Jürgen Kocka, and Hartmut Zwahr, 404–25. Stuttgart: Klett-Cotta, 1994.

———. "Mission to Happiness: The Cohort of 1949 and the Making of East and West Germans." In *Revisiting the Miracle Years: West German Society from 1949 to 1968*, edited by Hanna Schissler. Princeton: Princeton University Press, 1999. Forthcoming.

———. "Der Staat, die Jugend und der Westen. Texte zu Konflikten der 1960er Jahre." In *Akten. Eingaben. Schaufenster: Die DDR und ihre Texte: Erkundungen zu Herrschaft und Alltag*, edited by Alf Lüdtke and Peter Becker, 223–40. Berlin: Akademie, 1997.

Wildt, Michael. *Am Beginn der 'Konsumgesellschaft': Mangelerfahrung, Lebenshaltung, Wohlstandshoffnung in Westdeutschland in den fünfziger Jahren.* Hamburg: Ergebnisse, 1994.

Wilke, Sabine. "'Torn Halves of an Integral Freedom': Adorno's and Benjamin's Readings of Mass Culture." In *The Aesthetics of the Critical Theorists: Studies on Benjamin, Adorno, Marcuse, and Habermas,* edited by Ronald Roblin, 124–51. Lewiston, N.Y.: Edwin Mellen Press, 1990.

Willett, John. *Art and Politics in the Weimar Period: The New Sobriety, 1917–1993.* New York: Pantheon, 1978.

Willett, Ralph. *The Americanization of Germany, 1945–1949.* New York: Routledge, 1989.

Willis, F. Roy. *The French in Germany.* Stanford: Stanford University Press, 1962.

Willis, Paul. *Common Culture: Symbolic Work at Play in the Everday Cultures of the Young.* Boulder, Colo.: Westview, 1990.

Wissenschaftliches Institut für Jugendfilmfragen München, ed. *Film—jugendpsychologisch betrachtet.* Munich: Ehrenwirth, n.d.

Wittrock, Christine. *Weiblichkeitsmythen: Das Frauenbild im Faschismus und seine Vorläufer in der Frauenbewegung der 20er Jahre.* Frankfurt am Main: Sendler, 1983.

Wurzbacher, Gerhard, ed. *Die junge Arbeiterin: Beiträge zur Sozialkunde und Jugendarbeit.* Munich: Juventa, 1958.

Ziehe, Thomas. "Die alltägliche Verteidigung der Korrektheit." In *Schock und Schöpfung: Jugendästhetik im 20. Jahrhundert,* edited by Deutscher Werkbund e.V. and Württembergischer Kunstverein Stuttgart, 254–58. Darmstadt: Luchterhand, 1986.

Zielinski, Siegfried. *Audiovisionen: Kino und Fernsehen als Zwischenspiele in der Geschichte.* Reinbek bei Hamburg: Rowohlt Taschenbuch, 1989.

Zinnecker, Jürgen. *Jugendkultur 1940–1985.* Opladen: Leske und Budrich, 1987.

Zipes, Jack. "Die Freiheit trägt Handschellen im Land der Freiheit: Das Bild der Vereinigten Staaten von Amerika in der Literatur der DDR." In *Amerika in der deutschen Literatur: Neue Welt—Nordamerika—USA,* edited by Sigrid Bauschinger, Horst Denkler, and Wilfried Malsch, 329–52. Stuttgart: Phillip Reclam jun., 1975.

Index

Text:	10/13 Aldus
Display:	Aldus
Composition:	Impressions Book and Journal Services, Inc.
Printing and binding:	Edwards Brothers, Inc.